PRIMITIVE TECHNOLOGY

PRIMITIVE TECHNOLOGY
A Book of Earth Skills

From the Society of Primitive Technology
Edited by David Wescott

SALT LAKE CITY

06   10 9 8

Published by
Gibbs Smith, Publisher
P.O. Box 667
Layton, Utah 84041
Web site: www.gibbs-smith.com

Design by David Wescott

The articles in this book are reprinted from issues 1-10 of the *Bulletin of Primitive Technology*. The publisher bears no responsibility for their accuracy or content. Neither the publisher or editor bear responsibility for the results of any project described herein or for the reader's safety during participation. Caution and common sense are recommended for every activity.

Library of Congress Cataloging-in-Publication Data

Primitive technology : a book of earthskills / edited by David
    Wescott
            p. cm.
      Selection of articles from the Bulletin of primitive technology,
    issues 1-10
      ISBN 0-87905-911-7
      1. Industries, Prehistoric, 2. Archaeology–Experiments.
    3. Archaeology–Methodology. I. Wescott. Daved, 1948- .
    II. Bulletin of primitive technology.
    GN429.P75 1999
    930.1–dc21
                                        98-54428
                                          CIP

Contents

Section 5- PROJECTILES – Power From The Human Hand

Section 6- ART & MUSIC – Discipline and Meaning

Section 7 - Appendix

Cover photo by Mike Peters

Mike Peters

Foreword

The Fire Watchers. Leona Cave, Texas

THE SOCIETY IS FOUNDED

During the weekend of November 11-12, 1989, ten leaders in the field of experiential primitive skills gathered around the fire at the Schiele Museum's Center for Southeastern Native American Studies in Gastonia, North Carolina to organize a new national organization — The Society of Primitive Technology.

Conceived by Dr. Errett Callahan, pioneering reconstructive archaeologist and director of Piltdown Productions in Lynchburg, Virginia; the society seeks to promote the practice and teaching of aboriginal skills, foster communication between teachers and practitioners and set standards for authenticity, ethics and quality.

In his book, ***Ever Expanding Horizons***, Carl Swanson notes; "The linkage between biological and cultural evolution is an arena entered only at some considerable risk because it is middle ground". This is the same feeling we had when we established the Society of Primitive Technology; we were attempting to reach a middle ground.

Coming to a balanced consensus between scientists, teachers, practitioners and experiential learners is no simple task. However, Swanson has led us to an understanding of the similarities within the family of man and has founded these similarities in what he calls **"sociogenes"**, identifying those ideas that mature into shared concepts and interact with the expressed information encoded in DNA. After all, for 99% of human history our ancestors shared a technological phase called the stone age. We all have sticks and rocks in common.

He looked upon us as sophisticated children- smart but not wise. We knew many things, and much that is false. He knew nature, which is always true.
          Saxton Pope, <u>Ishi In Two Worlds</u>

Why Primitive

The very word has come, to many, to connote brutishness or backwardness. That is only one interpretation of a very formative word. Look at the dictionary definition:

primitive (prim´e-tiv)- 1a. Of or pertaining to an earliest or original stage or state. b. Archetypal. 2. Characterized by simplicity or crudity; unsophisticated: primitive weapons 3. Of or pertaining to early stages in the evolution of human culture: primitive societies.

(more)

The negative words that stand out are crudity and unsophisticated. But when we look closer at these words used to define "primitive", the definition of the word takes on a new light. **sophisticate** (se-fis'-ti-kat) - 1. to cause to become less natural or simple; especially to make less naive; make worldly wise. 2. to corrupt or pervert; adulterate; no longer pure. 3. to make more complex or inclusive. GREEK- sophistikos-from. -ed- having acquired worldly knowledge or refinement; lacking natural simplicity or naivite. -sohistry- a plausable but misleading or fallacious argument; faulty reasoning.

I, for one, would much rather be labeled primitive than sophisticated. Primitive implies first not worst. When looking at the degree of understanding and mastery of manipulation of simple materials to solve complex problems, we moderns have no advantage over those who, by design, choose to live a simpler life.

As our technological society rushes headlong to its dubious future, a new interest in primitive peoples has sprung to life...There have been thousands of societies on this planet and some of them hold secrets that we could well learn from. It is those secrets we are looking for. **The Challenge of the Primitives**

Why Technology

Many of the skills and methods presented in this text come from years of trial and error and personal discoveries by the authors. The benefit to you is that many secrets have been unlocked and are available through this collection of ideas and techniques. It is not our intent to give you shortcuts to what it may have taken decades for others to perfect, but merely guides to show you where they've been and how you can follow. As you can see, this book is not just a skills book. The technologies that are included are here to help you go through some of the same evolution as those who teach them. Listen to their words, and discover the process, not just the product.

The rediscovery of traditional skills and technologies brings a deeper appreciation for the people, places, and spirit of the times that laid the foundation of what we know today as a "lifestyle". The mastery of primitive skills comprises two factors - the method and the technique. The method is in the mind; the technique in the hands. Method is the logical manner of systematic and orderly processes, using a preconceived plan. Technique is the application of method (Crabtree). You have the mental capacity to grasp many of these universal principles without much effort due to the inheritance of thousands of years of experience. Unfortunately the last few hundred years have caused us to atrophy, as "lifestyle" has allowed technology to take over many of the very tasks that shaped us (We need to recognize that it is not the tool, but the inappropriate or overuse of the tool that has put us in this fix. There is nothing wrong with technology, more simply it is the inappropriate use of technology or the proliferation of inappropriate technology). It will take effort on your part to regain the skill and technique needed to master some of these arts, but isn't that the challenge?

Primitive skills move the technologist out of the realm of ideas and theory, into a realm of function and habit. If you're embarrassed by the idea of "doing the primitive thing", because it isn't modern or scientific, think about it for a minute. Our sciences and discoveries have made us masters of time and place. We have developed incredible technologies, yet we can never sever those indelible connections we have to our past.. We have been to the moon and returned. And what was the first thing we brought back......rocks ! **David Wescott, Editor**

Honoring Our Shared Heritage
By Steve Watts
"I am a human being, nothing human can be alien to me." Terance (154BC)

"Drawn near to the fires of aboriginal skills, we look to the indigenous peoples of the world for inspiration and insight. From the Aborigines of Australia's Western Desert. . .to their brothers in New Guinea and north and east throughout the Pacific to Southeast Asia and Old Polynesia. . .to the Ainu in the farthest reaches of Japan. . .to the Toda herdsmen of backcountry India. . .to the Berbers of the sand of North Africa and their black brethren to the south in the jungles and savannahs of the Mother Continent. . .to the Native Peoples of the Americas; in rain forests, woodlands, high deserts, and great plains. . .to the Inuits, Lapps, and Siberians of the frozen tundra. . .to all the custodians of unbroken lineages wherever they may be. . .Primitive Technology is their inheritance and we honor that here.

Yet no one is from nowhere. The blood of our ancestors flows in our own veins. Our aboriginal legacy is written in the very make-up of our bodies. The ancient caves and campfires of our pasts call to us from within. Primitive Technology is our inheritance as well. It is a world heritage which knows no race, creed, or color. It is foreign to no one. It is the shared thread which links us to our prehistory and binds us together as human beings. That we honor above all."

Section 1

Primitive Technology

WHAT IS EXPERIMENTAL ARCHEOLOGY?

By Errett Callahan

Experimental archeology may be defined as "that branch of archeology which seeks to interpret material culture, technology, or lifeways of the past by means of structured, scientific experimentation: (Callahan ms: 87). Reconstructive archeology, closely akin to experimental archeology, involves "interpretation of material culture and technology by means of physical reconstruction, using either experiential (Level II) or experimental (Level III) means" (ibid.). Only the latter may be termed "experimental archeology. Level I projects, although attempts at reconstruction, may not lay claim to the term "reconstructive archeology". [See below for explanation of the three levels.]

Experimental archeology started in the late 1800s, when a number of archeologists tried to duplicate the technologies they were finding evidence of in the soil. After this, experimentation went "out of style" until "rediscovered" in the 1960s by technologists such as Hans-Ole Hansen of Denmark. Hansen took it upon himself, as a teenager, to attempt an authentic reconstruction of a specific Neolithic house pattern (1962). This experiment gave rise, in time, to Hansen's prestigious Lejre Research Center in Lejre, Denmark. The center proved so popular that it was imitated all over Europe as projects in experimental archeology gained in popularity. It is still thriving there today.

In the mid 1960s, flintknapper Don Crabtree and archeologist Francois Bordes started working together (1969) to show archeologists that experimental studies with stone tools were important to science. Flintknapping quickly evolved from a quaint hobby into the serious field of lithic technology.

These studies inspired numerous technologists around the world to start taking experimental archeology seriously. College courses popped up all over and field school projects in experimental archeology appeared, mostly in the 1970s (DeHaas 1978, Reynolds 1979, Callahan 1976, 1981). For a detailed overview of who was doing what around the world, study John Coles' two synopses with care (1973, 1979). Survival schools also started gaining in popularity at this time, thanks largely to Larry Dean Olsen (1967). Although this was not experimental archeology, survival skills still involved many of the same primitive technologies which interested both groups.

During the 1980s, interest in experimental archeology and lithic technology in the States faded rapidly because of unwarranted, unfair, and harsh criticism mounted by archeology "guru" David Hurst Thomas (1986) and others. The fainthearted dropped by the wayside and the pioneers went into seclusion—ever improving their skills and methodology, but keeping the results of their work to themselves. Meanwhile, the survival schools were growing by leaps and bounds as interest in technology as an end in and of itself, not as a means to science, which was where the criticism lay, gained in popularity.

Finally, as the field was bursting at the seams for expression, the Society of Primitive Technology was born in 1989. The rest of the story you know.

So where does that leave experimental archeology today? Interest in Europe never diminished, but has continued to grow and gain respect. In the USA, however, experimental archeology is all but dead. Most of the proponents have changed direction and gone into more "respectable" professions. Others, the die-hards, are still out there plugging away, making better and better science, but, as I said, doing so in privacy until the time is ripe for fruition.

Perhaps that time has come. The Board of Directors of the SPT, at their last annual meeting, made a commitment to look into experimental archeology again, to dust it off, to give it a second chance. Realizing the common bond of interest between technology and experimental archeology, the Board is considering the sponsorship of exciting new projects in experimental archeology. For now the focus should be upon the methodology rather than the theory, upon the experiment more than its meaning to science.

Accordingly, I would now like to offer some suggestions as to how to distinguish three different levels of investment in doing physical reconstructions. (The following is condensed from Callahan ms: 35-46.)

These Levels dawned upon me as I personally examined projects in primitive technology and experimental archeology around the world. I came to realize that different attitudes and levels of quality were being expressed, often without the re-creators being aware of it. To avoid the pitfalls of claiming to be more or less scientific than you really are, I'd suggest a careful consideration of your objectives and a clear understanding of which level you are shooting for.

Level I: NON-AUTHENTIC AND NON-SCIENTIFIC
("Play" level). Reproductions which are unsuccessful or non-functional units, whether undertaken with the correct period tools, materials, and procedures or not. Such reproductions may vary between honest, failed attempts at authentic units or blatantly non-authentic simulations of authentic originals. Artifact examples might range from an arrow which is made with the proper tools, materials, and procedures but which does not fly straight (improper alignment of fletching, underspined shaft, or simply too crooked) to an immaculate, straight-shooting arrow made with modern tools from a commercial dowel.

These projects usually feature poorly researched, literal interpretations of ethnohistorical sketches or written accounts and are generalized versions of supposedly typical but usually imaginary situations. Although what the situation may pose to say and what it actually communicates may be at odds, I must add that the intentions of the designers are usually reverent and the mistakes often made in ignorance rather than by deliberation.

Level II: AUTHENTIC BUT NON-SCIENTIFIC
(Experiential level). Reproductions which are successful, functional units undertaken with the correct period tools, materials, and procedures. An artifact example might include the aforementioned arrow, made with the proper tools, materials, and procedures, which does fly true.

Level II projects vary between those which are private and short-lived to those which are permanent and open to the public. Thus their educational value may fluctuate between "learning by doing" experiences for the builders and the better living history type re-enactments for the media or general public. In general, the questions which are raised are of the experiential or "how" variety rather than of the experimental or "why" variety.

The value of these projects lies not only in their technological authenticity but in the critically important, experiential training which they impart to their practitioners—training which is imperative for gaining the experience required to attempt Level III reconstructions, which is where experimental archeology lies. (Level II is not experimental archeology.) It is my opinion that while Level II projects need not necessarily gravitate toward the Level II category, those who find themselves caught in Level I projects should work toward Level II status as rapidly as feasible. Likewise, and this is critically important, Level III projects should not be undertaken until Level II proficiency has provided adequate training (Kelterborn 1990).

Level III: AUTHENTIC AND SCIENTIFIC
(Experimental level). Reconstructions which are successful, functional units undertaken with the correct period tools, materials, and procedures and which are scientifically monitored. That is, objects are not just made, they are tested. An artifact example would again include the aforementioned arrow, still flying true. But this time it would be accompanied by data which documents its fabrication thoroughly enough that another could duplicate it. Without such documentation, there is no experiment. (Not only is data kept, but research reports, either in the form of lectures of publications, result so that others might have access to this information). The data might be supplemented with further information concerning the arrow's performance and/or damage patterns, which is then applied back to the relevant archeological situation so as to answer questions concerning the original arrow. This is experimental archeology.

Level III projects demand that the designer and participants be fully aware of the investment in time and energy required to follow such undertakings through and plan accordingly. It is also essential to have experience with Level II reconstructions before Level III experiments are begun, for if the basic skills have not been acquired before the experiment begins, learning will interfere with research, a valid point to which Thomas alluded in his criticism (1986).

It should not be forgotten that Level III projects include not simply the building of a dwelling or whatever, as physically exhausting as that may be, but the monitoring and the analysis of the associated data as well as the drafting up and presentation of a report. The latter task is the burden of the scientist. Unless the results of a test are made available so that it may be repeated by others, that test was an experience (Level II) not an experiment (Level III). Without such monitoring, however, there is no science. This is not to say that undocumented experiences with authentic reconstructions are not of intrinsic worth. They may indeed be. But they should not be passed off as science, as was all too often the case in the past.

While in the narrow sense, reconstructive experimental archeology is usually concerned with the re-creation of authentic and scientifically monitored technological projects, in the broader sense, the field embraces all types and levels of serious reconstructions. Therefore perhaps our discipline should provide models by which anyone interested in understanding that part of ourselves amenable to re-creation, which we feel has been lost in the past, may turn for guidance. If the new experimental archeology can help in this search for truth, then perhaps the time has come when it should be resurrected.

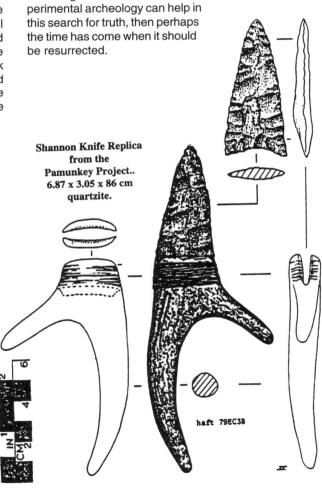

Shannon Knife Replica from the Pamunkey Project.. 6.87 x 3.05 x 86 cm quartzite.

haft 79EC3B

REFERENCES

Bordes, Francois and Don Crabtree
1969   *The Corbiac Blade Technique and other Experiments.* Tebiwa 12(2): 1-21.

Callahan,Errett
1976   *Experimental Archeology Papers #4. The Pamunkey Project Phases I and II.* E. Callahan, editor. Dept. of Sociology and Anthropology, Virginia Commonwealth University, Richmond.
1981   *Pamunkey Housebuilding: an Experimental Study of Late Woodland Construction Technology in the Powhatan Confederacy.* PhD dissertation, Catholic University of America. University Microfilms International #8121269.
ms   *The Cahokia Pit House Project: a Case Study in Reconstructive Archeology.* Manuscript.

Coles, John
1973   *Archaeology by Experiment.* Charles Scribners & Sons, NY.
1979   *Experimental Archaeology.* Academic Press, London, New York.

Dehaas, R. Horreüs
1978   *Living A Stone Age Life.* Typescript, Zwolle, Netherlands.

Hansen, Hans-Ole
1962   *I Built A Stone Age House.* John Day Co., NY.

Kelterborn, Peter
1990   *Preconditions and Strategies for Experimental Archaeology.* In Cahiers du Quaternaire no. 17— Le Silex de sa Genése á L'outil, Vth international flint symposium. Bordeaux, France. Edited by Séronce-Vivien and Lenoir: 599-602.

Olsen, Larry Dean
1967   *Outdoor Survival Skills.* Brigham Younh University Press.

Reynolds, Peter
1967   *Iron-Age Farm: The Butser Experiment.* British Museum Publications Ltd.

Thomas, David Hurst
1986   Hunter-gatherer archaeology. *In American Archaeology, Past and Future.* Edited by Maltzer, Fower, and Sabloff. Smithsonian Institution Press: 247-251.

The Society of Primitive Technology and Experimental Archaeology

By David Wescott

Introduction

The question, at this point, is still "who are we"? Is what we do limited to experimental archaeology, or is EA only a part of what we do ? For much of the SPT membership the answer would be "who cares?...I don't need more politics, I just want to have fun doing what I like." Others who are aware of the need for accuracy in materials, tools, procedures and context, would say "I've heard the arguments of the "scholars" and their goals have merit. But I've watched their infighting and petty battles to be at the top of the pigpile and tear each other down. I've also listened to their criticisms of what I do ("playing Indian"), and for people who have "created" entire cultural scenarios based on a single point type, they have no room to judge me for speculating.

At least my suggestions are based on practiced skills. "

And then there are those pioneers who have braved the slings and arrows of the traditional scientists in trying to bring the field to a respectable level of precision. Their response may be "we have the skills and capacity to offer far more than well practiced skills. What we do has interpretive value for a field (understanding mankind) that, in many ways, shares goals that are common to us all. By emulating the techniques of science and refining the outcomes of our projects, we can provide solid foundations of experience, insight and theory, upon which the entire field may build."

These responses represent much of the membership of the Society of Primitive Technology. To support one stance in favor of the others would be in direct opposition to

...continued on page 8

GENERAL OPERATING PRINCIPLES

from Cahokia manuscript by Errett Callahan, pages 157-159*

The Experimental Approach: More than Exercise

Experimental Archeology, as defined in Chapter 2-D, was employed on this project as a theoretical framework and practical application because it not only promised a means of clarifying the archeological record, but it promised to lend a degree of dignity to the project which a straightforward reconstruction exercise might not. The distinction between "experimentation" and "exercise" (which is also spelled out in Chapter 2-D) should be made clear to participants at the outset of any project (cf Callahan 1981:, 1987:). To reiterate, the exercise of reconstructing an aboriginal artifact, be it a stone tool or a house, should not be claimed as a valid experiment unless, first, the craftsmanship equals the original and, second, unless scientific methodology is followed. In my opinion, many of the so-called "experiments" so frequently seen within the discipline today are no more than craft exercises. As exercises, they may indeed have sound value because exercise builds the expertise needed for experimentation to claim credibility (cf Flenniken 1977: Callahan 1987: 4,5; Olausson 1987). But an exercise (i.e., a Level II project) does not automatically constitute an experiment simply because of the sincerity of the craftsman or the magnitude of the undertaking. An experiment (i.e., a Level III project) requires (1) the keeping of data under controlled conditions (enough data so that another may independently repeat the results: Hansen 1972: 11), and (2) the interpretation of that data in the light of the problem under investigation. A consequence of this interpretation should be one or more probability statements or inferences, pertinent to the unknowns. Thus it is the ordering of the details, the manipulation of the context within which the exercise operates, which determines its scientific merit or lack thereof.

On the Cahokia Project, we chose to adhere closely to the general operating principles espoused for experimental archeology by Dr. John Coles (1979: 46-48). These principles are widely accepted and form the very backbone of experimental archeology today. They may be summarized as [seen below] [cf Callahan 1981: 142]:

In 1981 I proposed a similar set of general operating procedures, which compliments Dr. Coles' list (Callahan 1981;142-147). Since this list provided additional guidance, I will summarize it here.

COLES PROPOSAL, 1979

1 - Use the same materials available in the past;
2 - Use the same methods appropriate to the past;
3 - Analyze the results using modern technology;
4 - Specify the scale of the reproduction;
5 - Repeat the experiment;
6 - Improvise and adapt to changing conditions;
7 - Do not claim proof. Evaluate with modesty.
8 - Be honest. Do not exaggerate.

*Please consult Chapter 1-C for additional
comments concerning principles of operation.

CALLAHAN PROPOSAL, 1981

1 - Use the same kinds of tools available in the past;
2 - Use the same kinds of raw materials available in the past;
3 - Use the same material articulation appropriate to the past;
4 - Relate experiments to hypotheses and use them in the construction of inferences.
5 - Seek a range of solutions rather than single answers;
6 - Test under field conditions which approximate those in the past;
7 - Document all pertinent experimental information;
8 - Build at full scale;
9 - Seek to reproduce technology, not social systems; avoid theatrics;
10 - Strictly avoid the reuse of prehistoric sites and artifacts;
11 - Document and register all experimental sites.

the goals and intent of the Society. In order to foster communication at the broadest levels, we have to provide a forum for including a variety of involvements, not a bully pulpit for those with the loudest voices or an axe to grind. Our membership represents a spectrum of participants ranging from trained professionals to the man in the street, and in the past five years with the SPT we have learned that everyone has something to offer. Membership in the SPT is not exclusive to any one agenda.

Science paints in shades of gray what is then converted to black and white.
Dick Hernstein

The Problem - Definition and Reality

According to Brian Fagan **anthropology** is the study of humankind's interacting social life, culture and natural environment. **Archaeology** is the study of human cultures and technologies , and is a subdiscipline of anthropology. Errett's definition of **experimental archaeology** - *"that branch of archeology which seeks to interpret material culture, technology, or lifeways of the past by means of replication, reconstruction or theoretical modeling"* - does not stop at the artifacts, but strives to also understand the intangible elements behind the artifacts.

In most of the world, the projects and theories of experimental archaeology have a long and respected tradition as being a complementary component of archaeological field work and research. It provides a solid experiential and scientific foundation for the assumptions and conclusions created from evidence unearthed through survey and excavation. These "two distinctly different means of data collecting", when merged at the level of interpretation, cross the sacred boundary between social and physical science, creating **anthropological archaeology** (read *Lightning Bird* by Lyall Watson for a better understanding of this relationship).

archaeologist - interprets evidence from sites, artifacts and features.
technologist - interprets evidence from reproductions, testing and experience.

During the late 60's and through the 70's, EA in the U.S. had a popular following. It wasn't until the early 80's that heavy criticism was leveled against the claims of EA. Whether warranted or not, the field of EA was not prepared to respond to the criticism, and to this date has yet to mount an adequate response. The foundation was weak, the guidelines were not widely accepted or adhered to, and the body was too busy playing the ladder climbing game to work together to create what was needed to move forward. The result - guerrilla technology and splintered efforts.

At this point, and accepting the above definitions, the problem takes on two separate facets; those criticisms from without, and those from within the field.

Criticisms From Without:

After collecting and reading all of the available articles on experimental archaeology, 5 common criticisms need to be addressed. Some of them we can do something about, others should be recognized as concerns, but there is little we can do other than learn from them..

1. Claims of being more than we are - How can we expect others to respect what we do when we have been unwilling to establish definitions and guidelines, and, either through ignorance or ego, ignore the writings of those (Coles, Kelterborn, Anderson, Callahan, etc.) who have tried to set models for us to adhere to. Until we accept guidelines to work within, we will always be susceptible to this criticism.

2. Claims are too sweeping - Science reduces the variables and at the same time focuses the results toward more refined interpretation by narrowing the field of speculation. However , the results are no less speculation. Heed Coles admonition that nothing can be proven with a certainty. This applies to both the technologist and archaeologist.

3. Too many liberties are taken on possible solutions - All we can present are possible or optional solutions to problems or questions. Controls are needed to narrow results to only those options that have a solid technological foundation, and a realistic possibility of working.

4. Too obscure testing - To avoid criticisms technologists are moving to more and more

TABLE 1

** Box numbers are for reference only. No hierarchy is implied.	DEVELOPMENTAL TECHNOLOGY	PRIMITIVE TECHNOLOGY	EXPERIMENTAL ARCHAEOLOGY
BASIS	**Adaptation - Model**	**Model - Artifact**	**Artifact - Evidence**
SIMULATION "What" Product - Visual Appearances	1	2	3
EXPERIENTIAL "How" Process - Production Methods	4	5	6
SCIENTIFIC "Why" Application - Theory	7	8	9

obscure projects. Callahan proposes that until we establish a solid foundation we focus on method more than theory, upon the experiment not the meaning. With solid guidelines and definitions we should be **free to pursue both**.

5. Jumping from applied to social science - The academics say that it is impossible for technologists (those who "play Indian") to recreate how people thought or acted, nor is it possible to explore the "why". Yet they are merrily engaged in creating computer models to explore those very questions. We need to be very careful what we claim, and we need to present our results in a very professional manner...or we need to be willing to blow off their criticisms and go about our business...or we need to seek a middle ground.

Criticisms From Within:

1. Until the rules are clear, we don't want to play the game - Critical review is necessary to improve and monitor quality, but review should be done against established criteria and not lowered to personal attacks. Both active technologists and archaeologists alike are unwilling to put forward many neat ideas because of their fear of criticism. This is a real blemish on the entire field, and an indictment against those who have let it become the norm and participate in its practice.

2. Guidelines and models to date are too limiting and exclusionary - Science, experience, and simulation are not above or below one another, they are simply different. Guidelines and models shouldn't be used to stifle the field or individuals, but better define where on the matrix you happen to be involved (by choice). No one should be able to criticize where anyone else chooses to participate, so long as we all understand the model.

Theory without practice is empty;
Practice without theory is blind.
Immanual Kant

A Proposal

I would like to propose the following as a model for how our field can proceed to define itself, and technologists can participate at a chosen level of commitment compatible with their skill, knowledge and interest.

1. As a body we accept the levels of experimentation (Callahan, Coles)

as: Simulation, Experiential, and Scientific. These levels can also be applied to the educational overlay of affective (coming to an appreciation of), psycho-motor (coming to a higher mental/physical ability), and cognitive (coming to a higher understanding and application).

2. In order to provide a broad and level playing field, we avoid a hierarchal model in favor of a spectral view of our field, based on a matrix of options rather than a pyramid (pyramids have limited space at the top, and invite a "king of the hill" attitude). The foundation

Developmental Technology
** Levels I-III based on a **generalized model or experimental design** that may be part of or derived from the prehistoric/ethnographic record.
** Levels I-III use **applicable** materials and procedures. The process of manufacture (the tool) is not important. The application of the design is as important as the product.
** Objective is to produce a **functional** replication/reconstruction/reenactment of the original template or new design.
** Level III requires the application of the scientific method, as well as documentation and reporting of the process, and provides theoretical insight into direct applications to the fields of experimental archaeology and primitive technology.

Primitive Technology-
** Levels I-III based on an **artifact or generalized model** that may be part of or derived from the prehistoric/ethnographic record.
** Level II uses **appropriate** materials and procedures, may use modern tools during learning stages. Level III stresses accurately researched material, tools, and procedures.
** Objective is to produce a **plausible** replication/reconstruction/reenactment of the original artifact/template, and gain insights and make inferences to related fields.
** Level III requires the application of the scientific method, as well as documentation and reporting of the process, and provides insight into possible applications to the many fields of social and applied sciences including: archaeology, anthropology, sociology, living history, recreation and others.

Experimental Archaeology -
** Levels I-III based on a **specific "artifact", features or evidence** from the prehistoric/ethnographic record. The weakness of Level I is in poor research or interpretation of the record.
** Level II uses appropriate materials and procedures, may use modern tools during learning stages. Level III limited to **accurately researched** material, tools, and procedures .
** Objective is to produce a **precise** (Level II and III) replication/reconstruction of the original artifact/evidence. Level II and III imply a broader understanding of the field. "Controlled creativity" can be applied "only in the absence of archeological fact".
** Level III requires the application of the scientific method, as well as documentation and monitoring /reporting of the process, and relates directly to the field of anthropology.

for classification is based on materials, tools, techniques, templates and objectives of the experiment.

3. We establish guidelines, definitions and models clearly enough that participants can "judge" themselves against criteria, and progress along a continuum as they feel the need, thus avoiding personality clashes and judgmental posturing.

Using the numbered boxes on the matrix (Table 1), levels of commitment can better be explained individually. The model not only strongly supports the efforts of experimental archaeology and allows for precision, but also provides an opportunity for involvement of technologists practicing at a variety of levels without getting caught up in politics and science.

1. Developmental Simulation - the spirit of what we do...the starting point for most people, especially kids. I see a picture of an atlatl in a book. So, I run out into the garage and build one. Since I have no wood or tools, or by choice, I make one from scraps of any material that may be on hand. I am interested enough to try it out and attempt to come to a better appreciation of what the thing is.

2. Primitive Simulation - the point where many of us are now. I want my new thing to look a little more like the "real thing", so I read more, find more pictures and a simple diagram on how the thing works. I gather some wood and a saw, and try again.

3. Archaeological Simulation - the place where most displays and educational programs are now. I go to my local museum and see an atlatl that was discovered in a cave just up the road from where I live. I go home and whip one out on the band saw.

4. Developmental Experience - the motivational point for many of us. I want better performance from my atlatl, so I can set a world distance record. I do some research to get a better understanding of the mechanical workings of the system, obtain materials that are best suited for the job, practice, and then call Guinness.

5. Primitive Experience - the heart of what we do...where most of us want to be. I want to live for awhile like the prehistoric residents of my backyard. I want to do it the way they did it. Total "primitive". I have to learn about wood, tool making and use, hunting, and more. If I choose to follow a specific culture, everything I do is based on what I can learn about them. I train myself to "think" and perform just like they did.

6. Archaeological Experience - the beginning of scientific experimentation. I want to know more about what I find in the field or behind museum glass. ...what's it made of, how is it made, and what does it take for me to reproduce it. I can really do it the way I think it must have been done before.

7. Developmental Experimentation - the realm of the thinker. I have an understanding of scientific process and a calculator, and I want to know the engineering and theory of what makes an atlatl propel its missile (Developmental Experimentation must have a subject and foundation that are directly related to Primitive Technology and Experimental Archaeology, otherwise, it has shifted into the realm of modern technology).

8. Primitive Experimentation - where wise men fear to tread. I want to explain to the academic that his diagram and explanation of how an atlatl works is incorrect, but just showing him doesn't always cut it. I have to accurately

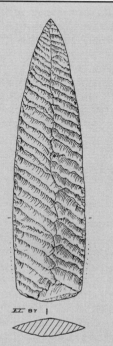

If I would study any old, lost art, let us say, I must make myself the artisan of it - must, by examining its product, learn both to see and to feel as much as may be the conditions under which they were produced and the needs they supplied or satisfied; then, rigidly adhering to those conditions and constrained by their resources alone, as ignorantly and anxiously strive with my own hands to reproduce, not to imitate, these things as ever strove primitive man to produce them. I have virtually the same hands he had, the same physique, generally or fundamentally the same actival and mental functions too, that men had in ages gone by, no matter how remote. If, then, I dominate myself with their needs, surround myself with their material conditions, aim to do as they did, the chances are that I shall restore their acts and their arts, however lost or hidden; shall learn precisely as they learned, rediscovering what they discovered precisely as they discovered it. Thus may I reproduce an art in all its stages; see how it began, grew, developed into and affected other arts and things — all because, under the circumstances I limit myself to the like of, — it became and grew and differentiated in other days.

Frank Hamilton Cushing
The American Anthropologist, 1895

record the results. Of course, while I was jotting down notes and tables, my dinner got away.

9. Archaeological Experimentation - the soul of the process. I want to reproduce enough tangible evidence that I've got a real good foundation from which to venture into the implications that suggest that "how to fling a stick with a board" is only part of the question.

*In the broad sense, an experience and a simulation can be a experiment. In the narrow sense, there can be no true experiment without science (structured, monitored, reported).

IN DEFENSE OF LEVEL II
Errett Callahan

It seems a lot of people have misunderstood what I was trying to say about the three levels of investment in experimental archeology (*PT Newsletter #1*). It's not a hierarchical progression starting at Level I and moving up to Level III. What level you are on usually has little to do with your learning or skill level. It's Level II, not Level I that the vast majority of our membership practices, and I've never thought otherwise. If you start out as a beginner and try to make an authentic reproduction in an authentic way, you're starting out in Level II. Hopefully, your results will keep you there. When you start out this way, your work automatically has integrity, even if it is fun and playful as well. And remember this — you can "play" or have "fun" in all three levels. When I said "play" before I was referring to such things as shelter reconstructions I've seen made with plywood and plastic sheeting, covered with branches or mats to make them look authentic. This is what you used to see in tourist traps around the country. That's what I mean by "play". I don't think a single one of our members is doing that. From what I've seen, most of our members are active in Level II learning and practice—authentic and proud of it. That's what our Society is all about. I just say, let's call it primitive technology, not scientific experimental archeology. It's not scientific experimental archeology unless you make science and that entails a lot of paperwork. If you're not up to this then do primitive technology and don't make any excuses. But don't give us plastic sheeting or copper billets and call it authentic.

Some Suggested Definitions*

simulation - honest, failed attempts to blatant forgeries.
experiential - focus on training and insight more than experimentation.
scientific - meets Kelterborns 7 criteria. Don't just make things, test things.

intangible - never a physical object...understanding of mankind.
tangible - actual evidence is present; measurable. Replicas can be made.
non-tangible - formerly tangible, but disintegrated. Reconstructions can be made.

template - mental image created by tangible, nontangible and intangible information.
model - design generalized or created from a template.
evidence - tangible information
artifact - complete is tangible, incomplete is nontangible.
feature - non-artifactual material evidence - post molds, hearths, etc.

reconstruction - dictionary- from given or available information.; falls within what is the inferred range of variation of the original, based on non-tangible materials; does not imply complete accuracy..one of many ways it could have been done.
replication/replica - dictionary- close to or exact copy or reproduction; falls within what is the range of variation of the original, based on tangible materials.
simulation - only approximates attributes of the original. does not fall within the range of variation of the original.
reproduction - dictionary - to make a copy duplicate, or representation; through reconstruction, replication or simulation.
recreate - cannot be done; anything beyond actual/tangible evidence is speculation.

*Many of the term definitions and explanations of the levels are from 5 different Callahan papers on experimental archaeology (see *Living Archeology: Projects in Subsistence Living,* 1975, and *The Maturation of Experimental Archeology: A Critical View,* 1981). In writing this paper, much of my attempt has been to align Errett's thinking about experimental archaeology (using excerpts and quotes from these papers) with what I feel to be the broader scope of the entire field. I take no credit for anything that sounds intelligent. I feel that we should embrace experimental archaeology as a major aspect of what we do, and work toward moving the entire field in new and exciting directions.

The construction crew in front of the completed Lower Catawba River Aboriginal House at the Schiele Museum of Natural History in Gastonia, North Carolina, 1988.

SHELTERED IN PREHISTORY

By Steve Watts

The peaks of the conical skin tents
of Lapps and Lakotas
The thatching of wattled and daubed
homes from Guatemala, to Africa, to
Korea...
The domed roofs of barks, mats and
ice arching over Iroquois, Kickapoo
and Inuit...
The layers of leaves shingled and
sloped to shed rains blown in from
the Pacific and Carribean...
And the painted ceilings—dancing
in the flickering light deep in
caves from California to the
Mediterranean...

All these and more have sheltered the Family of Man through millenia of dark nights and through generations of times good and bad. All these and more we see now as we look up, back, and within to that ancient architectural heritage which covers us all.

From the expedient use of an existing rock shelter for an overnight bivouac, to the scientific reconstruction of an entire Neolithic village—primitive technologists explore the wide variety of solutions to the age-old problem of protection from the elements. Aboriginal responses to the need for shelter are as different as the cultures and environments from which they come. The exercise of recreating these hearths and homes may thereby open new doors of perception into those peoples and places of the then and there, and ultimately, into we of the here and now.

Primitive house building projects may be undertaken for the sake of research, educational interpretation, sheer utility, or the pleasurable satisfaction of curiosity. All of these motives are valid in their own sphere and all require that many aspects of aboriginal technology be brought to application. Tools, techniques, use and availability of natural resources, seasonal considerations, and group/family/social structure all figure into the mix when planning, building and maintaining such reconstructions. It is an area of primitive technology which often calls for monumental effort and a drive to persevere against odds and the unknown.

Primitive house building projects may be undertaken for the sake of research, educational interpretation, sheer utility, or the pleasurable satisfaction of curiosity. All of these motives are valid in their own sphere an all require that many aspects of aboriginal technology be brought to application.

Hans-Ole Hansen began his house building experiences in Denmark alone in the 1950's which ultimately led to the Historical-Archaeological Research Center at Lejre. Here reconstructed prehistoric houses set the stage for a variety of primitive living experiments. The Butser Ancient Farm Research Project in England under the direction of Peter Reynolds likewise features housing projects in its research. And, in Holland, R. Horreus de Haas' Polder Project (done with such quality and lack of pretense) involved group living in houses built in the late Prehistoric style.

Though not nearly as well funded, publicized or long-lived as their European cousins, primitive house building endeavors in North America have produced important sets of data and experiences. From Errett Callahan in the east with more than fifty house reconstuctions to his credit, to John White in the Midwest with his emphasis on Woodland and Mississippian housing, to John Fagan's northwest coast plank house project (built completely with aboriginal - style tools), to the countless lesser known and unknown individuals and institutions across the country involved on many levels and in many ways—the desire to reconstruct the architectural past is fleshed out.

Within these pages you will meet some of these people and learn more of their efforts. Efforts which for the most part go unnoticed. Sitting with them beneath the roofs and within the walls they have constructed, we can rediscover the roofs and walls of our own lineages. Shelters—designed to hold back the wind, the rain and the intruders, and to house the fire, the knowledge and the sharing.

Come on in.

"*Any particular reconstruction may be almost right, or totally wrong, or any degree inbetween. This applies to the reconstruction of a structure, a tool, or a process. It may be proven right or wrong to a greater or lesser extent by evidence from the past, or functionally so, or not so by experimental use. In all cases it must be constantly re-evaluated.*"   *Steve Watts, 1988*

The Catawba Indian Village mat and hide covered house was made with stone age tools.

EVOLUTION OF AN IDEA

"House reconstruction - the physical realization of one possible interpretation."
Peter Reynolds, Butser Ancient farm Research Project, England

"They have other sorts of Cabins... that are covered overhead; the rest left open for the Air. These;;;serve for pleasant Banqueting-Houses in the hot Seaon of the Year."
John lawson, 1701

Quotes from an historic journal....
...stimulate an idea for a project.

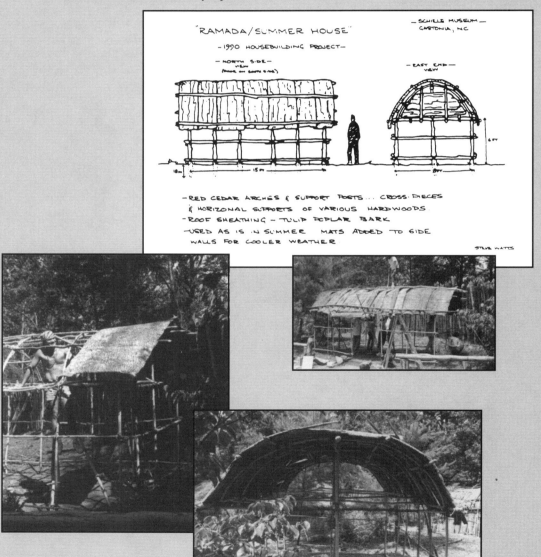

From: The Watts Notebook,
Page 21, June 28, 1988.

Studies of prehistoric technologies, tool forms, and artifact types have resulted in part from a desire to go beyond ethnographic analogy and to supplement the often sketchy field notes and interpretations of ethnographers and historians. In most cases the ethnographer or historical observer did not have the opportunity to observe a particular task from its inception to its conclusion and of necessity reported on conditions observed at only one point in time. Thus, detailed observations of complex processes or manufacturing procedures that require a specific series of activities performed over a period of time are often lacking, and the complexities of performing various tasks within primitive technologies are often misrepresented in the ethnographic and historical records.

Experimental archaeology, then is generally the only means of providing additional information about primitive technologies or potential solutions to questions to manufacture and use processes that have not been addressed adequately in the historical or ethnographic literature.

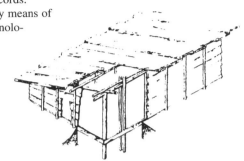

John L. Fagan
Experimental Archaeology and Public
Involvement: A Case Study

Living in the Past

In 1980 the BBC sponsored a one year project to see how modern people would adapt to iron age technology and living skills. The following is a brief excerpt from the project journal relating to living in the grass thatched common house (30' high and 50' across).

It is necessary to live an experience in order fully to comprehend it.
John Percival, *Living in the Past,* 1980.

The inside of the big round house was always filled with a thin haze of woodsmoke, which turned into a choking fog when the baking stove was fired in the early morning. Everybody was kippered by it. Skin, hair, clothes, everything, was deeply impregnated, so that they smelt, quite sweetly but distinctly of woodsmoke.....the round house was remarkably warm. In the daytime, even with both doors gaping to the cold air to let in what little light there was, the area round the fire was always warm. At night, with the doors closed it was almost to hot for comfort. After the evening meal people would spread their sheepskins on the uneven floor and gather close around the fire, chatting, spinning, one of the girls might be knitting and one of the men whittling a knife handle or making a thumb pot from clay prepared earlier in the day. The fire would be banked up brightly, not for warmth, but to provide extra light. So, as the evening lengthened, the circle widened as everyone withdrew from the heat, often to lie on the bare earth floor and gaze at the firelight flickering on the polished beams of the roof. Not that they were really polished, but the smoke had formed a shiny black carbon surface on the rafters and dyed the thatch a deep orange, the straw also seemingly varnished by the smoke until it shone. Thick black nets of cobweb, heavy with soot, spoiled the illusion of zealous cleanliness.

Archaeologists used once to believe that the fire hazard inside these round houses must have been a constant risk, and I had worried about myself. But the sparks which swarmed towards the roof seemed to die before they reached the black pocket of constant darkness, just beneath the roof cone itself.

On the nights that I stayed in the round house I would sometime spread my sleeping bag close to the fire as it slowly burned down. The villagers had a system for keeping it burning all night. The cooks for the following day - in practice it was always the man who was responsible for the fire - would cut and bring into the house a huge green log, an 'all-nighter'. The fire would be raked and scattered and the big log placed on the embers. The log would then smolder gently all night long and the cook in charge would only have to spend ten or fifteen minutes in the morning with dry twigs and split kindling blowing and fanning until it flared bright and hot to cook the breakfast of boiled wheat and cereal coffee.

WHY BUILD
TRADITIONAL HOUSES TODAY ?

By John and Ela White, Ancient Lifeways Institute

As a young boy I was fortunate to have relatives of my grandparents' generation who still spoke the Cherokee language. Proud of their Cherokee and Shawnee ancestry and culture-bearers in the truest sense, they filled me with an awareness of my responsibility to keep our lineage traditions alive. They communicated the importance of traditional culture and that it was not to be tampered with or joked about. These attitudes, which I absorbed as a young boy, are still with me.

Along with a wide range of oral traditions (stories), I also learned traditional technologies from them—pottery, cordage, flint knapping, wood working and details of house construction. My uncle told me that before the hewn log cabins there were those constructed of "poles" and that before them the Cherokee lived in clay-plastered wattle and daub homes with thatched or bark-shingled roofs. Behind each "summer" house there was the aw-si or winter house, a small earth lodge. He demonstrated its construction by using miniature timbers whittled with appropriate crotches for rafters and forks from which to suspend household goods and hunting equipment. A foot or more in diameter, it was large enough to learn construction techniques and sequences.

While on the hunt or in times of war, oval lodges of the age-old woodland pattern were built, covered with bark and canvas or cattail mats. Smaller structures based on the same pattern were used for sweat lodges, birthing and menstrual lodges.

The Gatiyi or great communal town house, was vividly remembered long after the last of them had fallen in decay or been burned by the Americans. Holding up to 400 or 500 people, ideally raised on a substructure mound, the town house dominated a Cherokee settlement. Basically an earth lodge with a steeper and higher roof than those of the Paw-

nee or Mandan, all serious community activity took place either within its vastness or in the plaza or square in front.

The stories I heard were in a kitchen by the wood cook stove or up in the hills of the Sequatchie Valley near Chattanooga. My father and his mother's people were born there only a short distance from the Chickamauga towns where our ancestors had lived and died to hold back the frontier for just a little while.

Several years later I talked at length with a Nanticoke woman in Pennsylvania who had been born in a thatched birthing lodge. Her family was one of the last to speak the Nanticoke language. As my mother's mother had a farm in the traditional Nanticoke territory, I took the opportunity to build a small thatched lodge as it had been described to me. I

Storytelling in the longhouse.

spent some weeks in 1951 or 52 living in it. Both the thatch and I were saturated with the delicious wood smoke. The old Nanticoke woman had talked in length of their great dugout canoes and of her people's extensive lore of the moon, tides and the ways of water creatures and migratory birds.

My memory of those kindly old people is that they would gladly share their treasure of traditional knowledge with anyone who was respectful and interested. At the slightest sign of inappropriate behavior or attitude, however, they closed up like a clam. They wanted their knowledge preserved but it was more important that it be respected. When the last of my older relatives died, it was like a door had been closed forever. Then one day I found where the old BAE reports were hiding in the library....

In graduate school at the University of Chicago and Stanford I was concerned with the anthropological study of the cultural transmission process itself. What could be learned from the experiences of others that would benefit those concerned with the survival of traditional culture in contemporary Native American Communities?

The approach of George and Louise Spindler, depicting the interrelationship of the many complex aspects of the cultural transmission process, did much to expand my horizon beyond the idea of some wise old person teaching tribal wisdom. I began to see more clearly how objects and the technologies required to make them formed linkages between a lifeway and its environment. An object, a "thing," carried with it many associated pieces of cultural data, like a bunch of grapes. My older relatives had seen this in a concrete form—that there were tiny threads that stretched through time connecting the here and now with whomever made the object in the past. It didn't have to be a family heirloom; it could be an arrowhead or potsherd in a farmer's field or an object in a museum.

But it was the accidental discovery of a small volume in the Stanford Bookstore that was to pull together these many threads. *Understanding Fire and Clay* by Arne Bjorn was a work concerned with the rediscovery of ancient Danish pottery firing techniques. But in the background of so many illustrations there were fantastic houses, many of them. A letter to Arne Bjorn led to a gracious invitation to visit the Historisk/Archaeologisk Forsogscentret at Lejre, Denmark. In 1972 the White family spent the summer at Lejre and several other programs that utilized reconstructed cultural environments.

At the Iron Age Research Center Ela, my wife and colleague, studied hanging warp loom weaving techniques with Ninna Rathje, whose replications of the Bog Peoples' woven clothing we saw in the National Museum in Copenhagen. I primarily worked with Arne Bjorn, who had developed the ceramic research program. These Danes were very interested in Cherokee pottery technology that I had been taught by my great aunt Sally Hicks. I had also learned how to chip arrowheads, scrapers and gunflints from my great uncle Charlie Copeland and demonstrated this. (In my family flint knapping, pottery and many stories never died out.) It was Arne Bjorn who impressed on me how lucky I was to carry this knowledge as a living tradition.

It was the houses, however, that had drawn us to Lejre and Ela and I were overwhelmed by their impact as a cultural environment. We lived, cooked and slept in one, together with our four children. We both knew immediately that this was how to teach a culture, that this was where

everything seemed to fall into place. Artifacts and traditional technology belong here. There is a natural flow in traditional technologies that rarely synchronizes with a modern classroom. Ever since Lejre we have felt that by far the most effective and appropriate educational environment in which to study ancient lifeways are reconstructed living environments.

As director of the project to build the Pawnee Earthlodge at the Field Museum of Natural History (Chicago), I intended to show how successful a replicated cultural environment can be within an existing museum facility. Working closely with tribal elders, existing ethnographic collections and the late Dr. Gene Weltfish, the Earthlodge project was a bridge between the Pawnee, an academic institution and the general population. It was intended to build trust as well as to communicate what the Pawnee wanted us to understand about their culture.

In 1976 I began to construct traditional woodland structures at the Center for American Archaeology in Kampsville, IL. Ela taught non-loom weaving technology while I taught ceramics. This led to the establishment of the ethnographic component to Northwestern University's Archaeology Field School that I directed until 1985.

1978 saw the construction of a village of five structures representing the houses of various archaeological cultures of the Lower Illinois River Valley. As originally conceived, the village would function as a research and teaching facility as well as being available to the general tourist. Technologies appropriate to the culture were a part of the living environment of each house.

The oldest structure replicated was based on a post mold pattern from an Early Archaic horizon (ca 6500 BCE) at the Koster Site. Groupings of four post molds in a rectangular formation had been interpreted as a scattering of small rectangular buildings, barely large enough for a nuclear family. As some of these posts were up to 2' in diameter, it was obvious that they were not corner posts but the center posts of substantial structures. Features, including small hearths, occurred in an oval roughly 24' x 26' around the center posts. As there was no sign of an external wall, as present in later earthlodges, we reconstructed it with rafters reaching the ground. The Archaic house was thatched and we intended to cover it with sod the following year. A major flood in the

spring of 1979 damaged the house severely, although it was repaired. The walls of a nearby Mississippian wattle and daub structure formed its own substructure mound.

Another major flood in 1980 proved the folly of further construction in Kampsville and we began to build houses on our own land in Michael, five miles south, located in a side valley adjacent to a spring-fed creek with lots of natural resources. The location proved ideal. The first house constructed was based on the double-walled structure from the Zimmerman site, a proto-historic to historic Kaskaskia village on the Illinois River.

When the Center for American Archaeology closed their year-round educational program in 1985, Ancient Lifeways Institute began to accept students in Michael. Whereas in Kampsville students lived in dorms, we were now free to utilize our structures as living environments and students could live in the "village."

Maketa Mahwa, Black Wolf Village in the local Tamaroa language, provides an appropriate context where cultural activities take place. Consisting of two Illiniwek longhouses, the Kaskaskia house, a large domed winter lodge, a small derelict thatched structure and surrounded by a palisade, there are enough structures to "feel" like a village. Attempting to capture the flow of traditional activities, Ancient Lifeways Institute's programs involve finding natural resources and then processing and manufacturing items in the village. Evenings are filled with social activities such as traditional songs, dances and perhaps a gambling game. Each evening ends with a traditional story-telling in the artifact-rich Kaskaskia house.

We use structures as environments within which cultural activities take place. They provide a context that gives meaning to the various aspects of an ancient lifeway through enhancing empathy as well as communicating the interweaving of various technologies. Ancient Lifeways Institute's approach to cultural ecology is to use traditional structures as the logical intersection of human activities. Our modern homes and schools insulate us from so many thing—heat and cold, the phases of the moon, the length of the sun's cycle, the direction of the wind. An evening that ends around the flickering flames of a central hearth allows us to reflect on the ways of our ancestors and to truly enter that world.

The Law of Fire
from, *I Built a Stone Age House*, by Hans-Ole Hansen, 1962 English edition.

Do you know the law of fire?

You will learn it now. From the day the first man fetched fire from a burning tree or from the flame-pewing mouth of the great volcano, he and his descenants for thousands of generations have been subject to the law of fire.

My companions and I had to learn the laws of fire too. We did not tend our fire as we should, we were irreverent and did not see that there was always someone in attendance. So, one day the fire rose, stretched up, and reached for the roof. Straw and rush heads began to glow and curl up in the ties. Then it got hold of the roof. Suddenly we saw its face appear over the ridge of the roof, and our hearts went into our mouths in horror.

We did what we could to master the fire, labored by the sweat of our brows. We fought for the house that we had toiled so hard to build and in which we had spent so many happy hours. But the fire grew and grew, became a giant. Hissing, it spread along the underside of the roof, then rose up like an ogre and took the roof up with it into the air....the heat became so intense that we had to withdraw quite a distance to watch our handiwork being destroyed and collapsing rafter by rafter.

At last the Fire God himself fell silent and sank down behind the now blackened daub walls. Then there was silence everywhere, except for the loud, clear song of the grasshoppers in the bushes. We felt as if the fire had embraced the whole world, although it was only a thing of our own that had burned. Carefully and respectfully we stepped into the fire ravaged floor, still hot and now open to the sky, to see if anything had survived.

The memory of that day is firmly imprinted on our minds, and our advice to you is: profit by our bitter experience and remember to respect the law of fire.

 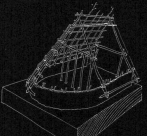 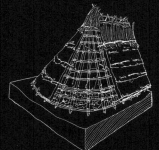

NORTH AMERICAN HOUSE RECONSTRUCTION PROJECTS

A photo collection of some of the projects undertaken by Errett Callahan. These project models are submitted as models for readers to review. The effort, skill, and dedication needed to complete a project like those presented in this issue is a common thread among those who undertake such projects. As we have stated earlier, there is much more to learn through the process than simply reconstruction techniques and design. One must also remember that everything above the ground is and "educated speculation" of what a house might have been like. Some evidence supports decisions, but a good deal of insight and "feel" direct alot of what gets done. The structure we build are resurrected from the remains of the old ones. It is in their tracks we must walk to do the job right.

__THE CAHOKIA PIT HOUSE PROJECT__ - **Sponsor: Cahokia Mounds Society, Collinsville, IL, 1983**

A reconstruction of a 1000 AD Emergent Mississippian pit house, based upon an exact duplication of the excavated floor plan. Construction took place between Oct. 1982 and Feb. 1983 and required 1300+ hours of work. Built predominately with stone tools, local natural materials, and technologies of the period.

View from the southwest.

The Floor Plan from John Kelly, __Formative Developments at Cahokia,__ 1982.

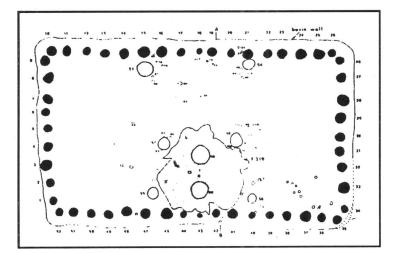

Interior view showing the wattle walls, major support posts, and stairway of graduated logs. Pit is 5.38m x 3.12m and .89m deep (18'x10' and 3' deep).

St. Mary's Longhouse Project, funded by the Maryland Humaities Council and Maryland Commission on Indian Affairs, St. Mary's City, Maryland. Built in 1984 for their 350 year anniversary.

Late Woodland Longhouse based on the great Neck site at the Virginia beach research center for Archaeology. Archway poles are constructed from cedar using an arch jig to bend them into form.

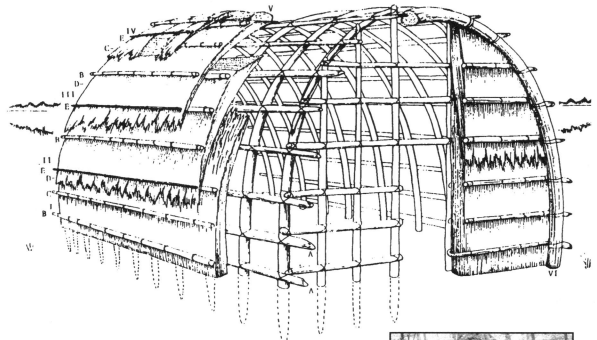

Schematic drawing of the PAMUNKEY INDIAN RESERVATION THATCH HOUSE.

A= Inner thatch lock pole
B= Lower thatch lock pole
C= Middle thatch lock pole
D= Upper thatch lock pole
E= Outer thatch lock pole

I= Thatch Row I
II= Thatch Row II
III= Thatch Row III
IV= Upper Thatch Row
V= Longitudinal Thatch Bundle along peak
VI= Eve Bundle

THE OLD RAG SHELTER - a Generic Woodland Structure built in 1972.

THE FLINT RUN PALEO-INDIAN HOUSE CONSTRUCTION
Thunderbird Museum and Archaeological park, Front Royal, VA 1985.

The Oldest Dwelling in the U.S.Reconstruction of a 10,000 year old, Late Clovis period dwelling excavated in the Shenandoah Valley in 1971. It is a reconstruction, duplicating the exact floor plan, using replicas of Clovis tools associated with the site. The structure measures 19' x 34.5' x 10' high. (5.8 x 10.5 x 3.0m).

Overhead view of the floor plan, staked out exactly as the original site plan.

Pounding holes for pole placement

Finished frame from same view as above.

Completed frame showing insulated wattle wall that deflects drafts from the entry, and pile of bark lashing material in foreground.

Completed frame with partial covering of deer hides.

Clovis biface axe hafted in elk antler handle.

MORE THAN JUST A SHELTER
THE MANITOGA WIGWAM ENCAMPMENT
By Susan Eirich-Dehne

You could walk right by it and never see it unless you took a hidden trail through the oaks and hemlocks. Suddenly you were in a clearing, transported back in time to a softly rounded bark house with hearth glowing; beautifully shaped pots steaming with fragrant stew, people going about their business; chopping, knapping, weaving, mending, stirring, laughing .... It was built using tools of stone, bone, and shell to cut wood, bark and grass; the very molecules reverberating with life. It was built from its surroundings and of its surroundings, blending so well that a stranger could walk close by and never know it was there. Tulip poplars stood scattered around the clearing and from tulip poplar bark it was made. It was built with tools of stone and wood and shell, so strong that a man could climb on top and dance. It would scarcely move- sturdy! Bone-dry and safe in the autumn rains; cool and shady in the hot-humid summer; warm and inviting in the winter cold; the hearth-fire beckoning, offering warmth, companionship and solace to the traveler in the snow.
A shelter!

Susan Eirich-Dehne

It came into being, as things, true things do, because of an urge rising from within - an urgency which, if attended to, will begin to crystallize into an idea one becomes aware of with a dawning recognition and then a shocking realization that it might be possible to make childhood magic come true. An idea which, if put into action, would get results we could not envision - in this case from a simple urge to a complete Prehistoric Native American encampment of museum quality, an authentic wigwam, an outside sheltered hearth, and areas for cooking, fiber processing, tool-making, pottery, and hide tanning. Supplies and beautifully crafted tools, weapons, mats and pots are stored around the encampment, making it ready to move in and live at a moments notice. A place to accommodate programs for professional (and un-

to a communion, a sensed knowledge of our ancestors and back even farther through the evolution of our animal heritage carried in the very structure of our brain and at the same time a searching forward and outward.

And because it came into being by following something within, it was essential that it be done well and beautifully, be authentic down to the last detail and tinniest process. Anything else would be a betrayal.

Living and experimenting in this setting speaks to an eons-old part of ourselves as we explore along lines laid down for us in our bones, genes and brain; a part, connected back through time to the mainstream of life larger than a family or culture. It touches so deep and true that it grabs you after exposure of only just a few hours. When doing a follow-up visit to their classroom in Brooklyn 6 months after a field trip to the wigwam, ghetto kids rushed toward me with tears in their eyes. I was stunned by the reception, surrounded by a crush of 20 kids all trying to reach out and touch and hug me - and I'd been with them only a few hours. I was a representative of something wondrous and real in their lives. The teacher noted " after the trip to Manitoga the children would go home and, without even letting you know, begin to come in with their own artifacts that they made. They found things on their own in the library and brought them to class - they talked about it with their parents. You know something incredible happened when their creativity was so stimulated".

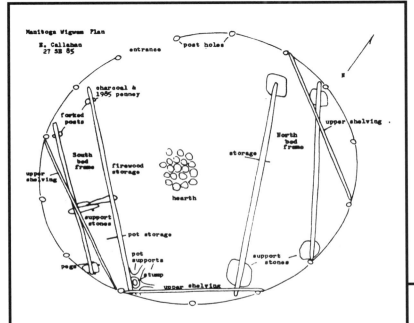

(more)

professional) "primitives" and seekers, graduate students, artists, potters, weavers, knappers, kids and families - fabulous aboriginal feasts and revelry.

It came into being through using our ancient brain until we came upon what we sought; feeling our way towards others on the same search, recognizing them with relief and delight - others who have explored a different dimension that will add to the emerging form and clarity of what we are creating.

It came about by following an inner quest, down deep into ourselves; down deeper through time to inner recesses that lead

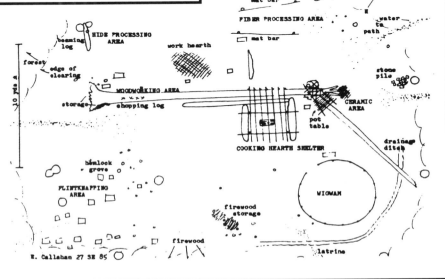

Site illustrations by Errett Callahan

For those of us fortunate enough to be able to experience this life for more than a field trip, the sensibilities sharpen and intensify as we settle into the culture of the wild - the culture we evolved from, and it is satisfying.

From a quest originating in the old part of our brain, spokes of fascination radiate out, different for each of us at the encampment, coming to fruition in the graceful shapes of a functional pot or the sharp, clear, well-defined edges of a fine stone knife as we followed the details of a technology - different spokes, all interconnecting in a larger circle of meaning and function; strands of seekings, meanings, and experience interweaving, contributing to a feeling of wholeness, "rightness" and community.

Exterior wraps hold bark panels in place.

As we worked there was a natural development of the encampment ... needs emerged... a separate area for cooking, for potting, for working with sharp edged flint, a storage place for tools...human needs...needs our ancestors must have had. As we looked for materials, made and used the tools, we understood more why they made things the way they did, and how they did. As we applied our intelligence to the tasks at hand we came closer to knowing how our forebearers might have thought, felt, figured things out; closer to their own delight in discovery and the leaps in evolution it led to as they applied their intelligence; closer to a sense of our own place in the evolution of life and culture.

With people going about their business fully absorbed body, mind and sole, there were moments of total peace and harmony - with one's self, one's companions and with the life around us; in the soil, the trees, the air - moments when we were one with the movement and pulse of life.

The taste of how it is possible to live left a permanent yearning for that seamless existence, a need for it never to be forgotten, to somehow be integrated into the rest of one's life forever informing and affecting it - there were days spent in the woods searching for the right woods and grasses and stones; Time spent digging in stream banks on hands and knees feeling for clay. There was the bittersweet sensuality of the sound and feel in peeling the living bark skin from a bleeding tree, peeling it off as easily as pulling back the skin of freshly killed prey. The living breath of the tree not quite gone, swearing that the sacrifice would not be in vain, that each part of the tree would be respectfully used. As we set the cedar poles in an upright circle ready to be bent and tied, the magic of a new presence - a shelter form - added to the landscape. While debarking poles with a sharpened shell, discovering the way different barks peel, smell, and feel we get a sense of the time and skills involved in living and building in the old way; the detail that makes up the whole; the spring and scent of hemlock boughs underfoot insulating the floor of the wigwam from the winter's cold in the ground; joining companions by the hearth-fire in the evening, around a steaming clay pot; sharing the days discoveries, sitting together in silence watching the soft green glow of phosphorescent molds, listening to the sounds of the night - a flying squirrel dropping acorns in its passage through the air, the soft hoot of an owl calling, the silent whoosh of wings,

Interior view shows insulating thatch and main frame.

finally retiring to the wigwam, waking in the deep of the night to softly glowing coals, and the sigh of the wind through the hemlocks signaling an approaching storm; odors of a damp night woods wafting in on breezes; looking up at the shadows cast by the wattled shelves; the rush of the creek in the distance - sounds, rhythms, textures, smells - unbearably rich and satisfying as we feel the stream of time flow through us soon to pass into the future as we live out our lives...sleepily pushing wood further into the fire, watching the flicker of the flames reflect on the warm golden walls and drifting off in fragrance, beauty and peace, to awaken to the sounds of the dawn...

DEVELOPMENT OF THE ENCAMPMENT

By Susan Eirich-Dehne

Board Member Susan Eirich-Dehne was executive director of Manitoga Nature Center in Garrison, N.Y. from 1981-1988. Manitoga was the former estate of Russell Wright who turned his house and land into a nature center in hopes of "bringing to American culture an intimacy with nature". For a more detailed description of construction and research, feel free to write to the author. While the wigwam itself only took a few weeks to build, the entire development of the encampment, from seasonal collection of materials to completion of the inside and outside areas and development of programs took place over a period of four years.

The majority of the development of the encampment was done under the supervision and direction of Errett ("if you're gonna make it, then make it beautiful") Callahan. The actual work was done by Errett, the author, and the Manitoga staff, with support from community and workshop volunteers. There were no shortcuts- "but we could dig this ditch so much faster with a metal shovel instead of a deer scapula"-"yes, but that wasn't the way it was done, and by the end you will have learned to use the scapula most efficiently and gotten a sense of the time involved" - it offered the benefit of being able to introduce people to prehistoric technology in an immediate, sensual way.

Programming was done by the author in conjunction with Maria-Louise Sidoroff (pottery and cooking), Alice Ross (cooking), Pam Weiland (fibers, cordage, basketry), Carol Hart (cordage and basketry), Susan Miller (school education), David Winston (Native American lore and ethnobotany), and Errett Callahan (flintknapping, tool construction, and general construction).

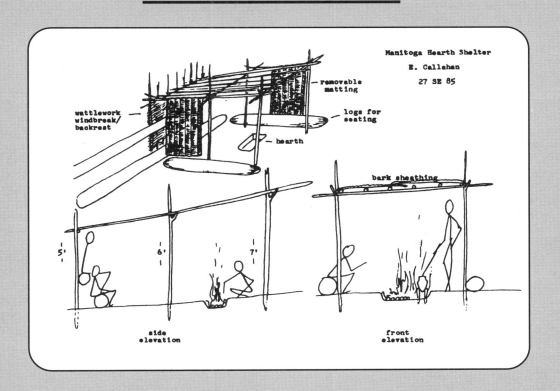

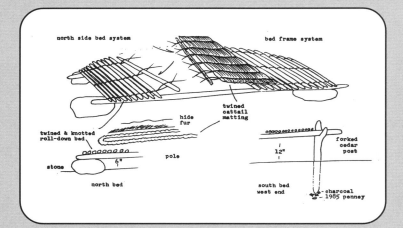

north side bed system　　　bed frame system

twined cattail matting

hide fur

twined & knotted roll-down bed

pole

stone

6"

north bed

12"

forked cedar post

south bed west end

charcoal 1985 penney

We first spent several days walking the land to select a site that could have actually been used as a site for a moderately extensive encampment; level, protected, near water. We selected a shaded glade on a level spot in a hemlock forest. Behind the site ran a seasonal rivulet for immediate use, and a two minute walk down the hill brought you to a lovely gurgling year-round stream with waterfalls and cool-clear ponds ideal for washing pots or collecting water. Some of the materials had already been prepared; the stone axe, the hickory cordage, the *phragmites* reeds cut with a sharpened shell and stored the previous year. We began the process in early spring, searching for straight-slender cedar trees suitable for a frame - cedar was the wood of choice because of the dampness of the forest floor. After locating, trimming, cutting, and dragging them back, we used a hickory spike and mallet to pound post holes to receive the cedar saplings. When we finished we had a rough circle of cedar trees standing straight up from the ground. We then bent two sapling from opposite sides of the ring, and tied them together with the inner bark of hickory - two more from opposite sides, until dome-like frame was completed. Tall slender maple trees about two inches in diameter (chosen for their flexibility) were used as horizontal lock poles and fastened in rings around the cedar frame with hickory cordage. *Phragmites* reeds were spread evenly around the frame and tied in place with more ribs and hickory cordage to the inner frame. These hollow reeds served as superb dead air insulation both in winter and summer in addition to adding wonderful golden warmth to the inner walls.

In late spring, when the sap was rising in that part of the country, large slabs of tulip poplar bark were collected, pried loose from the inner wood with sharpened green sticks and flexible deer ribs (the timing had to be just right - when tried at a later time of year the bark was almost impossible to pry off without cracking). The fresh and pliable bark was carried back to the building site and weighted down with stones to flatten it down while still flexible, until ready to use. These slabs were laid on the frame starting at the bottom and fastened with lock poles of maple (the hickory cordage was poked through the layer and fastened to the inner frame). The bark was shingled, all the way to the top, leaving a small space for the smoke hole. When completed a man could jump up and down on the top and feel the solidity of the construction. When complete the shelter was as dry as a bone in summer storms, and a small cooking fire was enough to keep it warm on winter nights.

Next we arranged the place for living; sleeping platforms (necessary because of the dampness of the forest floor), digging the post holes with fire-hardened sticks; making the wattled shelves, the drying poles, hooks, the inside hearth with a stone tripod to support the clay cooking pots, the deep bed of hemlock boughs on the floor in winter for insulation from cold, the thick cattail mats to lay on top of the sleeping platforms, gathering a ready supply of kindling and small firewood, a fire drill, black birch bark for tea and dried herbs for cooking.

Expanding outward from the wigwam were the outside sheltered hearth and working area, and the flintknapping, fiber processing, potting, cooking, and hide processing areas. The hearth area, protected under a bark roof and demarcated by logs for sitting, had conveniences such as cattail mats for kneeling while working, hooks and poles for hanging and drying, safe areas for pot storage, a stone tripod on one end of the hearth for pot cooking, a stone lining on the other end for other forms of cooking, hide pot holders, hooks, dipping gourds, -all the details that one needs when living the family life. Supplies were stored around the encampment in appropriate places-wood for fire and construction, bone and stone, sinew, and clay.

The encampment was of a generic form documented to be in use at the time of European contact, and reaching back several thousand years. Tools were replicated documenting human progress, starting with the atlatl and early biface up to the Late Woodland Culture existing at the time of contact, with its pots, bows and arrows, etc.

THE CADDO HOUSE RECONSTRUCTION
By Scooter Cheatham

The Caddo House sits as sentinal for all experimental projects to follow.

During the 17th century French and Spanish explorers traveled extensively throughout the south. From their journals, and reports attributed directly to Coronado, we have a vivid picture of what the distinctive houses of the Caddoan Confederations looked like. The unique manner in which they were built was also recorded in great detail. When a new house was to be built the Caddi (village leader) went to various families that were to participate in the construction. A sample of the main poles was taken to each as a model of what they were to provide. On the day of the raising, each family arrived on site with their pole as well as all the lashing, horizontal bands, and subordinate poles needed to build the house from their assigned position in the circle. In this manner, the construction of the house would proceed upward without workers having to move from their spot. The Caddi placed the first vertical pole. Workers climbed this pole and fastened a horizontal bar on which two workers sat in a seesaw fashion. Form this position they were able to cast a rope and lasso the tip of each pole and draw it to the middle. This communal work progressed in an exquisitely orderly manner and was completed in one day. The resident family did no building, but was responsible for feeding their guests.

The Caddoan house reconstruction conducted in Texas by Scooter Cheatham followed closely the methods of the past. The structure was duplicated from the post molds of Domicile #10 at the Davis Site. 3 mounds of a large Confederated Caddoan Center dating back to the 8-12th century were excavated here. The house was 25' in diameter, 30' high and contained 4 interior living levels. Tools for the reconstruction were prepared beginning in September, harvesting of the thatch took over two weeks in October, the poles cut, peeled and placed in position by the 1st of November, and the final touches were being added shortly before Christmas day.

The Caddoan House Reconstruction was one of the most ambitious projects related to the technology of prehistoric building techniques yet undertaken in this country. Information from the research and data collected on the project has yet to be published. This brief overview is included in the Bulletin as an attempt to illustrate the quality of work that has been done, and attempt to recognize the contribution of the workers to primitive technology.

The house was commissioned by the Texas Department of Parks and Wildlife for the Caddoan Mounds State Historic Site, 6 miles south of Alta, Texas. The tools are on display at the site interpretive center. It has withstood a tornado and 10 years of exposure to the elements and vandals, however, it is scheduled to be burned this spring (1994).

ANATOMY OF A HOUSE RECONSTRUCTION PROJECT*

*A Preliminary Outline Of The Construction Process Used In Reconstructing A Caddo House In Fall 1981 - Scooter Cheatham

PHASE I - Basic Tool Kit

Manufacture celts
Select tool model from celt artifacts
Select appropriate lithic material (greenstone)
Biface to gross scale
Shape to scale by pecking with hammerstone
Grind to final shape and sharpen
Polish final edge

Manufacture celt handles
Determine handle scale to fit celt replica
Select appropriate hardwood
 (*Quercus alba, Q. Stellata*)
Shape to approximate scale
Burn and scrape to finish
Cut hole to fit celt
Install celt

Manufacture digging sticks
Select appropriate hardwood (*Diospyrus texana*)
Cut to select length
Burn and scrape to shape ends for digging job
(wedge and point)

Manufacture Gahagan-style biface and handle
 (similar to celt and handle preparation)
Manufacture hafted sickles (deer mandible,
 flint flakes*)*
Select appropriate hardwood, flakes, blades, and
other necessary resources (*Diospyrus texana,
 Quercus fusiformis*)
Cut hardwood to shape
Groove slot for flint sickle or cut out mandible

for deer jaw sickle
Secure cutting blade to haft

Manufacture mallet
Select appropriate hardwood (*Quercus fusiformis*)
Cut to selected length and preliminary shape
Burn and scrape to final shape

Manufacture bone awls
Select deer metatarsals or ulna
Groove bone with flint flake or burin
Break bone along groove
Grind bone on sandstone to final shape

PHASE II - Materials

Harvest cane thatch (*Phragmites australis*)
Bundle cane
Trim and load bundles (two dump truck loads)
Transport cane bundles
Unload can bundles
Stack cane in crisscross pattern to season

Harvest structural members
Select pine (*Pinus echinata*) 35' tall 4"
 diameter at the base
 Oak (*Quercus alba, Q. stellata*)
 Hickory (*Carya tomentosa*)
Cut timber
Load timber
Unload timber
Sort pine into long, medium, short catagories
Debark pine

Prepare lashing- animal
Manufacture deer rawhide from deerskin
Cut deer rawhide for lashing
Cut cow leather (Mexican source) for lashing
Treat leather lashing with oil

Prepare lashing- plant (*Pinus, Vitis*)
Dig roots, transport roots, boil, pound and twist roots

PHASE III - Construction

Lay out house
Spread 6" thick dirt layer on former site excavation
Lay out house plan using radius from center
Line up main door SSE to Mound A
Measure hole spacing
Dig holes for structure foundation
    By stake and mallet - 10 holes
    By tractor auger - 38 holes

Install primary 16 poles
Determine location of main struts
Pair poles for lashing
Attach separate rope to top of each pole
Raise pole and put base in pre-dug holes
Tamp holes
Bend poles together with ropes
Lash tops together when desired bends are made

**Install secondary 16 poles
(similar to installation of primary poles except are attached below main crotch)**

Install tertiary 16 poles
Poles simply tamped but not bent

**Install 4 internal verticals
Plumb to locate bottom and top position of vertical**
Position vertical in ground dent
Attach top
Re-plumb verticals and complete external framework
*Tools added: plumb bob

Install major horizontal members
Install 13 horizontal members
Bandsequence:
3,1,2,4,5,6,7,8,9,10,11,12,13
*Tools added: levers, rope, tamper

Install decks A, B, C
Position beam, level, notch to fit, then lash in place
Install *Quercus* bands, inside structure to support
    portion of decks against wall
Select pine for deck A, and Oak for decks B and
    rack C
Split, trim, and notch wood flooring material
Position flooring and lashing in place

Install thatch
Manufacture wood needles (*Diospyrus virginiana*)
Manufacture chingaleras (4)
Hang thatch bundles
Clamp thatch bundles
Hang next row of bundles to cover clamp, then
    clamp above, etc. to top
Paddle thatch to straighten rows
*Tools added: needles, wooden awls, paddle

Finish house details and clean up site
Manufacture door
Install door
Dig run-off trench outer circumference
Clean up site

The primary construction crew on the finished frame.

TOOLS AND MATERIALS

USEFULNESS RATING OF TOOL TYPES USED IN PIT HOUSE CONSTRUCTION *

Critical	Desirable		Optional
Mussel shells	Forked Sticks	Thatching Needles	Mallets
Celts	Digging Sticks	Flakes	Hammerstones
Biface Knives	Rib Scrapers	Paddles	Feather Comb
Spade	Antler Tines		Cane Needle
Notched Hoe	Cane Sticks		Scapula Hoe
			Pry Bar
			Unnotched Hoe
			Chisel
			Deer Jaw Saw
			Adz
			Core Tool
			Wooden Hoe
			Charcoal Stick
			Bone Awl
			Antler Chisel
			Forked Pole
			Broom

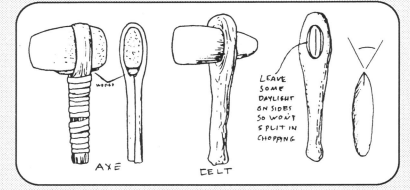

Tables on tool and materials are provided by Errett Callahan from "The Cahokia Pit House Project". Illustrations from APE 4, 1976 and Primitive Technology, 1989.

"Chopping the saplings down was easy with the handaxe. I found it was easiest to make two fair niches and then bend the tree to the ground and cut off the remaining fibers. Having used an axe about the size of my palm, I can see that a larger, but nearly as thin tool would have been far more efficient. That way I would have more weight behind my edge and less hassle with gripping the tool."
Walter Garde "Constructing a Shelter ".

Tools used in the Manitoga construction process.

Section 2

Fire
Where We Begin

The Miracle of Fire by Friction
By Dick Baugh

Introduction

Starting a fire by rubbing two sticks together. Why do I always get a thrill out of doing it? Is it because there are probably less than 500 people in the United States who can consistently start a fire with a hand drill? Is it the entertainer in me? I don't know. I assure you that the thrill is not diminished by knowing more about the scientific events that go on during the process.

The objective of this article is to provide some scientific insight into the events which happen when two sticks are rubbed together to start a fire. In particular, why is it that some woods don't work at all, some work with great effort and others with relative ease. The principals discussed apply equally well to the fire saw, fire plow, hand spun drill or bow drill. Will it help you start a friction fire more easily or quickly? Probably not. Will it give you a deeper appreciation of the process? I hope so.

Basic Principles

You have to get the char, powder that is rubbed off the wood, heated up to about 800 degrees Fahrenheit before it will start glowing (ignite). I measured this by sprinkling char generated with a bow drill on a soldering iron heated up to a known temperature. Below 800 degrees the wood dust would give off a little smoke but that's all. Above 800 it would smoke and then start to glow. Anything that prevents the char from reaching 800 degrees will interfere with fire making.

Composition and Structure

By this I mean what kind of molecules is the material composed of and how are the molecules arranged? If there is any volatile resin or tarry substance in the wood

The bow-drill fire set in action.

David Wescott

then as the friction heats the wood the tarry stuff will take heat away from the char (heat of evaporation) or will condense on the char and form it into a coarse gritty substance, preventing ignition. If the correct molecules are present and all the wrong molecules are absent there is still a problem if the molecules are not arranged properly. Imagine your best hearth board and hand spun spindle which will twirl up an ember with very little effort. The wood will be very light, a very poor thermal conductor (a good insulator). Now put your hearth board and spindle in a vice and compress the wood to 1/2 its original thickness. It will be twice as dense and its thermal conductivity will be doubled. You can still twirl up an ember but you will have to work twice as hard be-

---

Things that can cause problems:

a. If you don't have enough muscle power then you won't be able to raise the temperature high enough. Remedy: teamwork. Have someone else help you. Even if the helper can only get the wood temperature elevated to 300 degrees then it will make the job easier. Remember that a bow drill is the easiest in that it uses your muscle power most effectively.

b. If the structure of the wood is such that it disintegrates before it reaches 800 degrees then it is a wood that should not be used. I strongly believe that some softwoods such as willow and aspen don't work because they fall apart before they reach the critical temperature.

c. Volatile substances such as water or resin in the wood. Evaporative cooling will prevent the char from reaching the critical temperature.

cause you have altered the structure of the wood. You have made it a poorer insulator and you have doubled the amount of muscle power needed to reach ignition. For a person with limited muscle power attempting to start a fire by friction the use of low density wood is critical.

The simplest test for whether a particular piece of wood will twirl up an ember is the most obvious: try it and see if it works. A quicker test is to examine the char that is ground off as you twirl the spindle on the hearth board. The rule of thumb, literally, is to rub the char between thumb and forefinger. If it is coarse and gritty then reject that particular piece of wood. If it is very fine, like face powder, then you have a good chance of twirling up a fire. Both Kochansky and Graves mention this. What is the difference between these two classes of wood? Those that work and those that don't. We know that in the category of "good" woods there are soft woods, such as yucca, which can be easily dented with the thumbnail and hard woods such as sage brush which are much more resistant to the thumbnail test. Could it be that the "good" woods ignite at a lower temperature than the "bad" woods? That should be easy to measure. The straightforward way would be to measure the temperature of each tiny little particle of char as it is ground off the spindle or hearth board. Trouble is that it is very hard to measure the temperature of something that tiny without disturbing what is going on. The next best way is to measure the ignition temperature indirectly. Sprinkle some char on a piece of metal which has been heated to a known temperature. See what temperature the metal has to be heated to in order to ignite the char. As a practical manner I used a thermostatically controlled soldering iron as a source of known temperature. Tips with two different temperatures, 700 degrees F and 800 degrees F were available. I had observed previously that the char ground into the notch in a "good" hearth board would start glowing (ignite) if a pinch of it was placed on the 800 degree soldering iron tip but would not ignite if placed on the 700 degree tip. The conclusion from this was that if friction heats the char above 800 degrees it will ignite.

What about "bad" woods?

I used a piece of local willow sapwood, a material on which I have wasted countless hours in the past trying to light a friction fire. Never any luck. Always produces a coarse gritty char. This time I did a different experiment. I charred some of the willow with a match and then ground it off with a file. It was now very fine, much finer than the results of a bow drill. This very fine willow char would ignite almost instantaneously at 700 degrees. Conclusion: the more finely the char is divided the lower the ignition temperature. This hypothesis was tested further by grinding off some un-charred mule fat wood with a fairly fine file. This material was slightly gritty feeling compared with the char that falls into the notch of a mule fat hearth board. The coarser mule fat char failed to

ignite at 800 degrees. I did the same thing with char cloth, the favored tinder for flint and steel. Char cloth failed to ignite, even at 800 degrees.

Conclusions

The miracle of fire by friction is that you don't have to heat the char up to the temperature of a glowing ember to make it ignite. You only have to raise its temperature up to the point where it takes off of its own accord. When powdered charred wood is heated up to some critical temperature it begins to spontaneously oxidize. When it starts oxidizing its temperature rises, causing it to oxidize even faster. Eventually it reaches an equilibrium temperature limited by how much air is available and starts to glow, ignition. The critical temperature where this process begins depends on how finely the char is pulverized.

Fire by friction works only because these two events, pulverizing and heating, happen simultaneously. Woods that don't work disintegrate before they reach this critical condition.

Fire by Friction - The Spiritual Aspects

What is a cynical, agnostic engineer doing talking about the "spiritual" nature of something which can be fully explained by the laws of physics and chemistry? All I know is that there are some things that make me feel good and starting a fire the way my ancestors did 10,000 years ago is one of them. What makes me feel even better is getting a group of people to contribute towards the starting of a fire. I can think of no better way to bond a group of people. We all take turns at twirling the spindle, each according to his or her own ability, we all gently blow on the ember to bring out the flame and the smoke carries our thoughts and our hopes skyward. On the evaluation of a weekend course I gave a couple of years ago one of the students said "Starting a fire is a sacrament." I guess it is.

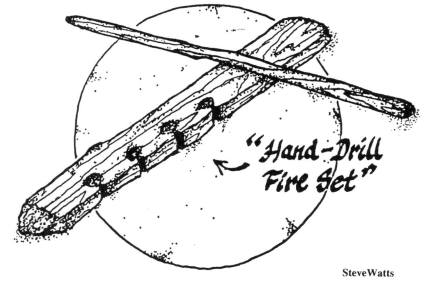

"Hand-Drill Fire Set"

Steve Watts

FIRE BY FRICTION MATERIALS of the San Francisco Bay Region
By Dick Baugh

The objective of this report is to list and describe the fire by friction materials that are found near San Francisco Bay. This is to fill a gap which is found in almost all the outdoor survival and primitive living skills books which I have read. They mention their favorite fire by friction material or materials, none of which are native to the area where I live. *My hope is that other "primitives" in different parts of the world would also write similar articles describing the fire by friction materials of their home territory.* This article is not intended to be a reference for plant identification, although several reference books have relied on my own experiences with using these materials. The opinions are obviously subjective and reflect my own prejudices and skill.

Materials that work

Selection of suitable materials is a matter of observing nuances. First, the wood must be dry. Second, just because one piece of wood from a particular species worked once is no indication that it will always work. Another parameter to consider is the degree to which the wood is decayed. Sometimes a small amount of fungal attack makes subtle changes in the ability to twirl up an ember. Heartwood very often works better than sapwood. Selection of woods is very critical. The material must be capable of being ground into a very fine powder. Any tendency for the powder being ground off to feel coarse of gritty is a signal that you are wasting your time and should reject that wood and find something else. Equally important is the ability of the wood to maintain its structural integrity at high temperature (up to 800 degrees Fahrenheit) before the char is ground off. This is discussed in great detail in *Bulletin #4*.

Materials
California incense cedar

Calocedrus decurrens makes the best hearth boards. A very soft, light wood which takes very little effort to twirl up an ember. Use a board or split piece with the annual rings perpendicular to the surface (quarter sawn). It also smells good. Incense cedar is native to the Sierra Nevada Mountains and is only seen in the San Francisco Bay region as a horticultural plant. It is, however, such a superior wood for hearth boards that it should be mentioned. The oldest, least dense heartwood is easiest to ignite with a hand drill.

I have never been successful in creating an ember with an incense cedar spindle twirled on an incense cedar hearth board. The char ground off is always coarse and gritty. My only explanation, albeit not very scientific, is that the wood is so soft that cedar on cedar wears away so quickly that the ignition temperature is never reached. *I would appreciate comments form anyone who has had experience with this material.*

Elderberry

The common elderberry of the San Francisco Bay region is *Sambucus mexicana*. It is seen along roadsides in the hills especially for a hand spun fire drill. Select shoots that are about 1/2 inch in diameter and fairly straight. Second or third year growth is best because the wood will be the correct thickness. Elderberry spindles work so well because they have a soft pith core of from 3/16 to 3/8 inch diameter. As a consequence when twirling the drill your muscle power is a rapid rise in temperature. Avoid first year stems which have too much pith and only a thin wood section. Cut elderberry shoots while they are green, heat them in an oven (250 degrees) and straighten them while still damp. Then leave them in the oven a few hours until they are perfectly dry. These "non-primitive" techniques can only be justified in that I need to prepare a large number of spindles at a time for the classes that I help teach. The slower alternative in preparing spindles is to straighten them with heat while they are green, tie them in bundles of 2,3 or 7 and leave them in a warm dry place. Elderberry wood which is larger in diameter is also good for hearth boards although fairly dense. As a consequence of its greater density it requires more "horsepower" form a hand-spun drill to reach ignition temperature. That is a non-problem for a bow drill.

California buckeye

California buckeye (*Aeschulus californica*) works well for hearth boards and bow drill spindles. I have seldom seen shoots which were long enough for hand drill spindles. There is a great variation in its hardness, depending on whether or not it was cut green or allowed to decay slightly. The less dense wood ignites more easily.

Mule fat

Mule fat (*Baccharus viminea*) forms long straight stems in stream beds in California through to Arizona. The soft woody stems are excellent for spindles and hearth boards. There seems to be a large variation in the density of the wood, meaning that some samples require more work than others to twirl up an ember with a hand drill. The only two times I have ever started a hand drill fire starting from essentially nothing have been with mule fat spindles and hearth boards.

Redwood

Redwood (*Sequoia sempervirens*). The heartwood works well for hearth boards. It is a relatively low density wood so little effort is required but I don't use it very often.

Cattail

Cattail (*Typha latifolia*) bloom spikes were used in prehistoric times in Eastern Oregon for hand spun spindles in conjunction with clematis hearth boards. Jean Auel, author of "Clan of the Cave Bear," etc. learned her stone age survival skills from Jim Riggs in Eastern Oregon. Hence Ayla, the heroine of Auel's books, used cat tail bloom spikes plus clematis to start her fires. I haven't had any success with cat tail spindles but I know a lot of people who have.

Typha leaves are also usable for cordage for making a bow drill. Cut the leaves at dirt level, ideally while they are still green and scrape off the slimy stuff that accumulates at the base of the leaves. Split them into long strips and then let them dry. Moisten and then twine them into a two-ply cord about as thick as a pencil. The finer you split the leaves the stronger cordage but will suffice for making a few bow drill fires before it breaks.

Mare's Tail

Conyza canadensis, a common weed makes excellent spindles for hand spun fires. It is a member of the sunflower family (compositae) frequently found near freeway on ramps. It forms straight, tapered shoots with relatively soft woody stems which are easy to straighten with heat. The combination of a mare's tail spindle and an incense cedar hearth board for me takes the least effort for a hand drill fire.

Box Elder

Acer negundo is a streamside tree in the maple family. The wood is white, medium hard and very reliable for bow drill spindles and hearth boards and spindles.

Cottonwood

Populus sp. are found near water. They are excellent for spindles and hearth boards.

Willow

Salix sp. are almost always found near a source of moisture, whether it is a stream or natural seepage. My experience with willow wood has been a complete failure. It seems to disintegrate before it reaches ignition temperature but not so fast! Norm Kidder learned from Peg Matthewson who read it in a book that local Indians used cattail stems for spindles and willow root for hearth boards. Norm tells me that this combination works well. Tree roots are another source of materials which should not be overlooked.

Tinder Materials

So, you have twirled up a glowing ember. Now what? Gather some tinder. Materials which I have successfully used are:
The husk from soaproot (*Chlorogalum pomeridiadum*) is excellent.
Dry pounded grass. It's ubiquitous.
Dry shredded cattail leaves (*Typha sp.*)
Rotten inner bark from cottonwood (*Populus sp.*)
Nettle fiber (*Urtica sp.*)
Milkweed fiber (*Asclepias sp.*)
Dogbane fiber (*Apocynum connabinum*)
Redwood bark (*Sequoia sempervirons*)
Powdered gall from oak trees (*Quercus sp.*) is useful if you don't have good tinder. It can be sprinkled on a glowing ember and gently fanned to obtain a very large ember. The shavings or dry pine needles and fanned into a fire. Powdered dry rotten wood can be used the same way as powdered oak gall.

Socket Materials

The socket for a bow drill can be made either from a pitch saturated knot from a downed rotten douglas fir (*Pseudotsuga taxifolia*) or very hard wood such as greasewood (*Adenostoma fasciculatum*).

Summary Chart

Common Name	Botanical Name	Uses
Incense cedar	*Calocedrus decurrens*	hb
Blue elderberry	*Sambuccus mexicana*	sp, hd, hb
Mule fat	*Baccharis vimnea*	hb, hd, sp
California buckeye	*Aeschulus californica*	hb, sp, t
Box elder	*Acer negundo*	hb, sp
Mare's Tail	*Conyza canadensis*	hd
Cottonwood	*Populus sp.*	hb, sp, t
Redwood	*Sequoia semervirons*	hb, t
Willow root	*Salix sp.*	hb
Cattail	*Typha sp.*	hd, t, c
Oak gall	*Quercus sp.*	t
Grass	various	t
Soaproot	*Chlorogalum pomeridiadum*	t
Milkweed	*Asclepias sp.*	t, c
Nettle	*Urtica sp.*	t, c
Dogbane	*Apocynum cannabinum*	t, c
dry, rotton wood	various	t
Douglas fir	*Pseudotsuga taxifolia*	so
Greasewood	*Adenostoma fasciculatum*	so

Key: hb=hearth board, sp=spindle (bow drill), hd=hand drill, t=tinder, c=cordage for a bow drill, so=socket for a bow drill

FIRE
By Norm Kidder

Anthropologists debate the proper place in the fossil record to make the jump from apeman (*Australopithecus*) to man (*Homo*). The current trend is to base this arbitrary quantum leap on the first appearance of manufactured stone tools. The earliest case for this so far has been named *Homo habilis* (Handy man), a being otherwise physically identical to nearby apemen. This approach continues the bias toward stone tools inherent in the term stone-age to describe the human condition until the advent of metallurgy. This bias is the natural result of stone tools being all that's left of ancient technologies, and thus serving the needs of archaeologists. Recently chimpanzee groups in the wild have been found using stone tools. shouldn't they also then be considered human? I suggest a different theoretical approach - the use of fire as a tool.

The ancient tool kit probably consisted of a crude digging stick, a sharp or pointed stone, a stone hammer, and pieces of bark or leaf used as a cup for water. These are little different from the tools known to be used by chimps. This kit did not change for vast stretches of time. I propose that the stimulus for change that jump started the behavioral evolution for our kind was the discovery of fire as a tool.

Pre-human hominids were omnivorous gatherers and scavengers, killing relatively helpless animals if discovered. They lived at a time of drought, when the great forests of the world were shrinking and being replaced by grasslands. They were forced to make dangerous excursions away from the relative safety of the trees out into the more food-rich plains. Foraging required that group size remain small, and lookouts be always alert for the many large predators. Another element of life a few million years ago was occasional fires, started by lightning or volcanoes, which would sweep across large areas unchecked. A burned area would provide a major windfall to hominid groups. The ground would be cleared of dead vegetation exposing seeds and tubers, as well as providing the occasional cooked dead animal (one advantage to cooked meat is its shelf life). Burning also tended to run off most predators, and make it much easier to detect any that returned. For millennia perhaps, our ancestors learned to seek out burning grasslands which might provide food, briefly, for large congregations of hominids (the first conventions).

The great leap forward that I feel justifies a new classification for humans came when the first of these ancestors took a burning branch and set a new fire, taking control of the process. This discovery that fire could be used to make food more readily available, to preserve some of it for the future, and help defend against predators, created the technological base for modern society.

Fire Stick Farmers

A study of aboriginal groups around the world gives clues to the advances in the use of fire as technology. One of the oldest uninterrupted cultural traditions known to science was found in the Australian Aborigines before they were 'introduced to modern civilization'. One anthropologist described their food gathering practices as fire stick farming. Using fire to determine the species of plants available to them for food. Specifically, they used fire to reduce less desirable plants, and encourage the most useful ones. The result was that most of the continents plant communities were, until recently, maintained by fire.

The evidence for California Indians indicates a similar use of burning to promote seed production in grasses and wildflowers; thatch removal to favor tuberous growth and other wildflowers; and thinning of brush to improve hunting by both increasing animal browse and decreasing cover.

Fire was also a critical element in the hunting process. Many ancient groups used fire to drive animals into traps (blind canyons, pits, tar pits, marshes, cliffs, etc.). In recent times, fire was being used by California Indians to drive ground squirrels from their burrows, bees and hornets from their hives and grasshoppers into a pit oven. Smoke and fire permeate most aspects of daily life. It is used to straighten arrows and spears, harden digging sticks, bend basket rims, waterproof tanned hides, purify and deodorize and of course to cook.

The importance of fire to all ancient people made it nearly inevitable that eventually someone would discover how to make fire. It is unlikely that anything in the fos-

The primitive "match" or coal extender.
See page 58.

sil record will enable us to know just when this change took place. Hearthfires started from wildfire are identical to those started by fire sticks. Even if by chance a set of fire sticks were to be found, it would only tell us when conditions for preservation existed, not the earliest use. As to how the secret of fire making was discovered, I have my guess:

The same process that produces fire will also eventually produce a hole. I believe that some-one trying to drill a hole in a board discovered fire making accidentally.

The wide range of the fire-drill throughout many continents (Australian aborigines use the same method as American Indians, etc.) implies that it may have been known before the great dispersal of humans carried out by *Homo erectus* around 1.5 million years ago, or at least by the migrations at the end of the ice ages starting around 40 thousand years ago (although it is possible that it arose separately and identically in many different places).

The basic technique for making fire by friction involves spinning a drill against the bottom of a hole in a hearth board. Friction from rubbing the sticks together produces heat and (if the correct woods are used) fine powdery sawdust, or char. The char is collected in a notch cut into the center of the hole. This concentrates the heat, the wood acting as an insulator. If the char is heated to 800° F. it will begin to smolder. (*Data courtesy of Richard Baugh*) Placing the smoldering char (ember) into a bed of tinder (fine, dry plant fibers) and blowing gently will cause the tinder to burst into flames. This is much easier to describe than to accomplish. Reaching 800° F. requires considerable pressure be applied to the drill.

The hand spun fire drill, the oldest method, accomplishes this through hand pressure against the drill while bearing down with the weight of the body while continuing to spin the drill as fast as possible. With practice, a strong, fairly heavy, well conditioned person can get an ember in a few seconds of hard work, under ideal conditions. Smaller or less experienced people can make fire through co-operative efforts and persistence. Mechanical advantages can be achieved through the use of a cap piece which is used to push down on the drill. To keep the drill spinning with one hand, a bowstring is wrapped around the drill and moved back and forth, spinning the drill. Another variant involves using **toggles** (and normally a second person)

to spin the drill. These methods probably evolved where conditions made fire making difficult.

Three other techniques for friction fire use lateral friction rather than rotational - **fire plow** (movement up and down a groove), **fire saw** (the edge of one piece cuts through the middle of another), and the **fire cord** (a vine is pulled through a notch). Two techniques are known using heating by compression - the **fire piston** (works like a diesel engine), and **flint and steel** (iron particles are crushed, and torn away, causing enough heat to ignite them). The last of these is the best known, but was probably not common until iron became available. Modern matches use materials which ignite easily with little friction heat. Lighters use miniature flint and steel sets to light their gas fumes. Three new ways to make fire have been developed in recent years - electric spark, electric resistance, and chemical resistance.

Friction Fires
#1 Fire saw
#2 Fire Plow
#3 Hand-drill

David Wescott Photos

UNDERSTANDING WOOD FIRE

By Mors Kochanski

The diffusion flame combustion process that is commonly known as fire is made easier to understand with the use of a graphic model known as the tetrahedron of fire. This approach to explaining fire usually applies universally to any form of combustible material and is one of the more popular concepts used in fire suppression theory. It is based on the work of W.M. Haessler, *The Extinuishment of Fire*, Dayton 1962.

In the four-sided tetrahedron the four entities are adjoined and each is connected with the other three. The four entities represent the four factors in the fire process: fuel (wood); air (oxygen), uninhibited chain reactions, and heat. By the use of the four-sided model we mean to imply that each of the four factors are equally related and of exactly the same importance. If any one factor is removed the fire process is impossible.

The fire process goes something like this: When heat is applied to a fuel, which in this instance is wood, the rise in temperature starts a break-down process known as pyrolysis. Some components of the wood are changed into gases and vapors, amongst other things, and become increasingly agitated until they break up into very active particles known as free radicals which are very intent on finding something suitable to latch on to. The free radicals interact amongst each other and go into an uninhibited chain reaction which now involves its own heat source and becomes self-propagating and continues as long as there are properly sized and arranged pieces of fuel to maintain pyrolysis, radical formation, and feed-back heat.

Fuel - Wood

Surface area or surface-to-mass ration: The ease of ignition and the promotion of combustion are strongly affected by the size of the wood used. The finer the wood, the more readily it will burn, and of course the faster it will burn. If a block of wood with a surface area of a square meter was split so that the resulting pieces would have a total surface area of ten square meters, these would burn up ten times as fast. The split pieces would burn with greater intensity to a higher temperature, but the amount of heat liberated would be the same for both, as this depends on the calorific value of the material. The way to be assured a good start for a fire is to use adequate fine material to get the intensities of heat and higher temperatures to make the larger sticks burn. Twigs and wood feathers should be about the thickness of a match stick to start with.

Fuel Spacing and Arrangement

It is not sufficient that the fuel be of the correct thinness but it has to be properly spaced in relation to the other pieces of fuel so that the desired heat concentration from the igniting source can be that the desired heat concentration from the igniting source can be achieved, oxygen has access to the combustible gases that evolve, and when the fuel is burning the adjacent fuel is involved to extend the fire process. Experience will eventually determine that you can not squeeze your fuel too close together or have it spread too far apart.

In lighting a fire, if the kindling is too close together the mass of the material in the kindling absorbs too much of the match's heat before it can be effective, and it physically obstructs oxygen access so that the oxygen combustible vapor mixture is too lean to catch fire, producing only smoke.

It is also helpful to light your kindling well off the ground. The coolest air is near the ground and there is more obstruction to the flow of needed air.

The best fuels are ones that are high in carbon and hydrogen content. The most common elements found in all living things are carbon, hydrogen, oxygen and nitrogen. Oxygen is not a fuel but it supports combustion. Nitrogen is not a fuel and neither does it support combustion; in fact it tends to interfere with oxygen. Combustion will cease when the atmospheric oxygen level drops below 15%.

The Composition Of Wood

Wood is composed of three major constituents: remicellulose, cellulose and lignin. Their molecular structure puts them in a class of chemicals known as polymers. A polymer is a relatively large molecule that is made up of a number of repeating (poly) smaller units called mers.

When wood burns the cellulose participates mostly in producing the visible flame and the lignin supports the major part of the glowing.

The cellulose is the main structural part of the cell wall of trees and plants. Wood has such an intricate structure, creating such an enormous surface area, that a cubic centimeter of wood spread out would cover an area of ten million square centimeters.

Wood heated up to 200 degrees Centigrade dries out, undergoes slow pyrolysis (break-down through being heated) evolving some carbon dioxide, formic acid and vinegar. Some heat is given off. At temperatures between 200 and 280 degrees Centigrade wood slowly undergoes pyrolysis with much the same evolution of gases as mentioned earlier and the wood is reduced to charcoal without flame. From 280 degrees up to 500 degrees Centigrade the mixture of gases are combustible and are readily ignited.

Wood will readily ignite from a flame at 380 degrees Centigrade. Spontaneous ignition occurs at about 545 degrees Centigrade towards the end of pyrolysis, as the emission of gas decreases and air can reach the hot charcoal. Above 500 degrees Centigrade carbon monoxide and hydrogen burn as a non-luminous flame and the charcoal burns until white ash is left.

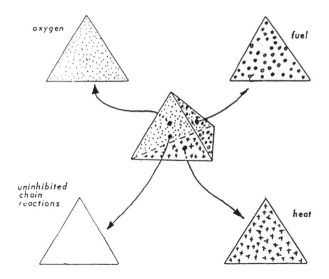

Figure 1. The Tetrahedron of Fire

Studies have shown that the average composition of the evolved volatiles remain constant throughout the pyrolysis. The calorific value was constant at about 4 Kcal per gram.

The yield of charcoal from wood is about 16 to 20 percent and the calorific value for charcoal is about 8 Kcal per gram.

Cellulose, which composes about 50% of wood, volatizes rapidly around 340 degrees Centigrade and exhibits typical polymer characteristics by degrading into nearly two hundred different chemical compounds. The situation is rather complex as numerous simple molecules form and diffuse to the surface where mixing with oxygen occurs and subsequent ignitions take place if the temperature is at or above the ignition point. All woods have similar ignition temperatures despite appreciable variations in their ignitabilities. Cellulose products burn without melting to form a char.

Rapid heating produces little charcoal, much tar and highly inflammable gases. Some of the compounds evolved through pyrolysis are very toxic, probably accounting for the headaches one often gets by breathing smoke, especially from black spruce and pine. Some of the compounds you are likely to find are:

    carbon monoxide
    acetaldehyde
    hydrogen cyanide
    butraldehyde
    carbon dioxide
    nitrogen dioxide
    formaldehyde
    acreolin

Smoke

Smoke is mostly composed of unburned carbon particles that are less than one milimicron in diameter and can be suspended in a gas. Anything larger would be considered a dust particle. Smoke is composed of clouds of particles, which when taken individually would be invisible, but taken as a cloud scatter light and are opaque to visible light. Smoke results when carbonaceous materials (and hydrocarbons) are incompletely burned due to a lack of heat or a restriction in the oxygen supply, and unreacted carbon molecules form. Soot is formed when these molecules lump together. When other intermediate gaseous products form simultaneously with the carbon, they may condense on the particles to produce uniquely acrid, toxic or irritating smoke. In a confined space wood smoke alone can produce lung damage and be lethal long before the heat of the fire would have any effect.

When a fire is producing excessive smoke, it is likely due to the condition of the fuel. It may be too green or too wet and so much heat is being used up in drying that there is little left over for volatization. The solution is to add good dry fuel on top of the smoky fuel and the products of incomplete combustion will be more completely burned in the improved fire.

Oxygen

The atmosphere generally contains about 20.9% oxygen and about 79.1% nitrogen. In the presence of oxygen almost all matter undergoes a change which is often termed oxidation. Oxidation can be as slow as rusting or as rapid as an explosion. With an increase in temperature, the rate of oxidation also increases. For each 10 degrees Centigrade rise in temperature the activity of molecules doubles. This accounts for the ease which a fire may be made on a summer's day at 20 degrees Centigrade as compared to minus 20 degrees Centigrade on a winter's day.

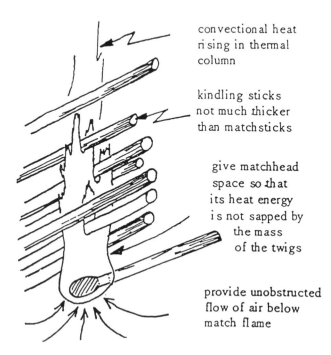

convectional heat rising in thermal column

kindling sticks not much thicker than matchsticks

give matchhead space so that its heat energy is not sapped by the mass of the twigs

provide unobstructed flow of air below match flame

Figure 2. Diagramatic sketch of how a match should be used.

Figure 3. The molecule structure of cellulose where it is in the orser of 5,000.

If the temperature of a fuel is raised continuously it will eventually burst into flame (the production of heat and light), an indication of its rapid reaction with oxygen. This is termed combustion. The rate of combustion is dependent on the ability of the molecules of fuel and oxygen to mix together in the appropriate proportions in spite of the interference from the nitrogen in the air.

In still air a fire will draw in surrounding oxygen through the circulation created by the hot convection currents (thermal column) rising above the fire. A fire suspended off the ground will burn better than one on the ground. For this reason a fire built on a mound will burn better than one in a hole.

A strong wind will force far more oxygen on a fire than convection draw could provide and thus make the fire more intense.

The thermal column formed above a flaming area establishes an airflow so that the oxygen is brought to where it is needed for mixing. The mixture thus formed has a flammable range within which it will burn. If the mixture is too lean in oxygen or too rich in oxygen for a certain concentration of fuel vapor, no combustion will result even if an open flame is present.

The too rich in oxygen phenomenon is often encountered in lighting a wood stove. When the door is open there is usually an imperceptible draw through the stove up the chimney. When the fine kindling is lit and the door kept open the fire does not seem to want to go. When the door is closed and the draft is reduced the kindling roars into flame.

It is interesting to note that when the oxygen supply, for any reason, drops from its 20.9% to about 15% combustion ceases due to the smothering action of the nitrogen in the air.

Ignition Continuity

Once combustion starts and is given ample oxygen, it becomes self-supporting:
a) as the fuel burns it creates more heat.
b) the increase in heat raises more fuel to its ignition temperature.
c) additional oxygen is drawn in by the convective column of heat forming above the fire. In a raging conflagration a windstorm can be observed drawing air to the burning source.
d) the oxygen increases the rate of burning and more fuel becomes involved.
e) this chain reaction continues until the fuel has been consumed. This is known as a fuel-regulated fire. Outdoor campfires are fuel-regulated in that you make it big or small by adding or withholding the fuel. In a stove the fire is oxygen-regulated, in that you can vary the air supply to make the fire burn slower or faster.

Heat Transfer

In an open fire heat transfer is carried out by either convection (flame created thermal column) or by radiation, with conduction generally being insignificant.

Heat Transfer By Convection

Generally, heated air or other gases produced by the burning process, being lighter than the surroundings, flow upward to warm or to dry and fuel above or even bring it to a kindling temperature. This transfer of heat through a circulation medium is termed "heating by convection". It is important to realize that when fuel is wet or green it must be put on a fire so that this convective heat can dry it out in anticipation of when it is needed.

Heat Transfer By Radiation

Any hot object sends out invisible infra-red waves that warm anything that intercepts these waves (if something is white hot it can emit ultraviolet rays that are even hotter, but this likely will never be encountered in a campfire situation). When you stand near a fire a wind may waft some convective heat your way but it is the radiant heat you should most benefit from. It is much like the warmth that we feel when the sun shines on our skin or on a dark item of clothing. Radiant energy can be blocked by a reflective material that bounces back these rays. A dark surface absorbs the rays and a light surface reflects them.

The Physics of Fire

In all these cases a fire occurs when a reaction is started that gives off more heat than was required to start it (exothermic), thus the reaction spreads through all the available combustible material or until the total heat falls below that needed to sustain the process. As heat radiates away from the point of fire in all direction, much of it is dissipated out into space (entropy). When two or more burning objects are placed close together, each captures part of the others heat, helping to sustain the fire. In the case of fires based on the oxidation of organic (carbon base) materials, if oxygen is used up, the fire will also die. Therefore, burning logs should be placed about an inch apart to insure enough oxygen while maintaining heat. A quick, bright fire requires lots of air flow, a slow hot fire occurs with minimal air flow.

N. Kidder

THE HAND-DRILL AND OTHER FIRES

By David Wescott

The mastery of fire technology, for many of us, has been an interesting devolution. For years it was thought that mastery of the hand-drill fire was beyond mere mortals and that it would never be tamed. However, once that barrier was breached by the likes of Scott Kuipers and Mike Clinchey (both masters of the hand-drill), the utility of the hand-drill has much surpassed the good old bow-drill that dominated the majority of teaching venues for years.

Little did we know that the level of technology and lack of physical control had impeded our regression to this simpler skill. With the bow-drill, the parts are complicated and precise, the body position and control is difficult, and these problems are compounded when the two are put together with a lack of understanding on what makes a friction fire work in the first place.

Fire By Friction Anywhere

Making fire by friction is a deceptively easy process once the principles are understood and the technique well practiced. It's a trip to watch a master walk over to a bush, snap off a twig and begin rubbing it on a log until smoke begins to rise from the resulting trough. Or a straight twig is cut, roughly straightened, and spun between the palms, while resting on a softwood hearth to create that magic spark. Or better yet, splitting a section of bamboo, scarping off the lacquered layer to be used as tinder, creating a notch with a slice of rock, and then rubbing the notch along the edge of the bamboo until the tinder ignites.

The materials may vary widely, and the technique corresponds to the materials, but the principles of what allows us to make fire by friction is the same wherever you go, with whatever materials you acquire. Bow-drills are still the best for overpowering inferior materials, or inclement weather. But, when the woods are dry and good materials are available, why waste time climbing the evolutionary ladder of technology to a method that isn't nearly as satisfying ?

Here is what you need: materials - read what Dick Baugh has to say about what will work and what won't. Woods that produce a fine powder (not granular flakes) are needed - good tinder is a given; **tools** - a simple cutting edge is all that's needed to rough out shapes and create required

Hand-drill "master", Scott Kuipers introduced us to such innovations as floating the hands and working up and down the spindle without ever removing the hands from the spindle.

notches and/or grooves - parts for these fire sets are simple and need little alteration from their natural form (not so with the bow-drill); **technique** - practice-practice-practice. Team work is a good idea, as the energy and frustration quotient parallel the learning curve...little skill= high rate of failure and big blisters.

Specific parts are very simple: 1. the manual piece which is spun or rubbed back and forth - spindle, plow, saw; and 2. The stationary piece which is held in place - hearth, log, split bamboo section.

Technique: 1. start out slow to warm up the set; 2. maintain pressure at the contact points; 3. gradually speed up and watch for ashes to accumulate (check them to see if they are powdery or granular); 4. increase speed and pressure; 5. don't forget to breath (by now you should be going anaerobic - carefully and quickly switch with your partner if needed) and watch for telltale smoke. Once the smoke appears, watch to see if the wisp comes from the pile of ash, not the set. Stop for a second and watch for smoke to rise from the collected ash. A slight blow or breeze should result in the spark glowing from the pile. Take a few breaths and let the ashes concentrate into a solid coal. Now you're ready for fire!

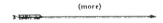

(more)

Tools of the trade - hearth, spindle, and blisters.

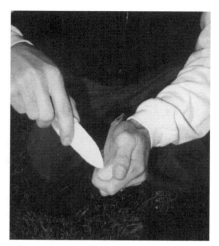

Create a small depression to hold the spindle in place.

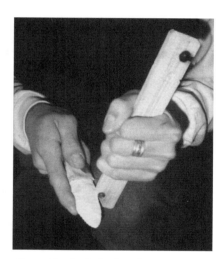

Once the hole is "set" by a couple of passes, carve a small notch into the center of the hole to allow the ash to accumulate.

Focus On The Hand-drill

The hearth and drill can be made of the same materials, but usually the long, straight spindle is harder to find. The bottom line is that all materials need to be dead and dry. The hearth needs to be quite soft (split yucca stalks work great) and at least twice the width of the spindle base. The drill needs to be as straight as possible and from 18 to 30 inches long. The diameter may vary, 1/4 and 3/4 inch in diameter (There has been a long and unsolved question as to what works better - a small spindle that spins faster,

or a fat spindle that provides more surface area for friction...any suggestions?) I might say that a very small spindle may be harder to learn with, and also allows the palms to rub together, resulting in huge beginner blisters. If a long spindle is unavailable, a soft plug may be added to spindles of harder materials to get the set you need as well as extend the life of the materials available to you.

Some materials may be: hearth - poplar, clematis, yucca stalk, cottonwood root, some willows and poplars; spindle - cattail, seep willow, teasel, sunflower, prince's plume, yucca stalk. You're looking for very soft yet stable materials. The should be light, dry, and solid not rotted.

Split the wood you chose for the hearth. One flat side will do, but you may flatten both. Leave hearth about 1/2-3/4" thick. Make a dimple in the middle of the hearth into which the spindle may be seated. The spindle should be scraped and straightened as well as possible.

Once the fire set is ready and the tinder bundle and fire lay are all in place, get comfortable and start to drill. The position you choose is up to you. Notice that Scott sits down, using his arms to do the work, while others kneel and use upper body weight to help with the process.

The trick to getting a spark is to start out slowly and spin the drill to warm it up. Start at the top of the spindle and work all the way down. Some pressure should be maintained at this point to keep the end from polishing. Once the set is warm, increase speed and pressure. Lean into it and maintain pressure. The spark comes from a combination of speed and pressure.

To avoid tiring too quickly and reduce blisters, spit on your hands to give you a

better grip without having to press inward too much. Use both arms equally. Flare the hands slightly and use the entire heel of the hand to avoid rubbing the hands together. Start out slowly and give it all you've got later in the process.

One other trick is to avoid pulling the spindle from the hearth or taking to much time returning to the top of the drill after each pass. Maintain timing to maintain the level of heat in the set and the ash. Move one hand at a time back to the top of the spindle and go again.

After one or two passes, cut a notch into the side of the hearth that extends into the middle of the whole created by the drill. This allows the ash to collect and increase in heat and mass as the spindle and hearth wear away wood fibers. Once the correct temperature is reached to kindle the coal (7-800 degrees, Baugh), the fibers will ignite and begin to smolder. At this point, sit back, tell a joke and let the coal grow and solidify. Not until then should the coal be transferred to the tinder bundle or transportation "match".

Making fire by friction is extremely satisfying process. The magic

Hold the hearth in place with the foot.

Continue to spin until smoke begins to rise from the pile of ashes. Bear down and increase preassure and speed at the last minute to get a coal.

Resist the urge to be in a hurry at this point. Allow the ashes a chance to glow and condense into a coal. Use the knife to release the coal if it sticks in the notch.

Working as a team allows partners to use maximum effort for short bursts and then get a rest. Try alternating every 2 or 3 passes to avoid exhaustion.

created by building your own set, mastering the technique, and then settling in to enjoy a cozy campfire, is truly one of the greatest of woodcraft skills that everyone should know.   **DW**

With the fire plow, the moving piece is moved back and forth in a trough created by the friction. There is no notch required, as the ash collects at the end of the trough.

The fire saw hearth is also the moving piece. The tinder is pressed into the concave side of the split bamboo, and the notch in the convex side is rubbed along a sharp edge on the staionary piece. The ash collects in the notch and ignites the tinder held in place by a small stick.

Tips for First Time Hand-drill Friction Fire Makers

Text by Paul Schweighardt, ©1995

1. Your biggest chore will be finding the right materials in your part of the world. If possible, find out what the local ancients used; they knew best since their survival depended upon these materials.

2. The char you produce will be your best clue as to whether or not the materials you have chosen will work. If your hand-drill is producing large amounts of very finely textured char quickly, then you have the right materials.

3. Use only very dry materials to begin with. Once you have become proficient in fire making, then you can experiment with damp, green or wet materials.

4. Choose your place well. Your area should be dry, sheltered from the wind, and clear of debris.

5. When twirling the spindle, twirling speed should be fast but not furious. Breath calmly and evenly,

6. Use only your palms to twirl the spindle, rather than letting it roll out onto your fingers. You will maintain greater speed and control this way.

7. Bear down on the spindle as you twirl it. Downward pressure is equally important as spinning speed. One without enough of the other produces no results.

8. Once you have your smoldering ember, remain calm. The ember will burn for quite awhile, giving you plenty of time to carefully place it into the tinder nest and gently fan it into flames.

9. Make fire in a responsible way so as not to cause bush or forest fires.

10. All motions should be performed in a calm, supple and graceful manner. Experiment, persevere and good luck!

THE GOYSICH HAND-DRILL
By Jim Allen

For those of you who despair over being unable to start a hand-drill fire, take heart—there is now an alternative! I'd like to tell you about a hand-drill method that is easier to do, requires no cordage, and can be set up in a few minutes.

The discovery of this method began several years ago, when I was visiting my good friend, Mike Goysich, in Lafayette, Indiana. Mike had been practicing the mouth drill method of fire starting, and had met with good success. I had always found this method to be awkward at best, and downright torture at worst. Nevertheless, Mike demonstrated his skill, and in the conversation, we began to brainstorm friction fire techniques. At this point I am not sure who came up with the technique I am about to present, but I've always attributed it to Mike. As Mike is now diseased, I have de-

cided to name the technique after him, as I'm fairly certain it was his idea.

The first step is to obtain a pole or log of approximately 25 lbs. This weight could be adjusted up or down according to ones strength. Nest, obtain a suitable spindle of mullein, yucca, willow, etc. The spindle can be anywhere from 8" to 24" long. Then construct an ordinary fireboard of suitable materials. The last step is to obtain four stakes of about 2-3 feet in length and a rock or log to use as a mallet for pounding stakes. (More than four stakes can be used as needed).

Next, pound the stake into the ground on either side of your 25 lb. log (or pole).

Drill a small socket at an oblique angle into the far end of the log, and you're now ready to start a fire (tinder, of course, will be needed as with any friction fire). Lift up the socketed end of the log and place the spindle top into the socket. Set the bottom end of the spindle into the fireboard such that the spindle is almost straight up and down. (A relatively stout spindle will be needed because of the weight of the log.) The log will now provide the downward pressure, and all you have to do is roll the spindle back and fourth between your palms! I have experimented with this method, and found it to work very well. I also discovered that with the heavy weight of the log, a larger spindle was easier to turn than a small one. The spindle I used was about 5/8" wide at the large end.

There are probably many other possibilities for a friction fire, including a cranking technique that Mike and I discussed. But for now, I'm happy to know a hand-drill method that works like a charm!

The ultimate fire starting gimmic - The Two-man Hand-drill set from Dick Baugh.

EXPERIMENTS WITH THE HAND-DRILL
By Evard Gibby

When experimenting with hand drill fires, I somewhat by accident discovered a useful technique.

I was using teasel for the drill and clematis for the fireboard. This is a combination that has worked well for me before. But this time the teasel spindle seemed to be drilling or cutting rapidly through the fireboard without producing an ember. Teasel has a hard outer layer and a pithy center, so as it is drilled it forms to the configuration as shown in the cross section (figure #1). So just as a change I grabbed a willow spindle and turned it a few times in the clematis fireboard with a bow, easily getting an ember. Spinning the harder willow spindle in the hole caused the fireboard cross section to look like (figure #2). Then I went back to the teasel spindle and again spun it by hand. To my surprise I was able to get an ember easier. After examining the equipment, the fireboard and spindle cross section looked like (figure #3). The now slanted sides of the fireboard hole caused the sides of the spindle end to conform to that shape.

Since then I have been able to start numerous fires with this same hole and spindle. The cross section has remained fairly constant, and at this time the hole has only worn down about halfway through the thickness of the fireboard, most of the wear being caused while obtaining the original configuration. I would say that well over 90% of the wear is to the spindle during operation of the equipment.

The reason, I feel, that embers are easier to obtain is that the slanted edges of the spindle and hole provide more surface area rubbing against each other, and consequently more heat, during the operation of the hand drill set.

It would be interesting to learn if others have the same results trying the same thing.

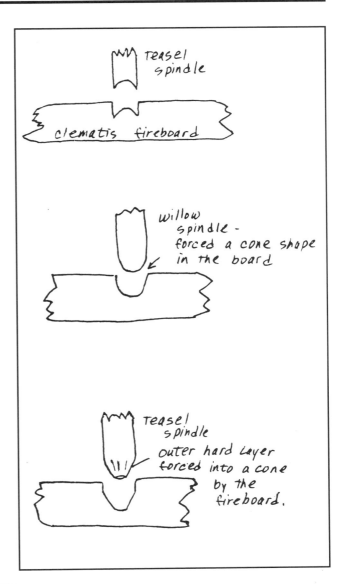

teasel spindle

clematis fireboard

willow spindle - forced a cone shape in the board

teasel spindle outer hard layer forced into a cone by the fireboard.

PUMP-DRILLS
Their Design, Construction and Attunement
Text and Photos By Anthony Follari

In the past, I have manufactured and used several pump-drills. I was never really impressed with their performance and used them mostly for drilling small holes which didn't require much torque. My opinion changed, however, when I met my now good friend and firemaking colleague, Charles Worsham. Charles demonstrated and let me operate a firemaking pump-drill he had made. It worked smoothly, effortlessly, and appeared to have substantial torque. To put it simply, I was impressed and became motivated to start construction on a new pump-drill. I set a goal for myself: to construct an efficient operating pump-drill that could be made quickly and easily using only stone

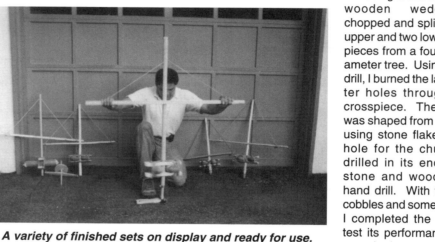

A variety of finished sets on display and ready for use.

tools. It had to be versatile so it could be used for firemaking and drilling, yet small and light enough to conveniently pack or transport. A tall order perhaps, but not an unreasonable one.

I had seen an unusual antique pump-drill that was used during the colonial period and its design intrigued me. It had two opposed weights outrigged on a crosspiece as compared to the more traditional round flywheel. This design appealed to me. I felt I could successfully reproduce it using stones for weight. This would give me the flexibility to easily adjust the flywheels weight by simply changing stones and decided to create a flywheel assembly out of two crosspieces which would hopefully sandwich the stones securely in place. (Stone flying off full speed at groin level would not be fun.)

I decided to construct a model out of lumber first to see if and how well this new flywheel design would work before I attempted one with stone tools. I also decided to make this test pump-drill extra large, trimming any excess off after I settled on effective dimensions. Since the weight was going to be adjustable, I decided to make the entire pump-drill adjustable. This way I could vary the height, width, weight, etc. and instantly see what impact these changes have. I could, in effect, test many different pump-drills, but only have to make one. This experimental adjustable pump-drill turned out to be a real educator. It confirmed for me that my method of securing the stones would work well. It also allowed me to study the physics involved in designing, oper-

ating, and tuning a pump-drill. After arriving at some dimensions for my new pump-drill, I gathered some basic stone and wood tools and began construction.

Using a stone axe and wooden wedges, I chopped and split out one upper and two lower crosspieces from a four inch diameter tree. Using a bow-drill, I burned the large center holes through each crosspiece. The spindle was shaped from a branch using stone flakes and a hole for the chuck was drilled in its end with a stone and wood tipped hand drill. With two river cobbles and some cordage I completed the drill. To test its performance, I inserted a basswood fire tip into the chuck and started drilling on a cedar fireboard. Within 30 seconds I had a substantial coal. The drill turned out to be a success.

Since that time I have made numerous pump-drills and have performed many experiments in an attempt to learn more about the elements that can affect the efficiency of a pump-drill. My favorite pump-drill to date was constructed with only primitive tools, it is durable, portable and very efficient, producing a coal in less than 15 seconds.

What I would like to share is my approach to constructing and tuning a pump-drill using only stone and wood tools. The design I have been using can be constructed with relative ease. To demonstrate this, we will start with a

All cutting was performed with stone tools.

While searching for the materials for this project I came across a three inch diameter tree that had been damaged and was dying. Although it was not the ideal tree I felt called to use it. Not only would it demonstrate that less than perfect materials can be used successfully, but it would be more in-line with my philosophical views regarding selection and harvesting. I hope you use the same approach and select a tree that can meet your needs while impacting minimally on the ecosystem.

Photo 3. Chopping out the spindle section.

tree and record our manufacturing time until completed. We will spend very little time on aesthetics as our focus will be on how quickly we can make a durable, efficient pump-drill. Please keep in mind that although I feel confident about designing, tuning and using pump-drill, I am not claiming to have all the answers. I am constantly experimenting and revising as I learn more. I welcome any and all comments and question. With this in mind, lets build a pump-drill.

Photo 4. Rounding the ends by abrading.

Constructing Pump-drills

To begin, first determine what you will be using your pump-drill for, then construct it with sufficient size and power to perform that job. If you intend to use it for more than one purpose, design it to handle the most demanding one. For example, if you are going to use your pump-drill only for drilling, design it around the largest drill bit you expect to use. For firemaking, select the largest and hardest fire tip you expect to use. Larger, heavier pump-drills have more power and can handle more difficult jobs. But bear in mind too large a drill can crush finer stone bits and fire tips and actually punch through wood. If portability is a concern, you should design the smallest, lightest drill that can be used for firemaking and drilling. We will design and tune it to handle a 3/4 inch diameter yucca fire tip. We will intentionally be overbuilding some components of the pump-drill and reduce them once it's completed. This is to prevent any one component from affecting the tuning by being undersize. If your pump-drill's purpose requires substantially more or less power then our example, you should proportionally increase or decrease the dimensions given in this article. The approach and tuning information would remain the same regardless of the size pump-drill you construct.

Photo 5. Tapering the ends on a stone slab.

The next step is to construct the components of the pump-drill. There are three main components: the vertical upright section or spindle, the large horizontal crosspiece which you place your hands on to operate the drill, and the two lower crosspieces which make up the flywheel assembly.

Spindle

Select a straight hardwood branch about 30 inches long and about 1 1/8 inches in diameter at the larger end (**Photo 3**). Remove the bark and slightly round both ends by abrading them against a large stationary stone (**Photo 4**). To ensure that the lower crosspieces wedge and fit tightly into place the spindle should gradually taper to about 7/8 inch at the tip. If your spindle doesn't naturally taper you can scrape it to shape using a large stone flake (*Photo 5*). Next, abrade a notch across the top end the same as you would for an arrow nock (**Photo 6**). This notch is for the crosspiece string to ride in. To complete the spindle you need a method of holding the fire tips and drill points. You could notch the bottom of the spindle and design your fire tips and drill bits to match. This method would require a lashing to be tied and untied each time you change fire

Photo 6. Notching the top end of the spindle.

Photo 7. Stone drilling.

Photo 8. Splitting the chuck.

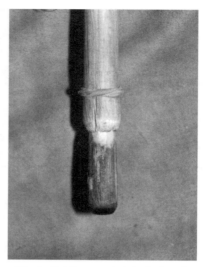

Photo 9. The completed chuck.

tips or drill bits and works well in situations where bit slippage is a problem. I have come to like a collet-type chuck best. It is a little more difficult to make, but if designed properly, works great. Shaping fire tips to fit this chuck is relatively simple. All your drill bits, however, must have the appropriate size foreshaft. This may require more work initially, but will make changing bits much more convenient.

To make the chuck, first pre-drill a hole straight into the bottom center of the spindle. I used a hand-drill with a 9/16 inch wide stone bit (**Photo 7**). This bit drilled a hole about one inch deep tapering to a point. Next I redrilled (actually burned) the hole with a 9/16 inch diameter wooden shaft to enlarge the hole a full 9/16 inch its entire depth (**Photo 10**). (If your hole is off center or drilled at an angle, chop it off and start again as a crooked or off center hole will not allow the drill to spin properly.) Next, split the spindle around the hole into six evenly spaced sections. The splits should run in about two or three inches deep, measured from the end of the spindle (**Photo 8**). To accomplish this I used a narrow, sharp bone wedge. Once the splits are com-

pleted insert your fire tip. It should be a snug fit, spreading the splits open slightly. Tie a piece of cordage tightly around the spindle about 1 1/2 inches from the bottom, then force the cordage downward against the taper to tighten the chuck. At this point the spindle is complete (**Photo 9**).

Crosspieces

In total you will need three crosspieces (**Photo 11**). One upper for the hand piece (approximately 30 inches long) and two lower ones for the flywheel assembly (about 8 inches long). My first primitive pump-drill was made out of hickory. I selected hickory because I thought it would make a strong durable pump-drill. It did. What I didn't anticipate was spending 45 minutes burn-drilling one hole, not counting rest periods.

Photo 11. The cross pieces.

Pre-drilling with a stone tip shortened my burn-drilling time to 35 minutes per hole. Remember you need three holes, so if time is a concern and you are willing to sacrifice some durability I recommend softer woods like sassafras, cedar, etc. All the crosspieces can be split out of one block of

Photo 10. Burn-drilling the chuck. Split stick vice is used to prevent the spindle from turing and splitting.

Photo 12. Selecting a section.

Photo 13. Starting the split.

Photo 14. Maintain even mass on both sides of the split.

wood. Select a straight, knot-free section of wood that appears to have all the bark furrows going in straight lines (an indication that the grain may also go and split in straight lines).

Chop out a 30 inch long section from the tree you have selected (**Photo 12**). You can use wooden wedges and a mallet to split the wood down into 1/2 inch thick strips (**Photos 13, 14 & 15**). Pick the best strip for the upper crosspiece and chop out two 8 inch strips for the lower crosspieces from the remaining strips. Abrade the rough edges by rubbing them against a coarse stone (**Photo 16**). With the crosspieces prepared it is now time to drill the large center holes.

I used a modified bow-drill arrangement to actually burn through the crosspieces. When burn drilling holes of this size I found that I needed a large diameter spindle which shouldered down to the size hole I wanted to burn drill (**Photo 17**). This allowed me the leverage to overcome the pressure and resistance I needed for burn drilling without the spindle binding or the cord slipping. (This and many other designs have many firemaking applications that will be discussed in a future article.) To facilitate the burn drilling you can pre-drill the holes with a stone bit. The size of the hole for the upper crosspiece should be about 1/8 inch larger than the thickest portion of the spindle the crosspiece must pass. The lowest crosspiece should wedge down and stop about four inches from the bottom of the spindle and the center crosspiece about 2 1/2 inches above that. If your weights are thicker or thinner adjust this distance accordingly.

At this point, the individual pieces are completed and you can assemble your drill. For a starting point, select two, 3/4 pound weights and lash them securely between the two lower crosspieces. For weights, I prefer river cobbles that are flat and longer than they are wide. Try to find two stones that match as closely as possible in weight and shape. If there are any irregularities, they can be flaked, pecked or ground off. For a quick fix you can wrap buckskin or cordage around an undersize weight to enlarge it. You don't have to limit yourself to rocks either. Once, for a demonstra-

tion, I used my moose billet on one side and two small hammer stones on the other.

Having completed the lower crosspiece assembly, tie each end of a piece of cordage to each end of the upper crosspiece allowing a slack cordage length of approximately 39 inches. Now place the crosspiece over the spindle and place the center of the string in the notch. Your drill is now ready to be tuned. Before I move on to tuning, however, I would

Photo 15. Select the fatest, most uniform piece for the handpiece and chop the lower pieces from the remaining split.

like to review the proper way to operate your pump-drill as the operator can greatly affect its performance.

Operation of Pump-drills

To get the most performance from your pump-drill, it must be operated efficiently. You should accelerate the crosspiece down authoritatively, yet smoothly, generating as much force as possible early in the stroke, as this is when the pump-drill has its greatest mechanical advantage for generating power (**Photo 19**). As the crosspiece approaches the bottom, the operator, anticipating its rise, offers and maintains downward resistance putting to work the flywheels momentum. Then, as the crosspiece reaches the top, the operator gets ready to start again.

Photo 16. Abrading the rough edges.

Photo 17. Burn-drilling the holes.

It's common for people not to apply any resistance on the crosspiece during the upward travel, thinking it will hinder the drills performance. This may be true with a poorly designed drill as it may lack the necessary momentum and stall, but a properly designed and tuned pump-drill will easily handle downward resistance during its rewind enabling it to more efficiently utilize and generate power.

Tuning Pump-drills

With the construction and operational aspects behind us it is time to concentrate on tuning. There are several factors which affect the pump-drill as the crosspiece goes through its upward and downward travel. Tuning consists of adjusting these factors to maximize the pump-drills efficiency. We will take a three step approach to tuning. If your pump-drill has the same or proportionally the same dimensions as our example these steps will apply. If not, refer to the trouble shooting guide as some of the components of your pump-drill may be undersize and prevent you from selecting the proper setting.

Step One - Adjusting the Revolutions Per Cycle

When the pump-drill is being operated the spindle rotates in one direction for a certain number of revolutions, then it reverses and spins in the opposite direction for an equal number of revolutions. By adjusting the number of revolutions that take place during a cycle you can have a tremendous impact on the drills performance.

The revolutions per cycle are determined and can be adjusted by the length of the string attached to the crosspiece. The shorter the string the fewer revolutions per cycle and conversely the longer the string the more revolutions per cycle.

A pump-drill with too many revolutions during its cycle will run out of momentum on the rewind and not be able to tolerate much downward

resistance. As we have already discussed downward resistance on the upward travel of the crosspiece is essential for maximum efficiency. Without downward resistance the drill will actually be coasting, waiting for its next power stroke. It will lack power, operate slower, and feel as if it can't keep up with you.

An ideal number of revolutions per cycle is somewhere between three and four. This will allow you to achieve a crisp, responsive drill as it is under more constant power by you. You will have sufficient time to develop maximum speed and momentum.

To adjust the revolutions per cycle on your pump-drill, wind up the crosspiece and slowly push down on it, counting the revolutions until the crosspiece reaches the bottom. It should be between 1 1/2 - 2 revolutions as this is only one half of a cycle. Adjust your string accordingly.

You will notice that I have been referring to string length and not spindle length. The spindle can be as long as you like as it is only the working area of the spindle that is important. That area is determined for the most part by the

Photo 18. Notching the ends of the lower pieces with a sharp rock.

Photo 19. Testing the finished, tuned drill. I got a coal in 19 seconds.

strings length. The spindle length only becomes a factor if you don't have sufficient length to adjust your string to the proper revolutions per cycle.

Step Two - Selecting the Flywheel Weight

The main criteria for selecting the flywheel weight is the amount of pressure you need. For drilling holes, you want to select a weight that allows for the application of sufficient pressure on the downward and upward phases to allow the bit to cut or abrade its way through the object being drilled. Too little pressure and the bit will not engage but spin idly. Too much pressure and the bit will punch or crush its way through doing little cutting. Smaller bits may even tend to shatter. For firemaking, you should have sufficient pressure to generate dark brown dust that flows freely from the notch. Too little pressure and there will be little or no dust or it will be too light in color. Too much pressure and the tip will tear apart or deform.

With this criteria in mind, test your pump-drill using different weights to determine if you are generating sufficient pressure. Starting with a 1 1/2 lb. flywheel, test your drill. Then increase the weight by 1/2 lb. and compare how each weight increase in the flywheel relates to its performance. As you get closer to your optimum weight you should increase the weight in smaller increments.

Ideally, it is nice to have an assortment of different weights to experiment with but almost any stones will do. Remember, you can make up for differences in size with buckskin or cordage. For small increases in weight, you can lash sticks along the crosspiece. Once you settle on the ideal weight, you can later replace them with nicely shaped stones of equal weight.

For our example, I found that a weight much below 1 1/2 pounds did not allow for the application of sufficient pressure to generate the color or volume of dust critical to firemaking. As I increased the weight, performance started to pick up until I reached 2 3/4 pounds. As I increased from there I started to experience more and more bit deformation and at 4 pounds had a lot of bit failure. I had a usable range between 2 pounds and 3 1/2 pounds with the ideal setting approximately 2 3/4 pounds.

Step Three - Determining the Crosspiece Length

The last factor we need to adjust is the amount of torque available as the crosspiece moves downward. The torque available on the downward phase (from here on referred to as downward torque) should match the torque the flywheel generates on the upward or rewind phase. By balancing these two forces the drill will take on a more consistent speed. Neither phase will overpower the other and the drill will operate more smoothly and fluidly.

The downward torque is a product of string angles. The more outward (closer to 90 degrees measured from the spindle) the pull of the string away from the spindle, the more downward torque the drill will have. The factor which we will be using to regulate the string angles is the length of the crosspiece. The longer the crosspiece the closer to 90 degrees the string angles will be and the more downward torque the drill will have.

We intentionally overbuilt the crosspiece in length and attached the string to the very end providing a high level of downward torque. This allowed us to select the ideal flywheel weight as a drill with insufficient torque is more limiting in its ability to handle weight. With the weight selected we now need to reposition the string on the crosspiece to the location which best balances the torque on upward and downward phases. Each time you move the string it impacts the revolutions per cycle. Therefore, you must also readjust the string length to return the revolutions per cycle to their original setting. This will ensure that you are only comparing differences in crosspiece length without any other factors influencing your comparison.

To find the ideal length move the string inward on the crosspiece in two inch increments (remember to readjust the revolutions per cycle each time). Test your drill at each interval and continue until you reach the point where the drills performance starts to drop off. At this point move the string back outward two inches, readjust the revolutions per cycle and your drill is tuned.

For our example drill, I tested each interval for about 20 seconds noting its performance. When I reached the 21 inch length the drill seemed sluggish and less responsive and it required more effort on my part to reach the same level of speed and power as before. In short the drill's performance dropped off. To complete the tuning I repositioned the string at 23 inches and readjusted the revolutions per cycle.

Keep in mind that there is a range if acceptable performance for every pump-drill and somewhere in that range is an optimum setting. The guidelines in this article will get you into that acceptable range. The optimum setting may vary from person to person and from drilling job to drilling job. You may want to increase or decrease the weight, revolutions per cycle or crosspiece length slightly to make any final fine tuning adjustments, personalizing the drills performance. Once you are satisfied with your final adjustments, you can cut off any extra length of crosspiece and/or spindle and go back over the drill cleaning up and reshaping any rough surfaces.

In testing the example drill, I was able to get a coal in under 20 seconds. From tree to completed pump-drill took under three hours using only stone tools. Using a softer wood for the crosspieces and a notch instead of a collet chuck could cut construction time down even further. Following is a breakdown of the time of construction:

Chop out section and split out crosspiece - 25 min.
Shape spindle, notch and make chuck - 40 min.
Abrade crosspiece, burn-drill holes, notch
crosspiece ends - 20 min.
TOTAL 175 minutes
(2 hours 55 minutes)

So, there you have it, an efficient, durable pump-drill that can be constructed in under three hours using only stone tools. Remember, this pump-drill does not require any searching for a special shape or certain type of raw material as any straight section of wood will do. The weight can be almost anything, even sections of wood from the same tree the pump-drill was cut from. The adjustability of the flywheel makes this a truly versatile design.

For those individuals who are not interested in fine tuning but want an efficient pump-drill for firemaking, simply use the following dimensions:

Fire tip	**5/8 - 3/4 inches in diameter**
Crosspiece	**22 - 24 inches in length**
Weight	**2 1/2 - 3 pounds**
String length	**31 - 35 inches in length**

What I have demonstrated is my approach to designing and tuning a pump-drill. It is not the only way, but I feel it is an effective one. As your experience and knowledge grows, you won't need to overbuild or adjust your drill to the degree we did in this article as you will know how to target closer to the final dimensions.

There are a few variables that I did not cover. Their impact on good pump-drill performance is not as significant as the variables we discussed and their inclusion would make tuning much more complex. It is beyond the scope of this article to cover these variables, but perhaps a future article can, along with discussing some additional pump-drill modifications. For those interested in doing some additional experimentation, these variables include:

1. Spindle diameter and shape
2. String diameter
3. String stretch
4. Weight placement

All in all, a properly designed and tuned pump-drill is a pleasure to use. Its consistent performance is great for testing different stone bits for drilling efficiency, the effectiveness of different fireboard notch shapes, the combustion time of woods, etc. It is a great camp tool, and the mechanical advantage it offers makes firemaking and drilling easy and fun for anyone. ***Happy drilling.***

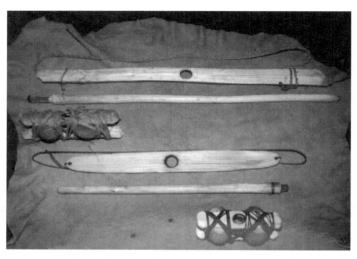

Finished pump-drill parts disassembled.

TROUBLE SHOOTING GUIDE

Before referring to this guide review the Operation of Pump-drills section to ensure that you are operating you pump-drill efficiently.

Problem	Remedy
Lacks power on the downward phase-	- Adjust revolutions per cycle +/- Increase crosspiece length +/- Lighten flywheel +/- Decrease bit or tip diameter
Lacks power on the upward phase	- Adjust revolutions per cycle +/- Increase flywheel weight +/- Increase crosspiece length +/- Decrease bit or tip diameter
Lacks both downward and upward power	- Decrease bit or tip diameter +/- Use larger, heavier drill
Excessive pressure, deforming or crushing bits	- Reduce flywheel weight +/- Increase bit or tip diameter +/- Use smaller, lighter drill
Insufficient pressure	- Increase flywheel weight +/- Adjust revolutions per cycle +/- Increase crosspiece length
Insufficient speed	- Decrease flywheel weight +/- Adjust revolutions per cycle +/- Increase crosspiece length

Problem	Remedy
Cycles fast, feels choppy	- Adjust revolutions per cycle
Non-responsive, sluggish	- Adjust revolutions per cycle +/- Increase crosspiece length
Bit does not spin true	- Crooked spindle, off center chuck hole, or crooked bit
Bit slips in chuck	- Increase depth and/or size of chuck
Flywheel assembly slips on spindle	- Wedge flywheel assembly down tighter on spindle +/- Insert a piece of leather between crosspiece and spindle before sliding flywheel assembly on +/- Elongate spindle and cross piece hole for a key fit +/- Insert a wooden pin through spindle and lash crosspiece to it
Drill lopes during use	- Flywheel weights are not balanced, one side is heavier than the other +/- Off center chuck hole

A NOTE ON TINDER BUNDLE CONSTRUCTION

Text and Photos By Charles Worsham

One of the most exasperating things in friction fire-making is to spin out a coal and then not be able to light the tinder bundle. Perhaps the tinder was a little too damp, or maybe the coal was too small to generate enough heat, or possibly the fire-maker blew too hard: cooling the coal and adding unnecessary moisture. Feeling the need to hurry the process is also a preamble to failure, as is not giving due consideration to what constitutes a properly made tinder bundle. Indeed, there is one aspect of tinder bundle construction which is often overlooked—the **COAL EXTENDER.**

The coal extender is one of several different ingredients which, when added to the core of the tinder bundle, will eliminate most or all of the problems listed above. It will extend the life of the coal; it will enlarge the size of the coal;

and it will allow more time for the fire-maker to carefully nurse and coax the tinder bundle to flame. Moreover, a coal extender, by increasing the life of the coal, will allow more time for residual moisture to dissipate from the bundle. Additionally, the increase in coal size and coal longevity will result in raising the core temperature of the bundle more rapidly and more substantially. And all of this can be achieved with little or no blowing on the tinder bundle.

In general, a coal extender will not break into flames itself. However, it will smolder and glow like a coal and will generate very hot temperatures which will aid in igniting the surrounding tinder material. Some of the better coal extending materials are illustrated in **Figure 1** and they are as follows: 1) cracked-cap polypore (lower left and lower cen-

Figure 1 - Coal extender materials.

Figure 2 - Cracked-cap polypore shavings.

more rapidly and the odds of producing a flaming tinder bundle will increase tremendously.

ROTTED WOOD

Next to the cracked-cap polypore, rotted wood can make an excellent coal extender. Most tree species are a source for tinder core material especially hollow, dead, or dying trees. Rotted wood, therefore, is much more available than cracked-cap polypore, but it has the disadvantage of not working well when wet or damp. A few dry pieces crumbled up in the center of a tinder bundle is all that is needed to enhance the quality of a coal and ensure success in creating flames. The first two examples illustrated in **Figure 1 (upper left)** are from southern red oak (*Quercus falcata*) and the third is wild cherry (*Prunus serotina*). The samples from red oak show two

ter); 2) rotted wood (upper left and lower center); 3) duff (lower right); 4)oak apple gall (upper right).

different forms of rotted wood. The first was taken from inside a large hollow tree and has the appearance of sawdust. When rotted wood has reached this state, it does not enhance a coal as well as more solid slivers of punky wood. However, by wetting this sawdust form and compressing it into a more solid ball, it will work almost as well as the more firm pieces of wood. Just put it somewhere to dry out, then break it up into little chunks and place in the tinder bundle. The second example of southern red oak and the piece of wild cherry illustrate the best type of rotted wood, punky but not too soft and solid but not too hard. It can be broken up in to slivers, all of which will turn into individual glowing coals when brought into contact with the primary coal.

CRACKED-CAP POLYPORE

The cracked-cap polypore (*Phellinus rimosus*) is a member of the Polyporacae family whose numerous species are noted for their use in various primitive skills. Some are choice edibles; others have medicinal value; a few can be used as dyes; and still others have importance as tinder materials. Mors Kochanski in his book, **Northern Bushcraft**, discusses some of the uses of these polypores (pp 16 & 29). The cracked-cap polypore is found almost exclusively on living or dead black locust trees (*Robina pseudoacacia*). Black locust originally was native only to the Appalachian Mountains from Pennsylvania to Alabama, and part of Arkansas, eastern Oklahoma and southern Missouri but now has been planted successfully in most states. Black locust cannot tolerate shade and will begin to die out when other hardwoods compete successfully for sunlight. Where black locusts are stressed and dying, the cracked-cap polypore is most likely to appear. In areas where black locust is scarce, other species of trees may supply additional kinds of polypores which will work well too. The cracked-cap polypore is an excellent coal extender, requiring no drying time before use and working well under any weather conditions. One small cracked-cap polypore will supply enough material for years of fire-making. Simply shave off a little pile of slivers (**Figure 2**) and place it in the center of a pre-constructed tinder bundle. Make a slight depression in the center of the polypore slivers and add the smoldering coal. The important thing at this point is to make certain that the coal is touching as many of the polypore slivers as possible. Each sliver, in turn, will begin to smolder and glow. Coal size will expand to include all of the polypore: heat will begin to rise

DUFF

When the word duff is mentioned, it usually elicits a dumbfounded expression followed by the word, "huh?" Duff (**Figure 1 lower right**) is the partly decayed organic matter on the forest floor. A forest fire which burns into the duff layer is a firefighter's nightmare; it is almost impossible to extinguish. A fire in this material can smolder unnoticed for days burrowing under fire lines and springing back to life with a vengeance. A duff layer fire is usually the product of long dry spells and, like rotted wood, it does not burn well when damp. Duff is hard to describe; it looks like dirt, but dirt will not burn. It is usually found on south facing slopes and seems to occur around oak trees. Duff tends to be grayish in color and, when lifted from the ground, it usually pulls up like little pieces of carpet. As a coal extender, duff generates incredible amounts of heat and will smolder for extended periods of time.

OAK APPLE GALL - The oak apple gall (**Figure 1 upper left**) is a growth which occurs on oak trees and is the repository for the eggs of the oak apple gall wasp

(*Amphibolips confluentus*). The gall grows as a chemical reaction to the wasp's sting, and the dry, spongy substance within the papery shell can be used as a tinder bundle core. However, the oak apple gall is listed here with some reservation; it is clearly not as good a coal extender as those listed above. It does not seem to generate as much heat, and its fire-making properties appear to decline as it is exposed to the elements over the winter; best results occur in the fall. Even so, this growth has possibilities and is worth experimentation. Crack open and remove half the outer shell of the gall. Take out the spongy core and compress tightly. Then add the compressed centers from several other galls and place all of them back into the half shell and it is ready for use. Put the half shell with the compressed centers into a tinder bundle and drop the coal into the oak gall shell. The spongy core will smolder and the papery shell will reflect heat back to the center of the gall. It is important here to make certain that tinder material is making contact with the inside of the gall, otherwise it will not catch fire. One of the advantages of the oak gall is that the papery shell will keep the inner material dry during wet weather (up to a point). In extremely wet weather, however, the spongy core will become damp and will be totally useless for fire-making until thoroughly dry again.

If the tinder bundle is carefully and properly constructed to begin with, and a good coal extender is added, no blowing on the bundle will be necessary. Simply add the coal, close the bundle up (not too tightly), and walk away; in a while the tinder bundle will erupt in flame without any further coaxing. Putting it another way, this means that the fire-maker can put a coal into tinder, place the bundle within the kindling tipi, go get a drink of water, make a phone call, address a few Christmas cards, and return just in time to see the tinder bundle catch fire and ignite the kindling. In terms of clock time, a tinder bundle made of red cedar inner bark with a cracked-cap polypore coal extender can easily sit unattended for over twelve minutes before catching fire by itself **(see Figures. 3 & 4)**. Now of course there are a number of factors which will reduce the chances of getting tinder to flame by itself: too wet; too much air; too little air; poor choice of material; too humid; too cold, etc. However, even when these factors make ignition difficult, a good coal extender can improve the tinder bundle to the point where a slight puff of breath or a gentle waving of the bundle is all that will be needed for success. Experimentation with various tinder materials and coal extenders will soon produce a list of those ingredients and combinations which will most often catch fire with little or no work after the coal has been inserted.

For a survival fire, the coal extender can give the fire-maker a larger, hotter coal, more time for drying damp tinder, and more of a chance for success under adverse conditions. For a ceremonial fire, the coal extender can give the fire-maker all of the above plus more time to patiently create a fire which can be a work of art. Graceful movement, an unhurried pace, carefully assembled equipment, and visually exciting moments from beginning to end are important aspects of a ceremonial or spiritual fire—the coal extender can help it happen.

Figure 3 - Smoking tinder bundle with coal extender core.

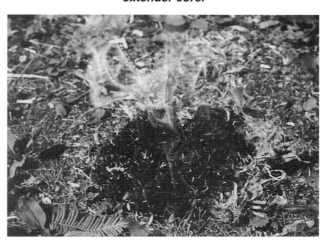

Figure 4 - Self-igniting tinder bundle with coal extender core.

NOTES ON POLYPORE FUNGI AS COAL EXTENDERS
By R. Alan Mounier

Charles Worsham identified polypore fungi (*Phellinus rimosa*) as effective coal extenders. My experimentation with a variety of such fungi indicate that he is correct. To know why, I took a close look at polypore fungi. A summary follows.

Polypore fungi, also known as bracket fungi or shelf fungi, comprise a family of pore-forming fungi that typically grow on stressed, diseased, or dead trees. Soft when young, they become firm, corky, or woody with age. My specimens

(more)

were harder and less resilient than cork but appreciably softer and more spongy than sound softwood, such as white cedar. The body consists of a woody mass which contains numerous, tiny, and closely spaced tubes or pores. This characteristic gives the material its name, polypore (literally, many pores). The specimens that I examined were gathered from black locust trees in Deptford Township, Gloucester County, New Jersey. This is the type of fungus noted by Worsham.

I prepared thin sections of the fungi for examination under a microscope. Freshly cut surfaces have a dark reddish brown color, closely approximated by the Munsell designation, 2.5YR 3.5/5 ("dusky red"). The transverse section revealed a regularly arranged matrix of tiny tubes in the woody body of the fungus. These tubes have an average diameter of 103.62ym (104 microns or micrometers = 104/1000 mm = 0.10mm). The intertubular distance on average is 70.65ym (**Figure 1**). In longitudinal sections the tubes have pinched and staggered closures, resembling the end view of an automobile radiator core or certain kinds of "Chex" cereals (see **Figure 2**). The tubes range between 47ym and 612ym in length. The staggered arrangement imparts strength that would be lacking if the tubes were substantially longer.

A glimpse of the sections reveals that the body of the polypore is very well ventilated. Since the woody material is both well aerated and combustible, the fungus catches an ember readily, even when damp. Once ignited, this material will continue to smolder for extended periods of time, thus making it desirable for the fire-maker. In open air, the smoldering pieces do not burst into flames, but they burn tenaciously, and hot enough to ignite even slightly damp tinder.

A sample cube, 5mm on a side, was impaled on the point of a small needle. Upon ignition this sample glowed brightly for 2 minutes, 37 seconds, then blinked out in a mass of fluffy white ash. Another sample cube, 10mm per side, burned for 21 minutes, 53 seconds. No open flames were observed, but bright red incandescence was distinctly visible in subdued light. The heat could be felt on the fingertips up to 10cm (4 inches) away.

An interesting property of this material is that, once ignited, the entire mass quickly becomes a glowing body. The bright red color indicates that the embers attain a temperature of approximately 1,250° F in open air. Forcing a draft on the ember causes bright reddish yellow incandescence, indicating a temperature of approximately 1,650° F. Temperature estimates are from a color chart in an old welding manual, where bright red is termed "Medium Cherry" and bright reddish yellow is equivalent to "Salmon" (Mackenzie and Card, *The Welding Encyclopedia*, 1922).

With samples of the sizes indicated, the entire mass continues to glow until all of the combustible material has been exhausted, whereupon the incandescence instantly vanishes—just like someone switched off a light. Very mystical.

The fact that the entire body glows indicates that combustion gases fill the tubular structure, which then radiates as the gases burn. In essence, the body of the burning polypore acts like the mantle in a gas lantern. Eventually, when the fuel is exhausted, the light just blinks out.

The residue is a soft, fluffy white ash, whose color is whiter than any chip in the Munsell Soil Color Charts (1992). The nearest color among the common soil colors is 5Y 8/1 (white), which is visibly more gray than the sample ash. The ash is easily crushed into a very fine powder that may have potential as a pigment for paint. But that is the subject for another inquiry.

Using polypore shavings, I was able to start a flaming fire outdoors when the temperature was only 9° F and the wind blew at 15 to 25 mph, with higher gusts. I made this fire by friction in the open, using a white cedar hearth and spindle. A seated posture permitted me to shelter the hearth-pit from the wind with my body. A kneeling posture would have made the hearth more vulnerable to the wind.

I placed the center of the hearth-pit well in from the edge of the board so that the powder would collect in the notch. This placement retarded the tendency of the wind to dislodge the powder pile from the edge of the board. I placed a sheet of paper beneath the notch to catch the fire dust. Once an ember was formed, six or eight slivers of thinly sliced polypore fungus were added. Once these slivers were glowing well, I added cattail fluff on top.

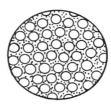

Figure 1: Sketch of magnified cross section showing porous structure. Pores are about 0.10mm in diameter.

Figure 2: Sketch of magnified longitudinal section showing porous structure. Tubes range from 0.47mm to 0.61 in length.

Figure 3: Sketch of glowing coal nested between two small Polypore Fungi.

The entire mass was then enclosed in the paper, folded to form a thin tube. Air was blown in an open end until the mass smoked vigorously, whereupon it was introduced beneath a handful of maple leaves, simply gathered from the ground at the time. These leaves had some moisture in the form of frost or snow. In a few seconds, upon receiving a gust of wind, the entire bundle burst into flames.

In other experiments with friction fires, I have noticed that a smoldering powder pile cupped between two small polypores (species unknown) is readily transportable and will retain a viable coal for an extended period of time (Figure 3). I have yet to complete time tests, but I imagine that the durability of the coal will be measured in hours or half-hours, rather than in minutes. The trick will be to deny the polypore any more air than is absolutely necessary to support its combustion.

Once ignited, the polypore burns tenaciously. I have found that the coal may spontaneously rejuvenate after being extinguished to the satisfaction of the naked eye. Therefore, due caution is necessary in the use of this material or your experiments may prove more incendiary than expected.

At any rate, polypore fungi are great aids to firemaking. I am entirely certain that there use extends back into ancient times. People living in the forest doubtless had an intimate knowledge of their surroundings and put that knowledge to use in their lives. I suspect that the polypore, because of its peculiar properties, was important not only in fire-making, but quite likely in magico-religious functions as well.

WHERE THERE'S NO TINDER
By E. J. Pratt

Where there is none of the commonly used tinder available, or indeed, where the tinder available is too wet, a fire can still be started.

If you have material for a friction fire set, you have a fire. In wet weather, dead (but not rotten) wood suspended above the ground can be used to make a fire set and the tinder. Whilst the outside of the wood may be wet, this can be shaved off to expose a dry inner.

Shavings of two grades are made from the wood itself. 1) A good handful of fairly coarse and 2) half a handful of fine scrapings (**Figures A & B**).

It will be appreciated that this form of tinder is granular rather than fibrous in texture and as such does not hold together on it's own and therefore needs to be kept together or it will disintegrate whilst the coal is being developed. Two containers are suggested as shown in **Figures C & D**. The construction is important. On dry ground, a hollow, as shown in **Figure C** can be scraped out. On wet ground the container in **Figure D** is formed that raises the tinder above the surface. The sides of the container should slope in towards the bottom. The sloping sides feed the tinder granules in towards the coal and help it to coalesce. If the sides are vertical the tendency is for the ignition point to disintegrate.

In **Figure D**, the container is constructed of about twenty green (to prevent their combusting) sticks pushed into the ground so that they extend outward about the length of an index finger. The construction forms a close knit circle with a narrow base splaying out at the top, to cover an area about the size of your palm. The bottom of the container wants to be covered with a couple of wood chips to raise the tinder above the wet surface

The container is now filled with the coarse shavings, and a hollow is formed in the middle to about half depth. This hollow in turn is filled with the fine scrapings. In the center of this make a small depression just big enough to hold the coal.

By blowing vertically downward and gently covering, the coal is coaxed to increase in size. Match sized slivers of wood are placed on top and the whole blown into ignition from the side.

All this may seem long winded, but on a seashore where there is only driftwood, or inland in wet conditions, this may well be all you have. If you have the wood for a fire set...you have fire.

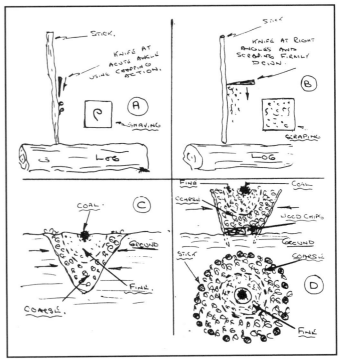

Fire Bundle or Primitive Match

By David Holladay, Photos By David Wescott

Once a fire is kindled, much of the work needed to build the next fire is already done. In order to maintain fire while traveling, a storage system can be created to transport the spark from the current fire to the site of the next nights camp.

All that is need is dry, fibrous material that can be shredded, then compacted into a large cigar-like "match". Lay out strips of bark for the outer layer of the match. Onto this, pile the shredded inner layers (Photo 1). Cattail down may also be added. It is an exceptional material for maintaining a coal without it igniting into a flame. The entire mass is tightly wrapped (Photo 2 & 3) and bound with other fibers (Photo 4). The Match must be wrapped very tightly to minimize air flow. The length of time that the match will last without igniting is a fine balance between reduced air flow to allow the spark to smolder, yet enough air to allow it to be maintained. The match should be sheltered from breezes, as these may cause it to bust into flame.

The spark is fed into one end of the match. Make sure that it begins to feed off of the inside fiber bundle and does not go out. A layer of bark can be lightly wrapped around this end to protect the spark from obtaining too much air.

Once you get to camp, the spark can be transported to a tinder bundle, or the match may be opened and the spark blown into a flame. The match is used to ignite the kindling and fuel.

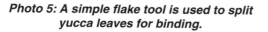

Photo 5: A simple flake tool is used to split yucca leaves for binding.

Section 3

Bone, Stone and Wood
Basic Elements

FIRST TOOLS

By David Wescott

Which came first, fire or the cutting edge ? Which came first, a wood, bone or stone age ? Which came first, core tools or flake tools ? Which came first, the chicken or the egg ? By the time you ponder all of those questions, someone else will have made the needed tools , collected their groceries, made a fire and cooked a hot meal, and bedded down for the night. Maybe thinking about it is as far as you want to go, but coming to a real understanding of how to do things takes action. By doing with your hands, you train your mind and body to work together. One is no more slave to or in control of the other...we come into balance.

Early tools were simple and field expedient. Early people picked up, modified, used for a specific task and discarded what tools they needed. They learned to seek out the best materials for a job later on, but at this point they used what was readily available to them...on the spot. "First Tool" or simple technologies require you to become familiar with what you have in your own neighborhood. Don't seek out the exotics or materials that would have to be obtained through trade or travel. Use what you have and master the skills that local materials will allow you to perform.

On our journey through time, we need to start at the beginning and work toward the present. Establishing a foundation in the "first skills" allows us to build not only our knowledge of materials, but to also train ourselves by starting with more large-scale tools and concepts and "evolving" into more refined tools as we travel through time. By mastering the broad-based principles first, we will then have the technical skills and insights to lead us through a natural progression of mental, physical and technological development.

Our Toolmaking Tradition

There is more to our connection with tools than simply making them. The ability to make tools is not unique to us. The fact that we create tools - to create tools - to create tools - to create tools - however, is a human characteristic. The way we alter and use materials as tools is what defines culture. Types of tools, techniques used and materials selected over a wide range of opportunities are what help us to identify a specific group of people. Since the total record of ancestral bones is composed of less than 1,000 individuals, our material heritage is the only other benchmark we have to mark our travel through time. The trait of passing on a collected assortment of technologies and traditions is what many define as the basic human niche - culture. Being culture-bearing is the essence of what makes us human. And our connection to tools - the longest recorded evidence of culture- has much to do with how we define ourselves and our relationship to the expanded range of environments and challenges we now experience.

You Are What You Eat

The question of herbivore, carnivore, or omnivore is a sticky one and will probably never be completely resolved. However, the majority of information points to the fact that early man was predominantly an eater of plants and that many of the expedient or "found" tools were used to access plant parts; i.e. roots, nut meats, fruits. Many of the early stone, bone and wooden tools were plant processors and harvesters that allowed man (an animal inadequately suited to compete with other animals in the same environment) to dig roots that required strong claws, crack nuts without powerful jaws, or prepare foods for those too small or weak to eat them without processing. Early choppers may have been used to modify wood and bone into gathering tools or as processors of what was found. Hand axes with

	TECHNOLOGICAL TIME LINE 5,000,000-10,000 years ago
5 mil	Pre-stone age industries of bone, tooth and wood Digging Sticks, Bone Shovels, Simple Pebble Tools
2.5 mil	**LOWER PALEOLITHIC** - old stone age Oldowan Tool Tradition - Earliest stone tools Stick, Bone and Found Tools
1.5 mil	Crafted tools and early fire hearths Acheulean Tool Tradition - Cleavers, Axes, Flake Tools Cooking Rocks, Seed Preparation
800,000	Man controls fire
400,000	Artificial shelters
100,000	**MIDDLE PALEOLITHIC** Skins for clothes and shelter Bones for utensils and tools Sophisticated core and platform production
60,000	Complex tools and ritual burials
50,000	Mammoths hunted
40,000	**UPPER PALEOLITHIC** Cave paintings Blade and Core Tool Tradition Atlatls and Spear Throwers Amulets and Adornments
35,000	Earliest known "written" records
33,000	Bone flutes
30,000	Sculpted Figurines - Food Storage Complex Language - Fire production tools
20,000	Bone, ivory, antler needles and harpoons
10,000	**MESOLITHIC** - old world

sharp edges on all sides work as well for digging as they do for woodworking or butchering.

The shift from plant eater to meat eater was most likely slow yet deliberate. Survival creates the drive to exploit all options to their fullest. This includes material and food sources. Much of what has been discovered in the form of early tools has been found in direct association with bones that can be dated for age, thus giving us a relative age of the tools. The majority of tools found have been with the remains of animals that were most likely used as food or raw materials for tool production. If we want to ignore the fact that early man became a meat eater, then do we assume that early tools were made by the animals with whom they were found?

The one asset we do have is a set of teeth that allows us to make use of a wide variety of food sources. Compared to other families we may not be the most expedient user of any one source, but our physical ability to create the tools we need to adapt, plus our built-in processors for almost any food type, keeps us fed wherever we go.

Man - The Sculptor

Manmade tools appear in the fossil record as far back as 2.5 million years ago and continue through time. Some, but not many, tool-using animals modify the shape of their "found tools", as well as select specific tools for specific tasks. Man, on the other hand, is able to conduct a mental process that allows him to see within the natural material the tool that is needed to complete a task, and can then modify the material to the shape that does the job best.

This process is basic to becoming a toolmaker. You need to be able to find the best material from among a variety of choices, see your finished product in the material, render it out - sculpt, knap, carve or otherwise reduce the material to the desired form that you saw - and then use the tool for the job that it was intended.

The basis of most simple technologies is the process of reduction. Each material must be able to undergo the process of removing excess mass until the desired tool is acquired, yet still exhibit the quality of the original material. Tools can also be worked into a new state created by preparing/processing the material. This reduction process follows a number of stages that can be predetermined and followed in sequence. The regular use of a selected sequence may be cultural (imposed by the worker) or natural (dictated by the material itself). Regardless of the source of the sequence, once it is discovered, followed, and taught, predictable results can be expected from similar materials, under similar conditions, by others with comparable skills.

The originator of this idea, Errett Callahan, was seeking a predictable pattern for working stone. His **Lithic Reduction Sequence** has been adapted by Steve Watts and expanded by the author for this book , following a number of staging sequences for each material group - stone, wood, bone, antler, fiber and shell - where possible to help pass on a better understanding of the basics of material use and predictable processes that can be incorporated into toolmaking skills.

Each material source used in this book has a regular pattern as to how it is worked. The stages may be combined (field expedient digger from a broken limb is only one step), steps can be skipped (harvested saplings twisted and wrapped to form a finished handle), but seldom are they rearranged. Thought and action should be learned together for best results.

In addition to these staging sequences for materials, there are also stages of manufacture for specific tools. These are suggested step-by-step sequences for completing certain projects from selected materials or combinations of materials.

STAGING SEQUENCE FOR STONE TOOLS
STAGE 1 - Obtain Raw Materials - quarry, gather, grade
STAGE 2 - Creating The Blank - core or flake created by hammer
STAGE 3 - Creating The Preform - shaping to center plane and margin with hammer
STAGE 4 - Secondary Thinning - creating generalized shape and thickness
STAGE 5 - Shaping - pressure and percussion to specific shape

STAGING SEQUENCE FOR BONE/ANTLER/TOOTH TOOLS
STAGE 1 - Obtain Raw Materials - hunt, scavenge, gather
STAGE 2 - Creating The Blank - break, score, flake, crack, bash to generalized shape
STAGE 3 - Shaping - grind, carve, saw to specific shape
STAGE 4 - Finishing - polish, notch, drill, sharpen, grease/oil

STAGING SEQUENCE FOR WOOD TOOLS
STAGE 1 - Obtain Raw Materials - select from category 1-5
STAGE 2 - Creating The Blank - break, throw, bash, split, pound, strip, burn

STAGE 3 - Creating The Preform - strip, bend/straighten, hack, adze burn, season, scrape, season
STAGE 4 - Shaping - carve, fine scrape, thin, bevel, sand to specific shape
STAGE 5 - Finishing - burnish, grease/oil, fire harden

STAGING SEQUENCE FOR FIBER TOOLS
STAGE 1 - Obtain Raw Materials - gather, scavenge, hunt
STAGE 2 - Creating The Fiber - pound, bend, ret, render, split to remove fiber
STAGE 3 - Twisting/Weaving - creating cordage, containers, fabric, mats or bundles
STAGE 4 - Finishing - sealing with pitch, wax, hide glue

STAGING SEQUENCE FOR SHELL TOOLS
STAGE 1 - Obtain Raw Materials - gather, scavenge
STAGE 2 - Creating The Blank - core or flake created by hammer
STAGE 3 - Shaping - notch, grind, pressure or percussion to shape
STAGE 4 - Finishing - abrade holes, etch, inlay, etc.

STAGE 5 or 6 - Combine any materials into compound tools

BONE WORKING BASICS
Text and Illustrations By Steve Watts

A possible reduction sequence for working bone...from the complete bone to the completed tool or ornament. This sequence was first presented in 1988 and has been used since that time both in personal replication projects and in the presentation of bone working workshops and demonstrations. It has been refined somewhat since that time and will continue to be re-evaluated as further applications are tested.

These bone working "stages" may or may not have been present in the mind and work patterns of the aboriginal craftsman, but may be helpful for replicators seeking to work with bone in a systematic way.

Knives of bone and antler made by the author.

Stage 1- Obtaining The Material

The material in this case, of course, is bone. It is: found/gathered in the environment, traded for, obtained as a by-product of butchering/cooking activities, or processed directly from the carcass for the intention of working. Fleshing, boiling, and shallow burial are common processing methods.

Stage 2 - Creating The Blank

Breaking, scoring/breaking, scoring/cutting, flaking, cracking, smashing, grinding, splitting, or otherwise modifying the bone in preparation for shaping. The "blank" may be the whole bone modified, or a part or piece of the bone obtained by one or more of the above methods. In some cases "ideal" blank-forms may be required, in others a more generalized shape/size may suffice.

Stage 3 - Shaping

Grinding, carving, sawing/abrading, or otherwise modifying the blank to shape it into the final outline and cross-sectional form. Many bone implements may be completed with this stage. Others may require Stage 4 work for completion.

Stage 4 - Finishing

Polishing, notching, fine sharpening, drilling, engraving or other modifications may be applied to the shaped piece (as holes in needles, fine points on awls, etc.). Finishing procedures are most often related to specific tasks required of the tool.

The piece in hand at each stage is referred to in this way:

Stage l...The Bone
Stage 2. The Blank
Stage 3. The Shaped Piece
Stage 4. The Finished Piece

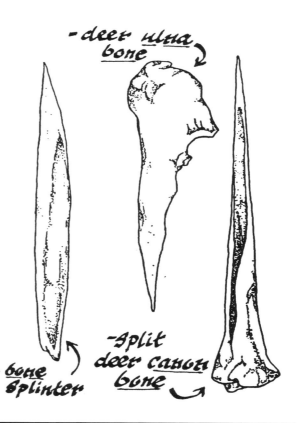

- deer ulna bone

- bone splinter

-split deer canon bone

Example: "Stages of Manufacture of A Bone Awl"

Stage 1	Stage 2	Stage 3	Stage 4
Cannon Bone (Whitetail Deer)	The Blank	The Shaped Piece	The Finished Piece

As in flintknapping, bow making, pottery or any other aboriginal technology approached in a systematic way; stages of manufacture may often be combined. Seldom however can they be rearranged in order. Stages may be omitted completely...as in the case of an expedient digging/stabbing tool created by the uncontrolled smashing of a long bone with a hammerstone. In this case the bone worker moves from whole bone to the completed tool with one swift blow.

Sources of Material

Bones of domestic and legally killed game animals can be obtained from hunters, ranchers, butchers and dairymen. Domestic and legally killed bird bones are rescued from the butcher block and the stock pot. Except in a survival situation, *avoid all bones from protected species* ..bird, mammal, reptile or human. No need for your bones to rot in jail !

Fresh or Dried?

The primitive bone worker may have little choice in his selection of raw materials in a given situation. When a choice is presented...which is better, fresh or dried bone?

Fresh bone seems stronger and more flexible than dried. Tools from these are less brittle and less likely to split and splinter. Yet, in manufacturing, a tendency to split can be an advantage if it can be controlled. Extremely weathered bone can deteriorate to a "spongy" state, making it the least desirable. Extremely fresh, uncooked bones can be excessively greasy, slippery and difficult to work with.

As with many things, a middle ground is best. In the "ideal" situation, where time allows, the best of both worlds finds the artisan using fresher bones through Stages I & 2 (where cutting, smashing, splitting, etc. are most utilized), slightly drier for Stage 3, and drier still for stage 4 (final grinding, polishing and sharpening). These Stage 4 tasks are best accomplished with dry materials. Fresh bone (somewhat like green wood) never takes the finer finishing processes well. It tends to "fuzz" and "feather" on the surface, resisting polish. Even a tool made from fresh bone will dry out over time, so completed implements should be oiled periodically to prevent weakening by checking, cracking, etc.

Raw or Cooked?

Raw bones are stronger than cooked ones...retaining their oils, structure and integrity. Baked or roasted bones may be used, but are often weakened considerably. Boiling (one of the preferred methods of processing found in Stage I) seems to weaken bone less than other "drier" cooking methods. Boiled bones are softened slightly in the process, allowing for ease of manufacture. Firmness is regained once they are dry. And, remember, all bones can be used for a smelly fuel (highly prized by aboriginal peoples living in wood-poor environments)—fuel for cooking, heating, or processing yet more bone.

Bone Working Tools

The aboriginal bone worker's tools vary from the simple (a hammerstone) to the sophisticated (a pump drill). Tools most often utilized in the various stages of manufacture typically are:

Stage 1...Digging sticks (wood or antler) for digging up buried bones; bifaces, unmodified flakes and scrapers for butchering and fleshing fresh bones; pots for boiling; packs, baskets, skins and cordage for transporting.

Stage 2...Hammerstones with flat, rounded or edged anvils; unmodified flakes, denticulated flakes and bifaces ("saws"); mauls, large-grained grinding stones, wedges, flakers and burins.

Stage 3...Medium-grained grinding stones, "saws", unmodified flakes, drills, gravers and burins, scrapers.

Stage 4...Finer-grained grinding stones, polishing stones, buckskin and sand polishers, drills, burins/engravers, pigments, oil.

Scraps

Cut-offs, splinters, partial halves from unsuccessful splitting attempts, etc. should be saved and examined. A "waste" piece from one project may become —upon close inspection— a perfect Stage 2 blank for another. The splinter becomes an awl or a needle, the cut-off a fish hook, or almost any piece a bead or ornament. Often a "useless" scrap is just a blank waiting for a yet to be thought of project. Toss these in a gourd, basket or bag with the other discards and wait for inspiration.

> The staging sequence presented by Steve was adapted from a reduction sequence for stone developed by Errett Callahan. It is an excellent way to approach all projects using natural materials and can be adapted to resources as diverse as shell and wood. Thinking of projects in stages gives you not only a predictable sequence of steps to a project, but also provides a blue print as to how a project may proceed in terms of processes.   The Ed

*****Brains, brawn, planning and perseverance are useful in all stages*****

Stages For Manufacture of A Fish Hook

Stage 1   *Stage 2*

Stage 3   *Stage 4*

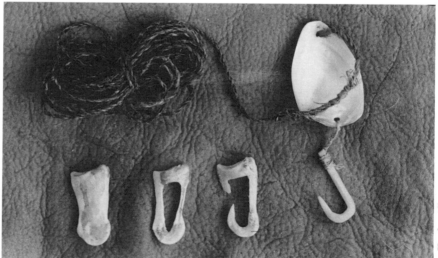

Hayden Allen

Using the toe bone (phalange) of a deer, the sides of the bone are abraded away until only one cut is required to create the hook.

Bone Splitting Tips
By Steve Watts, 1995

Splitting a rib bone using the bipolar technique.
(Photo: Michael Eldredge)

Scoring

For many bone-working projects (awls, needles, pins, daggers, large gorge hooks, knives, etc.) long sections of split bone are required. The nature of bone, however, does not lend itself to such splits. When unmodified and hit with a percusser, bone tends to split spirally instead of longitudinally. To overcome this the artisan carves/scrapes a groove the length of the piece (using a flake, biface or burin) before applying percussion. After scoring, the bone can be tapped with the percusser along the groove, encouraging the bone to split in this predetermined manner.

The Edged Anvil

John White (Ancient Lifeways Institute, Illinois) shared a bone splitting tip with me many years ago that I, in turn, have shared with many others since: Instead of a flat anvil, use an "edged" anvil—the edge of a core, large spall, biface etc. Partially bury this anvil in the ground or support it in some other way, placing the groove in the bone on that edge, and moving the bone back and forth as you tap with the hammer stone or billet. This concentrates the energy and results in high splitting-success rates.

Bipolar Splitting

Just hitting a bone laid on an anvil with none of the above preparations will yield unpredictable results at best. (For a possible exception see "Jacketed" technique below). Yet, I've discovered that large rib bones can be successfully split without any grooving or grinding preparation using bipolar percussion. Hold the rib on edge on a slightly rounded anvil. Moving it back and forth along the anvil as you work, whack it smartly with a hardwood or antler billet. You'll most often get nice long splits (sometimes even the entire length).

The "Jacketed" Technique

During a recent (Aug. '95) deer skinning, butchering experience we "discovered" a low-tech bone splitting technique that needs further experimentation. Having skinned the legs, a participant laid the bones on an anvil and smashed them without having removed the meat, sinew, membranes/tissues as would "normally" be done when using more formal bone splitting techniques. The object was marrow extraction, so the cleaning of the bone was neither indicated or suggested. The bones, to my surprise, split into long thin pieces producing instant needle, awl, pin blanks. The experience was repeated with similar results. Perhaps the adhering "jacket" of tissues affected the fracture-energy in a way different from "naked" bone? Or maybe it was just a fluke. Try it.

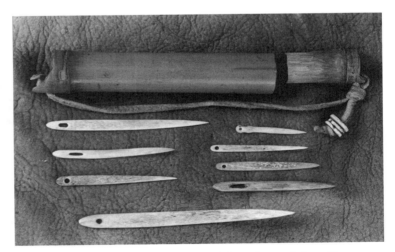

Replicas made by Steve Watts. River Cane vial and bone needles. (Photo: Hayden Allen)

An Experiential Exercise With Bone

By David Wescott & David Holladay

In anticipation of this issue, we had a question that we thought needed answering..which works easier with stone tools, fresh or aged bone ? Much like the adage "don't compare stone tools to steel tools..compare stone tools to no tools at all," there is also no comparison when it comes to working bone with stone. ...not all bone is created equal.

We have a great deal of experience working wood with stone and have come to the following conclusions. We found also that the same rules hold mostly true for working bone.

1. **Stone flakes or blades cut green materials best.**
2. **The drier materials become, the easier they take final shaping.**
3. **Planing and scraping to a smooth finish works best on drier materials.**
4. **Final burnishing and polishing is best done on dry materials with a polishing agent (grease/oil).**

Our chance to do a comparative study came one morning when a doe was killed by a passing rental car near our field office. We already had frozen bones on hand, and a whole yard full of dry bones gathered from the field, both of which we had used regularly. We immediately called the wildlife authorities to salvage the deer, and were given permission. We butchered the carcass on the roadside with stone tools. Skinning and quartering went quickly as we have done this regularly. We saved the hind quarters and front shoulders for food. The entire process took less than 15 minutes. Deboning the meat and fleshing the tendons with a cannon bone scraper took another 30 minutes. Then the test began.

The fresh cannon bone was skinned and ready for testing along with a frozen and aged bone. The exercise was to test the efficiency of stone tools on splitting a cannon bone. Simple burins were made from local flakes of jasper. Grooves were cut into the channel in each bone (front and back). We wanted to split the bone by graving, not cracking or splitting by pounding on an anvil. The dry bone went much as expected, and took over 45 minutes to complete a through cut on both sides. The frozen bone wasn't quite as hard to work, but took about 30 minutes to split. The fresh bone, on the other hand, was cut through to the marrow along its entire length (except the knuckle ends) in less than ten minutes.

After having worked lots of aged and frozen bone in demonstrations and classes, we were amazed (not merely impressed) at how fast the "green" bone worked in comparison. Creating the finished needle at right helped illustrate the other points listed above. Once the bone was split and a sliver removed, we had to let the bone dry or dried naturally as more refined steps to the process were completed.

More Bone Fish Hooks*

"The raw materials from which the bone and thorn hooks were made had been gathered prior to the project. The bones utilized were believed to be a cat (#1) and a possum(#2). These were chosen because only two cuts on each were necessary to form fish hooks. I employed a sawing motion with a slight rocking of the tool...in order to avoid wedging the tool into the cut.... A piece of sandstone added the finishing touches to the bone.

As far as field experimentation was concerned, the manufacturing of the two fish hooks was only the beginning [of the sets]. Fish lines and leaders were also made...attached to the hooks...[broken pottery shards were used as[sinkers were the last addition to the tackle.

The locations utilized for line fishing were usually from some vantage point along the shore. We were under constant demands from our diametrically opposed and assumed life-styles of scientist and pre-contact Indians. We had no time to sit upon the bank and play the fish lines. Therefore, the baited trot line and throw lines were left out at various strategic points. The lines were checked and baited three times a day...A variety of baits were tried; mussels, ground-hog organs, rotten fish flesh, minnows, and corn. Even though no fish were landed, the baits were always missing and some breakage did result.

After Modification

Fish Hook #1
Before Modification

After Experiment

Fish Hook #2
Before Modification

After Modification

After Experiment

Excerpt from APE 4, Edited By Errett Callahan. Bone Technology In The Pamunkey Project: Phase II, By Norman Jefferson

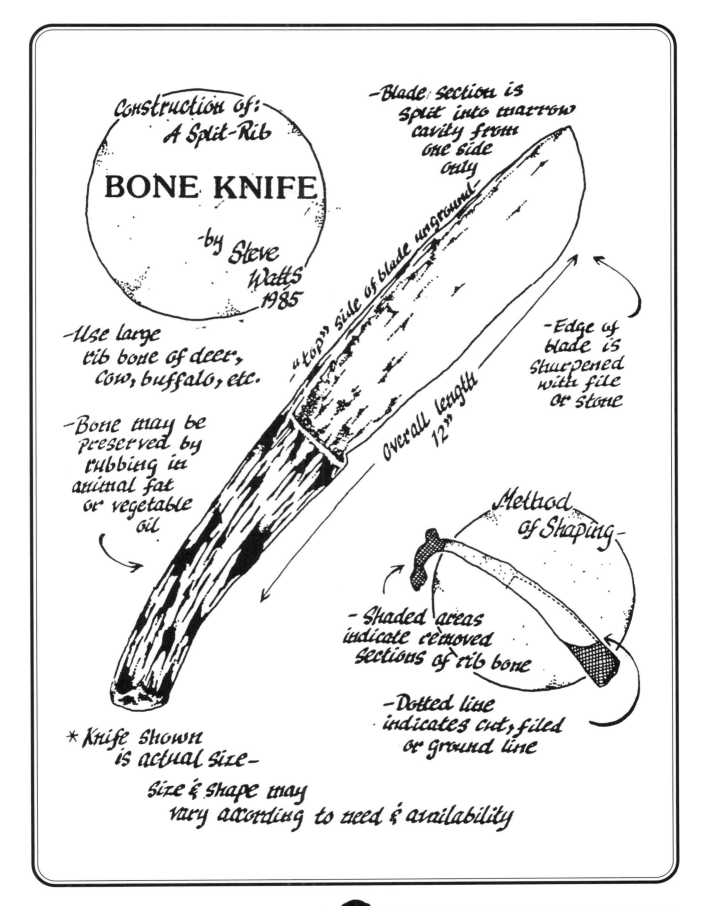

Construction of:
A Split-Rib

BONE KNIFE

-by Steve
Watts
1985

-Blade section is
split into marrow
cavity from
one side
only

"top" side of blade unground

-Use large
rib bone of deer,
cow, buffalo, etc.

-Bone may be
preserved by
rubbing in
animal fat
or vegetable
oil

Overall length
12"

-Edge of
blade is
sharpened
with file
or stone

Method
of Shaping-

- Shaded areas
indicate removed
sections of rib bone

-Dotted line
indicates cut, filed
or ground line

* Knife shown
is actual size-

Size & shape may
vary according to need & availability

FROM THE LEG OF THE DEER

Text and Illustrations By Roy H. Brown

During the summer of 1988 while working as a volunteer at an archeological excavation in Western Maryland, I uncovered an artifact that caught my imagination and hasn't let go. From the scattered debris of a Late Woodland midden emerged a portion of a split leg bone of a deer. The 3" long object had one end broken and the other ground to a beveled edge, polished smooth from use. I had found my first bone tool, the working end of a hide flesher. On returning home, I procured bones from a nearby roadkill and made a replica of my find.

Since that day I have examined numerous bone artifacts; awls, needles, beads, fishhooks, chisels, beamers and projectile points. The photograph shows a collection of tools which I have replicated from deer bone, a most versatile raw material. I recently mortised a hole in an elm celt using two green long bones. Breaking the upper end of the bone, I then ground a beveled edge on it with a sandstone slab. Blows from a heavy wooden mallet against the expedient chisels, cut a 1.5" wide x 2" high x 2" deep slot through the seasoned wood within an hour. The first chisel shattered during the process, thus requiring the second. The broken pieces were set aside for future tools.

I believe that the lower leg of the White-tailed Deer is one of the least appreciated and under-utilized parts of this fine animal. At the close of hunting season you can find deer limbs discarded the backroads throughout Appalachia. The ancient hunters of these hills were not so wasteful as we.

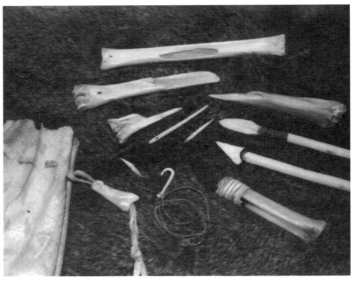

Bone tools replicated by the author: from the top - hide-working beamer, flesher/chisel, awls, needles, projectile point from bone sliver and one from hoof bone, bead from a foot bone used as a draw-string keeper, fish gorge, fishhook and bone-handled chert knife.

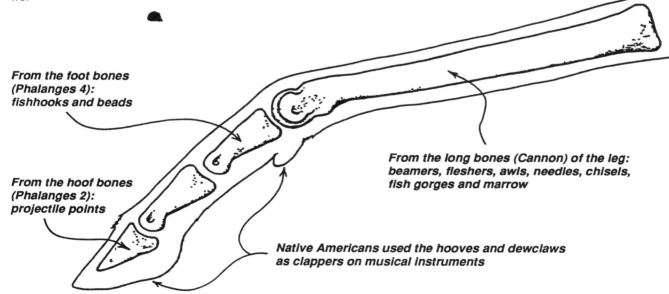

From the foot bones (Phalanges 4): fishhooks and beads

From the hoof bones (Phalanges 2): projectile points

From the long bones (Cannon) of the leg: beamers, fleshers, awls, needles, chisels, fish gorges and marrow

Native Americans used the hooves and dewclaws as clappers on musical instruments

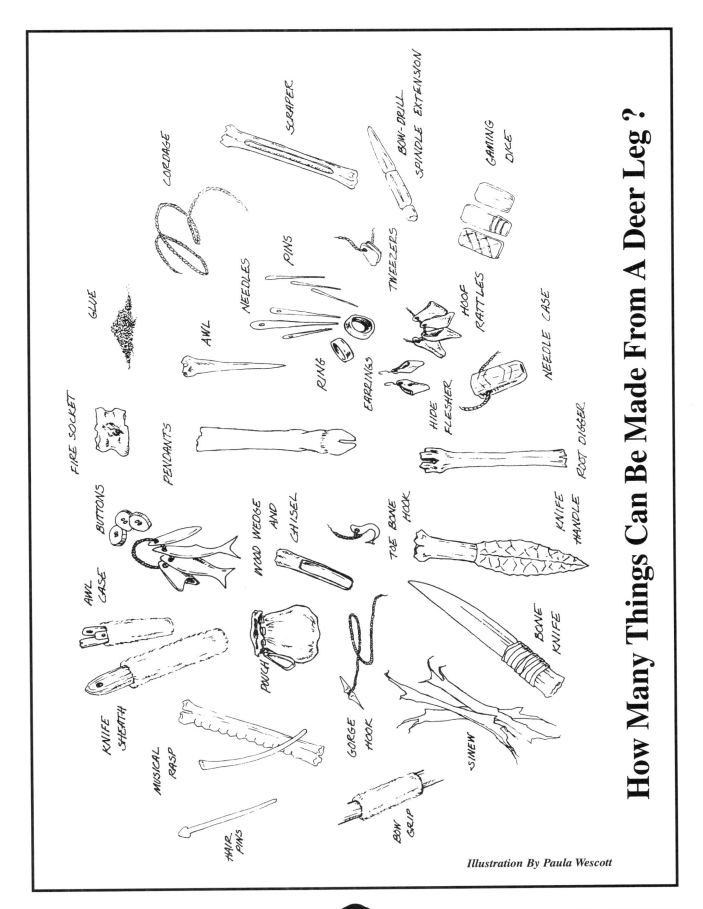

How Many Things Can Be Made From A Deer Leg?

Illustration By Paula Wescott

NOTES ON MAT NEEDLES AND CATTAIL MATS

By Chris Morasky

Some mat needles were made of wood, others of bone, cane, and a variety of other materials. Some were triangular in cross-section, and others flat or convexed. They ranged in length from a few inches to 3 feet long. Apparently, rib bone needles were more common in the east and the long, triangular needles were more common in the Pacific northwest. Some mats were creased on either side of the cordage to prevent the cattails from further splitting.

Cordage was common basswood bast where available, sometimes nettle. Quickie mats can be made with cattail or tule cordage used to twine the mat together.

Eastern mats were made approximately 12' long, but length varied, and 2-4 layers kept out all rain and wind. Mat lodges were often winter houses. One of the neat aspects of a mat lodge is its ease of relocation. The mats are simply rolled up, carried to the next site, a new framework made, and mats relaid. A one family, 12' diameter lodge can be built (including poles and tied into framework) in as little as 4 hours.

The top edge of a shelter mat was either twined or tied with half hitches as shown below. The bottom edge may be left unfinished.

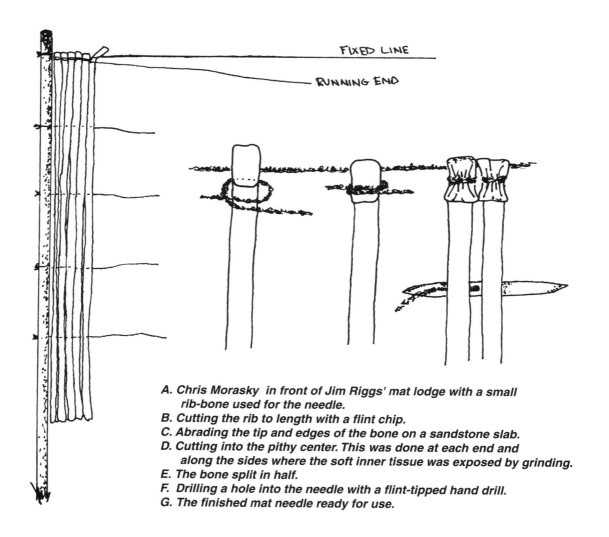

A. Chris Morasky in front of Jim Riggs' mat lodge with a small rib-bone used for the needle.
B. Cutting the rib to length with a flint chip.
C. Abrading the tip and edges of the bone on a sandstone slab.
D. Cutting into the pithy center. This was done at each end and along the sides where the soft inner tissue was exposed by grinding.
E. The bone split in half.
F. Drilling a hole into the needle with a flint-tipped hand drill.
G. The finished mat needle ready for use.

Making A Rib-bone Mat Needle

Production by Chris Morasky

A.

David Wescott Photos

B.

C.

D.

E.

F.

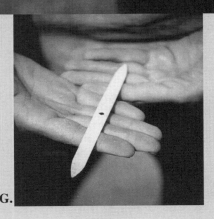

G.

MAKING A REDUCED ANTLER FLAKER

Text and Photos By Steven Edholm, © 1995

A few years ago I decided to wean myself from copper pressure flakers, figuring that I was cheating myself out of part of the stone tool making experience by not being in touch with real stone age processes. Using the various antler tines that I had lying around proved very disappointing and probably contributed to my not putting down the copper sooner. The curve in an antler tine doesn't allow for as controlled and accurate pressure to be applied to the work as in a straight tool, and the usually large diameter of the tine requires long and laborious grinding to resharpen, only to end up blunt again in short order. Also a short tool which doesn't reach past the palm lacks the leverage of a longer tool and doesn't always allow for the consistent removal of large even pressure flakes.

I knew that friend and knapper Jim Riggs used a slab of antler bound to a handle and in one of my favorite primitive technology references, *Indian and Eskimo Artifacts of North America* by Charles Miles, there is a picture of two of these tools.

The advantages seemed obvious so I made one and thus began my love affair with what I prefer to call the reduced or split antler flaker, that is, a section of antler which has been reduced to a smaller thickness and or width, straightened and bound to a wooden handle.

Then again, why not just use copper for pressure flaking tools? It's cheap, it doesn't require frequent sharpening, the tools are easy to assemble and it just seems to work a little better than antler. On top of all that, many people say copper was used prehistorically for flintknapping.

Prehistoric people in later stone working horizons may have used copper for pressure flaking, but they were certainly in the global minority. The vast majority of flintknapping through the eons has been done without the benefit of metal tools.

Sometimes I use copper while at other times I use

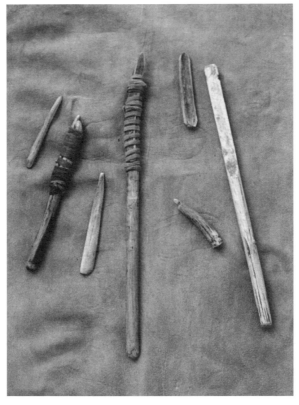

Reduced antler flakers with and without handles, and a notching tool. Good antler tools like these can improve metal free stone work.

antler and bone. It depends on what and why I am flintknapping. If my only reasons for flintknapping were to produce as aesthetic a piece as possible in a minimum amount of time, I guess I would use slab sawn stone, a diamond grinder and all copper tools. But I don't do primitive technology just because the stuff looks neat, I'm after an experience and a continuum. I want a glimpse into the past. I love to think about the multitudes of ancient flintknappers who have experienced the same problems and victories that I experience... like the buckskin thong that binds my flaker to the handle slipping off and unwinding or getting abraded when I sharpen the tool. My solution to some of these problems is sure to be the same as some of theirs, giving me further insight into the lives of stone age artisans.

Besides, there's nothing like the feeling of making something start to finish without the assistance of things made by other people or more especially by technology that we don't understand or can't duplicate. I think that most all flintknappers can benefit, in some way, from making and using a good antler tool and you may be surprised at just how well they perform.

A fine burinated groove by Scott Vandenberg.

MATERIALS

I prefer whitetail antler over mule deer. It seems to be consistently more dense and less pithy. Moose always seems dense and would probably be a good choice, I haven't tried it. Elk often seems soft to me and the one time I used elk it was too soft and performed poorly.

The longer you can make your flaker the better. A long tool is less likely to move around and work loose when bound to a handle, and of course a long tool will last longer.

Antlers, as you've surely noticed, rarely possess straight lines, therefore most reduced antler flakers will need to be straightened. There are two basic types of bends which may need to be removed. Imagine a long narrow slab of antler bent like a strung bow. This type of bend is easy to remove. Now imagine the same piece of antler bent like a boomerang. The removal of boomerang type bends is much more questionable.

If you make a light duty small diameter flaker (for removing small flakes) shaped more like a rod, either type of bend should come out pretty easily. However, I think a slabiform flaker about l/4" X 1/2" to 5/8" is very useful for

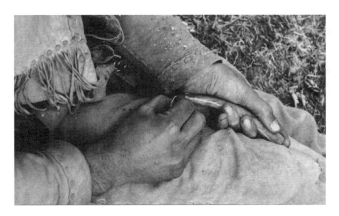

Matt Richards graving an antler with a burin.

working on larger pieces and in this type of stout flaker the boomerang type of bend will most likely not yield due to the extra mass.

So, look for a dense piece of antler from which a nice long bow curve shaped slab about 1/2" wide can be removed. A good thing to start with is a long deer antler tine (at least 5"). It will yield two flaker blanks when split in half. One or both of the resulting blanks could also be split again to yield small rod shaped flakers. (see photo #1 left side)

Antler is much easier to work when softened by soaking. Submerge it in water for 3 or 4 days in advance. Also remember that antler, even old antler, contains proteins which will begin to rot when wetted. I got a nasty infection once from a cut I inflicted on myself while working antler. The longer the antler soaks the more septic it will become. Changing the water helps and you need only soak it long enough to wet the material entirely through. Clean your hands as well as your situation permits after working with funky animal matter of any kind.

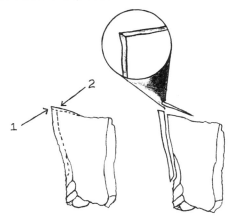

Making a burin. The burin is made from a flake with two blows of the hammerstone or baton. It can be resharpened if needed by removing further spalls in either direction.

TOOLS

I use stone flake and core tools, sand and a sandstone slab to work bone and antler. The tool that finds the most use is the burin or graver, a very ancient type of modified flake tool which works particularly well on these materials. When making a burin select a flake or blade (better tough chert or flint than obsidian) which is neither too thick in the center nor too thin on the edges. A burin has a strong blocky chisel type edge and a good one can move through soaked antler pretty quickly.

WORKING THE ANTLER

If the antler needs to be reduced into sections, as in removing a tine, use a sharp edge on a core of chert to chop the soaked antler or a biface to saw it. When you've chopped or sawn part way through, bend it, step on it, or hit it with a rock to finish the job.

(more)

Pick a point on the burin or another flake and carefully scribe lines in the antler where you want to cut it. Apply more pressure as these grooves deepen. Try using your burin at different angles. It should be removing long curly shavings not just mealy dust. Push it or pull it, whatever works best.

As the groove deepens the burin will bind up and stop cutting. This problem is minimized by using a burin in the first place instead of a sharp flake which would bind up even more quickly. Widen the groove as needed so that you can cut all the way to the pith of the antler. (The pith is the spongy looking core of the antler.) Avoid, however, making the groove excessively wide or you may find, in the end, that you have removed too much material.

You'll find that the antler dries out remarkably fast, even as you work. Keep it wet and your work will proceed quickly. If you take a break leave it soaking.

The ends of the grooves usually end up too shallow. I use a flake with small teeth chipped into it to saw through the ends. Once the pith is reached, this tool can also be used to finish cutting through the bottom of the groove and deeper into the pith.

Once you've reached the pith you have to split the tool blank off of the antler, or if you've chosen a single tine split the tine in half. If you use strictly stone age tools this can be a very frustrating job. A nice piece of metal would do the job expediently. I pound, lever, wedge, saw, pull and twist to separate the blank. A tool that has proved very useful for this job is one which I made for notching points. It is an antler tine the end of which has been abraded into a flat spatula shape (see photo). I pound it into the groove to break through the pith and also use it to pry the

My favorite flaker handle and a flaker that fits it well. These handles are easily made with stone tools if green wood is used. A shallow notch near the tip of the handle will prevent the thong from slipping off the end during use.

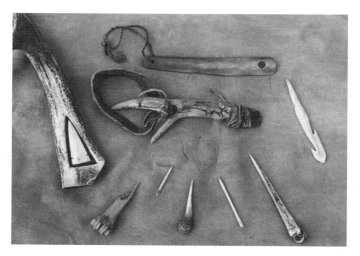

Bone and antler tools made with stone tool processes. Elk antler projectile point Hupa/Yurok (N/W California) style, elk rib shaft straightener, scraper/shaft straightener of antler, deer bone harpoon, and bone awls and needles.

blank off. Sometimes it breaks but antler is the only natural material I am familiar with which can undergo that kind of great bending stress. By the way, that tool also does make a good notcher. You may want to make one while you have soaked antler on hand.

Now you should have a blank with rough edges and burrs and chunks of pith. This needs to be further reduced to shape and thinned enough to bend easily. Use a gritty sand stone slab with plenty of loose, coarse sand and water on it for grinding to shape, as well as stone flakes with edge angles of 55 to 90 degrees for scraping and shaving.

Unless your blank has no bends, which is very unlikely, it will need some straightening. This is usually as simple as binding it to the handle or a straight stick while wet. However, some may have drastic enough bends or sufficient mass to warrant boiling or steaming to loosen things up. Don't boil or steam the antler for too long, just enough to heat it through and through. If I were in the field or even if I could just have a back yard without feeling like the neighbors would call the fire department on me, I would wrap the blank in six layers of green leaves and steam it in hot ashes.

While thoroughly hot from steaming or boiling, bend the tool straight as you tie it to the handle or a straight stick. Use a strip of buckskin or leather for the wrap. Allow the blank to dry and set this way for a few days. After a brief sharpening on sandstone the tool will be ready to use.

Lessons learned making the reduced antler flaker can be applied to a wide variety of bone and antler projects. Remember to use very fresh bone and soaked antler and be creative with tools and processes.

Antler billets with a thought for the pocket-book.
Text and Illustration By Charles Spear

It was after buying a moose billet for a hefty outlay of cash that I liked my copper-capped billets even more. However, when you knap for the public the same question is asked, "Did the Indians have copper tools like that?" My answer is the same each time,"No, they had plenty of deer and moose but they would have given their eye teeth for copper." With that introduction I solved the problem somewhat at least to my satisfaction by taking the antler tines from white tail deer which I pick up at 'rendezvous' for a couple bucks. I then take the handles from the hardware store for scissor-style bush trimmers to make antler billets. The pointed part of the tine is filed to a cylindrical shape which will fit into the handle socket. This end is epoxied in place with PC-7 a two mix 'grey' epoxy. When it is set overnight the other end is filed to a dome shape (the very best billets are made with the rosette of the antler as the rounded end) and it is ready to use. Replacements are easily made by drilling out the spent 'tine billet' and re-gluing a new one.

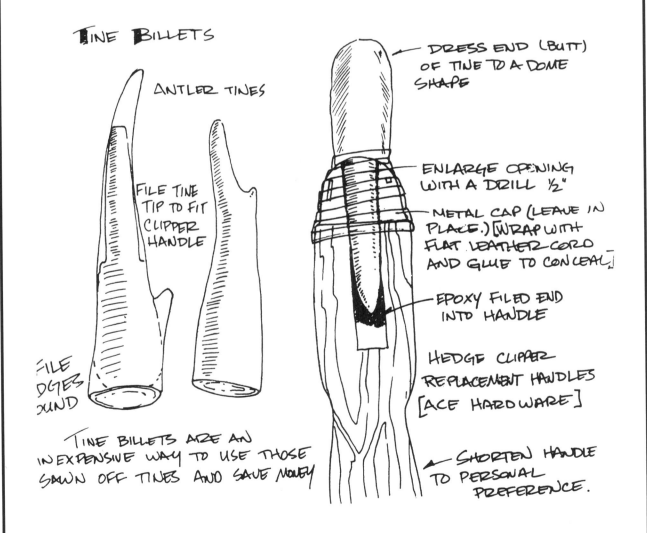

TINE BILLETS

ANTLER TINES

FILE TINE TIP TO FIT CLIPPER HANDLE

FILE DGES XUND

TINE BILLETS ARE AN INEXPENSIVE WAY TO USE THOSE SAWN OFF TINES AND SAVE MONEY

DRESS END (BUTT) OF TINE TO A DOME SHAPE

ENLARGE OPENING WITH A DRILL ½"

METAL CAP (LEAVE IN PLACE.) [WRAP WITH FLAT LEATHER CORD AND GLUE TO CONCEAL]

EPOXY FILED END INTO HANDLE

HEDGE CLIPPER REPLACEMENT HANDLES [ACE HARDWARE]

SHORTEN HANDLE TO PERSONAL PREFERENCE.

Selecting Bone-Working Materials
By David Wescott

The hunter-gatherer of old had materials available in tremendous quantity. Whether they hunted and killed an animal or simply made use of "found" sources, it was always there. Be on the lookout for whatever sources you can find, butchers, farmers, legal roadkill, etc. Think beyond mammal bones to include bird and fish as well.

Bone works much like wood - when it is fresh it can be scored, split and shaped easily, but does not finish as well until it is dry. Dry bone allows you to sharpen and shape it to extremely efficient points.

Fresh bone is by far the strongest to use. Tools made from fresh bone are less brittle than dry bone. In the animal it is strong, flexible and performs specific tasks....remember this when selecting the best bone for a tool. Fresh (green) bone is very waxy and works a lot like antler. Fresh bone can be rough-shaped, seasoned, finished (fine sharpening), and oiled to produce very durable tools.

Baking drys the bone out too much, and although boiling is less destructive, it does affect the bone. Soaking dried bone makes it easier to work in some ways. It improves the workability by making the bone more elastic and softens the surface to improve the bite of the tool.

Found bone needs to be selected and graded to be sure that it is not too dry, brittle, powdery or water logged.

Bones that have begun to decompose may be beyond use, but others can be rejuvinated by adding oil. When you find a bone, break it, and clean it out, and let it dry, then test it for strength. Bone is very brittle by nature and must be worked with carefully when making fine tools.

Bones have specific characteristics and capabilities. Bone working includes understanding where to look for the bones best suited to a task, how to modify them, and the tool options available.

Antler - stabber, club, billet, needle/pin, bow, purse
Skull - bowl or pendant
Jaw - Knife handel, saw
Vertebrae - slide, socket, beads (snake and fish)
Rids - knife, bow, buzzer, bullroar, batten
Scapula - shovel, hoe
Femur - needle, ring, stabber, flesher, awl, scaper
Ulna - knife, awl
Canon - multiple tools (see page -)
Ankle - bow-drill socket
Toes - rattles, amulet, arrow heads, fish hooks

The oldest known artifact on this continent is a 27,000 year-old caribou bone flesheing tool.

Working With Natural Materials

Working with natural materials as opposed to those processed and available in the store, introduces a variety of new problems. Since most processed materials are cleaned, sanitized (and approved by the EPA, USDA, etc.) they are free of many of the germs and other critters that natural materials may carry.

When working with bone, hides, brains, etc. remember that you are working with dead tissue which is prone to rotting and all its attendant hazards. Tularemia and Bubonic Plague and many other unfriendly diseases (most are treatable) are blood-borne, so be careful. Infection from rotting tissue (especially brains) is very possible. If you wish to process animals, make sure you protect yourself by using gloves and/or washing in an antiseptic solution when you're done. Tissue that is thoroughly dried and dead (tendons, rawhide, etc.) seems to produce fewer problems.

Harvesting roadkills is illegal in almost all states, although the laws are being changed to at least obtain some use from what would otherwise go to waste. Check with your local Fish and Game officials for regulations in your area. The use of parts from threatened and endangered species is illegal. The use of many animal parts for sale or trade varies with local regulations as well.

Flintknapping - the act of controlled fracture of a rock by another tool- is prone to produce flying debris, sometimes very sharp debris. This may rocket towards onlookers or towards yourself. The use of protective eyewear and gloves is recommended. Work in well lit and ventilated areas.

Some stone and shell may be hazardous when ground. Serpentine and Abalone, for example, produce asbestos fibers. Grinding should be done under water to reduce dust. Proper safety measures should be taken.

Many plants that provide usable fiber are poisonous. Know the properties of any plant you use. Do not leave plant parts, refuse, or stockpiles where those unaware may ingest them.

These and any other principles that apply to the safe use of natural materials should be followed. The authors recommend that you become informed of any dangers associated with materials specific to your area. Instructions contained in this work do not cover, imply or guarantee safety.

KNIFE HAFTING TECHNIQUES

By Charles Spear

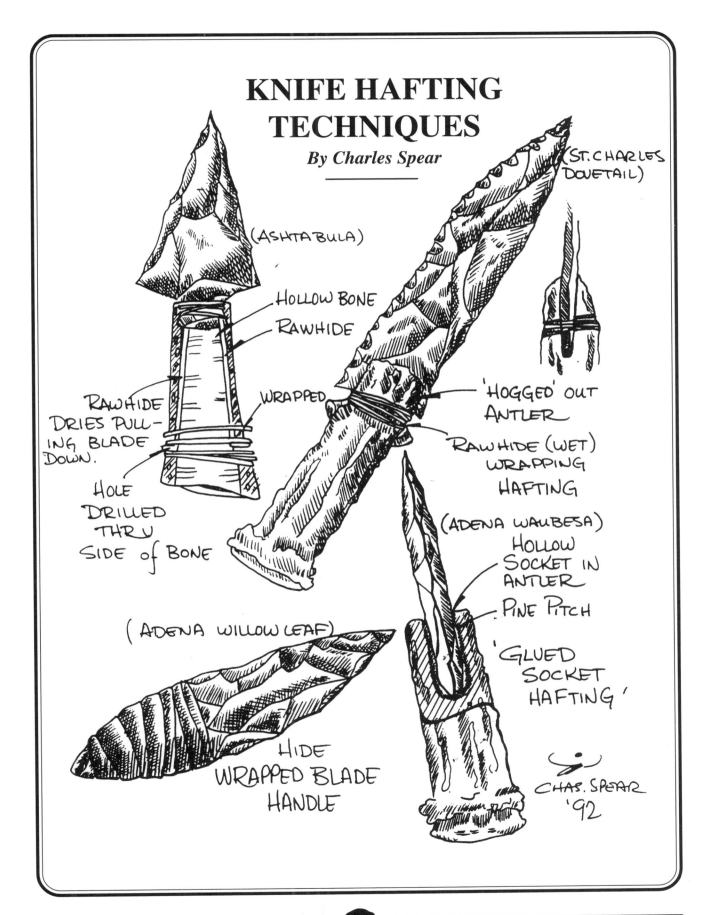

(ST. CHARLES DOVETAIL)

(ASHTABULA)

HOLLOW BONE

RAWHIDE

WRAPPED

RAWHIDE DRIES PULLING BLADE DOWN.

HOLE DRILLED THRU SIDE OF BONE

'HOGGED' OUT ANTLER

RAWHIDE (WET) WRAPPING HAFTING

(ADENA WAUBESA)

HOLLOW SOCKET IN ANTLER

PINE PITCH

'GLUED SOCKET HAFTING'

(ADENA WILLOW LEAF)

HIDE WRAPPED BLADE HANDLE

CHAS. SPEAR '92

STAGES OF MANUFACTURE - Percussion Reduction

By Errett Callahan

STAGE 1 - Obtain Material

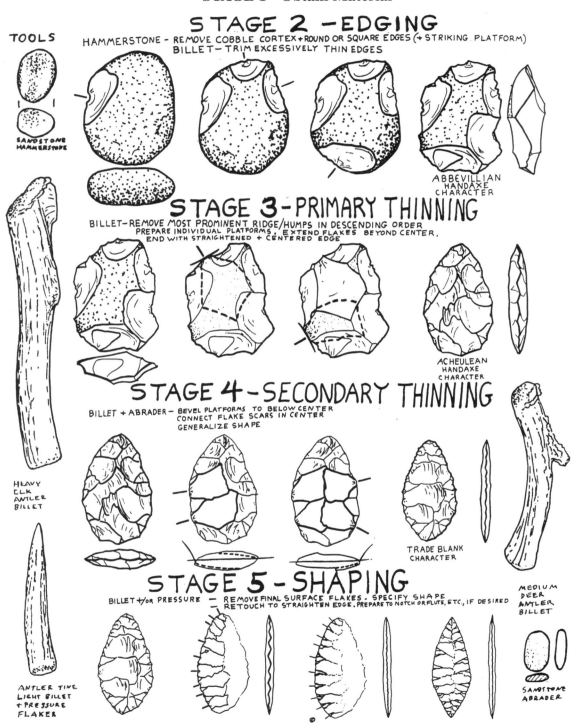

STAGE 2 - EDGING

HAMMERSTONE - REMOVE COBBLE CORTEX + ROUND OR SQUARE EDGES (+ STRIKING PLATFORM)
BILLET - TRIM EXCESSIVELY THIN EDGES

TOOLS

SANDSTONE HAMMERSTONE

ABBEVILLIAN HANDAXE CHARACTER

STAGE 3 - PRIMARY THINNING

BILLET - REMOVE MOST PROMINENT RIDGE/HUMPS IN DESCENDING ORDER
PREPARE INDIVIDUAL PLATFORMS. EXTEND FLAKES BEYOND CENTER.
END WITH STRAIGHTENED + CENTERED EDGE

ACHEULEAN HANDAXE CHARACTER

STAGE 4 - SECONDARY THINNING

BILLET + ABRADER - BEVEL PLATFORMS TO BELOW CENTER
CONNECT FLAKE SCARS IN CENTER
GENERALIZE SHAPE

HEAVY ELK ANTLER BILLET

TRADE BLANK CHARACTER

MEDIUM DEER ANTLER BILLET

STAGE 5 - SHAPING

BILLET +/OR PRESSURE - REMOVE FINAL SURFACE FLAKES. SPECIFY SHAPE
- RETOUCH TO STRAIGHTEN EDGE. PREPARE TO NOTCH OR FLUTE, ETC., IF DESIRED

ANTLER TINE LIGHT BILLET + PRESSURE FLAKER

SANDSTONE ABRADER

EC 72

STONE TOOL BASICS
Functions, Features, Form and Fracture
By Steve Watts

"The right tool for the right job" is perhaps a very ancient bit of wisdom. Define the task, then find or create the needed tool using the proper stone type, methods and techniques of manufacture. Although many stone tools are multifunctional (or can be easily modified to be so) few can function well outside their "Task" category. You will no more butcher a deer with a hammerstone than you would hammer a neal with a razor blabe.

Tasks Required	Tool Models:	Tool Types:	Stone Types:	Manufacturing Techniques:
Smashing, Bashing, Crushing, Grinding, Hammering, Pounding, Clubbing, etc.	Heavy and Blunt	Hammerstones, Nutting, Mulling and Grinding Stones, Stone Mauls, etc.	Medium and Fine Grained Stones –(From sandstones to basalts)	Expedient Gathering, Pecking and Grinding, Rough Flaking, etc.
Chopping, Hewing, Butchering, Ground Breaking, Hacking, etc.	Heavy and Sharp	Ground Stone Axes, Flaked Stone Axes and Choppers, Hoes, Adzes, etc.	Hard—Fine Grained, Stones, Cryptocrystaline, Stone (quartz, flint, chert, etc.)	Pecking and Grinding, Bipolar and Direct Percussion, Pressure Flaking, etc.
Slicing, Cutting, Saw, Trimming, Piercing, Drilling, Engraving, Scraping Carving, etc.	Light and Sharp	Modified and Unmodified Flakes and Blades, Bifaces, Projectile Points, Scrapers, Drills, Gravers,	Flints, Cherts, Quartz, Quartzite, Obsidian, etc.	Bipolar and Direct Percussion, Pressure Flaking, Notching Techniques, etc.

The Principle of Uniformity in Workable Stone

Not all rocks are created equal. Many have large grains that force energy produced by a hammerstone to travel around the individual grains. The energy may travel wherever the rock lets it, making the results very unpredictable for flaking, but servicable for other techniques such as pecking. Rocks with medium-fine grains may allow the energy to sheer each crystal and travel with more predictability, or may simply crush at the point of impact or crumblie apart. Neither of these types of rock works well for flaking unless the crystals are well bonded, allowing the energy to travel into and through the rock. Rocks that crush our crumble when struck work well for projects that require pecking and ginding, rough flaking, or abrading.

Hard fine-grained rocks work well for a variety of percussion techniques as well as pecking and grinding. Rocks with no grain are glassy or flint-like and allow energy to pass in very predictable ways. Rocks that have a glass-like quality are by far the most sought after for percussion work where a very sharp edge is desired. These rocks vary in hardness, but they allow a broad range of uses as simple tools.

No one rock type is usable under all conditions or for all tools, and not all rock types may be found in your location. Learn to use a variety of rocks with a variety of techniques. Start with simple projects like discoidal knives, simple choppers and flake tools and progress as your knowledge of available materials progresses.

Extremely fine-grained basalt like this works very similar to obsidian (shown below), but is much tougher and not nearly as sharp.

Each of these rocks range from coarse to medium grain and from relatively soft to very hard. A flake was attempted on each to test for flakability. 1 and 2 are soft, coarse grained and crumbled when struck. They will peck very well. 3 has obvious layers and broke unpredictably. 4. would flake, but the mineral seams caused some problems. 5. flakes very well and is extremely hard.

Lithic Grade Scale
Proposed by Errett Callahan

	.5	Opal
	1.0	Obsidian
	1.5	Coarse Obsidian
	2.0	Fine-grained Basalt
	2.5	Heat Treated Flints
	3.0	Fine Flints
	3.5	Fine Chert
	4.0	Silicified Slate, Coarse Cherts
	4.5	Fine Rhyolite, Quartzite
	5.0	Coarse Quartzite and Rhyolite
	5.5	Greenstone

Ease of workability increases up the scale — Antler Billet — Soft Hammer — Wooden Billet

TO WHOM IT MAY CONCERN

This is a letter of endorsement from the Society of Primitive Tehcnology for hunting with stone arrowpoints. Stone points have been used successfully for hunting since long before the dawn of history. They should continue to be allowed for hunting.

The sharpest material known to mankind is glass, such as obsidian, which is used to make the best stone points. According to the American Medical Association (AMA News 2 Nov 1984), obsidian is up to "500 times sharper than surgical steel" and may fracture to the last moecule. Dr. Saxton Pope consistently found that obsidian points penetrated 25% farther than steel points (Pope 1923: 368, 369).

The banning of such a superior cutting edge is ludicrous. We would therefore encourage approval of the use of stone points for bow hunting. For this endorsement, we would stipulate (1) that the points be newly made, not ancient artifacts; (2) that only the top grade of obsidian or the finest-grained flints (lithic grade scale 1-3) be used; and (3) that the points be knapped to the lowest feasible edge-angle by experienced flingknappers, rather than by beginners. The other attributes (ie. width, design, etc.) should conform to local laws.

Errett Callahan, PhD.
President, SPT

from Primitive Archer, Vol. 2, No. 4. The Broadhead of Stone, by Sam Fadala

" Dr. Payson Sheets did a fantastic study of the flint head....using a scanning electron microscope, the dullest edge was shown to be that of chert produced by percussion flaking. The quartzite flake was far sharper than chert, almost ten times so....The stainless steel razor blade used in Sheet's test proved two times sharper than the scalpel in fact.
But the obsidian blade was sharper than either the razor or the scalpel - far sharper, in fact....obsidian was 100 to 500 times sharper than the razor blade, and 210 to 1050 times sharper than the surgical scalpel".

David Thompson

Surgical scalpel and obsidian blade photographed by a scanning electron microscope at a magnification of 10,000x. Brigham Young University.

EXPERIMENTAL REPRODUCTION OF PREHISTORIC SICKLES

By Manuel Luque Cortina,
Asociacion Nacional De Technologia Primitiva Y Supervivencia
and Javier Baena Preysler, Universidad Autonoma De Madrid

A sickle could be defined as serrated flint or as a couple of serrated flint teeth embedded in the grooves of wooden hafts and fixed with "cement" (Spurrel, 1982). Sickles have probably been used since the early neolithic to the present, and are almost always related to the origin of agriculture in such tasks as threshing, reaping and cutting of cereals.

The type of denticulates we have reproduced for this experiment are based upon archaeological microliths found in the site of the grave of a Spanish forger, near Madrid (Baena, J. and Luque, M., 1994). No attempts were made to analyze microwear, gloss or polish of the reproduction. Sickle morphology and hafting procedures were just experimental and simply de-

Plate I. Sickle morphology and flakes employed. h=handle, f=forearm, a=arm.

signed to test the cost of production and efficiency of this kind of instrument. The model presented in Plate I is a reconstruction based on archaeological data. It does not mean that this particular form was documented in the past.

A more complete development typology of sickles located in different archeological deposits from the Old Continent and Near East, illustrating the historic development of the experimental works with this kind of tool, can be obtained from the works of Jule Jensen, H. 1993 and Steenberg, A. 1943.

In our example, four main aspects were pointed out; wood employed in the production of the sickle, lithic reduction sequence of denticulate sickle flakes, glue and hafting, and the cordage to reinforce the whole structure. Finally we demonstrated the efficacy of the tools made by non-systematic experimentation in cutting bracken, nettle (Urtica dioica) and grass (Avenua fatua and Aegilops ovata). The primary results are shown at the conclusion.

EXPERIMENTAL REPRODUCTION
Wood Shape

In order to describe the methodology of the project, three parts to the experiment were identified: handle (h),

arm (a) and forearm (f) (Plate I). This configuration can be made by using a fire-moistening treatment of the wood selected, but materials with natural features (boxwood roots, fallen branches, etc.) can also be used. Thereby, no particular skills are required to get the desired shape.

One of the most important features of the sickle, is the resistance of the wood to breakage. The wood employed in the experiment was broom, (Cytisus scoparius). We also tried other materials such as cherry wood, boxwood and common elm, all of which gave us the same results. Due to the short length of both arm and forearm of the sickle, the strengths needed to withstand flexion during reaping is highly independent of the wood selected. Thus, good woods for making a sickle are quite common and available. What is always important, is to avoid gnarled branches, which can accidentally fracture while working.

The handle must be wide enough to provide a fitting surface for easy handling; neither thin, nor bulky; our haft is 3.5 cm of diameter, which decreases in width, gradually to the distal end of the arm. The transition between forearm and hafting area can be right angled, slightly obtuse or even absent, it depends on the sickle morphology, and use.

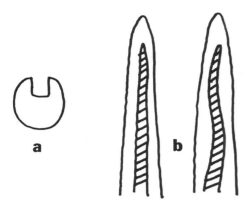

Figure 1. Groove a. section of the arm. b. Groove well centered and irregular groove.

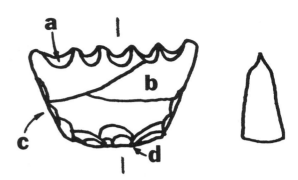

Figure 3. Morphology of a sickle tooth, and section. a=notch, b=dorsal surface, c=ventral surface, d=flank.

For hafting the teeth, a slit is produced lengthwise by scratching the arm with a burin. In spite of the fact that we can employ a simple flake or blade for the same purpose, burins seem to be suitable and effective for shaping a longitudinal fissure, as well as an accurate section at the same time (Figure 1a). In order to make a better seat for the teeth, it's important to avoid an inverted triangular section in the groove. The cross-section usually shows a rectangular profile.

The outline of the slit must be well centered; curvilinear delineation should be avoided as far as possible (Figure 1b). A poorly made haft will cause accidental detachment of the microliths while reaping. Microliths can also be pulled out, if the crack depth is too shallow, or if microliths extend too far beyond the upper limit of the crack, normally caused by the creation of an inverted triangular section on the groove.

Width and depth of the fissure are a function of the microliths dimensions. Groove depth might be at least, half of the microlith width and no longer than the radius section of the arm, which would probably weaken the whole structure of the sickle (Figure 2).

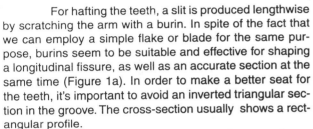

Figure 2. Depth crack and cordage application.

Lithic Reduction Sequence and Tooth Manufacturing

Sickle teeth are flakes with a saw-like edges formed by numerous small, closely spaced notches (Juel, 1993), (Figure 3). The lithic reduction sequence for produc-

ing these teeth is quite simple. No complex strategies are required except for the production of the blades that will provide the blanks.

In our case the lithic samples found at the archaeological Calcolithic site are made from random flakes. Our goal was to get small pieces, roughly similar in dimension to the originals. For this process, a couple of polyhedral cores were produced (Plate I).

1. Shaping a preform from a single flake is the first step towards the final morphology; hammerstone, soft hammer and even antler billet are quite useful. The flake is simply reduced by flaking until a fragment about 5 cm long and 3 cm width cm is obtained. Generally this step can be avoided by selecting flakes that are already close to the desired shape.

2. Final shaping and flake preparation. The back of the flake, that is to say, the side that will be inserted into the groove, is made (according to our archaeological sickle-flakes) either by pressure or by bipolar percussion (Figure 4), using an anvil and hammerstones of small dimensions (60mm x 36mm x 27mm for the hammerstone). The goal is to make this edge abrupt, avoiding undesirable bending fractures. When reaping, both, lateral surfaces of the groove and the tooth itself, produce flexural strains, due to the effort of cutting.

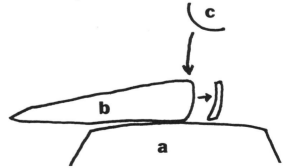

Figure 4. Bipolar percussion using an anvil. a=anvil, b= sickle tooth, c=hammerstone.

Plate II. Notch retouch of teeth with antler burin.

3. The final step is creating the teeth by simple retouch, usually made by pressure, with a sharp flint edge, a bone punch, or even an antler burin. This retouch must be produced from the dorsal to the ventral face and vice versa (Plate II).

In our archeological pieces, we have found many of this kind, although some of them presented very small individual notches upon the ventral side, very closely spaced.

Before creating the teeth, it's recommended to prepare the cutting edge, **avoiding diversions (?)**: both transversally and longitudinally.

The sections of archaeological sickle-flakes found, are normally triangular or of a triangular trend, while their morphology was quite varied. We have noticed semicircular shapes, trapezoids, rectangles as well as many other type variants. We have reproduced, sickle-flakes having a trapezoid shape to help the coil of cordage bind around the arm of the sickle (Plate II).

We have spent from four to six minutes in the manufacturing of each tooth.

Glue and hafting.

Glue was obtained from a treatment of red deer tendons, but there are many ways to produce it (see BPT #2).

Before filling the slit with the glue, it's recommended to try a "dry" haft in order to set up the final positioning of every tooth. This allows the modifying of the flank of the tooth or the groove. Each position must be well defined before final hafting.

Before pouring the glue into the fissure, reinforce the groove by daubing it with a thin layer of liquid glue. A second deposition of glue will serve to hold the denticulates in place, in a straight line all along the crack.

Next, fill the entire fissure with glue and arrange the teeth in the final lateral morphology. The result is shown in the Plate III.

Cordage.

In order to establish a better seat for the teeth, and also to reinforce the sickle which is slightly weakened because of the groove, we tied cordage around the arm, passing it between holes defined by the microliths (Figure 2). This reinforcing may not be necessary with a good covering of glue.

Our cordage was made with sparto grass fibers (*Stipa tenacissima*) and stinging nettle (*Urtica dioica*), common species of Spain. Better results could be obtained when using cordage impregnate with the glue described above.

First experimental use

Reaping of *Avenua fatua* and *Aegilops ovata* lasted 30 minutes, cutting 16 square meters (Plate IV). The

Plate III. Filling up the groove.

final result was the loss of one lithic piece and the breaking of five teeth into three pieces. While reaping brackens for ten minutes, two microliths were pulled out and five flakes sustained accidental indentations.

Plate IV. Reaping *Avenua fatua* and *Aegilops ovata* with the sickle.

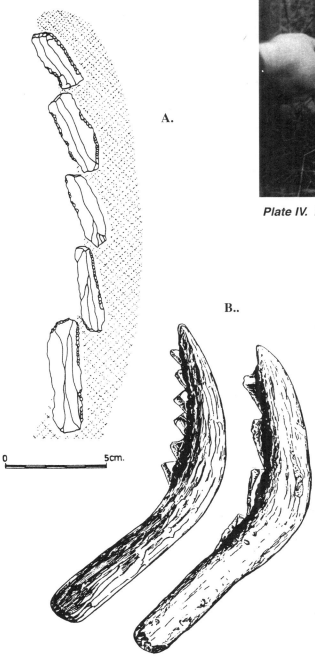

A.

B..

0   5cm.

Figure 5. Reconstruction of sickles using blades. a= Spanish Neolithic from Cueva de la Sarsa (Fortea et al. 1987). b= two Bandkeramick sickles (Behm-Blake 1963, in Jensen 1994).

REFERENCES

Baena, J. and Luque, M.
1994 La produccion litica durante fases Calcoliticas: analisisdel conjunto del yacimiento campaniforme del Campo de Futbol (Getafe, Madrid). In C. Blasco (ed.) El Horizonte Campaniforme de la region de Madrid en el Centenario de Ciempozuelos, Universidad Autonoma de Madrid.

Bocquet, A.
1980 Le microdenticule, un outil mal connu. **Bulletin de la Societe Prehistorique Francaise** 3, 76-85.

Curwen, E.C.
1930 Prehistoric flint sickles. **Antiquity** 4, 179-186.

Fortea, J. et al.
1987 La industria litica tallada del neolitico antiguo en la vertiente mediterranea de la Peninsula Iberica. Lucentum VI, 7-22.

Gijn, A.L.
1992 The interpretation of 'sickles': a cautionary tale. In: P.Anderson (ed.) **Prehistoire sw l' Agriculture. Nouvelles Approches Experimentales Ethnographiques.** (Paris: Monographie du CRA. Editions du CNRS), 363-372.

Juel Jensen, H.
1993 **Flint tools and plant working; Hidden traces of stone age technology.** Aarhus University Press (Denmark).

Spurrel, F.
1892 Notes on early sickles. **Archaeological Journal** 49, 53-69.

Steenberg, A.
1943 **Ancient harvesting implements.** (Kobenhavn: Nationalmuseets Skrifter, Arkaeologisk-Historik Raekke I).

KNAPPING ILLUSTRATED

Text and Illustrations By Charles Spear

I am a knapper and author of <u>The Illustrated Flintknapper</u>. Recently, I thought: "What if I couldn't order that nice Texas and Missouri flint, do I know enough to use the 'crud' around here?"

So I will give you my experience blow by blow. First, I found a stream near home and searched out some quartzite and granite and basalt. They ranged from 2" - 4" in diameter or length. They were my first tool kit. I chose them on the "soundness" of the material for bashing.

  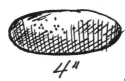

Next, I began to pick up rocks that looked like they had potential to be knapped, around here that's basalt (fine grained) and creek chert. I found a nice cobble from a spillway, split by concussion on the stream bed. Here's where it gets critical. I needed a knife more than an axe so I had to do more than knap one end.

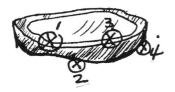

I began to hit the edge of the stone on the "x" mark then reversed the stone to the other side "x2" then reversed the stone again and hit "x3" continuing to repeat hitting and reversing until I had a wavy edge around the center of the stone. I am holding the one "knife" chert in my left hand and striking downwards with my right hand and the 3" egg hammerstone. (See **Fig. 1**) After I had created a wavy edge around the stone I had what is called a rough *biface preform*.

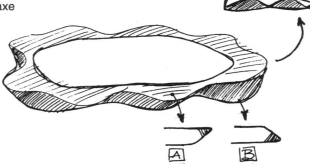

Next, I ground the preforms edge on an abrasive piece of sandstone (any gritty stone will do.) From this point I needed to center the way the centerline ran around the stone. 'A' and 'B' are the two extremes on the biface's edge. On 'A' I knocked off the shaded area as well as on 'B'. This more of less evened up the centerline of the biface preform.

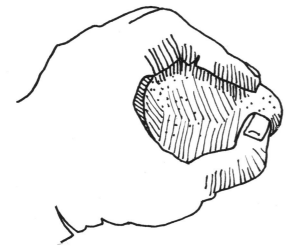

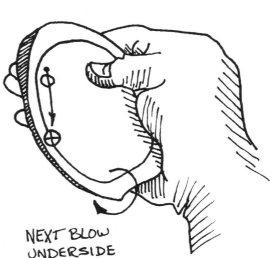

NEXT BLOW
UNDERSIDE

Figure 1

This preform's edge is somewhat sharp now and I could quit here but the stone was still a little bulky.

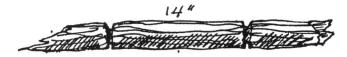

Now I needed another tool and there weren't any deer around and it was already spring, alas no antlers for billets. However, I do know osage orange is very dense and I knew where a tree was that had died a year ago. When I found the hedgeapple tree I removed a limb about 1 1/2" in. diameter and cut a groove around the parts I wanted. I used my preform to groove the branch.

I was then able to snap off the center 14" piece for my billet. I scraped the bark off the branch and ground one end on a large gritty rock near the tree. Now I could complete my "knife" preform. Holding the biface like I held it in Diagram 1 I hit the centerline in 3 well placed blows removing flakes on the underside of my knife.

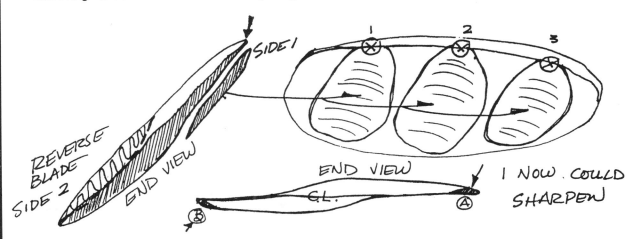

I now could sharpen this thinned blade by pushing off flakes at 'A' and 'B' using a smaller osage branch 1/2" diameter ground to a dull point. I knew I would need this later. So you see knowing stuff sure helps.

George Stewart's "Hands-free Vice"

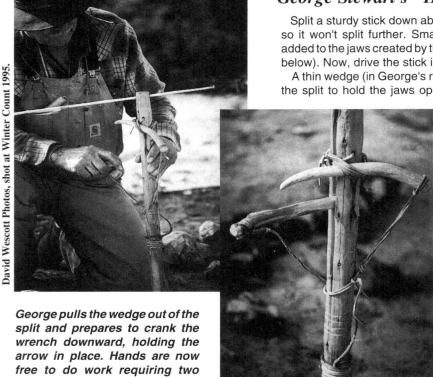

David Wescott Photos, shot at Winter Count 1995.

Split a sturdy stick down about 10 inches, and bind so it won't split further. Small leather pads can be added to the jaws created by the split (see top of photo below). Now, drive the stick into the ground.

A thin wedge (in George's right hand) is placed into the split to hold the jaws open until your work (an arrow, atlatl, or other project to be worked) is positioned into the open jaws. The wedge hangs from the cord while not in place.

The antler "wrench" is pulled down, tightening the leather binding around the split and clamping the work in place. As the antler is torqued downward, the cord attached to the end of the antler is slid down the stick and friction holds tension on the leather binding.

George pulls the wedge out of the split and prepares to crank the wrench downward, holding the arrow in place. Hands are now free to do work requiring two hands.

"George Stewart's "First Switch-blade Knife"

So simple ! Split a handle (bone, antler, horn) and bind the butt ends togther. The blade is slid point-first into the handle and bound in place when not in use. When needed the handle is unbound, the blade turned around and positioned as desired. The blade is compression hafted into the handle with a few quick and simple wraps of cord.

To sharpen or replace a blade that is more disposable than a good handle, simply release the compression wraps and start again.

Variations on a theme. L-R . Handles of split bone, pronghorn, and antler.

A Basketmaker II Knife System
Text and Illustrations By David Holladay

This endeavor started out about a year ago as a project to replicate a knife found in Sand Dune Cave, on display at the Museum of Northern Arizona in Flagstaff, AZ and three similar knives found at Edge of the Cedars in Blanding, UT and it has continued into the present. The materials and design of these knives were common enough for me to want to find out why they were made the way they were. Rather than make an assumption about the design of the knives, hafts and handles, I decided to make the knife with all stone tool technology, which would place automatic limits on how I could work and also make a difference on what the outcome would be. . . I then began using them for daily tasks.

First I made blades that were similar in thickness, width and materials to the museum examples. Then I made the handles. In making a handle, which is about as wide as the base of the blade (Fig. 1), my only limitations were locating accurate materials and my lack of knowledge about the original method of manufacture. From there I entered the void. I used the unhafted blade to make the notch. I was glad to find that the handles of the Basketmaker originals were all made from light, soft woods - agave stalk (Agave spp.), sunflower stem (Helianthus spp.), cottonwood root (Populus spp.). I chose cottonwood root, the hardest of the three, to make the handles on my knives. I noticed that one of the "old" handles had a hole drilled in the middle with a fragment of string still in it. When I saw it several questions immediately came to mind . . . Why is the hole in the middle? How long was that buckskin cord before it rotted off? Isn't the blade kind of small? Was it a neck knife? Did they slip the string over their heads for safe, accessible keeping? Why such soft handle materials? I liked what I saw but I didn't know why.

I went back to Boulder, UT and started making, wearing and using the "Sand Dune Cave" style neck knife. I got poked in the chest several times due to some strange dynamic that I was sure had to do with the hole being more to the center of gravity, so I stopped hanging it around my neck. As I thought on it for the next few months, lots of ideas came to me on how to use and carry this style of knife. In the mean time I kept them in my shirt pocket.

Prior to seeing this design, I was always knapping out longer, thicker blades which I used unhafted and then disposed of, leaving me free to carry something else or nothing at all. Later, I began keeping especially well made blades, modifying them as needed. They gave me more cutting edge, better grip, and were excellent for wood working, drilling, scoring, splitting, chopping, skinning and digging and didn't snap off while I was sliding down talus slopes or climbing trees and rocks. They cut excellent notches in fire boards and all in all seemed like a caveman's best friend. But, this winter my wife and I butchered a lot of sheep, cattle, deer and elk and we found that an unhafted knife was much harder to hold onto without cutting yourself. We ended up hurting our palms and forefingers. The hand-held blades don't feel sharp for the first few minutes of use but after a while our hands would become tender unless we dulled the grip side of our knife or wrapped it with leather. So, when my wife and I were butchering and jerking out a steer one day we switched over to the "new" kind and were pleased to find out after 45 minutes of fast cutting with our "Sand Dune Cave" knives that our hands and knives were in great shape. In fact, we did it again the next week when a perfectly healthy steer ate itself to death on too much good hay. The learning continued . . . . . .

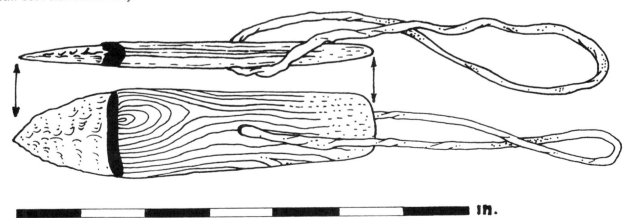

Figure 1. Basketmaker II style knife made by David Holladay from Cottonwood root, Yucca cordage, and blade made from heat-treated yellow Hogsback jasper. Reduced 78%

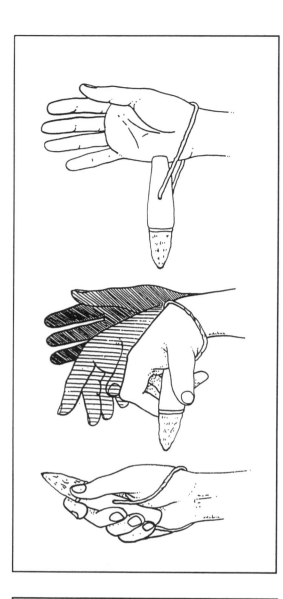

I tried to use my "Sand Dune Cave" hafted knife to do wood working like cutting notches in a fire board or harvesting willows. It worked great as long as I depended on a fast-light sawing action rather than hard, pressure slicing. When I did the latter, the dung and pine pitch glue holding the blade gave way, and the blade broke off part of the wooden handle.

Then I made some handles of bone and some like the Iceman's knife, with hardwood handles of mesquite (*Prosopis spp.*) and cat claw (*Acacia greggii*). They were great for skinning but were much heavier to carry around. They looked good but when used incorrectly the blades snapped off at the haft. Then I made some handles out of elk rib. They were easy to haft, light and the pitch and bone broke out rather than snapping the blade when misused — and they looked real good! But that wasn't what I saw behind the glass. The Basketmaker people used light, pithy woods. So I went back to their style and obsessed about stone age life some more.

I learned that if you haft stone blades in a rigid, durable handle and put the wrong kind of action on the knife (torque the blade) you could easily "snap the rock". But, if you mount one into a softwood handle that provides sufficient resistance to apply good cutting pressure and is strong enough to do the job (which I feel this style of hafted blade was meant to do...which is cut flesh) the handle breaks out before the blade snaps when used incorrectly. If I was using my knife wrong I wouldn't loose my blade which can take a long time to produce. That's an advantage! Especially if thought of in today's cutting edge scenario (steel and lasers). Handles were expendable, blades weren't!

I began thinking about the terrain where the "Sand Dune Cave" knives were found (the Colorado Plateau desert) on the Navajo Reservation, where you have lots of sandstone and sand, but not much good rock for making stone blades. Good rock had to be brought in. Good knapping materials are not always available...even in the best locations they can be frozen in the earth or hidden beneath the snow, or it can be night time and your whole world is only as big as the glow of your campfire and you aren't finished butchering.. And I suppose the Paleo people had thousands of years to pick over all of the best materials, so surface gathering has been tougher ever since.

I like to imagine. I imagined living in Sand Dune Cave or some other area where good rock was hard to find and thought to myself that if the beautifully made, imported, wide, thin, long stone knife I owned broke I would save the pieces, rework them, and haft them. So I did just that. I found out that a small blade could butcher out a huge animal if I could get a grip on it (the animal and the blade). One can take total advantage of what materials he has and turn them into a knife he can work with. With a small hand-held blade you can't get enough power behind it to do a lot of work. But if you add a handle to it, and if you can get the blade into the handle far enough to make a strong haft, you get a mechanical advantage. That small blade becomes a very powerful ripping tool. You also create a material advantage— every little piece can be hafted. Thus the "Basketmaker" system extends the blade life expectancy, is super light, and helps modify, and utilize marginal materials. Good idea!

Continued on page 44 ....

in.

Here's How

If you want to feel what I'm talking about, let's make one,
and then you can get behind the wield of your very own
Basketmaker II Sand Dune Cave Self-Accessing Model AD 1-500, 2000BP knife.

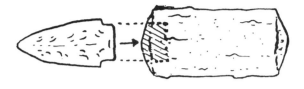 

Cut a hand-width or longer length section of a soft-dry branch, root, stem or stalk, about 2" thick. Knap out a blade with slight shoulders at the basal end.

Fig. 1. Dig and scrape, or force a hole into one end of the handle. However you choose to make your slot, make it snug, but not too tight of a fit. Gently test it out as you go.

Fig. 2. When you've got a good fit remove the blade and fill the empty cavity with hot pitch/dung glue and let it cool.

Figure 3

Figure 4

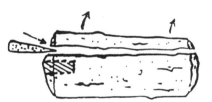

Figure 6

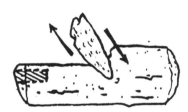

Figure 5

If you want to shape the handle, use a flat-abrasive rock and sand it down (Fig. 3), or try your hand at splitting off the excess girth with a stone, bone or wood wedge (Fig. 4). You may also use the unhafted blade to saw/cut the sides down (Fig. 5). Another method would be to whittle the sides to shape using a chisel-like or razor-sharp flake (Fig. 6).

Heat the blade until it is hot to the touch, and firmly and slowly press it into the glue-filled slot. If you're worried about splitting the handle out at this stage, wrap the haft end of the handle before forcing the hot blade back into place. Then as the excess glue

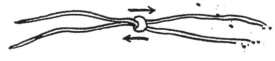

cools a little, push it up around to seal the joint between the blade and the handle.

Finally your ready to drill, poke or burn a hole in the center of the handle and put a cord through it. Try out different distances to find out your "knife to wrist ratio" before tying a permanent knot. Or put an adjustable slide on it like a tight fitting bead (Fig. 7). Now you have it.

(more)

I was still curious about the hole in center of the handle, so I made a section of cord from yucca fiber, but remembering my first experience I knew I didn't want it to be long enough to go around my neck. I thought about trying one that was shorter. One I could hang on a tree branch or go around my wrist. For years I had been drilling holes in the end of my knife handles to put thongs through so that I wouldn't drop my knife onto the ground if it slipped out of my hand. And besides, it looks cool...it gives you something else to do to your knife while resting in the shade...drill, polish, paint, sculpt, rub in some wax or fat, fiddle, fiddle, fiddle. At the time I though maybe that was a good enough reason for the hole. I didn't have enough material to make a long-thick yucca loop, so I made a short one and threaded it through the hole and put it around my wrist. I wore it there while I worked at doing something else but the handle kept poking me in the wrist....the loop was too small. So, I made another handle with the hole near the end, like I've always done, and wore it like that, still on my wrist. It felt better, but that wasn't what I had seen in the museum. So then I made a slightly longer cord and tried the hole in the middle again. I began working on something else and forgot about the knife being on my wrist. While I worked I would occasionally put my hand down and the knife would be right there...it would literally fall into my palm. Each time I put my arm down, with-out even thinking about it (which is when I am at my smart-est) the knife would be there, ready to use. I could use my hands, drop my arm or hand down and the knife handle went right into my palm. I got chills!! That hole in the middle helped facilitate control of the knife when it wasn't being used and then because of its location in the handle, it swung the handle directly into my grip when I wanted it. This would be great for skinning an animal in the snow or sand or deep grass or mud. When you need your fingers free to pull back a hide, push open a rib cage or grope for some entrails, you don't want to lay your tool down where it could get buried, lost, muddy or sandy. No matter how busy I was, my knife was always available and my fingers were free at an instant for some other task by just letting go. But, then as if by magic, my knife was "at hand."

In closing, the Sand Dune Cave knife uses a haft-ing system specific to this area. My article is not an explana-tion or recommendation for all uses or an argument against alternative hafting methods and materials. Rather, it is a record of my experience with some thoughts and opinions attached. The original specimens, dated at 1-500 AD, were found intact in a dry cave. This type of knife needed to be tested in a real use situation to determine what the advan-tages and disadvantages of the design might be. I'm still working and having fun with it. I trust you might also.

DRILLING STONE
By Larry Kinsella

The most common use of stone drilling in my area, the Midwest, is the manufacture of bannerstones (atlatl weights). Many different types of stone, from soapstone to quartzite, are used for bannerstones but banded slate seems to dominate. Banded slate is beautiful and strong, yet soft enough to drill. The hole in bannerstone is roughly 7/16 inch (12 mm) in di-ameter and allowing the atlatl sections to pass through the hole. It is possible that the bannerstone is used to join different sections of an atlatl together as well (i.e. wood handle to an antler hook etc.). This area of study is just one that needs more experi-mentation.

The stone slab, core and drill.

To drill a stone the ancient way, a piece of cane is used in conjunction with an abrasive to slowly cut a hole through the stone. A by-product of stone drilling is a cylindri-cal "core" which survives the drilling process by remaining inside the cane drill. These are found archaeologically and look exactly like modern reproductions.

Steps to Stone Drilling
1. Cane Selection and Straightening - The selection of a cane drill is crucial to stone drilling because it will become a tool you will use for many hours. Choose a piece of cane with as much length between the "knuckles" as possible so

> *Items Needed for Stone Drilling*
> *1. stone - banded slate*
> *2. cane - Southern Illinois river cane*
> *3. grit - sand, flint dust, quartzite, etc.*
> *4. vise - a split limb or branch*
> *5. cordage - 5 to 10 feet*
> *6. chert flakes*

you have as few "knuckles" as possible to grind off later. Straighten the cane by applying heat where the cane is to be straightened. Heat until the cane "sweats", straighten by bending, then cool the area as soon as possible. I use a damp cloth. After the cane is straightened, scrape and grind off the "knuckles" until smooth. Some-

Scraping the shaft and nodes.

Note the clamp device used to hold the piece being drilled.

times, they take a lot of grinding, so I always straighten before grinding to prevent snapping the cane during straightening. The tool should be smooth to prevent abuse to your hands while drilling.

2. Grit Selection - If using sand, choose a sand with sharp edges, not river sand. River sand is rolled downstream and is therefore rounded like ball-bearings and will not cut unless crushed. My personal preference now is chert dust because it is readily available to me (from kapping debatage) as it must have been prehistorically. Some grits I intend to experiment with include ground up quartz and granite debris left over from the making of stone axes.

Grit needs to be sorted as to size. Too small and it doesn't cut well and too large it tends to damage the cane and bind in the stone. I sort the grit by winnowing. I lay a deer hide on the ground and pour the grit onto it from about 5 feet above. The wind will blow the fines to one end of the hide while the heavier coarse grit falls on the nearer end. I select the grit in the center area (about 1 mm).

3. Stone Selection - The stone you use should be roughly shaped to the finished product you want. You don't want to spend 10 or 20 hours drilling a hole through a stone that may break while shaping. On the other hand, you wouldn't want to drill a finished piece and risk the hole being crooked or coming out the side.

4. Vise Construction - Select a tree limb 2 or 3 inches in

diameter and 1 or 2 feet long. Split it and tie one end with cordage. Place the stone between the halves at the other end and tie securely so the stone does not move. Sometimes it may be necessary to notch the limb halves to allow more area to contact the stone.

5. Starting - Since the stone has a smooth surface, the cane will not stay in position. The surface must be prepared by scratching a circle into the stone with a chert flake. This circle must be deep enough to steady the cane and cannot be accomplished in a few minutes. The flake should be pointed and may have to be resharpened repeatedly, but the hole will, eventually, get deep enough to hold the cane in position.

6. Drilling Technique - The cane should be placed on the prepared area and revolved by rubbing between the palms. If the cane stays on the prepared surface, you are ready to add grit. If not, the surface must be scratched until it does stay.

Add 10 to 30 granules of grit to the surface, position drill and begin to drill. As you drill, the grit will fall out of the hole or ride up into the cane. Drill as long as you feel the grit cutting. If you feel it has stopped, lift the cane and put the grit back into the hole. Eventually, you will be able to feel when the grit is no longer cutting and the cane will usually start squeaking. This is a sign that the grit is becoming rounded or slipping out of the hole onto the ground. Blow out the dust away, add more grit, and continue drilling.

From here on out it is just elbow grease and persistence. I encourage you to treat your drilling as an experiment and keep your time in a log. Also, save your "core" so you can compare it to those found archaeologically. You will find, after the time and effort you put into it, just how prized a well made bannerstone must have been to early man.

Other drilling methods: 1. A stone thumb drill used to drill bone; 2. stone-tipped pump-drill also used on bone; 3. stone tipped hand drill used on shell and many other materials.

CELTS
Celts used in the construction of a fish weir at Pamunkey.

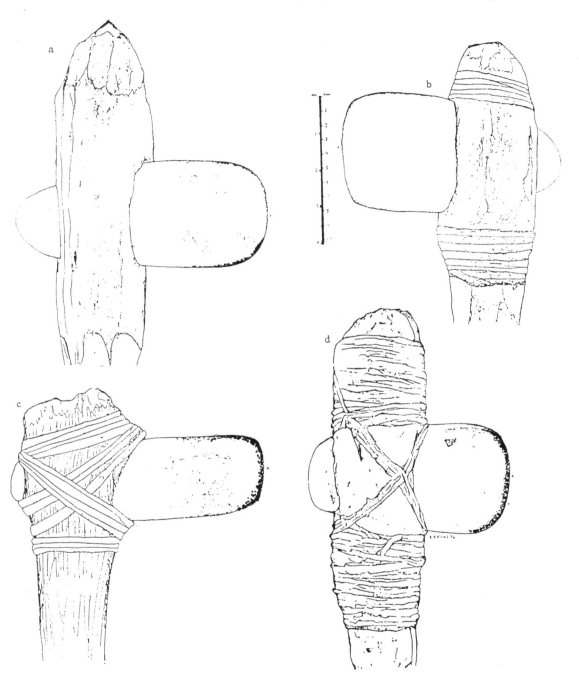

These celts were all made from Catoctin greenstone and are hafted with sweet gum and red maple (handles average 17"). Some have rawhide wrappings to reinforce the haft. Their bit angles were 70, 66, 61, 58 degrees respectively. The heads are all slightly more than a pound. This drawing by Errett Callahan was reduced 78% from scale to fit this page. From APE #4, The Pamunkey Project: Phase II, 1976.

CELTS AND AXES

CELTS IN THE PAMUNKEY AND CAHOKIA HOUSE BUILDING PROJECTS
By Errett Callahan

WHAT IS A CELT ?

The term "celt" is used to refer to an ungrooved, tapered, ground stone axe with a centered edge at one end. An average size is roughly between 3 to 6 inches (8 to 16 cm) in length by 1 1/2 to 3 inches (4 to 8 cm) in width by 3/4 to 1 1/2 inches (2 to 4 cm) in thickness. Raw material is typically Catoctin greenstone. Optimum edge-angles for wood cutting range between 60 degrees to 70 degrees. Technique of manufacture could be as simple as selecting an appropriately sized river cobble and grinding a cutting edge or as elaborate as complete bifacial flaking of the surface, followed by complete pecking of the flaked surface, followed, in turn, by complete grinding of the pecked surface. Edge polishing comes with use.

wooden swords, and even small knife handles; knots on housing poles; notches at ends of housing poles; measurement nicks on poles; poplar bark slabs; (hickory bark for baskets); walnut bark for cordage; cattail roots against chopping log; various trimming, pole splitting, and fine woodwork. other - used as plumb line on one house (any other rock would have done as well)

One celt was used for chopping a total of 333 poles--or the equivalent--for use on the project. Most poles were used on the Bark House. The remaining cuts were used for making tools and miscellaneous woodworking.

During the first summer's use, very detailed records were kept on the use of celts for chopping 63 saplings.

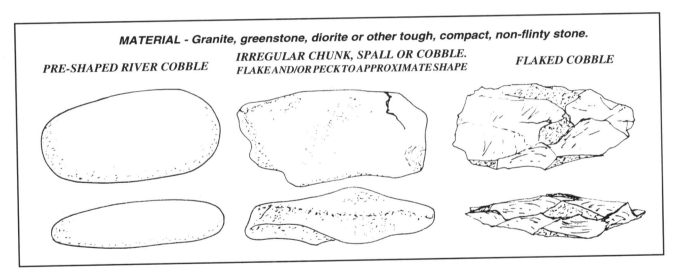

MATERIAL - Granite, greenstone, diorite or other tough, compact, non-flinty stone.

PRE-SHAPED RIVER COBBLE

IRREGULAR CHUNK, SPALL OR COBBLE.
FLAKE AND/OR PECK TO APPROXIMATE SHAPE

FLAKED COBBLE

Ethnohistoric references to celts include vocabularies in which a "hatchet" is called a "taccahacan", a "tamahaac". Archaeologically, celts have been recovered in many Late Woodland Coastal Plain sites. Surface finds of celts are common and their attributes may be readily distinguished. Middle Woodland celts seem to have a wider range of variation in size, especially toward the upper (larger) range.

OBSERVATIONS FROM PAMUNKEY

Hypothesis: Celts are tools of critical importance for felling and sizing saplings and for shaping wooden tools and implements needed for house construction.

Experiments: chopping - sapling poles for houses, outbuildings, and benches; (fencing for gardens and village); wooden tool parts such as mallets, post stakes, celt hafts,

While poles were cut up to 3 1/2 inches in diameter (8.8 cm) the average pole was 2 inches in diameter (5.49 cm) and 6 3/4 inches in circumference (17.23 cm). The average

Some of the text and drawings for this article are from reports published in 1976 about projects conducted on the Pamunkey Indian Reservation and Old Rag mountain in Virginia by founding Board member Errett Callahan and his students from Virginia Commonwealth University. These are landmark publications, long out of circulation. The information on Cahokia will be available in Errett's new book, now in pre-publication.

time for felling and trimming a 2 inch sapling was 4 1/4 minutes, of which 3/8 of the time was spent felling (till it fell of its own weight) and 5/8 of the time was spent trimming (removing limbs and limb stubs). The average number of single chops or swings per 2 inch pole was 85.7.

According to calculations made above, at 4 1/4 minutes per cut and 85.7 chops per cut, the 333 severance cuts would have taken, on standing trees, the equivalent of 23.35 hours of continuous chopping and 28,538 chops.

OBSERVATIONS FROM CAHOKIA

Celts were used at Cahokia for 59.39 hours or 13.2% of the total time. Three celts were employed. Two were full-sized and made for the project, the other was rather light and had been made beforehand.

To display the efficiency of these tools, one celt was used for 29.39 hours of work during the project. Controlled field testing was done on felling and trimming cedar trees of 3", 4 1/2", and 6" (7.6, 11.4, and 15.2 cm, respectively) diameters.

In the above tests, all variables were kept constant except tree diameter. The results show that as the diameter is doubled, the work time increases more than four-fold because of rests required between chopping spurts on the larger trees. (Note that mathematically, doubling of the diameter exactly quadruples the volume). It is therefore postulated that, in the past, decisions as to post diameter may not have been made haphazardly. That is, the difference between a 2" post and a 4" post is significant indeed in terms of work expenditure and may have reflected a conscious decision on the part of the wood cutter. Presumably, cultural norms would temper all such technological considerations.

ONE CELT'S HISTORY

One of the most extensively documented tools used in the Pamunkey study is celt 77EC5L. This celt is described in some detail due to the importance of both this tool unit and the tool kind to the project. This celt was made of Catoctin greenstone in 3.5 hours by a combination of overall percussion flaking, pecking, and grinding with sand and water. Polishing came with use. Upon completion, the celt measured 14.1 x 5.6 x 2.83 cm, weighed 345 g (12 1/2 oz.), and had an edge-angle of 55 degrees. The haft was made of seasoned Southern red oak in 5.10 hours by burning and scraping. The hole was made by burning, chiseling, and scraping. The haft measured 40.3 cm (length) x 5.36 cm (head width) x 3.21 cm (head thickness) x 2.4 cm (minimum grip thickness). It weighted 345 g, the same as the head. The combined weight of head and haft was 690 g (l lb. 9 oz.).

During this considerable usage, the celt underwent 14 resharpenings. The edge-angle fluctuated between 55 and 65 degrees as the optimum cutting angle was sought for chopping the woods needed for the tasks at hand. Steeper angles were desired for chopping seasoned hardwoods such as hickory and oak while lesser angles would suffice for chopping softer, green woods such as cedar and maple. It was decided that an angle which would serve for multi-purpose chopping was more feasible than an angle which fluctuated with the particular wood being cut; for the less the celt was resharpened, the longer it would last. I concluded after three years of experimenting, that an edge-angle of between 63 degrees to 65 degrees is the optimum angle for felling, sizing, and otherwise working a variety of woods relating to house construction and tool preparation.

The 14 resharpenings added 1.49 hours to the "manufacturing" time. In all, a total of 1.08 cm of length was lost while the weight dropped 25.3 g. Use was terminated when the celt was accidentally dropped on a rock and severe damage was noted on the bit. It would have taken a major resharpening effort to have repaired it at this point.

From the above, excepting the final damage to the bit, this celt--in the haft--would have been quite servicable until about another two cm. had been lost in length. Beyond that point, the sides of this haft, at the bit, would have interfered too much with the proper chopping angle. Accordingly, I would postulate that a celt such as this one could have, if it were not severely damaged, been used to cut the equivalent of 1000 poles (333 poles per cm. of celt head length) before it became too short for further efficient use. (One could, if one cared, calculate how many houses this might represent. I hesitate to do this because of the many unseen variables.)

CONCLUSIONS

Celts were assigned a use-rating of 1 (extensive/critical use) for both village and overall project. The majority of time went into cutting and sizing house poles. This was followed by considerable time doing woodworking on tool handles. Most of our wood was cut green, as mentioned by Beverley (1968: 229), who says "By the help of these [axes], they made their Bows of the Locust Tree, an excessive hard Wood when it is dry, but much more easily cut when it is green, of which they always took the advantage." Nevertheless, completely seasoned locust, hickory, and white oak were successfully chopped with our celts. Downed wood was chopped against a solid chopping log. All celts were used hafted except for the plumb line experiment.

In summary, the celt, as a tool kind, was an indispensable tool to the project. Without the celt, the poles would have had to be felled by a combination of fire, coretools, and /or choppers--none of which would have allowed more than a fraction of the speed or efficiency experienced with the celt. Furthermore, the versatility of the celt practically made many other tools unnecessary. On the other hand, the making of a celt could involve a considerable expenditure of time, an expenditure which the other tools, being more quickly made, might avert.

Inference: From our experience, it is felt that the celt was no less than a critical and indispensable part of our housebuilding tool kit. Accordingly, there is a high degree of probability that, in the past, similar celts were tools of critical importance in house construction tasks and that they were employed for a variety of work related to material acquisition, processing, and basic construction.

(more)

CELTS
Celt 77EC5L and Haft

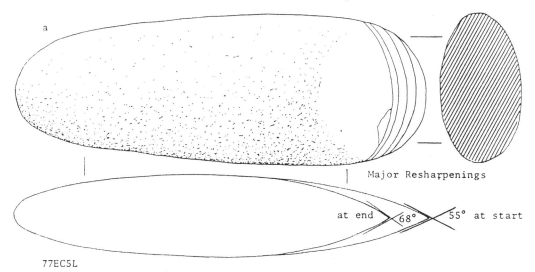

Major Resharpenings

at end 68° 55° at start

77EC5L

The variety of edge angles and shortening of the bit were recorded, as subsequent sharpenings reduced the overall size and varied the bit angle.

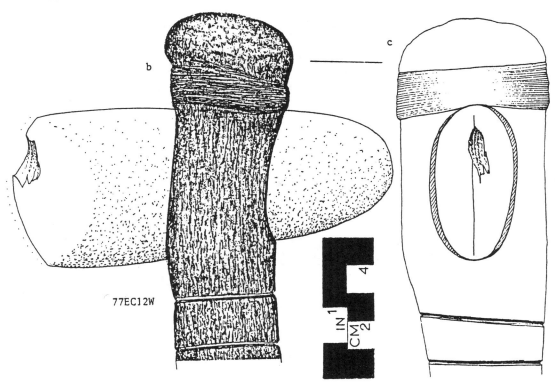

77EC12W

The chip in the bit came late in the use of this axe and inadvertently shortened its potential use substantially. This drawing by Errett Callahan was reduced 78% from scale to fit this page. From APE #4, The Pamunkey Project: Phase I, 1976.

Using Stone To Work Green Wood

A comparative exercise in the use of a south-western grooved axe (E) and a midwestern celt, (A) conducted by Larry Kinsella (C) and David Holladay (B) at Rabbit Stick 1992. The exercise was to test the efficiency of both models while chopping a black poplar approximately 9" in diameter. It took slightly longer than 4 minutes to fell the tree, and less than 3 minutes to limb it (D). To anyone who has not seen a stone axe in action, it was a most impressive experience to bring home the prize (F). Photos by David Wescott

Personal Notes On Celt Use
By Larry Kinsella

I started using stone axes during the reconstruction of a pit house by Errett Callahan at Cahokia Mounds in 1981-1982. Three celts were constructed for the project. Each has a unque history. One celt was broken in 1983 by an 8-year-old boy while cutting an 8" log. A lot was learned about stone axe breakage from that single incident. In local fields, axes have been found broken in apparently the same way. It appears that "side slap" broke that specimen. The young boy's hands could not control the "side slap" while cutting inside a four inch wide and six inch deep notch. His blow landed on the right side of the V-shaped cut and his wrist could not control the handle, so the stone struck the opposite side of the notch , and a large chunk was knapped from the bit. To avoid this problem I now fashion the handle's grip so it is twice as wide as it is thick. This has decreased but not eliminated "side slap."

The second celt has lasted to this day (see   ). It has cut 3000 limbs and trees from 1/2 to 12 inches in diameter and has never been resharpened. In 1983, it was used to construct the stockade around the Callahan pit house. 420 black locust logs were limbed to form a stockade, and two large swinging gates made of hickory were constructed as well, all using that celt. This celt was also used in the Cahokia Woodhenge reconstruction (48 trees, 22' long and 1' diameter). It cut and limbed 1/3 of the logs, twenty-four black locust and 24 red cedar logs. It was also used to reconstruct a Late Woodland pit house in the author's back yard.

A third celt was made by Dave Klostermeier and the author, and it was used for another 1/3 of the Cahokia Woodhenge project. Since the Woodhenge project, I have made and used 4 other celts. Two are in museum displays and two are still being used. One was hafted in an over-sized handle to see if the handle size could overwhelm the stone (see   ). So far it has really been laid into and neither the handle nor the stone has been hurt.

The method used for constructing stone axes comes partially from insights gained at an Archaic site about 1/2 mile from my home. The site was located on a low bluff above a major stream that eventually flows into the Mississippi. On the edge of the site is a smaller stream that cuts through a glatial till at the botttom of the stream. Granite axe material can be found in that glacial till along with chunks of chert. At the top of the hill, axe parts can be found in association with chert balls used to peck them. Twenty chert balls and a few granite hammerstones were found there indicating that mostly chert balls were used at that site for pecking the stone axes. One advantage of using chert is that it works better around the bit, because you don't have to hit as hard, cutting down on breakage.

The celts were hafted so that the wedging of the stone into the handle is done in a way that exerts pressure on the top and bottom of the haft only. Allowing the sides to touch, splits the handle. Callahan taught that technique during the Cahokia Pit House reconstruction. Reinforcing of the handle by leaving knots or heavier amounts of wood above and below the stone, was personally noted by observing a surviving celt at the Museum of the Red River in Idabel, Oklahoma. Greg Perino had the axe on display in 1985, and the specimen showed reinforcing "humps" in the wood on both ends of the stone with enough removed on the top of the stone to allow removal by hitting the butt of the stone over a log.

The celt removal technique was being demonstrated at Illinois Lake Carlysle in 1988. The celt was knocked out, used as a wedge, then replaced in the handle. On the next chop, the handle was split, so a back-up celt was used. The head was removed, then reinserted, and the celt handle was split again on the next chop. Several weeks later, Dave Klostermeier and I were flintknapping and discussed why the handles had broken. We concluded that the stone heads had inadvertantly been installed upside-down, and since the handle did not fit tightly, the handle split. For years we had seen what were known as "tally marks" on many celt artifacts. From experimentation to conclusion came the idea that "tally marks" would show the correct way to re-insert the stone and stop handle breakage.

In the Cahokia Mounds area, "tally marks" occur on the bits of celts that are symmetrical. "Tally marks" are simply scratches made near the celt bit and sometimes in the butt. They only occur on symmetrical axes, because if the shape was odd or flaws in the stone were noticeable, it was easy to replace the stone the same way every time the tool was used.

CELTS
Celt # AIb10/EC/1 --- A MODEL

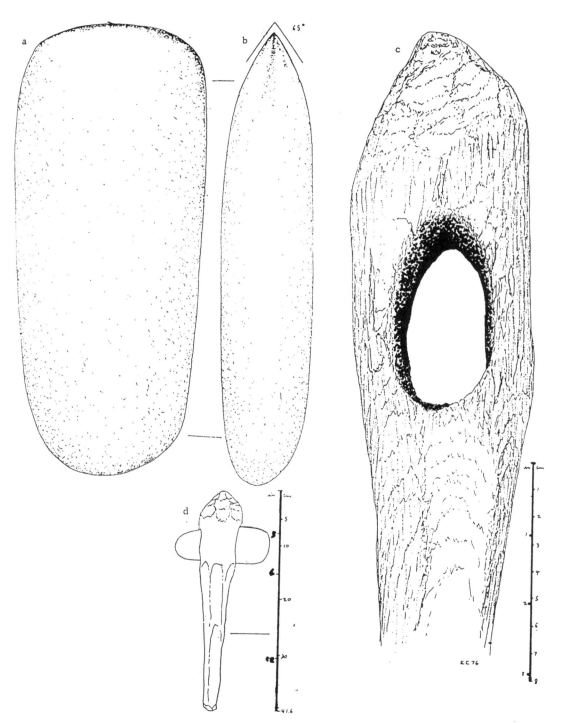

This drawing by Errett Callahan was reduced 78% from scale to fit this page.
From APE #4, The Pamunkey Project: Phase I, 1976.

CELT RAW MATERIAL - Catoctin Greenstone cobble, Madison, VA

TOOLS USED -   Heavy billet, quartzite abrader, hammerstone, granite boulder, duck oil.

PROCESS - Flaking of river cobble, bifacially, with billet to
Stage 3. Direct percussion....   40 min.
Pecking all over with hard hammerstone..... 1.45 hr.
Grinding all over on granite boulder (15 min) and sandstone
    abrading stone with sand and water.....   45 min.
Polishing on wet slab without sand....   5 min.
 Rubbing with duck oil (rendered from duck fat).....1 min.
    TOTAL celt head preparation time.....   3.16 hrs.

NOTES: The often-overlooked key to holding the working time down on pecked stone tools is selecting for a hard enough hammerstone for pecking. The harder the hammer, the less time required for completion. In addition, the more pecking done at the bit, the less time required for grinding. Edge-damage potential is high, however, so one must work quite carefully. It could be said that each 15 minutes pecking will save about an hour's grinding. Pecking with a pointed portion of the hammerstone and striking toward the basal end (with bit facing the worker), rather than perpendicular to the edge, will reduce the chance of fracture. Maximum feasibility, however, comes with soft hammer flaking of the bit. A well-formed bit so flaked will require little or no pecking within 1/2" of the bit. This considerably reduces the danger of edge damage and total time expenditure. (The above observations are based on experience gained by the replication of over 50 grooved and ungrooved axes and celts.

HAFTING RAW MATERIAL - Sycamore from a tough, 3' long, beaver-chewed log found by the Pamunkey River.

TOOLS USED -   Hafted, 3 lb. grooved axe for sectioning and trimming grip; moose antler tip chisel and heavy billet used for hole.

PROCESS - Stick was cut to length (41cm; 16 1/8")
    with grooved axe...   5 min.
Handle was trimmed from 6.5 cm (2 1/2") diameter at
    base to 3.2 cm (1 1/16"), reduced weight from
    2 lb. to 1lb. 40oz. Grip was octagonal in cross-
    section for better grip.....   15 min.
A 3' hole (7.7cm) was chiseled out with antler chisel
    (resharpened 15-20 times to 70 degree bevel)
    + billet.....   1 hr.
Handle trimmed to 15 oz....   15 min.
    TOTAL handle preparation time.....   1.35 hrs.
    TOTAL axe preparation time....   4.51 hrs.

NOTES: Handle was retrimmed into a square shape on day 10. This was needed for optimum grip with medium slip. The octagonal grip eventually became rounded off and polished from use. The square handle was less slippery.

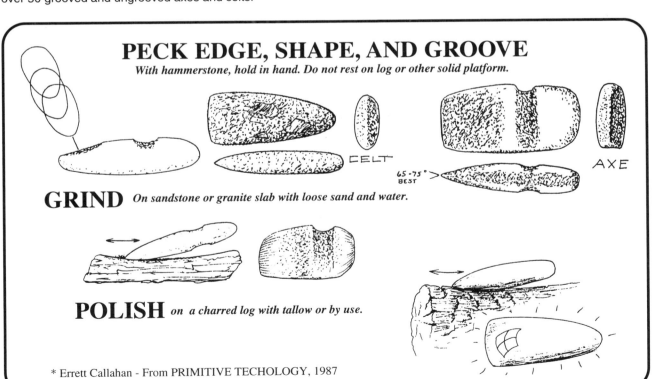

PECK EDGE, SHAPE, AND GROOVE

With hammerstone, hold in hand. Do not rest on log or other solid platform.

CELT

65-75° >
BEST

AXE

GRIND *On sandstone or granite slab with loose sand and water.*

POLISH *on a charred log with tallow or by use.*

* Errett Callahan - From PRIMITIVE TECHOLOGY, 1987

CHOPPERS

AXES

A

B

C

D

E

A. Arizona Rhyolite chopper and knife.
B. Greenstone blanks at various stages.
C. 20-minute hafted hammer.
D. Various celts by Errett Callahan.
E Scott Silsby's celts.

CELTS

HAMMERS

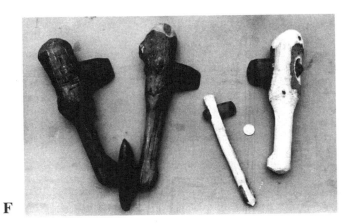

F

G

H

I

F. Hadzets by Scott Silsby.
G. Celt showing spacing detail.
H. Hafted grooved axe with shim in place.
I Choppers and hand axes by David Wescott.
J. Celts by David Holladay. Also C, G & H.

**Photos by David Wescott and
E. & F. by Scott Silsby**

J

MANUFACTURE OF GROUND STONE AXES
By Paul Hellweg

It does not take a great deal of skill to manufacture a stone hammer or axe; however, it can require a fair amount of patience. Crude hammers can be produced in less than an hour, but a finely crafted axe can take more than forty hours of repetitive effort — one should not undertake such a task unless he or she is in the proper frame of mind (think of your efforts as relaxation, not work).

1. SELECT ARTIFACT BLANK - (See Silsby)

Select a blank which closely approximates the shape of the hammer or axe you intend to manufacture (thus saving working time). The blank should be course-grained for a hammer; more finely-grained for an axe. Also, the blank should be homogeneous (that is, of like texture throughout), and it should be free of cracks.

2. SELECT HAMMERSTONE

Stone hammers and axes are made by pecking them into desired shape through repeated blows of a hammer. A proper hammerstone will speed up the process, and care should be taken in its selection. A siliceous mineral such as quartzite makes an ideal hammerstone; however, any very hard stone will suffice. A good hammerstone is fine-grained, comparatively heavy, and free of cracks.

3. PECK ARTIFACT INTO DESIRED SHAPE

If you are making a stone hammer and if you have found a blank of ideal proportions, all you will need to do is peck out a hafting groove. But if you are making an axe, you will also need to peck the blade into approximate shape (thereby speeding up the grinding process — see next step).

Peck your blank into shape with short rapid blows of the hammerstone. Try to develop an effective but relaxed rhythm, and the work will proceed steadily. While pecking, support the blank on a wood anvil - this can be a tree stump, log, simply a piece of thick board *. Progress will be made quite rapidly on a course-grained hammer blank, but results will be slower to appear when working with a fine-grained axe blank.

4. GRIND AXE BLADE

If you are making a stone hammer, you will probably not have to do any grinding. But if you are making an axe, the blade will have to be ground into a smooth and sharp cutting surface. A sandstone slab is ideal as a grinding medium; however, a concrete patio stone will suffice—if that is all you have available. If you are using a concrete slab, you can speed up the grinding process by periodically sprinkling it with small quantities of sand.

Grinding is no more complicated than pecking. Simply abrade the artifact blank back and forth, while periodically rinsing the slab clean of accumulated waste material with water. You should exercise increasing care as the blade nears its final shape so as not to nick its cutting edge.

5. SHARPEN THE AXE BLADE

You will not be able to grind an axe blade truly sharp on a rough grinding slab. Thus the final step in manufacturing an axe is to sharpen the blade with a small sandstone pebble (or wetstone—if you're not a purist). Keep the pebble wet and abrade it in a circular fashion along the axe's cutting edge—do this by holding the pebble at about a 20 degree angle to the axe blade (much in the same manner that a steel knife blade is sharpened). Assuming that you started with a sufficiently fine-grained blank, you should be able to grind an impressively sharp edge onto your stone axe.

CONCLUSION

Admittedly, this discussion of manufacturing techniques has been brief. However, all the basics have been covered, and you should be able to fabricate your own stone hammer or axe with this information. Most likely the hardest part of the whole process will be finding suitable materials: artifact blank, hammerstone, grinding slab, and so forth. Once you have these in hand, the actual work should proceed without too much difficulty.

GREENSTONE WOODWORKING TOOLS

Text and Photos By Scott Silsby

"Greenstone" (Catoctin Metabasalt) with minor Flint Run Jasper from near Front Royal, VA.

The name "greenstone" is a wonderfully archaic field name used by geologists the world over to describe a wide variety of volcanic basalt related rocks containing minerals that usually impart a greenish color to them. Throughout the Eastern Appalachian mountain range a formation known as the Catoctin provided (and still provides) the rock formally known as Catoctin metabasalt as the premier axe grade stone.

Fresh basalt or those only a few tens of millions of years old have but little strength advantage over easily worked flint family stone. Certain highly metamorphosed greenstones in many regions throughout the world have been literally forged into an extremely tough and tenacious rock by natural actions.

In the northern regions of Shenandoah National Park from Front Royal, VA south to Luray, VA the Catoctin Metabasalt averages 1800 feet thick. Its estimated age is 600 to 800 million years old.

In a geological report about this rock it is stated "generally present are chlorite, epidote, amphibole (actinolite) albite and pyroxene. Magnetite in sufficient quantity to deflect a compass needle, is present at some localities" (Allen '67). In another report (Reed '55) it is stated "only the pyroxene and

part of the magnetite are believed to be primary minerals of the original lava" and further describes alterations of various other minerals that "attest to the highly altered mineral character of the Catoctin."

Unfortunately, this metamorphism along with severe tectonic buckling destroyed the vast majority of this rock from an axe makers point of view. Only the greenstone originating from or occurring at or near the highest elevations along the northern crest of the Blue Ridge in warren and Page counties of Virginia appear to have escaped the destructive aspect of this vulcanism. Within this region are

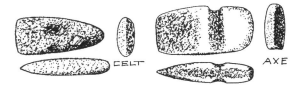

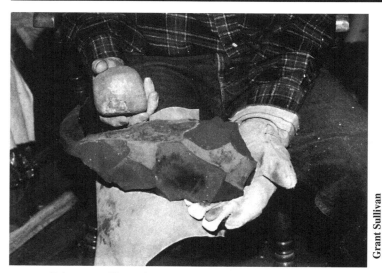

Primary spalling of a cobble using a greenstone hammer

Courser, more crystalline grade after primary spalling.

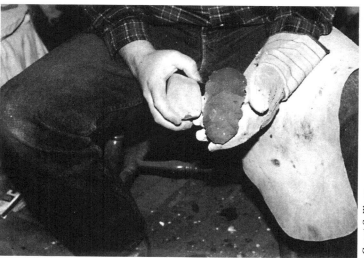

Finer grade after primary spalling

found the extensive celt shops described by W.H. Holmes in an early report (Holmes '97).

The greenstone from this restricted area can be found in large flawless pieces in great quantity although collecting of it must be from outcrops and talus off of park land. Greenstone to the south of this area is ruined by epidotization while rock from further north is highly layered and folded (Gathright '76).

What makes greenstone tick?

Each component of the rock serves a vital role in making it the classic it is. Amphibole in the form of micro fibrous actinolite acts like glass or graphite fibers that impact flexible strength. (Nephrite jade is a highly pure fibrous actinolite) Chlorite serves as a shock damper while epidote, albite and pyroxene lock them all together and provide hardness. Magnetite copper (native form), hematite, jasper and piemontite provide density, weight and also visually enrich the various varieties of rock. The mixture of these minerals and rock into the internal form that makes up true greenstone, allows it to be knapped as one would knap a strong flint. The softer minerals allow pecking (referred to a bushing in the stone trade) with little risk of fracture and further allows it to be highly polished where, if shaped correctly, it can withstand a great deal more shock than any other knappable stone. Jade is stronger but can't be flaked with control.

Tips for Working Greenstone

Think safety from when you start to whenever you use your finished item. Wear eye protection and avoid knapping, pecking, and grinding dust.

Primary spalling and flaking can be done with slightly softer greenstone hammers. Large dense moose antlers work great as well as native copper ones. Very tough flint type hammers work well as pecking stones but soon shatter if used as flaking hammers.

When flaking greenstone with antler avoid grinding platforms as it strengthens them too much. Use the billet to scrape into the platform thus stacking up the back of the platform with a number of micro hinged flakes. Ground greenstone is amazingly strong and ground platforms can split a moose billet.

Don't over thin your preform. You can always peck and grind away any excess later. Once you have roughed out your preform and flaked away most of its cortex or weathered surface, soak it in hot water a couple of minutes then towel it dry in good light. Cracks and unhealed fractures will retain moisture and allow you to see if they are in critical area. Unless very severe or at the bit edge most will have little effect on the tools finished strength. Pecking destroys your ability to use this "flaw proofing" technique so do it during flaking. Healed veins and recrystallized cracks can be Two ignored. They are often stronger than the rock.

Pecking is very tedious. Use a lot of leather as cushioning and match your pecking stone weight to the tools weight. As your greenstone tool takes shape and loses weight switch to a lighter stone. Avoid pecking near the bit edge. Rely on just grinding to shape it there. Avoid "karate chop" type blows which tend to bend the rock where its weakest attribute is tested. Support your tool well while you deliver small decisive sharp blows. Start in one spot and peck out a depression. Then keep pecking into the depression from one edge and work it all the way across the tool's surface.

Three blanks on left show progressive stages of pecking. Top right lacks secondary flaking, while the rest are ready for pecking.

Hafting

Axes and "hadzets" are socketed into a mortise such that the top and bottom sides of the celt wedge into the hole making contact only on the up and down faces of the handles long axis. The more rectangular the celt is in cross section, the more surface area to absorb shock and transfer it into cutting force. Your bit should be slightly tapered from bit to pol so that the more it is forced into the mortise the tighter it will be. Avoid any taper on the tools side that would act as a wedge by making the tools bit a rather flat arc. Don't make it completely flat but keep the arc low.

Overly tapered celts tend to pop out of the haft from misstrikes or rebounds. Very square, parallel sides can be driven through. Refer to the photo's for suggested angles. If the side edges are too smooth you may have problems getting the celt to "hang in there". Peck overly smooth edges rough to get the bite you need.

Grinding and Polishing

Because hafting involves the constant insertation and removal of the celt from the mortise while you're banging away with abandon, the celt receives a lot of abuse and neglect at this stage. I usually peck and rough grind the celt to near finished form then fit it to the haft. Then lastly I do the final grinding and polishing.

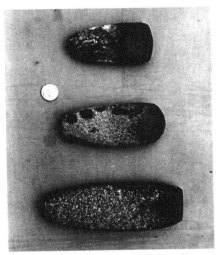

Top: beveled edge celt flaked to shape. Bottom two show extensive pecking.

Grinding can be done on any gritty rock that contains quartz or harder minerals. Not so hard, rotted rock can have a slurry of hard grit smeared on it as you wet grind. Grinding rocks that are too hard slick up while rotted ones constantly wear away exposing fresh sharp material. Some creeks and streams carry very hard mineral sands such as garnet, corundum and topaz. You'll need a hand lens and a book to find them. Finer grits are used in the last stage of grinding with particular attention paid to the bit area running back to where the celt makes contact with the wood. Stone can withstand tremendous compressive forces but is weak in tension. The smoother the surface is the stronger it is but I don't mean waxing it! Ignore any advice you hear about shining 'em up with wax, tallow or oil You want a true polish and that's obtained only by using elbow grease and sweat.

Within the secretive fraternity of faceters is held knowledge of more ways to shine up a stone than our abo ancestors knew ways to knap flint.

Examples of head shape and lateral view showing suggested bevel.

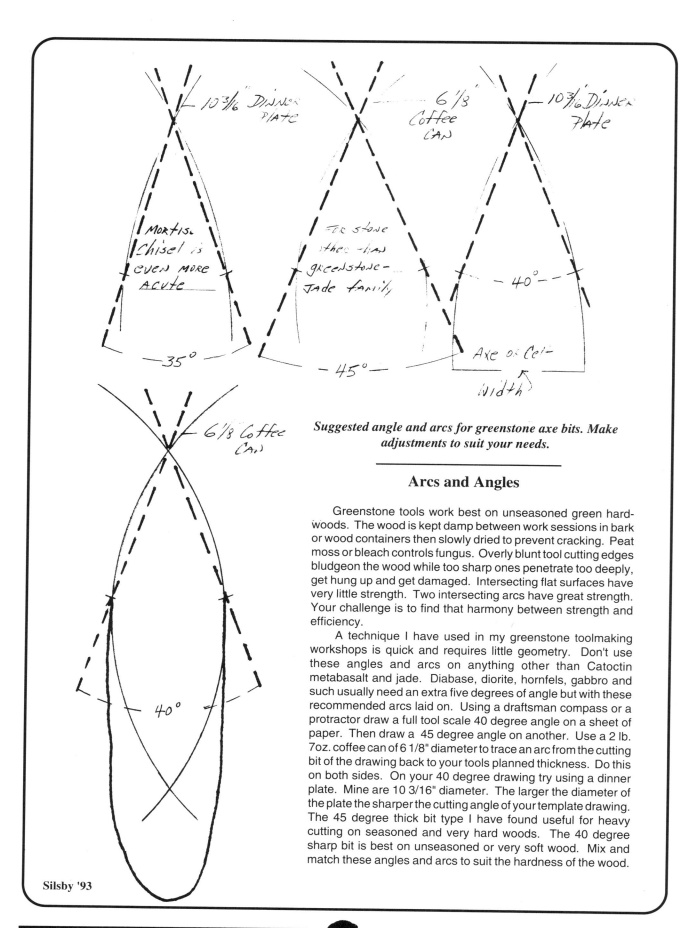

Suggested angle and arcs for greenstone axe bits. Make adjustments to suit your needs.

Arcs and Angles

Greenstone tools work best on unseasoned green hardwoods. The wood is kept damp between work sessions in bark or wood containers then slowly dried to prevent cracking. Peat moss or bleach controls fungus. Overly blunt tool cutting edges bludgeon the wood while too sharp ones penetrate too deeply, get hung up and get damaged. Intersecting flat surfaces have very little strength. Two intersecting arcs have great strength. Your challenge is to find that harmony between strength and efficiency.

A technique I have used in my greenstone toolmaking workshops is quick and requires little geometry. Don't use these angles and arcs on anything other than Catoctin metabasalt and jade. Diabase, diorite, hornfels, gabbro and such usually need an extra five degrees of angle but with these recommended arcs laid on. Using a draftsman compass or a protractor draw a full tool scale 40 degree angle on a sheet of paper. Then draw a 45 degree angle on another. Use a 2 lb. 7oz. coffee can of 6 1/8" diameter to trace an arc from the cutting bit of the drawing back to your tools planned thickness. Do this on both sides. On your 40 degree drawing try using a dinner plate. Mine are 10 3/16" diameter. The larger the diameter of the plate the sharper the cutting angle of your template drawing. The 45 degree thick bit type I have found useful for heavy cutting on seasoned and very hard woods. The 40 degree sharp bit is best on unseasoned or very soft wood. Mix and match these angles and arcs to suit the hardness of the wood.

Silsby '93

One particular "trick," practiced world wide for centuries, is to withhold water during the final few seconds of wet lap polishing. Many minerals respond by developing a brilliant glaze that has proven to be a very hard surface as well. The phenomenon is called Beilby's Flow and a few specialists in the field have proposed that under very high frictional forces molecules are ripped off of high points, changed, then bonded back to the surface at low points. All other polishing is the simple method of producing progressively smaller and finer scratches. Old, flint dust impregnated knapping pads of leather work great, dirty leather will do. Crush hard minerals to a fine powder, winnow out the grit and smear the finest powder on a damp leather pad. Rub like crazy for an hour longer than you think you possibly can stand and you will have a decent polish. Try crushing various rocks and minerals in you abo mortar and pestle until you find one that works. Refer to the Moh's scale of hardness in rock books as hard minerals work best.

Adzes - Top-left: Gouge bit hafted to honeysuckle bush handle. Right: Plano-convex head hafted to plum wood with suede and cinched with latigo.

Adzes

An adz is a flat bottomed ax turned sidwise. The top curved back of the bit is the critical area and should follow the same suggested angle and arc of an axe. The platter (lower arc) bottom side receives less force when used correctly. Any method of hafting that prevents compression between the bit and poll can be considered. Pinch the two ends together with force and you are in danger of buckling it. Wrapping with buckskin is the best or substitute suede leather. Both provide a good grip whereas rawhide is too slick for my taste. Once wrapped as tight as possible, give it a cinch wrap. After use the leather will stretch some so recinching is usually called for.

I prefer an angle of just less than 90 degrees between the handle and head. More acute angles work fine with razor sharp steel tools but not with stone ones.

Handles that are oval to rectangular allow you to control the cutting angle whereas round handles tend to be harder to manage. Smooth wood seems to be the best finish although built up handles of leather and cane work fine if smooth and friction free. A completed greenstone tool should have a scabbard made to protect the bit and someway of assuring that a fine touch-up whetstone accompany the tool wherever it is taken. Using a damaged bit for further work is inviting tool destruction.

A few types of adzes. Top row, second from left has proven to be the most efficient type for me.

MORTISING A CELT HANDLE
Photos By Scott Silsby

A

B

C

D

A. *A finished mortise in Bitternut Hickory. It took about an hour and an additional ten minutes of sawing and rasping with a quartzite knife to clean up.*

B. *Beveled edge celt hafted as a carpenter's hatchet ("hadzet")was used to cut this green hickory.*

C. *While an adze would work better here, the hatchet gets by. Chips of stone are death on cutting bits, hence the admonishment.*

D. *Handle is roughed out and ready to mortiise.*

E

F

E. A narrow bited chisel of greenstone. Pecked grooves help in holding.

F. An extremely tough mallet of Hop Hornbeam (Ironwood) is used to gently cut the mortise.

G. Hatchet and axe handles in various stages of production, with mortising chisel and mallet.

G

HAFTING A GROOVED OR FLAKED AXE

Cut down desired limb, sapling, or root. Trim handle to final length (not too long, one usually holds just under the head) cut forks or split to correct length by chopping or sawing against a solid log or tree.

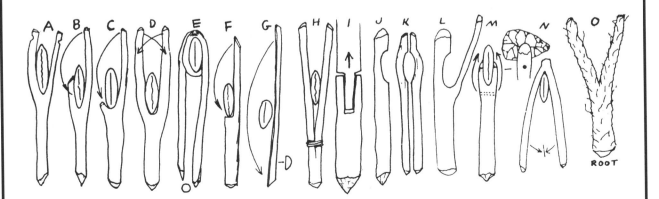

From Primitive Technology, Errett Callahan, 1987.

111

Live Tree Hafting - Scott Silsby

This photograph of the greenstone axe bit set in a bitternut hickory branch (two years growth) illustrates a long held misconception of stone tool technology by the general public. But now you know that you were not the only curious fool alive who pondered the possibilities of this highly impractical technique. I think I have a good amount of experience with trees having had a career dealing directly with them for a couple of decades not to mention a couple other decades as an avocational woodsman. I have met a lot of trees in my life yet I have never run across one with just the right sized hole for mortising an axe. I have seen plenty of rotted, insect or bird damaged ones but always the wrong shape or condition for axe hafting. Somewhere out there I would guess one exists but lacking it, I decided to make one just to learn from the experience.

Mental notes gleaned from this are as follows:
1. Pick a tree at a comfortable working height (I didn't).
2. Make sure you will have room to work at both ends of the mortise (I didn't).
3. Assure the tree (or limb) will retain enough strength to survive gutting it and still remain intact in a storm or from icing (I did).
4. Once the head is wedged in it must be held in until enough growth grips it as the wind moves the wood somewhat. (Eventually had to hammer it back in and bungee cord it.)
5. Guard your creation from vandals and thieves.
6. Plug gaps in the mortise with resin or gum to deter insects. (I used beeswax and replugged it as needed.)

Is it worth all the bother? Most likely not but stay tuned for further updates as the "creation" is turned into an axe after the upcoming sap flow allows bark stripping.

For those interested in prehistoric Native American examples I recommend an article by Gregory Perino which includes a photograph and drawings of several types including one that illustrates hafting incorporating secondary growth around the mortise. Whether it was cultivated or discovered is not clear. (Perino '79)

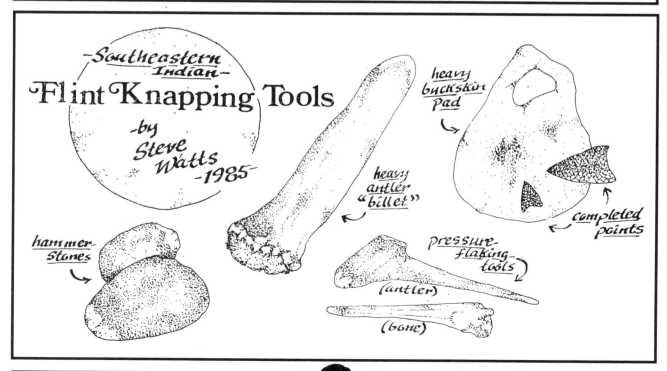

-Southeastern Indian-
Flint Knapping Tools
-by Steve Watts -1985-

hammer-stones

heavy antler "billet"

heavy buckskin pad

completed points

pressure-flaking-tools

(antler)

(bone)

A PEEK INTO THE PAST:
AN ANCIENT WOOD CARVING KIT CACHE
Text and Illustrations By Steve Allely © 1995

Ever wonder what some ancient tool kits might look like if you could go back in time and see one? If you're anything like me you've probably wondered about that sort of thing before a time or two and applied it to your favorite subject or particular area of interest.

Well thanks to a friend of mine by the name of Steve Wallman and his keen eye for archaeological clues, we have some pretty good insight on what is almost certainly an ancient wood carving kit. In brief, it consists of an elk antler splitting wedge, a beaver jaw or at least the remains of one, nine jasper flakes and a sandstone abrader. Steve first told me of this find, and how he felt certain that it was a wood carving kit, quite a number of years ago. Some time later I was able to actually see it for myself and had to agree. In short, you have tools for splitting, carving, gouging, scraping, sawing, planing, rasping and sanding. Personally I'd have to say that if this isn't a wood carving kit, then I don't know what one is. Later, he graciously gave it to me since he felt it would mean more to me than him and I've been itching to write something about it ever since.

This find was made in the forested region southeast of LaPine Oregon a number of years ago in the middle of a logging operation. This region of Oregon sits on the immediate east side of the Cascade range and is a relatively flat area interspersed by volcanic features such as cinder cones, buttes, and periodic rimrock and lava outcroppings along with a few isolated springs. The area is covered with ponderosa pine and lodge pole and lies just to the west of where the tree line stops and the sage and juniper take over to form the northwestern edge of the Great Basin. It's likely that the people who lived in this area were quite migratory and their yearly routine probably led them west into the forested regions and up into the Cascade range during the summer months and then back out into the Great Basin region just to the east to spend the winter much like the herds of game animals still do even to this day.

The site in which the find was made was near a spring as most sites in the area are. There is a great deal of pumice and ash throughout the entire region that overlays many of the older archaeological sites, from both Mt. Mazama to the south and from Newberry Crater only a short distance to the north. Usually the ash and pumice along with the duff on the forest floor keep sites buried and fairly undisturbed but logging operations had uncovered this particular one as they often do.

Steve happened to be looking over the site and noticed in a section of uncovered ground something that didn't look quite right. Upon further careful investigation he found a small cache pit with the items stashed in it as shown.

The timely discovery of this cache was fortunate since the heavy equipment in use would have surely destroyed the items within and scattered them if they hadn't been removed. As it was, the sandstone abrader had already been broken by being run over prior to its being found.

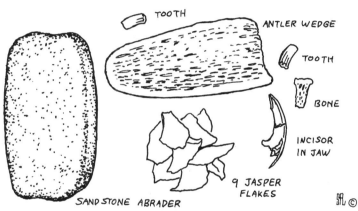

Figure 1. Position of items found in cache.

A brief description of the items from the cache is as follows: The elk antler splitting wedge is 5" long by approximately 2 1/4" wide and is fairly decomposed as are the rest of the bone items found. The nature of the decomposition makes it appear as if it had been eaten away by acid to some degree and it's original surface highly pitted and etched away. Possibly this was due to an acidic content in the surrounding soil. It's outer surface and inner marrow are still readily apparent though.

All that was left of the beaver jaw was one incisor tooth incased in a small amount of jaw bone, two molars and another fragment of bone which may be a part of the same jaw. Beaver teeth along with other rodent teeth have long been a documented part of wood carving for years among

(more)

many tribal groups. I'd read this before in various places and also had it confirmed by Errett Callahan in a recent phone conversation that I had with him about the widespread use of beaver teeth amongst native peoples. I have a modern beaver jaw and incisor tooth that is nearly identical in size and shape to the old one. The rear teeth or molars, in the modern jaw are identical to the two found in the cache, although there are a total of four rear teeth in a beaver lower jaw so two are missing. It's possible that they may have been removed by the former owner or had fallen out or were disturbed and scattered in later years by burrowing rodents, or by the disturbance that uncovered the cache in the first place. Experimenting with my beaver jaw led me to wrap the base of the incisors with sinew for reinforcement, smooth off the rough portions of the jaw bone for a more comfortable grip and then wrap it with a thick thong of brain tanned leather. It makes an admirable wood working tool, and is most effective if the wood is still green.

The nine jasper flakes all found clutched together, are a brownish yellow heat treated jasper and appear to be percussion flakes from biface manufacture. What's interesting about sites in this region is that obsidian was almost exclusively used for knives and points due to the availability of several good sources of it nearby, only 25 miles or less, while jasper and agate was generally used only for such items as drills, gravers, and other "hard use" bone and woodworking tools. The reason of course is that obsidian while being extremely sharp, doesn't hold up nearly as well as does the harder non obsidian materials. So here we have jasper flakes that could be used for carving, sawing, drilling, scraping, and planing. None of them had been altered or used yet in anyway and appeared to be "fresh" with no edge wear apparent. Perhaps they were intended to be altered into whatever carving or shaping tools were needed at a later date.

The sandstone abrader is 6" long, 2 3/4" wide and is 3/4" thick. It's really the equivalent of a modern sanding block in about 60 grit. It was broken as was mentioned earlier probably by heavy logging equipment passing over it and was restored by Steve Wallman. This is definitely an abrader and not a misidentified mano used in conjunction with a metate. It's made from a very gritty and abrasive sandstone and shows definite use wear on both sides and along the two longer squared edges. I would tend to think that this would be used more after the wooden item being shaped was dry since sanding while wood is still green simply loads up sandstone (or sandpaper for that matter), with wet wood fiber. So quite possibly this is a final finishing and shaping tool at least for wooden items. Additionally, it could be used for bone and antler items as well and may well have been used to shape and sharpen the elk antler splitting wedge it was found with.

It's unfortunate that this find couldn't be more precisely dated with some possible obsidian hydration dates from the associated lithic scatter nearby but the disturbed nature of the site makes this speculative at best. There were some fragments of point bases also found nearby which are quite old, possibly several thousand years or more but since they weren't found in direct association with the cache and could have come from a deeper level in the site, its difficult to be certain. It's quite possible that the cache is very old and may be well over several thousand years, but no real firm date can be assigned.

So there you have it. A splitting wedge which was an important wood working technique amongst native peoples especially for removing the initial piece of wood to be worked, a beaver jaw, with the incisor tooth for carving and gouging, nine jasper flakes for carving, scraping, planing or whatever else you choose to do with them, and a sandstone abrader for rasping and sanding with the dual purpose of being useful for bone and antler as well as wood. All of us who are interested in aboriginal life skills are indebted to Steve Wallman for granting us a glimpse into an ancient tool kit.

LEFT - Figure 2. The wood working cache found by Steve Wallman. A - Beaver incisor and molar teeth showing outline of lower jaw bone. B - Bone fragment which may be part of jaw bone. C - Nine heat treated jasper flakes. D - Elk antler splitting wedge. E - Sandstone abrader. All items shown to scale.

Iceman's Tool Kit

Scraper

Blade

Flint tools found in waist pouch. Drawn to scale from photos in The Man In The Ice, by Konrad Spindler, 1994

Drill

0 1 2 3 4 5

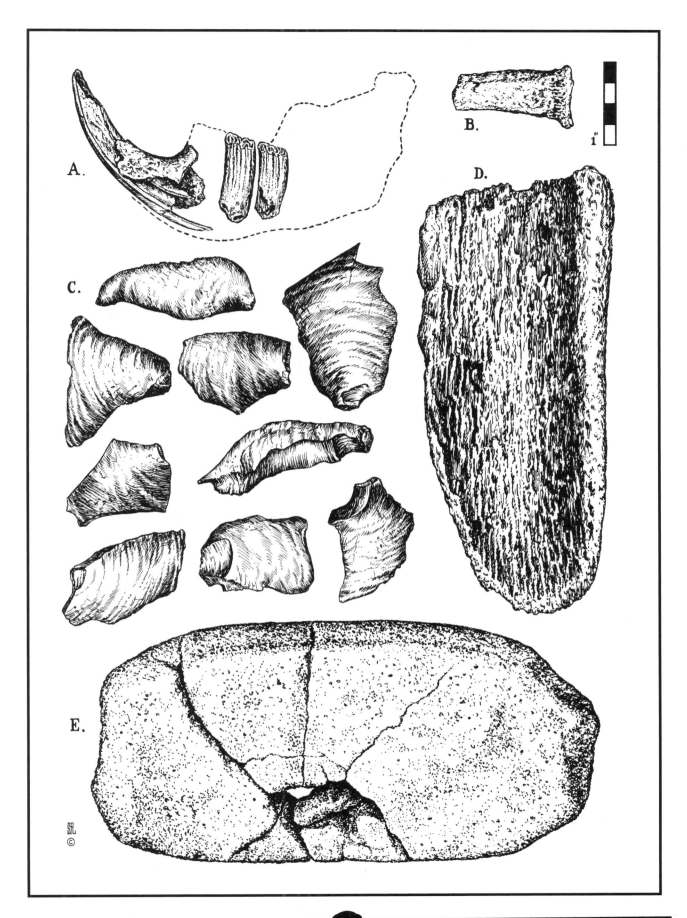

B.

C.

D.

E.

1"

FUNCTIONAL MOTIONS *
Working Wood With Stone Tools
Text and Illustrations By Errett Callahan

This article is provided for those who wonder what happens to stone when it's used to work wood. It has been taken from Experimental Archaeological Papers #4, June 1976 (APE#4) edited by Errett Callahan. These were papers compiled from the field studies of participants in Phase I and II of the Pamunkey Project (Virginia Commonwealth University Field School), a landmark effort in this country in the field of living/experimental archaeology.

This information is provided for two reasons: 1. to provide scholars and practitioners with solid research data about edge damage, and 2. to establish a model of what can be produced by adding the scientific process to good field work. ED

I. Percussion
A. *Rectilinear (in a near-straight line downwards, up and downwards, or otherwise)*

1. Chopping (dicing) - uni-directional arced movement usually directed downward into objective piece at oblique to perpendicular angle (45° - 90°) to that piece, as severing a standing or fallen sapling, breaking sod, or dicing carrots, etc.

2. Chop-sliding - uni-directional movement usually directed downward into objective piece at oblique angle (30° - 45°) blending into a pushing of the tool's edge along the cut away from the body, as severing a standing sapling.

B. Random

3. Agitating (tossing, spinning, shuffling) - bi- or multi-directional movement of 2 or more objects at random angles (0 - 360°) one against the other in air or liquid media, perhaps with aid of a container, as tossing flakes up and down in a basket for a musical rattle.

II. Pressure
C. *Longitudinal (parallel to lineal edge)*

4. Cutting (incising) - uni-directional movement parallel to lineal edge and usually directed toward body with tool held near perpendicular (90°) to objective piece, as cutting a sizzling tenderloin steak.

5. Sawing - bi-directional movement parallel to lineal edge, with the tool held near perpendicular to objective piece, tilting from side to side (80° - 100°) as/if needed to widen the gap and prevent binding, as severing a small branch from a sapling.

D. *Transverse (perpendicular to lineal edge)*

6. Scraping, uni-directional - uni-directional movement perpendicular to lineal edge, directed either toward or away from body, with tool held at 45° - 90° to objective piece, as removing scales from a fish or fleshing a hide.

7. Scraping, bi-directional - bi-directional movement perpendicular to ineal edge, directed both toward and away from body, or from side to side, with tool held at 90° to objective piece, as scraping bark from a willow twig.

8. Whittling (carving) - uni-directional arced movement, near perpendicular to lineal edge, directed away from body, with tool held, by one end, at up to 30° to objective piece, as sharpening a pencil by hand.

9. Planing (shaving, away) - uni-directional movement, generally not arched, perpendicular to lineal edge, directed away from body with a pushing motion, with tool held, at both sides, at up to 30° to objective piece, as planing down an arrow shaft with a snapped blade, flake, or biface.

10. Drawing (shaving, toward) - uni-directional movement, arched or not, near perpendicular to lineal edge, directed toward body with a pulling motion, with tool held by one end or both sides, at up to 30° to objective piece, as sharpening a pencil toward the body.

11. Digging - uni-directional movement perpendicular to lineal edge, usually directed toward body with tool held near or beyond perpendicular (90° - 135°) to objective piece, as scooping out a hole in the ground. May accompany initial chopping movement.

E. *Longitudinal - transverse (partly parallel and partly perpendicular to lineal edge)*

12. Rasping - bi-directional movement at oblique and varying angles to lineal edge, with tool held near perpendicular to objective piece, tearing fibers in a sawing/scraping manner, as rasping down a tool handle.

F. *Perpendicular (perpendicular to center plane of tool)*

13. Trampling - uni-directional movement perpendicular to center plane (or to any given surface, perhaps varying over time) and perpendicular to objective piece (ground), possibly accompanied by sudden force, as walking or stomping on a pile of flakes by man or beast. When a flake is pressed against another flake or stone, the latter may act as an anvil, causing fracturing either at an edge or across the center of the flake.

G. *Revolutionary (revolving around longitudinal axis)*

14. Boring (drilling, twisting) - bi-directional movement revolving around longitudinal axis and focused into a single given point or area, directed downward into objective piece at near 90°, as piercing an eye hole in a bone needle.

Functional Motions and Expected Damage

Functional Motions

Expected Damage

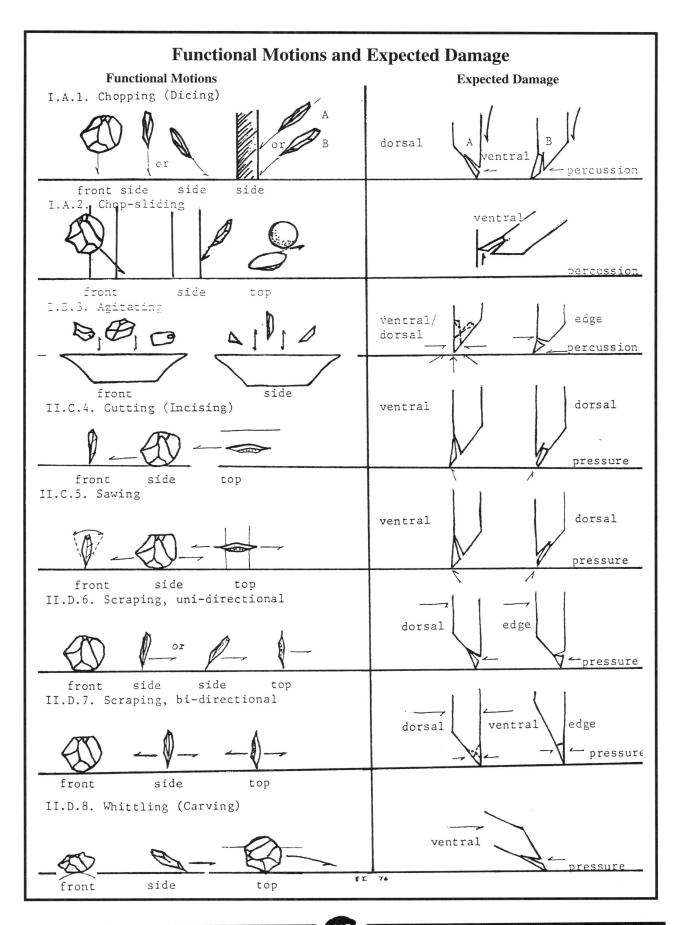

I.A.1. Chopping (Dicing)

dorsal   A   B

ventral   percussion

front   side   side   side

I.A.2. Chop-sliding

ventral   percussion

front   side   top

I.B.3. Agitating

ventral/ dorsal   edge   percussion

front   side

II.C.4. Cutting (Incising)

ventral   dorsal   pressure

front   side   top

II.C.5. Sawing

ventral   dorsal   pressure

front   side   top

II.D.6. Scraping, uni-directional

dorsal   edge   pressure

front   side   side   top

II.D.7. Scraping, bi-directional

dorsal   ventral   edge   pressure

front   side   top

II.D.8. Whittling (Carving)

ventral   pressure

front   side   top

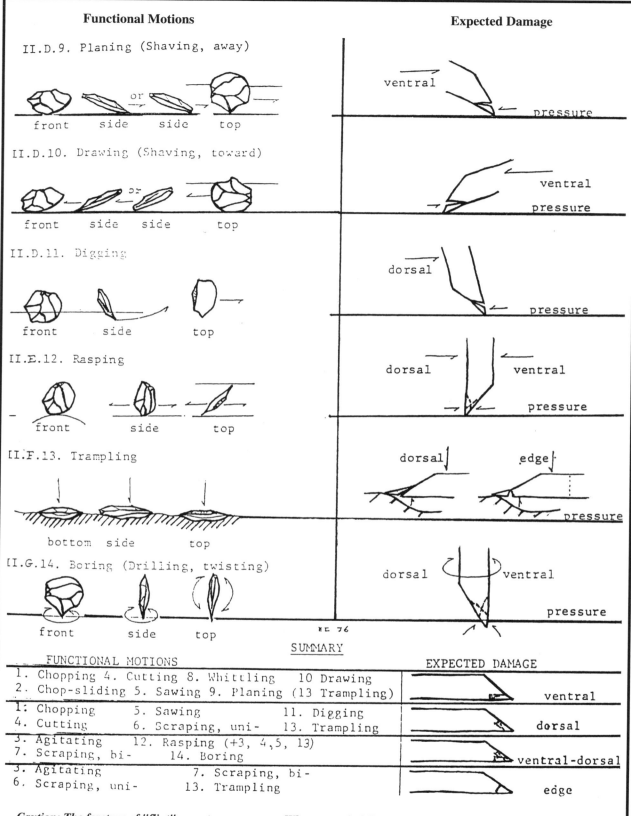

Functional Motions	Expected Damage

II.D.9. Planing (Shaving, away)

front   side   side   top

ventral — pressure

II.D.10. Drawing (Shaving, toward)

front   side   side   top

ventral — pressure

II.D.11. Digging

front   side   top

dorsal — pressure

II.E.12. Rasping

front   side   top

dorsal   ventral — pressure

II.F.13. Trampling

bottom   side   top

dorsal   edge — pressure

II.G.14. Boring (Drilling, twisting)

front   side   top   FIG 76

dorsal   ventral — pressure

SUMMARY

FUNCTIONAL MOTIONS			EXPECTED DAMAGE	
1. Chopping 4. Cutting 8. Whittling 10 Drawing				ventral
2. Chop-sliding 5. Sawing 9. Planing (13 Trampling)				
1. Chopping 5. Sawing 11. Digging				dorsal
4. Cutting 6. Scraping, uni- 13. Trampling				
3. Agitating 12. Rasping (+3, 4, 5, 13)				ventral-dorsal
7. Scraping, bi- 14. Boring				
3. Agitating 7. Scraping, bi-				edge
6. Scraping, uni- 13. Trampling				

Caution: The fracture of "flint" operates as a system. Whereas each different functional motion might produce slightly different wear characteristics under the controlled conditions above, more often than not a number of inter-related mechanical and micromorphological factors interact to cause any given type of damage.

Wood Tool Basics

By David Wescott

THE WOOD AGE

Not only is there speculation and evidence to support a developmental Bone Age, there are also a number of supporters for a Wood Age. Nowhere is this level of development more evident than in Australia. This phase of development was not only practiced archaically, it remains as the foundation of Aboriginal technology today. The Wood Age is proclaimed by many to be the "greatest untold story of mankind". As we begin the story we immediately begin to lose parts along the way...we speculate on what is in and what is not in the record. The lack of wooden tools in the record is the start of the process of leaving it out of the big picture entirely. But if we accept the Stone Age record we also need to accept the fact that these stone tools related directly to plant/wooden tools - they were used to process plants or plants were used as tools to process new tools. In order to make the record complete we should add the development of wood-based cultures and technologies to the record. The problem with this idea is that there is precious little prehistoric wooden evidence upon which to base the story... there has been no preservation to give us clues. Or has there?

Too many times we think that unless the record is dug up from beneath 200,000 years of dust that it doesn't exist. This is a difficult process to support when we have living archives among us today. We need to avoid thinking of these stewards as vestiges of the Stone Age, they are as modern as you and I. They have simply chosen not to adopt the same contrivances and distractions that we have. The fact that they have chosen to live as they do, and that their entire basis for doing what they do is based on the directions of the old ones, we need to take a careful look at what they have to share with us. Many areas of the world, especially in those places that have shown late or no development of stone tools, were covered with plants that produced edges every bit as sharp as stone. Many cultures used bamboo to create razor-sharp edges that are not in the record. We assume that they were primitive or slow developers, when the truth is that they probably chose and continue to choose to do what they do for reasons that were best for them.

Early ethnographic reports were more interested in the products of the culture than the processes of the culture. We have volumes of information on customs and material culture, but can only speculate on the daily tasks that drove them. We can speculate how things were used and why, but it is only through experimentation and comparison with living links to the old ones that we come to a more clear

understanding. It's time for us to look to the keepers of the Wood Age for the clues they can provide that shed light on this great quest for rediscovery. (Rediscovery ? Hell, we were never lost !)

We need to realize that technology is evolutionary. And in order for there to be levels of technology for us to use today, those technologies must have had ancestors....food gathering tools possibly lead next to defensive tools. Since materials were only available in their natural form and needed to be processed by hand, it is those processes and relationships with the natural materials we need to experience for ourselves. For years ethnobotanists have championed the legitimate complaint that plants have been left out of the story of the foundation of life. Plants manage and store the energy from the sun. If we only had rocks and no plants we wouldn't have soil to stand on or oxygen to breath. We also need to realize that there is no more direct link to the primal times than those plants that still survive which are relatively unchanged from their very beginnings.

Plants were the most familiar connection to the earth for early man. They came down from the trees...the first nursery. They provided refuge, shade, food, and ultimately tools.

WOOD TOOL BASICS

The first wooden tools were most likely designed to dig, reach, poke, or hit. They were field expedient (easily made, used and discarded) but evolved into prized tools that when cared for could last from father to son. Wood is sub-

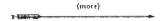

STAGING SEQUENCE FOR WOOD TOOLS
STAGE 1 - Obtain Raw Materials - select from catagory 1-5
STAGE 2 - Creating The Blank - break, throw, bash, split, pound, strip, burn
STAGE 3 - Creating The Preform - strip, bend/straighten, hack, burn, scrape, season
STAGE 4 - Shaping - carve, fine scrape, thin, bevel, sand to specific shape
STAGE 5 - Finishing - burnish, grease/oil, fire harden

ject to weathering and aging and must be "treated" on a regular basis. The craft of wood working beyond simple tools was not a daily task, thus making it something that could be done with forethought and skill.

The Lower Paleo Tool Kit contained such items as digging sticks -found/expedient, beveled, chopped and shaped, fire hardened - simple spears, and gathering poles used to reach high spots or into holes, and bug switches.

Selecting the Materials- Green / Wet vs Dead / Seasoned

Green woods afford you the ability to work them with stone tools. Once the wood dies or seasons it becomes very hard and difficult to work. Therefore woodworking with stone tools should be done while the wood is green or wet. This allows the stone to cut the soft fiber of the wood. However, for finishing or final shaping that involves scraping, grinding or polishing, the wood must be allowed to dry adequately. Woods that are worked green can be seasoned more rapidly by shaping the tool roughly and evenly, and either allowing it to dry, or forcing it to dry by heat treating. The process of seasoning or heat treating is very important for pointed implements, as dry wood holds a point and penetrates better than green wood.

Greenwoods are pliable and springy. They can be used as is, bent to form after rough shaping, or they can be heated for straightening or bending. The sap in the wood allows it to bend more freely without cracking or splitting. Dead, dry wood is good for knife handles and other tools that need to be shaped, carved or ground.

Collecting the Materials

- Small twigs and flexible shoots are simply twisted from their source and used as is, to bind and attach components, or bent and woven to form simple open-weave containers. They may also be pounded to process fibers used in other ways. They may be sliced or split by sharp edges of stone, bone or shell. Broken branches with sharp points, large knots, or other useful natural shapes may be used as is. Branches or saplings being collected for straightening into spears are best done green. A hand axe or chopper may be used to remove small limbs, outer bark or otherwise shape larger branches or billets (sections of logs that have been chopped or sawed to length). Billets may be split by pounding an axe or chopper with a wooden maul into the end grain. Billets that have been split and seasoned may be split again and reduced down to the preform that best suits them to shaping.

Note: When splitting wood, if you want to end up with nice straight splits, always split the wood in the middle of the mass - ie. split a round billet in half, split a half in half again, creating quarters, etc. Do not try to split a round into thirds. Any splits made other than in half will have a tendency to force the tool away from the center and run out at an angle, creating an uneven split.

When cutting saplings or small branches, bend the wood away from the side being cut. This puts tension on the fibers and allows the tool to cut through the material much more quickly and evenly.

For simple field tools you may take the bark off to

season the wood more quickly. If checking or cracking from uneven drying is not a problem, simply dry the piece in the sun for a day to remove excess moisture from the outer layers. This method has seasonal considerations to be aware of. When the sap is up, bark peels quite easily, but when it is down, the bark will hold on tightly making it difficult if not impossible to remove without a lot of extra work. Bark that can be removed in sheets can often be split for bindings or weaving, while shreddy barks may be used for bedding, clothing or tinder.

LOWER PALEO TOOL KIT - WOOD
Staging Sequence for Wooden Tools
For tools found in the first tool kit. Tools requiring minimal alteration

Stage 1 - Obtaining Raw Material - the nature of the project determines the choice of materials.

Category 1 - live and standing, dead and standing, or dead and down

Category 2 - dried or seasoned

Category 3 - rigid or flexible

Category 4 - new shoots or mature growth

Category 5 - soft wood or hard wood

Stage 2 - Creating The Blank - burning, breaking, throwing, bashing, splitting, pounding or otherwise collecting or preparing the material for shaping. The blank may be used whole (as is), rough shaped to a general form, or split for further reduction. All woods require some level of cutting or chopping to remove the desired piece of material from its source. Burning may be used, but has more limits. Ripping and breaking shoots and branches will work for smaller pieces of material. Dry wood can be thrown or levered in the crotch of a tree to section it up. Longer pieces that need to be shortened in a controlled way can either be burned, chopped or sawed (cutting across the grain). Billets (sections of wood) can be worked from this point, split lengthwise to reduce the mass and/or access inner materials, or seasoned to be worked later. (Note - working wood with stone tools is best done green. Since seasoned woods are much harder, it is likely that very little seasoning was done in the form of large billets, but rather were shaped preforms that could be dried quickly and finished after they dried slightly)

STAGE 3 - Creating The Preform
- strip, bend/straighten, hack, burn, scrape, season. The staging sequence for wood is much like that for bone, except for the added element of seasoning. The variability of wood in choosing between those that are green or dead, wet or dry, fresh or seasoned, rigid or flexible, hard or soft can determine how it is to be worked and for what projects it can be used. The complexities of wood are well covered in the pursuit of Paleo skills. The one exception is the need to work within the grain when working the back of a bow stave. Since we stop our progression short of the bow and pottery, it will not be addressed in this book.

Seasoning enters into the sequence, but is limited to its being controlled for the variety of tools and functions in the Paleo Tool Kits. The majority of tools are field expedient and can be done without waiting a long time for materials to season or cure, or can be "forced" by heat treating The stages may be combined (field expedient digger from a broken limb is only one step), steps can be skipped (harvested saplings twisted and wrapped to form a finished handle), but seldom are they rearranged. Thought and action must be sequential for best results.

STAGE 4 - Shaping
- carve, fine scrape, thin, bevel, sand to specific shape - **Digging Stick--** Expedient wooden tools are not in the archaeological record, but they most likely predate the Stone Age. Functional wooden tools can be made quickly and simply without the aid of stone, but tools that need to withstand hard and repeated use bring to bear the application of stone tools to create a more efficient wood tool. A simple broken branch used as a digging stick will work well for a while. But after digging in the damp and rocky ground for fresh spring bulbs, the tip becomes soft and pliable, and is no longer useful. However, a nicely beveled digging stick with a fire hardened tip that has been scraped, greased and burnished will last for much longer without needing to be reworked.

Throwing Stick - - the beginning of projectiles extending your power and increasing it beyond yourself - eloving from round to flat and straight to curved - heavy ended stick - the center of the length of the stick and the point of balance are not the same- spins off center

At this point of development any dense stick that would carry a wollop will do. The process of manufacture is simple, like that of a digging stick. In fact, a digging stick will work as a throwing stick and perhaps was used on occasion. A gatherer wouldn't hesitate becoming a hunter simply because he was carrying the wrong stick.

STAGE 5 - Finishing
- burnish, grease/oil, fire harden
Fire-hardened Spear - Primary weapon for a quater of a million years - spear used into the upper paleo times in Europe

The best tools are ultimately seasoned and dried for the longest lasting service. Since working green woods is best with stone tools, you will need to dry the wood as quickly as possible to use it as a tool. If you have the luxury of time, you can simply let nature do it. However, waiting for wood to season isn't an option at this point.

Once the tool is shaped to a rough blank stage, it can be heated near or under a fire to drive-off excess moisture. It is not held in the fire or allowed to char unless there is so much material to be scraped off that the inner layers are protected from the flame - charring weakens the wood. Forcing the stick into the super heated dirt under the fire or into the ash at the base of the fire exposes it to heat, but does not allow air to get to it, so it can't burn. As the outer layers dry out the stick can be scraped into a more refined shape - bevel, point, etc. The wood will be hot, but have a slightly damp feel to it as layers are removed.

BASIC NEEDS	TECHNOLOGY	MATERIAL
FIRE	CUT, SPLIT, DRILL	SOFT, HARD, DEAD
HAND DRILL	SHAPE/GRIND	DRY, NON-RES
	JOIN/BIND	BARK, FIBER
		BRANCHES, STEMS
SHELTER	SPLIT, TWIST, CHOP	SAPLINGS, FLEXIBLE
MATS	GRIND, PEEL, CARVE	LIVE, THATCH
BED	LACE, BIND	DEAD SPIKE
WILLOW FRAME	MAUL/STAKE	ROOTS, GRASS, VINES
SANDLES		
HAFTING	BEND, NOTCH	
BASKET	CUT, AWLS, SAW	DRY
BURN BOWL	BURN, CHOP, CURE, SPLIT, WEDGE,	
	BLOW PIPE, CONTROL, SCRAPE	
DIGGING STICK		
RABBIT STICK	BRANCH, LIMB- BEND, HEAT, CHOP,	
ATLATL, HANDLES	SLICE, SAW, BURN GLUE, TIE, SAND, GREASE	

A Simple Shaving Horse For Bowmaking
Text, Photos and Illustration By Douglas Macleod

Finished shaving horse with bow in place. To decrease the angle of the bench, simply shorten the dimension of the upright.

Anyone who has ever seen or used a shaving horse will call to mind the traditional dumbhead type. It's origin dates back to 1556 in Germany according to Roy Underhill's **Woodwright's Work Book** (1986). German woodworkers called them a "Schnitzelbank". Later American chairmakers referred to a shaving horse as a "drawbreak" and used the bench for leg and rung production. With a drawknife occupying two hands, the foot operated clamp was also useful for dressing split oak roof shakes, making rake or ax handles and more recently is found to be well suited for bowmaking.

My interest in building shaving horses began as a resident of Errett Callahan's "Cliffside" cottage. He had asked if I could build two traditional red oak horses', based on Underhill's instructional article in **The Woodworker's Shop**. I then began to look into variations of the principle by studying models from books, living history museums and arts and craft fairs. I sought a design that would not have the limitations of a "fixed bench", in relation to the assorted sizes of people using a shaving horse. Dr. Callahan's concern was to furnish students a bench that was easy to store and transport, lightweight and adjustable.

Last fall, a friend and I came up with a simple design to meet these requirements; borrowing from **Fine Woodworking** magazine (March/April 1982) and the first **Foxfire** book. Students of a ladderback chair workshop in North Carolina used rough sawn boards supported by a clamp at one end and weighted with a rock on the ground at the other. The seat was separate from the clamp. The only changes we made were to use lighter kiln dried lumber, make the board length shorter and to stake it with iron pipe. This more conventional type shaving horse allows direct leg leverage in comparison to the more awkward under-the-bench leg position with a traditional horse.

To quickly and easily build a 2x10 portable shaving horse; cut two 12 1/4" cross pieces. Attach these blocks at the top and bottom of two 30" 2x4 legs, as though rungs of a ladder. Drill pilot holes for the screws to prevent splitting.

Attach a 9 1/4" 2 x 4 block at the bottom of the clamp, flush with the ends of the legs for added strength and smoother travel.

Next measure down 6" from the top of the clamp and drill a 1/2" hole, on center, in the sides of the clamp legs and ream a bit larger as dowels swell with humidity. This measurement provides a 1 1/2" clamp opening for finish work. Drill another two holes at 7 1/2" for a clamp opening of 3 1/2" for rougher shaving on a larger stave. A 6 1/2" measurement may be ideal for both.

Then drill two 1/2" holes into the edges of a six foot 2x10, approximately 8 1/2" from one end (on center) and ream about 4" deep. Insert dowels through clamp legs into the 2x10. With a 1 1/8" spade drill bit, drill a hole about 5" from the other end of the 2x10 to accommodate the 1" pipe stake. Drill holes through the pipe with a 5/16" metal bit, beginning at 22" and continue every 8 to 10", depending on rocky or soft soil. Drive the pipe into the hole in the 2x10 and insert a 16d nail, or the like, through the pipe to prevent the board from riding up the stake while working on the bow. Additional weight is required when drawknifing a rough stave

Note the position of use and the securing peg.

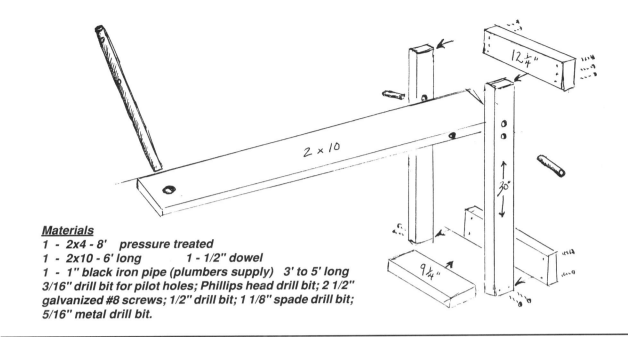

Materials
1 - 2x4 - 8'   pressure treated
1 - 2x10 - 6' long   1 - 1/2" dowel
1 - 1" black iron pipe (plumbers supply) 3' to 5' long
3/16" drill bit for pilot holes; Phillips head drill bit; 2 1/2"
galvanized #8 screws; 1/2" drill bit; 1 1/8" spade drill bit;
5/16" metal drill bit.

if the stake works loose. A longer stake might solve this problem.

Use any seat 20" - 24" height or whatever is suitable to work comfortably. If the bowstave slides toward you while working it, use a "chock" to raise the work behind the clamphead or cut an inverted "v" into the bottom edge of the top crosspiece to catch knots or irregularities in the stave. To prevent the stave from swinging from side to side while drawshaving; us two 16d nails driven into the 2x10 to hold the work stationary. Attach strings to dowels and chock to keep readily accessible.

David Wescott Photos

Full-size shaving horses may be made from natural forms, dimension lumber, or finely crafted from native woods.

The Three-Stick Roycroft Packframe

Text, Photos and Illustrations By Dick Baugh

How would you like a pack frame that is comfortable, strong, and can be made from natural materials in less than 1/2 hour? We were introduced to the Roycroft pack by Mors Kochansky at the Rabbitstick Rendezvous a few years ago.

Its an excellent lesson in self sufficiency, outdoor survival skills, knifecraft, lashing, multiple use of an object (blanket) and use of natural materials. What more do you want? But is it primitive? I don't know if our stone age ancestors actually made this type of pack frame. We do know, however, that the "Iceman", whose remains were found after 5300 years in the Alps between Italy and Austria, had with him a wood pack frame(1,2,3. See drawing also). The archaeologists have released very few details on his pack frame but say that it was an inverted U shape. I also saw a photo taken in the Himalayas early in the 1900's of a simple inverted U-shaped pack frame. The Koreans have been using A-frame packs for centuries.

Essentially we are lashing together a triangular wood frame, wrapping our belongings in a blanket and tying the bundle to the frame. A single piece of thick cordage is then used as combination shoulder straps and waist band

The Frame

The FrameCut three sticks for the frame. They should be about as thick as your thumb. The length of the bottom piece should be the width of your buttocks. Ideally it should also be slightly curved to fit your back. The length of the two side pieces should be equal to or slightly longer than the distance from your buttocks to the back of your head. I have heard of other ways to select the lengths but this works for me. In the past I have used green willow (*Salix sp.*) because it was available in the correct diameter, straight, plentiful and easy to cut and if necessary, bend. The Iceman's pack frame was made from hazelnut and larch. Hazelnut is a much tougher wood than willow. The three sticks are held together by a combination of joints and lashing. Figure 1 shows detailed dimensions of the pack that works best for me. As a reference point I am 5' 8" tall and weigh 140 pounds. If the pack frame is too short then a greater fraction of the weight will be carried by your

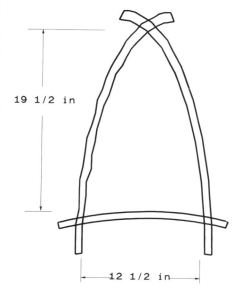

19 1/2 in

12 1/2 in

Figure 1.

shoulders. If it is too long then the shoulder straps will be very loose and the load will wobble from side to side.

Figure 2 shows two different kinds of joint that can be used to hold the sticks together, the lap (Abe Lincoln) joint or the butterfly joint, another Mors Kochansky original (4). I don't see much difference between the two but the lap joint is possibly more appropriate if you have weak wood and strong cordage whereas the butterfly joint works well if you have stronger wood and/or weaker cordage. My frame uses a lap joint on top and butterfly joints on the two bottom joints.

The lashing material can be any kind of vegetable fiber cordage or rawhide. It doesn't even have to be very strong if the joints are tight. One joint on my pack is put together with finely shredded cattail leaf fiber, another with New Zealand flax and the third with willow bark cordage. Figure 3 shows one possible way of lashing. It isn't very critical since most of the strength should come from the joint.

The original strap for my pack frame was made from a worn out Volvo seat belt plus a piece of nylon rope. Strong, durable and comfortable but it wasn't very primitive. The strap I am now using is two-ply shredded cattail (*Typha sp.*) leaf rope. It is made with the middle part, used for the shoulder straps, thicker than the ends. For comfort the straps should be at least one inch (2.54 cm) in diameter. The straps should taper down to 1/2 inch after they leave the shoulders to facilitate tying them around your waist.

Making straps out of cattail leaves is a good lesson in cordage techniques. Making a piece of cordage can be an abstract exercise which doesn't mean much if you have no specific application for the cordage however making a piece of cordage for a particular application combines the "how to make it" with the "What do I use it for after I've made it?". For optimum results gather the cattail leaves late in the growing season, before they have died and turned brown (5). Shred them into narrow strips. A coarse "comb" made by driving nails into a board is a useful tool for the shredding. Otherwise it can be done by hand. Finely shredded fibers will be stronger and more flexible.

After shredding the fibers should be dried and then moistened before twining.

Three-ply braided versus two-ply twined straps: take your choice. The important things are that the cattail leaves should be shredded finely to give flexibility and the straps should be thick enough to give comfort.

Packing and tying on the load: You want to pack your load in such a way that it is comfortable and everything is readily accessible without having to take it all apart. The

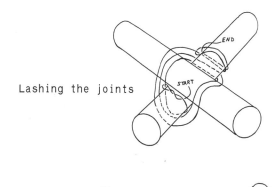

Lashing the joints

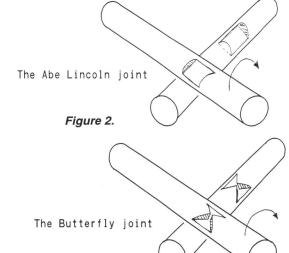

The Abe Lincoln joint

Figure 2.

The Butterfly joint

best way I have found so far is to wrap up your gear the same way you would a baby. Another analogy is to say the blanket is folded like an envelope. Fold your blanket into a square and place it on top of the pack frame with the corners up, down, left and right. place something soft such as a coat or sweater at the bottom for padding where it will contact your lower back. This is very important. Otherwise the crosspiece digs into your lower back. Put the rest of your gear on the blanket. Fold up the bottom corner, and then wrap the left and right corners around the

gear. Last, fold the top corner down. This way it is easy to access anything by lifting up the top corner.

Gear secured to the pack frame.

Tying the pack to the frame: Begin securing the load to the pack frame by first tying a rope to the center of the crosspiece. The load is then tied on in accordance with Figure 4. It is critical to tighten the rope sufficiently that some of the soft padded portion of the pack protrudes through to keep the crosspiece from contacting your lower back. That is shown in Figure 5.

The pack all ready to go.

(more)

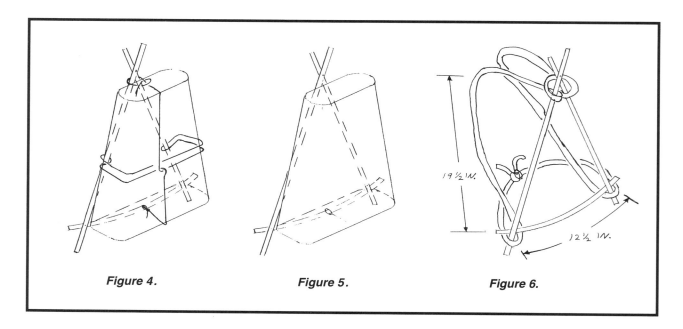

Figure 4.   **Figure 5.**   **Figure 6.**

Securing the straps: Secure the center of the straps to the top of the pack as shown in Figure 6. It can be done as illustrated or with a "lark's head" knot. The straps then go over your shoulders, around the bottom of the side pieces and then are tied around your waist. Once the straps are tied together you can leave the knot in place and remove the pack simply by slipping the straps off the bottom of the side pieces.

Field testing: My first real experience with a Roycroft pack was on a two week BOSS walkabout in south eastern Utah. I was using the Roycroft whereas my compadres were using very simple blanket packs. None of us had very heavy loads. One big advantage of the Roycroft over the simpler pack was the ease with which you could untie the pack, add something or take something out, and then re-tie it and be on your way. The other advantage was greater comfort.

My next test of the Roycroft pack was to see how it did with a heavier load. I packed a heavy coat and 25 pounds (11.36 kilograms) of books in the Roycroft and took off on a 1 1/2 hour hike in hills. This is where I learned that narrow straps don't work well. It is also important that there be enough padding in the bottom of the pack to keep the cross piece off your tail. Other than that it works great.

Footnotes

(1.) 1993, _The Iceman_, **National Geographic**, June, page 36.

(2.) 1993, _Who Was the Iceman?_, **Popular Science**, February, page 46.

(3.) 1992, _The Long-Lost Hunter_, **Audubon**, September-October, page 92.

(4.) Mors Kochansky, **Northern Bushcraft**, Lone Pine Publishing, ISBN # 0-919433-51-0.

(5.) 1994, **SPT Fall Bulletin**, pages 10-17.

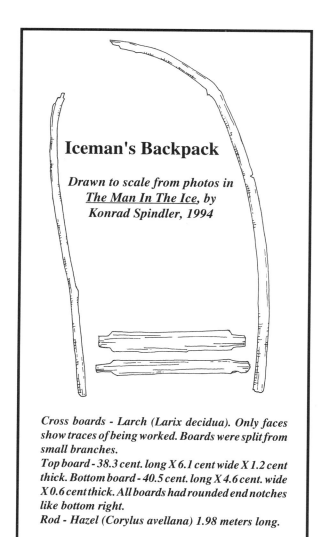

Iceman's Backpack

Drawn to scale from photos in
The Man In The Ice, *by Konrad Spindler, 1994*

Cross boards - Larch (Larix decidua). Only faces show traces of being worked. Boards were split from small branches.
Top board - 38.3 cent. long X 6.1 cent wide X 1.2 cent thick. Bottom board - 40.5 cent. long X 4.6 cent. wide X 0.6 cent thick. All boards had rounded end notches like bottom right.
Rod - Hazel (Corylus avellana) 1.98 meters long.

THE MANUFACTURE OF PRIMITIVE PRIMITIVE THRUSTING SPEARS

By Steve Watts

Our Homo Erectus ancestors possessed both flake and core stone tools. That much is certain. Beyond that, we can only speculate about the wood, bone, fiber and other technologies at their disposal. Our first evidence of wooden thrusting spears does not appear archaeologically until Neanderthal times. Yet, to envision Lower Paleolithic humans without a sharp stick in hand is pretty difficult. They were most likely there, and their use was probably multifunctional-for prying and digging up food and flakable stone, for defense against predators, and (even though our earliest ancestors were most likely scavengers, not hunters) for the occasional killing of a maimed, sick or dying animal. The requirements were simple—sturdiness and a sharp point or bevel.

Perhaps the first of these tools were not created by man at all. Wind and water can splinter saplings and tree limbs which can in turn become lethal weapons in the hands of humans. Whatever the circumstances, the thrusting/jabbing spear was born. It is both the ancestor of all piercing weapons that would follow and an important and viable tool for the primitive hunter still. (See "Reconsidering the Thrusting Spear")

Primitive Primitive Manufacture:

"Primitive Primitive" as used here has both temporal and technological connotations. Temporal—as in "first first"—reflecting on the earliest possible prototypes and functions. And, technological—as in "basic basic"—exploring the simplest tools and techniques needed to manufacture such spears. Having already offered up the possibility of expedient/found thrusters, we turn now to three basic methods of primitive manufacture—methods available to us and to the men and women of the Old Stone Age.

John Latham

Fig. 1. A bent sapling explodes under the forces of bending. . . resulting in a properly splintered thruster.

The "No Tools" Method:

The technique is simple: Bend it 'til it breaks. Select a dead standing sapling or an accessible limb on a larger tree. Finding just the right tree at just the right stage can be tricky. You are looking for a wood that will "explode" under the stresses of compression and tension, resulting in a splintery break (Fig.1). Green wood is too flexible for this technique, and wood that is too far gone will be either too weak or will simply snap off cleanly. Experiment with a variety of species to discover the possibilities. Your failed experiments can be used for firewood. Eastern Red Cedar (*Juniperus virginiana*) fills the need in my part of the country. It's plenty strong enough. It is not very heavy, but remember, we're looking for a thruster not a thrower. And, it splinters into some wicked points and bevels (Fig. 2). Break off the butt end to the desired length and you have created one of the most basic of weapons.

Fig. 2. The "No Tools" method of thrusting spear manufacture results not in a point, but a sharp bevel.

Credit: John Latham

The Hand Axe Method:

Much has been written about the possible uses of flaked stone choppers and hand axes in the Lower Paleolithic. Like the thrusting spear, their use was most likely multifunctional: butchering animals, defense, bone breaking for marrow extraction, use as a prepared core for flake removal, etc. Some people have eliminated the use of the "axe" label, altogether, citing too much of an inference of wood chopping functions. But, chop wood they will! It's not a lot of fun, but hand axes can indeed by used to fell and trim trees.

Select a suitable sapling and begin chopping in a downward direction, working your way around the tree. You are in essence cutting down the tree and shaping the spear's point simultaneously (Fig. 3). Support the tree with your body as you work so that it will not fall under its own weight too soon and splinter or "fuzz up" the point (Fig. 4). Cutting it all the way to

Credit: Richard Rosenfeld

Fig. 4. Supporting the tree as you chop helps to steady the vibration and keep the point from splintering out.

the last fiber will result in the desirable strength and sharpness. If you need it sharper, you can use the edge of the hand axe in a scraping fashion (Fig. 5). Lay the downed tree on a log and chop it to the

Credit: Richard Rosenfeld

Fig. 3. Chopping has progressed completely around the tree. Continuing in this same manner, the point is completed as the tree is felled.

Credit: Richard Rosenfeld

Fig. 5. Sharpening the point with the edge of the hand axe.

desired length.

Dead, seasoned wood will be harder to chop, but will produce a spear that is ready to go. Green wood cuts much easier, but will require seasoning or fire hardening to keep the point strong and sharp.

The Fire and Stone Method:

This is basically a "burn and scrape" or a "burn and grind" technique. Select a standing dead sapling and either break it off or uproot it. The spear is sized by burning at the desired location. To create a point, rotate the blank as it burns. A little scraping with an unmodified flake (struck from your hand axe perhaps), or grinding on a coarse stone will remove the char and expose the hard wood underneath. Keep burning and scraping or grinding until satisfied. A very sharp point can result (Fig. 6).

Steve Watts

Fig. 6.   The combination of fire and stone can produce a sharp point efficiently.

Steve Watts

Three completed "primitive primitive" thrusting spears. Left to right: No Tools Method, Fire & Stone Method, Hand Axe Method.

RECONSIDERING THE THRUSTING SPEAR

The standard progressive train of thought runs something like this: First, hunters used thrusting spears for the taking of large game. Sometimes these spears were thrown. Lighter and more flexible atlatl darts replaced the heavy spears, only to be replaced themselves by the even speedier arrow. And so, the lowly thrusting spear is left behind in the ever-evolving tool kit of the hunter.

Yet, if we look at the ethnographic evidence from hunter/gatherer cultures which survived into the twentieth century, we find that a place for the thruster remains in the arsenal—in spite of the presence of both atlatl and bow and arrow technology. Inuit hunters of the arctic used short thrusting spears for the dispatching of sea mammals taken by harpoon—much in the same way that a modern hunter may carry a pistol to dispatch an animal wounded by his rifle. Clubs and mauls of various designs were used for this "final blow" function in a multitude of other cultures.

Has the use of thrusting spears as dispatching weapons come and gone several times throughout prehistory? This question is raised by the sometimes confusing assemblages of "spear points" (of various sizes and edge angles) which occur together in a given time period. Were some of these meant for "thrusting" only, while others were designed more specifically for cutting and/or aerodynamic flight? Or, have thrusting spears been there all along, becoming from time to time archaeologically invisible as they periodically alternate back and forth between stone tipped models and the all wooden Lower Paleolithic form?

"What we should be doing is trying to understand how a cultural system handled resources... Most people's thinking goes on the assumption that when something newer and better comes along, the people discard what they did before. This clouds a lot of the ways that tribal cultures are perceived."   John White
Early Man, Archeological Quarterly
Vol. 2, 1978

BULLROARERS

By Tom Hackett

"There is hooting, drumming, singing and shrieking and, as a climax, the head Kani (Bullroarer) is swung. . . . by itself; then follows a whole chorus of "short-legged" Kani so that, for the first day and night there is an infernal howling. . . . Through its swinging movements the large head Kani produces a distinctively soothing rumble; the small "short-legged" Kani are swung with such skill that they sound like the furious yelping of enraged curs. In still weather one can hear the humming from Tami even in Yabim, three or four hours walking distance away." (Bamler 1911:501 in Gourlay 1975)

(IMMERGUT)

Few things in life are as enjoyable as furiously yelping like an enraged cur, hence the bullroarer. As this journal is concerned with technical rather than mythic or ethnographic endeavors I will only touch on the ideas and mystery surrounding the bullroarer.

Bullroarer, Rhombus, Lightning Sticks, Prayer Sticks, Whizzers, Kani, Rokut, Churingas, etc. (see Drumming On The Edge Of Magic for a list of over 60 indigenous names for this simple tool) are often clouded in the ceremonial/spiritual mystique of special societies and celebrations, yet also appear in some cultures as childrens' toys. In some cultures it portrays a monster to be feared, in others the voice of the ancestors, and yet in others a tool to summon the Gods. From the manifestation of the spiritual world to the source of life giving rain, the bullroarer is truly a pandemic tool. Found on each of the populated continents in various cultures, the bullroarer's functional menagerie is matched only by the wide variety of forms it takes. However, the common function of all bullroarers, regardless of ceremonial significance, is the production of sound.

An attempt has been made here to describe the making of a clear, loud, crisp, bullroarer.

Material Selection

The range of materials used ethnographically includes wood, metal, bone, and antler. Wood is by far the most common material available for the construction of the bullroarer as variety of source and style becomes unlimited. Virtually any kind of wood when shaped to the rough dimensions described herein will produce a sound. However, to make a bullroarer that will be heard for miles one must use a wood with a relatively high concentration of lignin. Lignin is a specialized sclerenchyma tissue found in the secondary cell walls of many plants. Basically, lignified cell walls equate to heavy, dense, wood. The heavier and more dense a piece of wood

the better the sound and flight of the bullroarer. Some primitives sought blanks from the trunks of lightening-killed trees in order to take advantage of the magic from the sky.

The availability of such dense wood varies from region to region. One might be considered lucky, in some respects, to live in the deciduous forests east of the Mississippi.

Unfortunately, the very best sounding woods are also those which are the

Included is a list of the woods the author has used for bullroarers. This is a mere smattering of the woods available. Starred woods are those that have proven most successful so far.

Apricot	Balu *
Black locust	Desert holly
Juniper	Freemont's cottonwood
Mango	Gambles oak *
Mesquite	Mountain mahogany **
Palo verde	Osage orange *
Purple heart	*River Hawthorne
2 x 4 pine/fir	White pine
Wood lathe	

hardest to work. One gains new appreciation for the reverence attributed to an aboriginal bullroarer when one starts to shape a section of Mountain mahogany with an incisor-tooth scraper.

Tools

The level of technology in producing a bullroarer is purely one of personal choice. Scrapers of various lithic and tooth derivation would have been the norm in pre-history, and in some cultures are still in use today. The tools of choice in a more modern context are the machete, hatchet and wood rasp. In addition, an occasional belt sander or band saw should not be discriminated against. A small blade of some sort is also useful for the final touches, as well as some type of sanding tool; paper, rock, etc.

Design

An ongoing study of the design, weight, dimensional ratios and sound, of (as of now) about forty separate bullroarers, has suggested a general shape and mass as outlined below. Again, it must be emphasized that virtually anything tied to the end of a string and swung around ones head will make a sound. The data here presents one way in which to shape a bullroarer.

Start with a dry relatively knot-free section of wood from forty to fifty centimeters (For an excellent reference on drying times of suitable woods see Time Baker's article in BPT #2). Green wood will work but

(more)

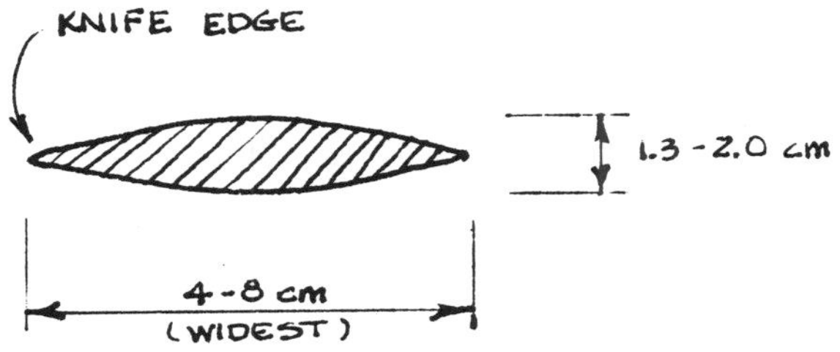

KNIFE EDGE

1.3 - 2.0 cm

4 - 8 cm (WIDEST)

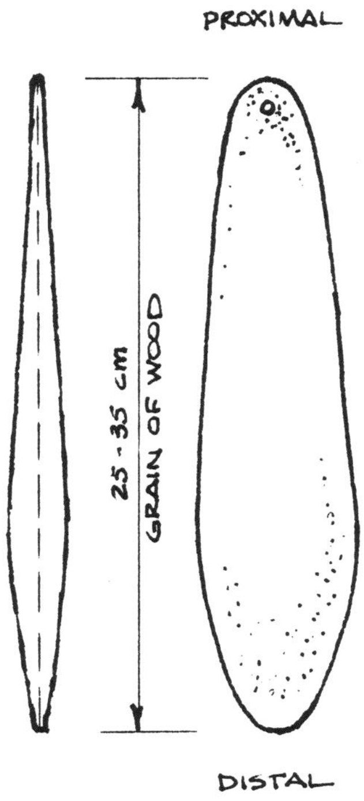

PROXIMAL

25 - 35 cm

GRAIN OF WOOD

DISTAL

TROUBLE SHOOTING

Problem	Possible Solution
Fluttery/wobbly spin	Center the string in the hole/Bevel edges more
Won't spin at string end	Pre-spin the bullroarer string prior to swinging or bounce bullroarer off soft ground to initiate spin
Feels heavy - muted sound	Thin it down more
Noise not loud enough	Shape might be too wide for the length, try reshaping and reduce the width to length ratio
When in doubt	Try another string
Thin! Thin! Thin!	

without the ease of dry wood. In addition a dry blank of wood should not offer as many splitting surprises.

Split the log or branch in half. If the halves of the once whole log are thicker than five centimeters split one of the halves again. Always split the section you are working on at the center of the mass. Trying to split the edge of a section will only result in "grain run-out", making the piece more difficult to work.

Using the tool of choice thin the blank evenly on both sides. Look for the straight longitudinal plane within the wood and then use this straight plane as the center-line of the blank. Thin on either side of the center-line so that the distance from the center-line to the outer edge of the blank is even on each side.

The straight plane is as critical in this early stage as it is in the final stages of finish work. Establish this midline for both side to side, and top to bottom. The center-line plane is the reference for all subsequent shaping throughout the making of the bullroarer. It is the baseline, and must be established early on.

Continue thinning the blank to about one and a half centimeters then start thinking about the shaping. At this point the blank should roughly resemble a rather thin rectangle.

The surest way to shape and avoid any unfortunate shaping errors, is via modified thinning. This is accomplished by working the thinning tool at an initial angle of approx. 45 degrees to the center-line. Thus shaving down the edges of the rectangle from a squared edge to a convex surface. The angle of work allows the scraper to across grain ends rather than "catching" an end and diving into the work surface or tearing off an edge grain.

The convex-convex, or lenticular shape of the board is the basic design essential to the finished bullroarer.

The final thinning and shaping can now be done. A template of a selected shape may transfered to the board, or a freehand outline can be applied. As you can see from the photo, the variety of design varies within certain limitations. See the drawings * to get a feel for the overall shape.

In general:
1. Leave distal end thicker than the proximal end.
2. The proximal half should taper in thickness from the center of the bullroarer to the thinnest section at the base.
3. The center-line and margins of the biface bullroarer

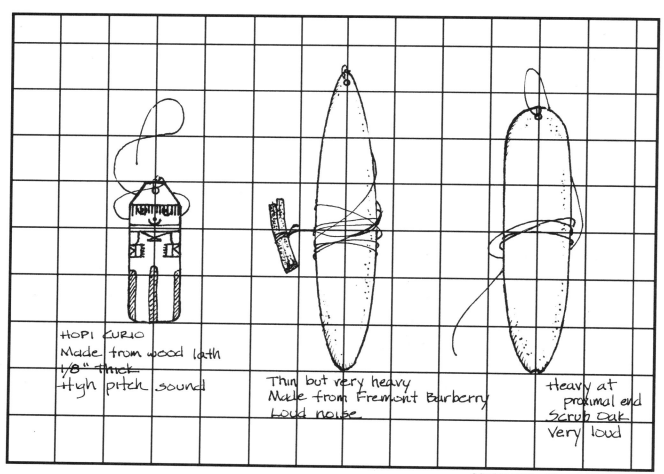

HOPI CURIO
Made from wood lath
1/8" thick
High pitch sound

Thin but very heavy
Made from Fremont Barberry
Loud noise.

Heavy at proximal end
Scrub Oak
Very loud

SCALE: 1/2" = 2"

should be straight as an arrow.
4. The bevel from edge to the midpoint of the bullroarer should be equal at all points.
5. An overall shape of 3 or 4 to 1 (length to width) is generally acceptable for best results.

String

Intrinsic to the propulsion of the bullroarer is the string and the hole the string is attached to. The average distance from the base to the center of the hole on the bullroarers under study is 0.9 cm. The placement of the hole is exceedingly important. For the bullroarer to spin without fluttering the string should be an extension of the midline of the bullroarer. Therefore proper centering of the hole for the string is paramount. One easy and safe knot for string attachment is the girth hitch.

Traditionally, the string for the bullroarer was made from flax and various other plant fibers, rawhide, and even human hair (refer). Their lengths were as varied as the cultures they came from. A manageable length is about 180 cm, just longer than the fingertip to fingertip distance on outstretched arms.

The string can greatly effect bullroarer performance. Because the actual physics behind the motion of the bullroarer are partially dependant on string performance, the intrinsic values of various strings can make or break the bullroarer's roar. For a prehistorically correct (PC) string, rawhide or buckskin is recommended. For a really high performance bullroarer use the modern day artificial sinew. Artificial sinew is a waxed nylon which lends itself nicely to bullroarer performance. A small stick or hide handle on the hand-held end of the string can be useful in avoiding blisters and raw fingers. In some cases a long stick may be added to the string to produce extra force in the spinning of small specimens.

The actual swinging of the bullroarer is fundamentally easy. Hold the string high above the head and swing the bullroarer in a plane horizontal to the ground. Take note of the changing pitch and frequency of the sound and its relation to the string action.

A note of caution. Bullroarers build up significant centrifugal force and when unintentionally released (or strings break) can cause serious damage or pain to those around. Please use two strings of artificial sinew, or two strands of rawhide, and experiment with any PC method alone before amazing you friends. Let me know what you discover! Send any new design ideas, comments on performance, records on ethnographic uses, etc. to me c/o BOSS. A study investigating the actual physics of the bullroarer and what's behind the sound is currently in progress.

Matt Immergut doin' the bullroarer shuffle at Rabbitstick.

Carving Green Wood and Curing Wood Carvings
By Gregg Blomberg

Green wood is readily available and inexpensive or free. Beautiful local woods can be found almost everywhere in the US. Salvaging and using this material can be more satisfying than buying some exotic piece at a high price from the lumber yard. All the fruit and nut woods I know of are quite suitable, as are many other species. Here in the Northwest, red alder is our "trash" deciduous, growing rapidly to over two foot in diameter. The wood is splendid for carving green, and if cured correctly is quite beautiful. Another advantage of green wood is that green wood of most species is considerably easier to carve than the same wood fully cured. Some woods, once fully cured, do not carve well at all.

This discussion assumes the carver is working with hand, not power, tools. When working with power tools, there are some advantages to working with fully cured wood. Besides the curing method here described, the use of PEG (polyethelyne glycol) can eliminate checking problems. Although in some cases PEG and/or power carving may be necessary or desirable, I usually try to preserve the quiet and simplicity of carving.

Many carvers stay away from carving green wood because they are worried about the problem of checking. Curing a carving without checking is always an important consideration for a carver. It is more difficult to successfully cure a carving that has the core or heart of the tree in it, since that is the concentrated center to which all checks run. In some woods, the heart itself is so full of stress that checks can begin there.

Checking is of course due to stress in wood. The crack opens up to release the stress. Stress increases with squirrely grain, knots and other irregularities. The checking that happens as a carving is drying is usually the result of unevenness in the drying process. If the wood on the outside of a carving is quite dry while the inside is still damp, the outside wood will not have enough elasticity to absorb the internal movement and must release it with a check.

An examination of early Northwest coast work shows the aboriginal carvers understood their medium well. Most Northwest coast work is hollowed out: bowls, masks, rattles, canoes even the backs of poles. This hollowing allowed for a uniform thickness and thus even and unstressful drying. In some cases, carvings were pierced and relieved in what would otherwise be a heavier area hard to cure without checks. These relieved areas were integrated into the carvings to enhance the design.

If you are carving solid work, is it possible to relieve the carving by hollowing out the bottom, running a drill up through it and/or piercing the heavier areas? If not, you may need to work with fully cured wood and probably should avoid the heart as well.

...continued on page 137

Making A Northwest Coast Ladle
Text and Illustrations
By Gregg Blomberg ©1987

A Northwest Coast spoon or ladle is a useful and fun carving project, simple enough for the novice and interesting enough for a seasoned carver. Carving a ladle is certainly a useful introduction to work in the third dimension.

To make a ladle I would use a marks-on-wet-wood pencil, a small hatchet and a crooked knife. A shaping adze would also be very helpful to start the hollow and shape down close to the drawn line.

Traditionally these ladles were made from a round of wood just large enough for the object. The advantages are obvious- a small round of wood is easy to come by and there is minimum waste wood to remove. The large ladle in the drawing will require a round of wood 12" long by about 3.5" in diameter (after removal of the bark). Don't hesitate to make your own templates if you have a different size block of wood.

I recommend using red alder and carving it as green and fresh as possible. In other areas, birch, beech or other woods may be more available. Examine your round foe flaws. Often you can lay out so as to evade problems with knots, etc. To avoid checking, keep the carving in a plastic bag between carving sessions. Carving through the center of the block will rarely cause any special checking problems if the methods used are correct (see "Curing and Carving Green Wood", this page).

Begin by peeling the bark off with the crooked knife and lay out the top view of the template with the pencil. Cut out the templates and center the top view template on the blank wood. Draw the line freehand while "eyeballing" where it should be on the round (If you fold the template, you will have a different shape). Do it as neatly as you can, keeping the ladle centered. After the initial drawing, refine the land freehand. Then waste the excess wood with a hatchet or adze. Keep cuts square and parallel with each other. After roughing the first dimension, carve right down to the lines with the crooked knife. Next, lay out the side view template. Hold the template flat and eyeball the lines onto the block. This really isn't difficult, and you continually take every opportunity to refine the work. The carving doesn't have to be exactly like the template to be correct. Waste the wood in the second dimension, then carve the hollow and round off the back.

Leave a crooked knife texture on the piece and finish with mineral oil. Look in museums and books on the Northwest Coast for other ideas and variations. Good luck and have fun.

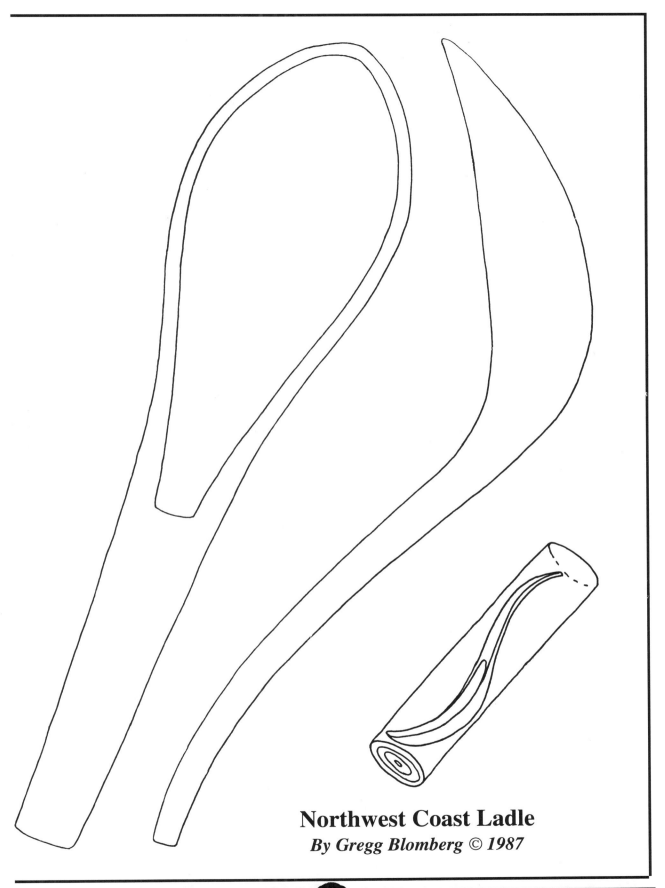

Northwest Coast Ladle

By Gregg Blomberg © 1987

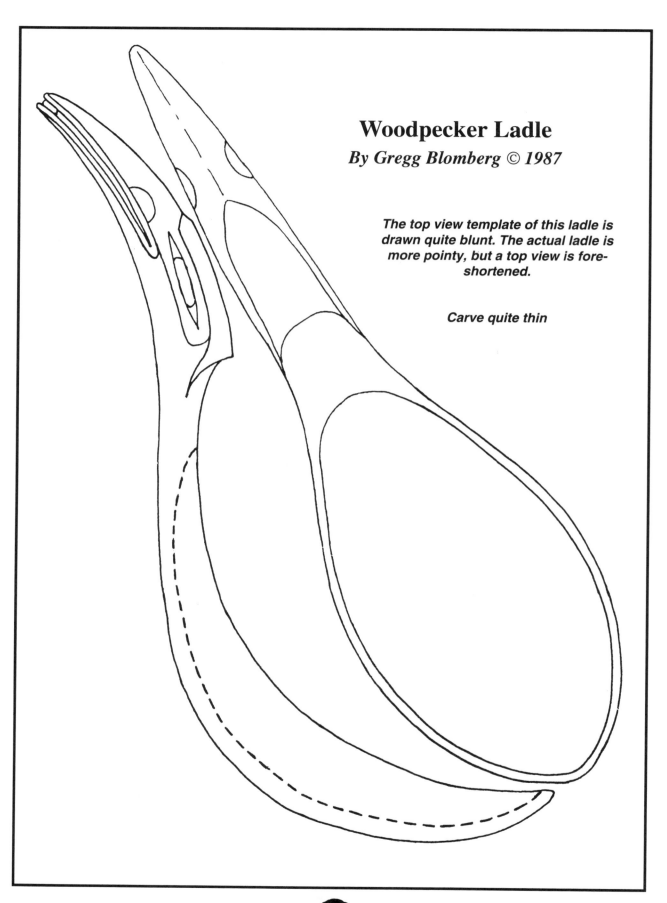

Woodpecker Ladle

By Gregg Blomberg © 1987

The top view template of this ladle is drawn quite blunt. The actual ladle is more pointy, but a top view is foreshortened.

Carve quite thin

... continued from page 134

If you procure a piece of green wood and are not able to proceed with carving it right away, it will be important to preserve it from checking. When curing in the round, checks may start on the ends of the log but they will usually run into the block only to the place at which the moisture transmission through the bark equals that through the log ends. Try to obtain the log with extra length. Painting the ends while leaving the bark on will usually contain the checking. Bruce Harvy of Orcas Island cures a lot of wood for instrument making using a mix of half paraffin and half paint thinner to coat the log ends. Any material that slows down the movement of moisture will help. Wood prepared in this way should be stored in the shade in a cool place. It will take years for most wood so stored to fully cure.

Another way to preserve wet wood for a short time is float it in a rain barrel or some such. Wood saturated with moisture will take up color from minerals if they are present in the water, and once it is removed it must be carved in a fairly short period of time. The loss of this artificially-induced moisture seems to take place more rapidly than the loss of the original tree sap would.

Yet another way to hold green wood for a short time is by placing it in a plastic bag or wrapping it in damp moss. Alder and many other woods are quite prone to rapid spalting and break down under these conditions. Likewise they cannot for any length of time be cured in the round as described above. A month or two will be the maximum you can hold most wood species under these conditions. To lengthen this time, remove the wood from the bag for an hour or two every few days and turn the bag inside out each time you wrap it back up. In other words start a slow cure.

When carving green, the carver does everything the same as with dry. The difference is that in-between carving sessions, the carving is kept in a plastic bag. Upon completion, the carving is treated to longer periods of time outside the bag. Each time it is replaced in the bag the moisture in the piece is equalized, as is the stress brought on by unequal drying. I usually leave the bag open a crack in between as well. Depending on the carving, it will take a week or two to fully cure the piece. I do all but the final strokes, mostly cure the work and then finish it.

Some checks do not detract from the value of a carving, but if checks do start to open up that threaten to compromise the value of your work, try stabilizing them with super glue. Super glue has very low viscosity so it can penetrate deeply. I have used it quite successfully in wood, bone and other materials.

Once I needed a mask in a hurry. I had but three days to work with. To my dismay I didn't even have a block of wood to use, so I cut down a green alder (June). I carved the mask to about 3/8" to 7/16" thickness. To cure, I left the mask on the table and, examining it hourly, patted water on to the end grain where the checks were wanting to open up. Overnight I placed it in a plastic bag. By the third day I had it fully cured and painted (acrylic of course). To this day the piece hasn't checked. From growing tree to cured carving in three days!

OBSERVATIONS ON A HAFTED ADZE

By George Price

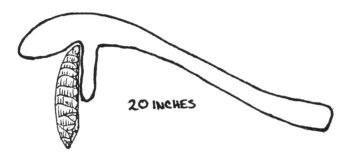

20 INCHES

I carve a lot of soapstone sculpture, pipes, containers, etc. Usually I rough out the piece with a hatchet and finish with a rasp and sandpaper. Recently, while chopping out a bowl, I ran into a problem. The hatchet head wouldn't reach into the deepening bowl cavity. I needed an adze. I had lots of raw material but I chose some tough Morrow Mountain rhyolite, thinking harder to make, harder to break. I modeled my adze roughly after pictures I had seen of Dalton adzes, small, thick, parallel-sided oval bifaces. My adze was also plano-convex in cross section, the flat bottom would seal firmly against the haft element of the handle with the distal end buttressed. See illustration. The handle was made from a fork in a dogwood branch. The head was lashed on with a single strip of soaked rawhide 1/2 inch thick. The rawhide shrunk around the contours of the blade. No adhesive was used nor was it needed. This tool has been through some rigorous pounding and the haft has held firm.

This is a very effective tool for gouging out soapstone bowls and for finer shaping on sculpture because it gets into tight places that a hatchet can't reach. Its main advantage is that the blades are readily interchangeable. Just soak the business end in water for about two hours and unwind the lashing, haft the new blade, let the rawhide lashing dry overnight and the tool is ready to use. No messy adhesive.

I have two blades for my adze. The small rhyolite blade, which is good for late stage bowl manufacture such as thinning walls and final shaping, and a larger blade made of Fort Payne chert. It is heavier and packs more of a wallop making it preferable for early stage roughing out and shaping, like an axe instead of a hatchet for chopping wood. The blades have taken on the characteristic adze wear pattern, polished bit with micro step fractures. The more vitreous chert adze is more prone to step fractures and occasionally large spalls fly off which effectively resharpens the blade in use. You can't get that with a metal tool The smaller rhyolite adze does not have this feature which renders it less effective in terms of time spent resharpening the tool. It is a very difficult tool to resharpen because of the angle of the haft. I could not resharpen the rounded bit of the rhyolite adze using an antler tine but again it can be unhafted and resharpened. The cost being the extra time spent.

It is interesting to note that the shape of the haft element of the handle dictates the shape of the haft area of the blade. The blade has to fit! The handle is more time consuming to produce and blades are easily and quickly made by an experienced knapper. This presents the knapper with a set of constants to achieve in the finished form. In this case those constants are plano convex cross section and width of the haft area. That leaves the cutting part of the blade the only portion open for variability. Perhaps similar experiments could lend insight into projectile point and knife hafting elements in relation to function.

The rawhide was obtained from a large doggy chew toy. Just soak it in water until it unravels and cut into strips. They can be purchased for as little as one dollar or a strip of innertube might do the job.

Using a stone adze to rough-shape a bow stave.

David Wescott

Section 4

Fibers
Holding The World Together

Gathering and Preparing Plant Fibers

By David Wescott

Fibers are manufactured by plants to aid in stability, protect vulnerable plant parts such as the vascular bundles (the circulatory system), and aid in the dispersal of seeds, and possibly deter herbivores. The primary cell wall of plants is a layer of cellulose chains* which mat together to form a semi-rigid structure. As the cell is actively growing, longitudinally up the stem, the microfibers tend to be stretched and laid down predominantly along or slightly off the axis growth. In plant cells that produce secondary cell walls, such as fiber cells, new layers of cellulose are laid down with the microfibers lying in different angles to the last layer deposited. These alternating layers can number up to seven. This "cross helix" orientation of microfibers, added onto the strength of the microfibers themselves and the cellulose chains, gives fiber cells great mechanical strength. The fiber cells of flax are about 30 microns in diameter, and up to 30mm in length: a length to width ratio of 1000:1. (Mathewson, 1985)

According to Kroeber, **material culture follows traditional paths thus making patterns of change or experimentation slow**. In order to avoid this problem, here are some suggestions for stimulating experimentation.

1. No plant list or description is complete until you have experimented with it yourself. Try all new sources of fiber. Any strong, flexible plant fiber makes good cordage. Do not get stuck on lists. Try anything. If it has the right properties to do the job of a fiber, it's a fiber!

2. Try new ideas for fiber rendering until you have mastered them. Take someone else's discoveries as only a springboard to advance your own.

3. The only time to ignore #1 is when you are recreating an artifact and exactness applies. Know the bio-regional demands of the people who created the artifact and do enough research to match all materials.

4. Learn some simple tests to aid in your exploration.

A favorite quote of those who teach cordage making is from Margaret Wheat's Survival Arts of the Primitive Paiutes. Speaking of those who practiced the traditional lifeways she said "they literally tied their world together." When you begin to count up the variety of ways that fiber materials were used. it's easy to see how true this statement is.

When novices learn the techniques of rendering plant fibers into useful tools, the experience is, like fire making, almost magical. One can reach out and grab a fiber bearing plant and then twist into cordage without doing anything other than working it to a flexible state. The product is improved by making the cord thicker or refining the fibers further into a tighter twist.

Learning the basics of fiber collecting, preparation and processing liberates the outdoor traveler by compensating for any need for "attachers"...string, thread, even rope.

Where To Find Fibers

Thousands of years before the domestication of cotton or flax, native people were already gathering and spinning plant fibers. Over 1000 species of plants in North America have served as fiber sources (Buchanan, 1985). Due to lack of commercial value, many common and valuable sources of fiber have been overlooked by modern opportunists. The ability to recognize, harvest, and utilize plant fibers from their most simple form should be important to all interested in primitive technology.

Fibers come from a number of sources, but 5 types are the most common:

leaf fibers - hard fibers surrounded by fleshy structure.
bast fibers - soft vascular fibers located between outer bark and woody stem.

root fibers - underground fibers.
bark fibers - both wet inner bark and dry outer layer.
whole plant - including shoots, stems, roots and vines.

Seed fibers are also common but are far too small to be of use for making cordage. Bast fibers on the other hand are the most common fiber source dealt with in articles about cordage making. Bast fibers from woody plants (the phloem or inner bark) are also common.

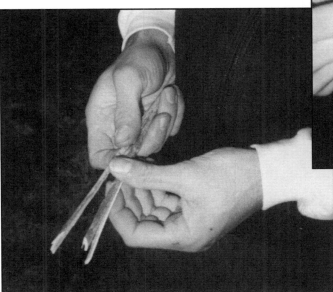

Know When To Gather
Many people are of the opinion that useful ropes cannot be made from fibers close at hand, but they are wrong. Native people who are often referred to as primitive were able to manufacture cordage from grasses, plant fibers, and hair which were strong enough to capture el

Testing Fibers For Use
* Tie a knot in the plant/fiber to check for flexibility.
* The Flexibility Twist Test - spin a bundle of fibers clockwise at each end while the ends are grasped between the fingers. Pull slightly on the ends to provide tension on the bundle while twisting. Twist until a kink is formed (Kochanski, 1987).
* Remember that all fibers have their own idiosyncrasies. Some are weakened when wet while others bind tighter and become more flexible with moisture. (Mears, 1990) Try all samples both wet and dry.
* Try small and large bundles of fibers.
* Check the minimum bend result before fibers kink or break.
Check fibers for length. Test by gently pounding on bast fibers until they can be separated, or peel a sample of inner bark or leaf fiber to see length and flexibility.
* Test for strength and durability by twisting a sample length of cordage and pull until it breaks or you give up. More twists per inch in a length of cordage in-

creases strength and stiffness (Kochanski, 1987). But remember, it is possible to over twist some fibers and actually lessen their tensile strength.

Some Plant Fiber Sources
Dry outer bark: bulrush, cattail, willow, clematis, sage, cliffrose.
Wet inner bark: basswood, aspen, cottonwood, juniper, sage, willow, saskatoon, cedar, walnut, cherry, aspen, ash, box elder, hawthorn, cliffrose, mesquite, slippery elm, big tooth maple.
Bast fibers: dogbane, milkweed, nettle, evening primrose, fireweed, thistle, flax, hemp, velvet leaf.
Leaves: yucca, reed grass, cattail, agave, iris, sotol, palmetto.
Roots: spruce (conifers), poplar, dune roots, lupine.
Shoots: ash, birch, willow, oak, grape, clematis, squaw bush.
Seeds: cattail, cottonwood, fireweed, milkweed.
Whole plant: rush, grass, cattail, sedge.

ephants, to harpoon whales, to climb cliffs, and build bridges (Mears, 1990). Other uses include trap triggers, bowstrings, fire cords, fish line, snares, shelter lashings, snares, pack ties. Plant fiber was also used extensively where stronger sinew fibers would rot.

Fiber quality is determined by condition of plant, time and method of harvest. Most bast fibers are best obtained at the end of the growing season and prior to winter. Nettle, for example, begins to degrade almost as soon as it dies so it is best gathered green as is flax (This does not

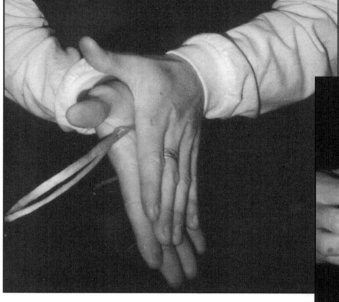

How To Obtain Fiber From Plants

I can still remember, after hours of work to make a 6" piece of string, the amazement and new appreciation I felt as I looked at a picture of a dogbane rabbit net that had recently been unearthed at a local dig. It was 4' high and 140' long.

Fibers can be extracted from plants mechanically or via the retting (rotting) process (see Gibby article on flax). Most extraction is fairly obvious....use as is....break, scutch or hackle.....soak and split.....split green and use......ret.

However, when it comes to removing the soft bast fibers from their woody stalk a simple understanding of this specialized technique is in order.

Step #1 Lightly scrape the stalk with a knife held perpendicular to the stalk. You are trying to remove the papery

work in some areas. Air must be allowed to dry the stalks so they don't mold and rot). Dry or slightly green stalks can be bundled and stored until needed. Leaf fibers such as yucca can be gathered green or dry. I prefer to gather them green and pound them lightly so that fibers are separated from the tissue. They are then set aside to dry for storage. When they are to be used they can be soaked more rapidly than if they were gathered dry or if they were left intact.

Inner barks and shoots are easier to gather and are more flexible in the early spring as the sap begins to rise and prior to wood production. Both are best used while they are green and damp and allowed to dry in place. Some shoots and branches such as sumac (Rhus trilobata) can be used all year by simply heating the woody branch over hot coals until the bark begins to slip. Any grasses that resist crumbling when worked may be used. If they are dampened before twisting they are more manageable. Grass is at its best soon after death. Cattail leaves are best in fall and early winter. The flowering spring shoot may be split and twisted as is.

outer sheath without damaging the bast fiber itself. If the surface begins to "fuzz-up" you are into the soft fiber bundles.
Step #2 Buff the stalk over a smooth green limb or your pant leg to remove the remaining outer bark. This also aligns any fibers separated by the scraping.
Step #3 Crack the woody stalk with a dull rock or between the fingers. Do not pound so hard as to cut the fibers with the broken woody core. Simply crack the stalk in half or in quarters lengthwise to expose the inner material.
Step #4 With the bast fibers against the skin, bend the stalk over the fingers until the woody core cracks inward (toward you and away from your finger and the fibers). Do this for the length of the stalk about every inch or two.
Step #5 Gently peel the short pieces of woody material away

from the remaining fibers and discard. To do this, work the wood at both ends until it releases without taking fiber strands with it.

Step #6 Roll the fiber bundles between your palms or palm and thigh to align the fibers and remove any remaining outer bark. If large pieces of bark remain, work them between the fingers until they are removed. Chunks of garbage left in the fibers looks bad and will also weaken the cordage you worked so hard to produce.

Step #7 Roll the fiber bundles into coils and store for future use.

REFERENCES

Kochanski, Mors
1987   NORTHERN BUSH CRAFT.

Mears, Raymond
1990   THE SURVIVAL HANDBOOK: A Practical Guide to Woodcraft and Woodlore.

Buchanan, Rits
1985   Using The Fibers Of Native Plants, SPIN-OFF, Vol. IX, No 5, Winter

Mathewson, Maragret
1985   THREADS OF LIFE: Cordage and Other Fibers Of The California Tribes, Senior Thesis, Univ of Calif.

Natural Fibers Preparation
By Steven Edholn and Tamara Wilder

MATERIALS	PREPARATION
DOGBANE/INDIAN HEMP	
(*Apocynum Cannibinum*) • An excellent native US fiber. Widespread but uncommon. Prefers wet areas. • Harvest reddest stalks dry in autumn/early winter after plant has died back completely.	• Crack into four equal parts by squeezing or tapping up and down the stalk with a rock. • Crack out the woody center and buff the outer bark off between hands and scrape with nails to clean.
MILKWEEDS	
(*Asclepias species*) • Excellent silky, white fiber. • Harvest dry late summer/early fall before it rains.	• Remove fibers from stalk like dog bane and clean them by rubbing them between hands
NETTLES	
(*Urtica species esp. Breweri, Gracilis, Holocoricea*) • An excellent native fiber source. Some species are much preferred. Plants with wet feet but sunny leaves make better fiber. Not good for nets as rots when wet. Used in wartime Europe as a linen (flax) substitute. • Harvest at peak height or dead but not rotten.	• Sometimes requires retting (rotting slightly to break down the starchy elements) but not so much as to rot the fibers. • Clean by rubbing between hands or pounding with a mallet to loosen the fibers, especially at the nodes.
YUCCAS	
(*Yucca species esp. Mahavensis* (Best) *Bacatta*) • Widely used in desert areas for nets, ropes, sandals and fiber skirts. • Harvest anytime.	• Pound leaves on a smooth log with a smooth, peeled 2-3" billet. • Wash and pound repeatedly until fibers are clean and separated. Save washings as soap. • Also sometimes retted.

OTHER MATERIALS

• Agave (sisal), coconut fibers, Iris macrosiphon and tenax, cannibis sativa, mulberry bark, willow bark, primrose, sagebrush, ribbonwood, mountain mahogony, western red cedar, giant cedar, redwood bark, beach lupine root, elm bark, leather root, cattails, tules, maple bark, plus many more.
• Experiment •

REDISCOVERING FLAX
BY EVARD GIBBY

When I was a young boy my father gave me the bow that he had used as a Boy Scout. The bow didn't have a string anymore, so instead of buying one, Dad took me to town and we purchased a roll of flax shoemaker's thread and some beeswax. He explained that flax was the best material he knew of to make bow strings. He then taught me how to make one from these materials.

Back then I didn't know what flax was or where It came from. I still knew little more than that until recently, when certain events prompted me to do some research. In early 1986, I watched Larry Olsen demonstrate the technique of making primitive reed arrows. While working on the arrows, I began thinking about making a primitive bow. It was then that the flax bowstring making technique came back to mind. I decided I had to find what flax was and if it could be obtained and used under primitive conditions. Olsen's **Outdoor Survival Skills** did not mention the use of flax for cordage, nor did other survival literature that I checked. Then checking in the encyclopedia, I discovered that flax is a plant with blue flowers and stems containing strong fibers. These fibers can be spun into thread and woven into linen cloth. I also learned that several species of flax grow in the United States. During my research I was happy to discover a flax plant growing in my own yard in a patch of wildflowers that my wife had planted. To her dismay I chopped out part of it and began to experiment with it.

During a field trip with Olsen and others a plant was found with blue flowers like the flax in my yard. It had to be flax! Larry, interested in this new plant encouraged some experimentation with it. I then Picked a few plants and soon had a short length of cordage twisted from the fibrous skin.

Linum lewisii

Flax belongs to the Linaceae family. It is an annual or perennial herb having simple alternate leaves, five stamens, five sepals, and five petals that are usually blue or yellow and soon fall off the plant. The ovary is superior and the capsule is ten loculed and 10 seeded. Local plants (Great Basin) have several stems arising from the base, sometimes branched, that are a foot or more in height. There are over 200 species of flax in the world with about six species in the Utah-Idaho area alone. The most common flax found in this area is Linum lewisii. This is one of the most common and widespread native species and was discovered and named by Captain Lewis of the Lewis and Clark Expedition. It has attractive blue flowers.

Larry's questions prompted further research. "Is this a native plant?" he asked, and if so, "Did the Indians use it for cordage material?" I found the answer to be yes to both questions.

Several authors confirm that flax is native to America and Indians used it for cordage. Also according to Jim Woods of the Herrett Museum in Twin Falls, ID, flax and linen have been found in some pre-columbian American archeological sites.

Flax fibers are among the strongest natural fibers known, and the plant is one of the first useful fiber species known by man. Many stone-age people used flax to make cordage and linen cloth. The flax plant could have been cultivated as early as 7,000 BC in Syria and Turkey. Egyptian mummies were wrapped in linen cloth.

Flax is processed commercially by retting (rotting) the plants in water, drying them, and then mechanically crushing, beating, and combing them to separate the fibers. The fibers are then spun into thread. From this information and experimentation, I developed two methods to separate the fibers from the plant via simpler means.

Preparing Flax Fibers

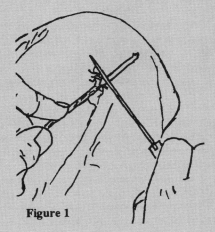

Figure 1

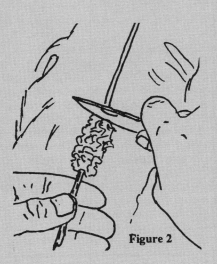

Figure 2

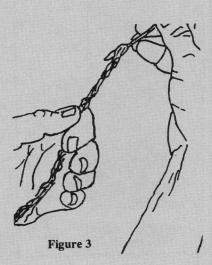

Figure 3

The first method is best suited for immediate production of small quantities of cordage. Strip the leaves from the green stem. With a knife blade or stone flake, start scraping at one end of the stem, removing the fibrous skin from the woody core. Hold the knife perpendicular to the stem, scrape with short strokes, and allow the fibers to form a ball or "cocoon" in front of the blade as you proceed (Figures 1 & 2). An easy method is to place the stem on your knee and rotate it back and forth as you scrape to remove all the fibers. When the cocoon is about 1/2 inch from the end of the stem, carefully pull the free end to unravel and remove the yarn-like fibrous mass from the stem (Figure 3).

The second method involves the retting process. Submerge bundles of flax in water and allow them to ret from several days up to about two weeks. The fibrous skin can then be easily peeled off the still wet stems by hand. Once removed, the fibers can be twisted into cordage either wet or dry, but twisting fibers while slightly damp seems to work best. The strongest fibers are obtained when the plant reaches the seed stage, but fibers can be used any time after the plant blossoms.

Future projects will be to compare fiber quality, quantity, and workability for cordage from various species. None of the references I researched gave any indication of variations among the different species. For more information on cordage, see other articles in this issue, or *Outdoor Survival Skills* by Larry Olsen.

AGAVE FIBERS

On recent visit to remote villages of southern Mexico and Guatemala, BOSS staff Carrie Wilson and Michael Ryan were fortunate to see a number of skills with ancient tradition still in use today. One village in particular was completely dependent upon an industry based upon the fibers obtained from giant Agave plants grown on the steep hillsides surrounding their homes. Photos of the plants show how plants from 6-12' high were cultivated on the high coastal steppe.

Each day, the entire village (men, women, and children) was busy harvesting, preparing, and weaving the fibers. The huge green spikes are brought to a rendering location where they are pounded with a dull wooden mallet to separate the fibers from the fleshy part of the leaf. Once the fibers are exposed they are left to dry.

Finished fibers are resoaked and used by the villagers to produce rope, bags, tumplines or other serviceable items. Being so remote, most items are for utility rather than the tourist trade. The streets are filled with teams of workers producing rope with "Pomo rope twisters", a simple mechanized method of rope production from long fibers. Other workers were involved in dying and weaving fibers into bags and tumplines examples of which were brought back to use on the trail. Tumps are a vital part of village life and used to carry huge loads of wood or other products

Mike Ryan standing by the giant Agaves cultivated in Guatamala for its tough fibers. (Wilson Photo)

Native craftsman preparing Agave fiber for rope and tumpline weaving. (Wilson Photo)

MEMBERS RESPOND - Fiber Preparation

AGAVE FIBER PREPARATION ON THE TRAIL
By David Holiday

On a trip through the Mogollon Rim in Arizona this past summer, we were unable to find our usual source of cordage material (dogbane, nettle, milkweed, or primrose) for the students that were with us. As an alternative we tried the large spined leaves of the Agave plant.

They are plentiful and very thick and fleshy in this area of the country, and average over 3' long, but can get up to 5' long. We knew they were full of fibers, as we regularly pulled needles and threads from the core of the leaves. The problem was getting the fibers out of a fresh-cut leaf fast enough to use on the trail. We cut one three foot leaf and pounded it lightly on the rocks of a small running creek. The mallet we used was a section of Arizona Black Walnut that we found in a flash-flood debris pile (it was later made into a celt handle). As the fleshy part of the leaf separated from the fibers, it was washed down stream and away from the process. Along with it went the majority of alkaloids that are contained in the Yucca Family and cause severe itching from contact irritation among some people.

Without even letting the fibers dry, we taught a streamside class in simple cordage techniques, splicing, thigh-rolling, fishline and hooks, and needles and thread. One leaf provided more fiber than we could use for the class of 15, so we coiled up the leftovers and used them along the trail for Paiute trap triggers and netted bottle carriers.

The most interesting insight gained was the fact the high quality fibers could be obtained through field expedient means without taking the time to ret the fibers as is the method most often described for Yucca fiber preparation.

How do you get a needle and thread? Bend the tip of the leaf back and forth until the outer tissue slightly separates from the fiber at the terminal spine. Next, carefully bend down to the plant and gently place the spine into your mouth. Caution! Be careful not to get poked by other spines! Close the teeth in the side of your mouth over the fibers at the break between the spine and leaf. Place them over the fibers so that they go between the gaps in your molar alignment. This allows you to pull the fibers from the core of the leaf without damaging the contact between the needle and fibers. Begin to pull back steadily and strongly (don't do this if you have week teeth).

It may take a fair amount of pull, but once the fibers "release" they will begin to pull right out of the leaf. When you get them far enough out to grasp them you can take a small stick to wrap them around and use as a handle. The bundle of fibers that extend from the tip can be twisted into cordage to make a "bomb-proof" stitching cord. Good Luck.

Working agave fibers on the banks of Clear Creek, AZ.

David Wescott

RETTING BASSWOOD BARK FOR BAST FIBER
By Scott K. Silsby

In Vol. 1, No. 2 Bulletin of the Society of Primitive Technology, Phillip D. Moore described and explained in his article The Basswood, many of the trees uses. What follows is offered as a supplement and is my experience with the process of retting the stripped bark to obtain highly flexible, rot resistant fiber of good strength and natural beauty.

As Phillip stated, basswood prefers moist woods, often on north facing slopes. I'll add it also thrives on limestone. My place along the Shenandoah River is but a handful of miles from the town of Linden, VA., another namesake of the basswood. There the soil is more acid but also rich and moist.

Abundant as they are I'm reluctant to assault them for their "hides". Fortunately they have a habit of sending up suckers and the more suckers you take, the more they return. Now isn't Nature great. This past spring one of my larger four foot diameter basswoods located too close to our local railroad, failed to leaf out normally. By summer it had managed to generate numerous leaves directly from the bark, mostly on it's lower trunk. By mid summer these leaves had turned yellow and I realized the railroad had been more than generous with it's herbicide application the year prior. The tree was too massive to drop across the tracks so I decided to salvage what bark I could.

When it's sap is up, basswood has one of the easiest barks to strip. But on an eight foot tall, four foot diameter tree perched on a limestone ledge hanging twenty or so feet from the tracks it's a challenge. I cross cut the bark near the base with a greenstone axe then scored the bark vertically in half foot wide strips as high up the tree as I could reach. I then used the axe to pry the bark strips free at the base. Antler or wood bark spuds are more efficient but the axe was available and worked adequately. In order to get strips as long as possible I backed off away from the tree while ripping the strips up until they ran out. These half-foot by twelve foot strips were too stiff to roll up so were carried on the shoulder like boards. With bark from immature trees it is convenient to roll the bark strips up like a giant roll of tape. When doing this, position the outer bark to the inside of the roll to prevent kinks in the desirable inner bark portion.

Retting for Bast

The retting process requires that the inner bark be filled with sap so late spring through summer are your safest times for harvest. Also needed is fresh water, lots of oxygen, plenty of warmth and a system for controlling mosquitoes. A bubbling brook in full sun with enough depth to submerge the bark is ideal so long as it doesn't get subjected to a freshet. Chasing bark down a flooded stream is not retting, it's foolish. Lacking a suitable stream or pond you can use kids wading pools. Double them up for added strength and use a garden hose to flush and oxygenate the batch at least once a day. I did a late fall batch once in the Nature Center Lab using aquarium heaters and an air pump hooked up to a couple of air stoves. It's best to avoid iron buckets as the tannic acid reacts with iron compounds producing something similar to the old colonial style ink. For a very colorful effect try adding lye from hardwood campfires. The ashes should be mixed with water, soaked a while then the liquid is poured through a screen or tight basket into your retting pool. The lye reacts with the tannin producing a burnt sienna color in the bast. I've gotten similar color reactions from osage and locust bark as well. Use care handling and splashing lye as it's very caustic, especially in the eyes.

There is no hard and fast rule on how long the bark should stay in the water. With lots of oxygen and temperatures staying up in the eighties, I've had batches done in as little as a week. Low temperatures and low oxygen can slow the batch down to many weeks. You can speed the process up by removing bark strips and gently beating them against a smooth log or rock with a smooth mallet. This physically breaks the bark down and allows the biological process to invade the bark deeper and sooner. Don't overdue the beating. I've never heard a definitive explanation of
what's going on in the retting process but thought it may be a combination of yeast fermentation and bacterial orgy. Perhaps one of our member has the bottom line on this?

As the process proceeds you will observe the individual fiber layers of bark begin to separate. They are very fine close to the wood, gradually becoming courser towards the outer bark side. Once I can separate the course outer layer it goes on the mulch pile as I have no need for it and it tends to use up too much oxygen, slowing the batch down.

Retted bast from trees in my area are paper thin. If you're getting thicker layers you are either into healthier trees or you are not letting the final layers separate. Properly finished bast will weight like crepe paper but will be smooth, flat and have exceptional strength. Once all the food has been consumed by our micro "whatevers" there is nothing left for fungi to eat as long as the bast is not exposed to excessive dampness for extended periods of time. Check to be sure that there is no mucilage-like sap left in the bast and test this by feeling it. If it feels slippery and slimey, leave it in longer.

Practically all bark can be retted as basswood is, especially slippery elm. My sons witch hazel bow has a slippery elm root bark string that is going into it's sixth year of service. These root fibers were very fine and short but held together very well once corded. Shortly after finishing this string and while it was still damp I gave it a heavy smoking over a campfire rich in oak bark and mountain laurel leaves with the intent of impregnating it with preservatives.

Locally, Ailanthus (Tree of Heaven or Tree of Hell as some folks now call it) is invading the landscape displacing a lot of desirable native species. It has a most foul smelling bark that is thin and easy to strip when the saps up. I stripped some small saplings of their bark and added it to a batch of basswood bark that was about a week old. The Ailanthus retted in less than two days and I was able to lift out some pure white bast fibers that upon drying had the feel and strength of short fiber linen, which is processed from flax. The Ailanthus bark that I left in the batch rotted away over the next two days. Monitor it closely. I corded up a short section and tested it for strength. It was very strong and had a nice smooth feel to it. Not all fibers are as comfortable to handle and work with as basswood is. Some produce fibers that have a tendency to deliver minute slivers into your hand.

Skeeter Management 101

As for mosquitoes it's best to survey the surface of your container and watch for what looks like little rice sized pieces of floating ash which are their eggs. I daily skim them off with a fine meshed aquarium net. You can rig one up using a coat hanger and panty hose. Once the larvae appear as the familiar little wrigglers, it is best to drain your batch, hang the bark-bast to dry thoroughly before refilling with fresh warm water. Filling a garden hose up and letting it sun itself a few hours is a good way to start batches warm without wasting energy. Just don't forget the hose if you leave it under pressure in the sun as I did. Boy it looked like a giant greensnake had eaten one of my cats.

Once you're convinced the batch is thoroughly retted, take it out of the water, rinse it off with fresh water and dry it in the sun. When stored dry it will last as long as wood does. Wet the bast prior to cording and when it redries it will hold whatever shape you formed it into. Because the fiber swells when wet, cord will shrink a little in diameter as it dries leaving a little space between the strings in your cord. Twist it tight and stretch it out very tightly as well to obtain the final cord.

I've used it for may tasks and found it serviceable for bowstrings up to forty-five pounds weight. Weights beyond that required that the strings diameter be made too large in size to fit comfortably in a normal sized nock. Braided bast makes a lightweight, quiet and comfortable quiver strap as well as straps for ceramic ware and gourds. Use your imagination and enjoy one of nature's finest gifts.

CORDAGE

By Steven Edholm and Tamara Wilder

Fiber and Cordage

The aboriginal world is tied together, though often with things other than actual cordage. Buckskin and rawhide thongs, strips of bark, supple twigs, cattails, tules, spruce and pine roots, long leaves like palm, etc...are among the things used to wrap, tie or lash shelters, bundles and packages together. Materials too weak and/or brittle to tie in a knot can be wrapped and tucked several times to secure them and even relatively weak materials can make a strong lashing if wrapped many times.

Figure 1

To start a piece of cordage, grasp a length of fibers near the middle with your hands about 4 inches apart. Twist the fibers away from you with your right hand (B) and towards you with your left hand (A). (Twisting is best achieved by rolling the fibers between your thumb and forefinger.) As you twist the fibers tight, they will want to buckle in the middle and curl upon themselves forming a little curlycue (D) which will be your start.

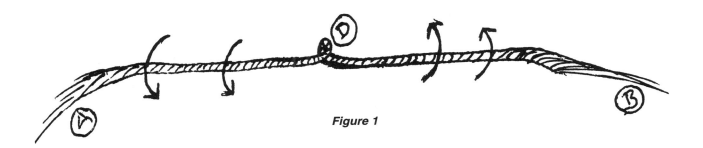

Figure 1

Actual spun cordage, however, is needed for bowstrings, nets, ropes, snares and lots of other things you can't think of until you need a piece. Different shapes and sizes of nets are made for fishing, entrapping large and small game, carrying, for storage in the home and as sleeping hammocks. Netting can be done either knotted or knotless and among these there are many different weaves.

Ropes are used in association with boats and horses, fishing for big fish, harpooning, snaring large game, lashing large beams and posts together, etc. Middle and large sized ropes are usually made from many 2 ply cords twisted together. For instance, 9 two ply cords are twisted into 3 three ply cords which are twisted into one three ply rope. In many parts of the world rope is made on a rope machine (see ***Bushcraft*** by Richard Graves, 1978, Warner Books, Inc.).

Making Cordage

Two ply cordage can be produced by several methods; leg rolling, hand twisting, and mouth rolling. Hand twisting and mouth rolling make very tight cordage which is desirable for bowstrings and more aesthetic pieces of cord, but hand twisting entails twisting each twist one at a time and is very slow. Mouth rolling, however, produces the same results and is much faster, so I will attempt to relate this method, as I have found it to be very efficient.

Hold the start (D) in your teeth, grasping each bundle of fiber (A) and (B) between a thumb and forefinger. This movement should sort of start to make cordage, however the two elements (A) and (B) should be twisted up tightly <u>before</u> they are allowed to wrap around one another as cordage. Practice will allow you to feed them together evenly. Play around with this until you have at least an inch of something resembling string..

Figure 2

Next grasp the junction of the elements (C) and hold it as you twist the already completed section of cordage between (C) and (D) tight so that it has a lot of spring tension. (The tension is critical in this method of cordage because it releases itself by spinning (A) and (B) into cordage.

So, holding the tension thus produced, place (D) back in your mouth and spin on. You won't get very far for this time before you have to take it from your mouth and twist (C) to (D) tight again, but as the space between (C) and (D) gets longer (i.e. more cordage completed) you can make more cordage at a time.

Continue until one or more strands need more fiber.

(more)

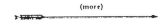

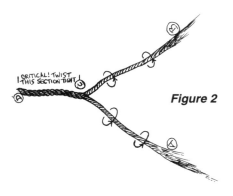

Figure 2

Splicing

Figure 3 shows two types of elbow splices. If you add big wads of fiber at one time or wait until you are almost completely out of fiber before you splice, your cordage will be lumpy or weak. It is important to add fibers Gradually and to stagger the fibers so that they will run out gradually instead of all at once. Good splicing is frequently and in small amounts.

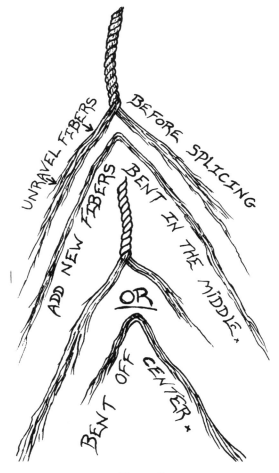

Figure 3

Leg Rolling

Leg rolling is done on the naked thigh (pants don't work). Leg rolled cordage is looser than hand twisted or mouth rolled cordage and therefore is <u>somewhat</u> weaker and less durable. However it is quite serviceable and I would think that it probably accounts for the vast majority of cordage made by "real" primitives because it is so much faster to make. It is used particularly when vast amounts of cordage are required as in nets, hammocks and for the many cords required make rope.

Figure 4

For leg rolling the cordage is always grasped at point (C). (Right handers grasp cordage with left hand and roll with right). The two elements (A) and (B) lay at the top of the thigh about one inch apart. The rolling hand lays over both of them and rolls them down the thigh thus twisting the elements (A) and (B) tight, keeping a good hold on point (C). Ideally, by the time that you roll the two elements to your knee, the two elements (A) and (B) will no longer be one inch apart, but instead, will be lying right next to one another and touching. If not, set them that way without letting the fibers untwist. With the rolling hand, roll back up your thigh. This action should create some inches of cordage. In places like Micronesia and Central/South America people leg roll miles of cordage for nets and hammocks and can roll over 6 inches of cordage per stroke.

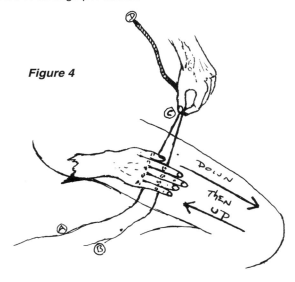

Figure 4

Persevere.

When you need to splice while leg rolling, which you often will, roll the elements up your leg thereby unraveling them to prepare for your splice. Then add fiber as before and continue rolling.

Good luck.

WOVEN TUMPLINES, CARRYING NETS, AND BELTS
By Alice Tulloch

Tumplines, carrying nets, and belts are important tools for managing resources. They free the hands by shifting the loads to a stronger point on the body's frame. They consolidate the load and they allow a greater weight to be carried. They have been found archaeologically dating back many thousand years in the Great Basin and California. Their utility has undoubtedly been known far longer throughout the world. Tumplines and belts have been made from leather and other materials as well, but this discussion will focus on the woven straps of California and the Great Basin.

A tumpline or burden strap is simply a band, about one to one and a half inches wide and more than 9 feet long. It is long enough to tie around the body and the load.

A carrying net is a small net with straps at each end. The net is large enough to hold a basket or bundle. In either case, the strap needs to be wide enough and soft enough to spread the load at forehead or shoulders.

In California and the Great Basin, tumplines traditionally have been made of dogbane (Apocynum cannabinum) or milkweed (Asclepias speciosa and other sp.) bast fibers. These are commonly available cordage plants in this area. Other bast fiber plants such as nettle (Urtica holosericea) or other vascular fibers such as iris (Iris macrosiphon) might be suitable, provided the fibers are long and strong, and an abundant quantity is available.

Preparation of the cordage is the most time consuming part of tumpline production. The cordage needs to be strong and a uniform diameter throughout its length. It needs to be tightly spun, with few tag ends from splicing.

California's ethnographic tumplines typically have five or six warp cords, twice the length of the finished product and approximately 3 1/2 mm in diameter. Approximately 10 yards of slightly smaller diameter cordage is needed for the weft.

For weaving, a needle, awl, or shed stick is used. Weaving does not depend on a loom, just like most of California's pre-contact textiles. Basically, one end of the work is tied to a tree, and the working area is tied to a belt or cord at the weaver's waist, an arrangement called a belt loom.

Work begins at the loop. The mid-points of the warp cords are aligned side by side. Six or seven inches of strap are woven by passing the weft cord between the plys of the warp cords. The loop weaving is centered on the center of the warp cords. The loop is then formed by folding this section over on itself.

The belt loom is now re-tied with the loop near the tree. The warp cords are then alternated, side-by-side, and needle weaving between the cordage plys is resumed. The work proceeds on twice the number of warps as on the beginning loop, making the main band twice as wide as the loop.

It is impractical to weave with more then two yards of weft at a time. Splicing of wefts, as needed, is accomplished, not with a knot, but by overlapping the old and new weft ends for two or three rows of weaving.

Near the end of the warps, for approximately the last foot of weaving, the warps are customarily divided into two parts, apparently for decorative purposes. At the very end, the warps are wrapped to secure them. The tumpline is complete. With use it becomes soft and glossy.

Figure 1: Loop Formation

ESTIMATED TIME	
cordage making	40 hours
weaving	4 hours

(more)

The photos on the next page show how the tumpline is used, with the strap at either forehead or shoulders. The half twist between the head and load provides a hinge that keeps the strap from sliding off the head while walking. A twined hat was often worn in the Great Basin to further cushion the forehead, and as protection from the sun.

The carrying net was fabricated using a similar technique for the straps. The net section would be made using a regular netting technique with shuttle and gage.

Belts are universal. Not only do they support clothing, but they continue to be used today for hanging small tools and pouches at the waist. Among the Wakchumni Yokuts of California (Southern Sierra Nevada Foothills), belts were woven of the same technique as described above. These belts were worn by both sexes to support a breechclout. The belts were plain for every day, decorated with clam shell disk beads for special occasions. The belt was made with plain ends and no loop.

The tumpline and clam disk bead belt shown in the photos are probably the first ones made in California in the last 50 years. The tumpline's utility has already proved out, carrying loads backpacking through three feet of snow. The simple appearance of these tools belies the great increase in carrying effectiveness they give the user.

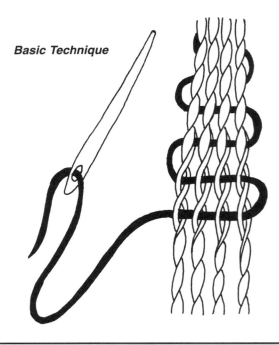

Basic Technique

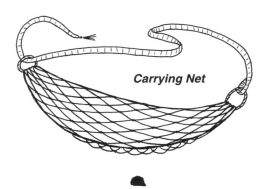

Carrying Net

REFERENCES

D'Azevedo, W.L.
1986   ***Handbook of North American Indians,*** *Vol. 11, Great Basin, Smithsonian Institute, Washington, D.C.*

Gayton, A.H.
1948   ***Yokuts & Western Mono Ethnography,*** *University of California Archaeological Records, Vol. 10, No. 1, October 1948, Pg. 83-85.*

Latta, Frank F.
1977   ***Handbook of Yokuts Indians,*** *Bear State Books, Santa Cruz, Ca.*

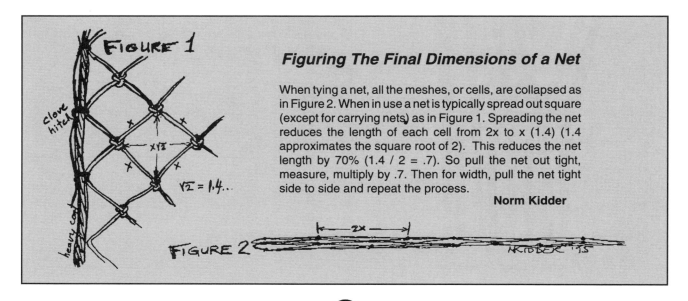

Figuring The Final Dimensions of a Net

When tying a net, all the meshes, or cells, are collapsed as in Figure 2. When in use a net is typically spread out square (except for carrying nets) as in Figure 1. Spreading the net reduces the length of each cell from 2x to x (1.4) (1.4 approximates the square root of 2). This reduces the net length by 70% (1.4 / 2 = .7). So pull the net out tight, measure, multiply by .7. Then for width, pull the net tight side to side and repeat the process.

Norm Kidder

Tumpiline carried on forehead (L) and shoulders (R).

Clam disc bead belt in process (L).

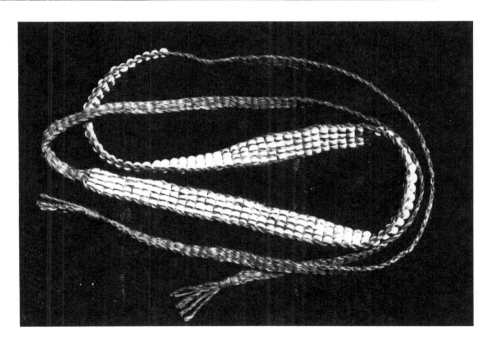

...and completed..

Photos by Ray Echols

NETTING NOTES

Text and Illustrations By Steve Watts, 1992

No one knows when, where and how our prehistoric relatives first brought their fiber skills together to form the Ancestral Net. Perhaps it was a child's string figure gone awry. . .or the sartorial pause in which order was discovered in the chaos of tangled cordage on the shelter floor. . .or the creative combination of knots necessary to secure the previous bundles of food, medicine and tools for the treacherous crossing of a river approaching flood stage. . .or the attempt to recreate the symmetry of the orb web weaving spiders' traps hung by the water's edge highlighted by the dew, sunlight or an early frost.

Yet, sometime, somehow-in all places where our human antecedents dwelled—patterns expressed themselves with fingers, shuttles and string. . .and, the Net became a part of our common technological heritage.

It has brought food to our hearths, born our burdens, bound our hair and when stretched between trees and house posts lulled us to sleep and dreams. The rhythm of mesh upon mesh survives — a symbol of our connectedness—"networked". . .we are joined.

"Net tying, like all traditional skills, is best learned firsthand."

net- n [ME nett, fr. OE; akin to OHG nezzi net, L nodus knot] 1. a. an open-meshed fabric twisted, knotted, or woven together at regular intervals b. something made of net as (1): a device for catching fish, birds, mammals or insects. . .

Although loose weaving and string looping methods are sometimes referred to as "netting" (generically as in Webster) what we are focused on here (more specifically) is a technique most commonly labeled "knotted netting". These true nets are created by the repeated tying of knots in a measured pattern resulting in a series of square or diamond shaped spaces called "meshes". In this respect nets are "tied" — not woven.

Knotted netting can be accomplished by freehand techniques alone, without the use of specialized tools (See the next article in this issue). The first nets were most likely constructed in this way. But, at some point, net makers throughout the world developed two simple devices designed to control the string delivery and the mesh size and thereby increase the speed and uniformity of their work. These tools were and are—the netting needle and the mesh stick.

NETTING NEEDLES

Netting needles (also called "shuttles" and "bobbins") come in both "open" and "closed" styles. Variations in design and ornamentation occur, yet remarkably similar models are found worldwide. This has led many to present complicated and convoluted diffusion scenarios designed to explain this uniformity. But, finding common solutions to common problems seems to be a more likely and straightforward answer.

The needle's purpose is to transport stored (yet easily released) lengths of cordage throughout the knotting series smoothly, with speed and control. Well made needles therefore tend to be strong, yet light in weight and in possession of a certain undefinable "grace" which allows them to turn, slide, glide (or swim?) through the tight spaces they must. Hardwoods, bone, antler, horn and ivory are the materials of choice when making netting needles. These media allow the craftsman to create thin, springy tools capable of taking a smooth finish. A fine polish develops with use, further eliminating snag and drag problems. The patina of a well worn needle attests to the net maker's skills and commitment.

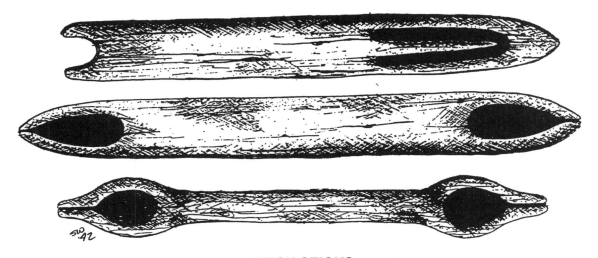

MESH STICKS

Mesh sticks (also called "gauges" and "sizers") are used to control the distance between knots. This insures that the mesh size meets the requirements for the net's function (not too small or too large). It also results in a finished product which exhibits symmetry. The net makers familiarity with his variously sized mesh sticks allows him to predict the amount of cordage and the number of meshes required to produce a net of given size for a given purpose.

The mesh stick's width and thickness determine the mesh size. Length is a matter of personal choice. Some traditional net makers prefer a stick only long enough to sit in the single mesh being tied. Others opt for a longer tool which rests in several previously formed meshes at once.

Smoothness of finish is important here as well; so hardwood, bone, horn, antler and ivory once again prove to be the chosen materials for mesh stick production.

Flat, oval, lenticular and teardrop cross sections have all been observed in aboriginal models. This may reflect personal or cultural preferences. Some mesh sticks are simplicity itself, while others (the Inuit types come to mind) exhibit various sized sections, handles and awl or marlinspike type points for knot separation. While some veteran net makers can, by their experience, tie a very uniform net using fingers and eyesight alone to gauge mesh size, a mesh stick is used by most and could be considered a must for the novice.

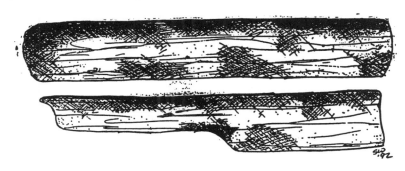

Mesh and Tool Size Considerations

The size of net's mesh is determined by the net's use. In fishing this is related to both the size of the fish and net type (dip, trap, gill, drag, etc.). Mammal and bird nets (as in Great Basin and Australian Aborigine examples) exhibit mesh size appropriate to specific species. Burden nets (bags, gear slings, etc.) have meshes related to the size and weight of the anticipated articles to be contained. And, so on. . .

A mesh stick's width reflects the length of one of the four sides of the mesh it produces. Is it too obvious to say that the mesh stick determines the size of the finished mesh, and/or the size of the mesh is determined by the mesh stick width? Maybe so, but I said it anyway.

A netting needle's width should be narrower than the mesh stick being used.

The String

The most time consuming aspect of net making in the aboriginal style is not the net tying (which goes steadily and smoothly once mastered), but rather the making of the string itself. Materials must be gathered, processed and then spun or laid into thread or cordage of the correct dimensions — in adequate quantity for the size and style of net desired. Several yards to several miles may be required (from a small bag to a gill net which spans the river's width). A net maker working on a major project may pass the work of many others through his fingers—the needles loaded with the efforts of an entire community.

Rawhide, sinew, flax, dogbane, cedar, milkweed, cotton, wool. . .the list goes on. Throughout man's history nets have probably been tied from almost every fiber capable of being made into string. There are cultural preferences, of course. The Paiutes insist on dogbane for their rabbit nets, while Northwest Coast peoples look to stinging nettle fibers for their large deep-water nets.

Once again the importance of string becomes paramount when considering the aboriginal lifestyle. If a net means food, then indeed the string is the "thread of life" itself.

The Knot

Overhands, figure eights, square knots and others are often found in traditionally tied nets. But, it is the sheet bend (also called the "mesh knot") that is pandemically the net maker's knot of choice.

An excellent knot for joining two lengths of rope, the sheet bend serves in netting to link the meshes. When properly tied it will not flip or slip as will a square knot, and it is better suited to use with a mesh stick than are overhands or figure eights.

What may seem difficult at first, soon becomes a familiar task. With each tying of the sheet bend the pattern is reinforced.

*These are "netting notes"—not step-by-step instructions. Net tying, like all traditional skills, is best learned firsthand.

Two styles and sizes of netting needles.

David Wescott photos

The Knot

My thanks go to John White for teaching me and to Pegg Mathewson for inspiring me. They are my connections to the ancient world of net tying—the most recent knots in a series of meshes reaching back. . .back to the first net and beyond.

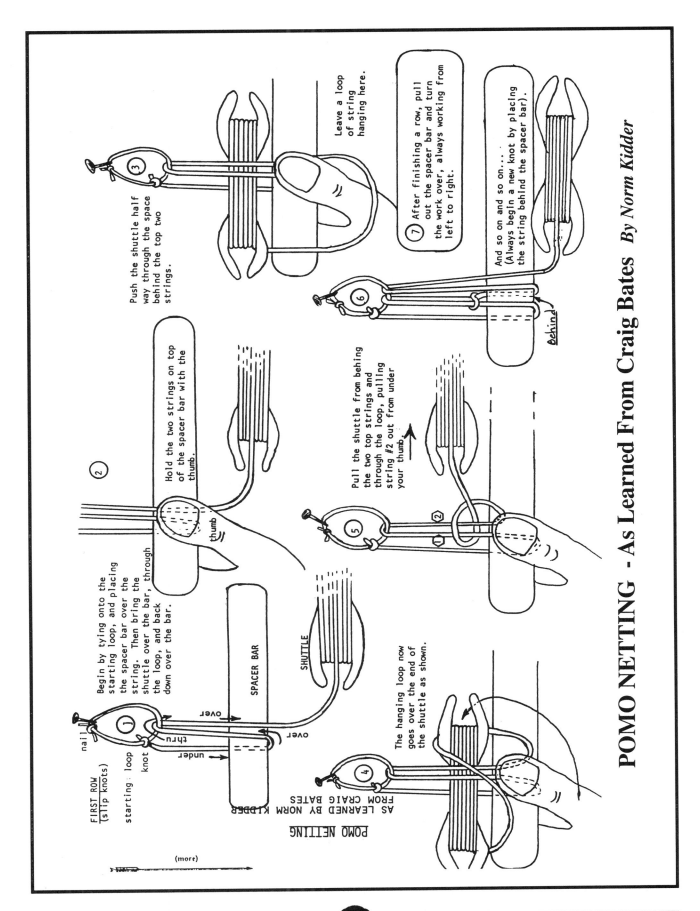

POMO NETTING - As Learned From Craig Bates *By Norm Kidder*

Push the shuttle half way through the space behind the top two strings.

③

Leave a loop of string hanging here.

⑦ After finishing a row, pull out the spacer bar and turn the work over, always working from left to right.

And so on and so on...
(Always begin a new knot by placing the string behind the spacer bar).

behind

⑥

② Hold the two strings on top of the spacer bar with the thumb.

thumb

Pull the shuttle from behing the two top strings and through the loop, pulling string #2 out from under your thumb.

⑤

FIRST ROW
(slip knots)

starting: loop knot

nail

① over
thru
under

over

SPACER BAR

SHUTTLE

The hanging loop now goes over the end of the shuttle as shown.

④

POMO NETTING
AS LEARNED BY NORM KIDDER
FROM CRAIG BATES

(more)

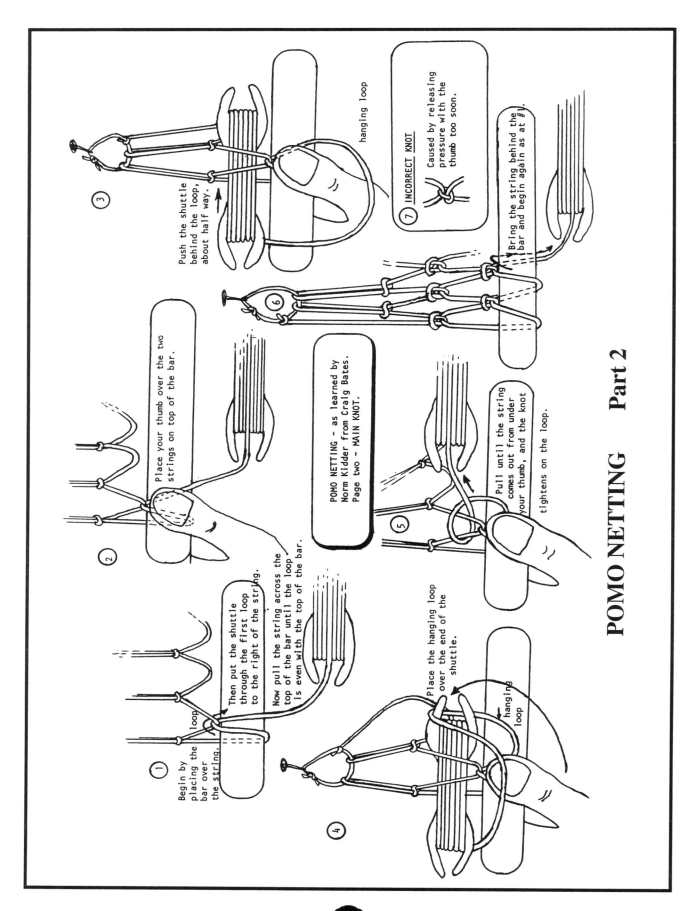

POMO NETTING   Part 2

③ Push the shuttle behind the loop, about half way.

hanging loop

⑦ INCORRECT KNOT
Caused by releasing pressure with the thumb too soon.
Bring the string behind the bar and begin again as at #4.

⑥

② Place your thumb over the two strings on top of the bar.

POMO NETTING – as learned by Norm Kidder from Craig Bates. Page two – MAIN KNOT.

⑤ Pull until the string comes out from under your thumb, and the knot tightens on the loop.

① Begin by placing the bar over the string.

Then put the shuttle through the first loop to the right of the string.

Now pull the string across the top of the bar until the loop is even with the top of the bar.

④ Place the hanging loop over the end of the shuttle.

hanging loop

A DOGBANE NET
Photos and Text By Jeff Gottleib

In the Fall of 93 when the dogbane was ready to pick, I started making and storing cordage. I got the idea to make a net. My friend Barry Keegan sent me the Pomo netting techniques published by Norm Kidder (see pages 81-82).

The sizable spool I had collected was all done in the hand. I would not like to speculate how long it took to make per foot.

If I was going to make a net, I wanted something useful, so I settled on a seine. I had used them many times as a kid, to collect fishing bait. And if I was going to make a seine, I might as well make a good-sized one. My "lever" looked long enough at 12 1/2 feet. That big fat spool of cordage made only 3 rows of 1 1/2" meshes. I decided not to make a gauge stick, and to use

Thigh-rolling dogbane (Apocynum) fibers.

my fingers, because I would always have them with me. I just formed each loop around my left index and middle fingers. I soon could eyeball a mesh I was making and tie its knot so as to make it a uniform size (see next page).

I thigh-rolled the rest of the cordage. Taking a dozen dogbane stems, I quickly stripped the bark off the wood, and buffed all the bark fiber together in a bundle, taking care not to tangle it into a ball. Dampening my left pant leg made thigh-rolling easier. Practice increased speed considerably.

I discovered that 12 stems made approximately 25 feet of cordage, which filled my netting needle. This was enough to knot one row of meshes. With practice, I could turn 12 stems into a row of meshes in two hours and 15 minutes. The net, at 30" deep, consists of 33 rows of meshes. This means it contains approximately 825 feet of cordage and took more than 75 hours to make. Knowing how slowly I made the first 10 rows, it was more like 90 hours total. It required approximately 400 stems of dogbane. This does not include the lengths of two-ply, three-lay heavy cord that hold the row of sinkers at the bottom and floats at the top.

The floats are sections of the trunk of a basswood

sapling, drilled out like spools. The weights are flat cobbles of a soft schist, in which I ground notches for tying places.

Cordmaking grew tedious as the months wore on. Knotting the meshes was a pleasure, very soothing and satisfying. I took the net with me where ever I went and worked on it while commuting by train into New York City, at meetings, while watching TV. Of all the primitive skills I practice, this project was, for more people, a part of their living memory. Several people volunteered information about their families in Cuba, South America and elsewhere, who had been fishermen and had worked on their nets in the same way.

The Hudson River Museum expressed interest in exhibiting the net. I had to rush the last 10 rows or so. That took a lot of the pleasure out of it. I had to deliver the finished net immediately in order to make the exhibit deadline. This meant that it never saw water! When I get it back in January '95 I will add ten more rows of meshes, making the depth a little over 3' and replace the sinkers with spool-shaped soapstone ones. I think they will work a bit better, although the flat cobbles are more regionally authentic. Once I am finished in the spring, I will take it to water and catch something in it! Readers, feel free to write me to find out the results.

Using a netting neddle to create the mesh.

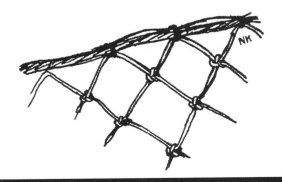

THE FIRE WATCHERS
Text, Photos and Illustrations By Doug Elliott, ©1992

SWAMP DANCERS: Cattails

"Supermarket of the swamp" — that's what Euell Gibbons, the dean of American wild food foragers, called the common cattail.

It is said that you could never starve living next to a cattail marsh. I think this is close to the truth. You can hardly find a more versatile wild plant.

Young, tender cattail shoots, when they first poke out of the cool water in early spring, have been called "Cossack asparagus" because it is a traditional spring food among country folk in Russia. Sturtevant's extract from Clarke's **Travels in Russia** tells of people " devouring cattail shoots raw with a degree of avidity as though it had been a religious observance. It was to be seen in all the streets and in every house, bound into faggots. They peel off the outer rind and find a tender white part of the stem which for about its length of 18 inches, afford a crisp, cooling and very pleasant article of food."

If you want to try this spring delicacy, just head for your favorite swamp when the weather warms and look around the edge of the old faded, winter-beaten cattail leaves and stalks for the new green shoots poking up out of the water. Just wade on out and start pulling. Each shoot usually breaks off at the base where it joins the rootstock. The base

of these shoots have a tender core a few inches long. They are mild flavored and can be eaten raw right out of the swamp (Be sure of the water quality.), or they can be stir-fried, steamed, added to soups, or used in salads.

In late spring or early summer, the part that later becomes the "cattail" is forming. It is composed of two cigar-shaped spikes, one above the other. The one beneath is the seed-bearing pistillate, or female flower, that later turns into the brown "cattail." The top one is the pollen-bearing staminate, or male flower. The dry stem that protrudes from the top of the brown cattail later in the

Yellow pollen blowing from the spike.

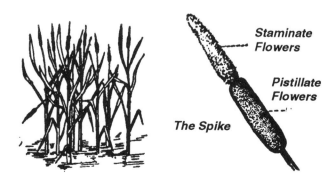

The Spike

Staminate Flowers

Pistillate Flowers

A ready snack of tender spring shoots.

season is the remains of this male flower. Just before they come into bloom, both members are green and wrapped in a sheath or husk. At this stage the top, staminate spikes can be picked and steamed for twenty minutes and served with salt and butter like miniature corn-on-the-cob. I call them "cat-on-the-cob" and they are one of my favorite wild foods. They have their own unique flavor which to me is reminiscent of corn, though some folks say they taste like artichoke hearts. Even if you don't like artichokes, or corn, there still is a good chance you will like cattail tops.

Horizontal rootstocks contain a starchy core that may be used for flour.

A little later in the summer the spikes will shed their wraps and the nuptial delights begin. The green staminate spike swells and begins a lusty shedding of powdery yellow pollen which spills down over the pistillate flower spike below and, with the help of a breeze, is dispersed across the marsh to insure a health cross pollination of the rest of the cattail population. You too can share in the pollination celebration if you are willing to wade out among the blossoms. By inverting and shaking each swollen, yellow spike into a bag, a substantial amount of pollen can be collected in very little time. This pollen is as smooth and fine as talcum powder. It can be mixed with equal

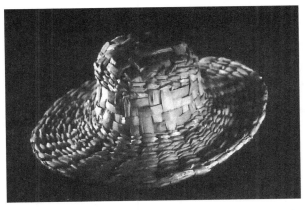

Cattails may be used to create headwear as simple sunshades or fancy hats.

parts of flour and made into wholesome yellow-tinted bread, pancakes, biscuits or pastries, and can be used like saffron to color rice dishes. Cattail pollen is also used in various native American ceremonies.

The high-priced "bee pollen" that is sold in health food stores as a nutritional supplement is simply pollen gathered by bees from various flowers (including cattails, sometimes). What you are collecting from cattails is essentially the same, except that it is gathered by you. You might call it "people pollen."

While this "celebration of pollination" is going on in the upper levels of the marsh, down below in the muck and mire, the cattails' rootstocks are also rapidly growing, producing tender, white growing tips. These tips, if caught before they shoot upwards into the light, are good eating. Just peel them and munch them fresh, right out of the marsh, or use them in salads or cooked dishes.

The long sections of horizontal rootstocks between the leaf clumps have a starchy core that can be utilized as flour. Even today cattail flour is still an important food for some Native American groups. One method of extracting the flour is to dry the roots, grind them up, and sift them to separate the flour from the fibrous cortex. I have also used the "Euell Gibbons method" which entails washing and peeling the fresh roots. The cores are then put into a bowl of water and crushed by hand until the fibers are all separated. The sediment is allowed to settle for about half an hour and then the water is carefully poured off, leaving the starchy residue on the bottom. More water can be added and subsequently poured off after further settling to more fully refine the product. After the last settling, pour off as much of the liquid as possible, add a little regular flour to thicken it and use it to make your favorite breadstuff.

At the junction of the stalk and the rhizome is a thickened area of starch which, after peeling, can be eaten raw, or cooked like a potato and added to stews or soups.

Cattail leaves have long been used as weaving material, not only for mats, baskets and hats but also to make rush chair seats. If you want to weave with cattails you need to gather the leaves when they are full grown but still green. They must first be dried under cover and then moistened before use.

Some folks call cattails "punks" because the dried brown heads slowly smolder when ignited. The pleasant smelling smoke will repel mosquitoes.

If you want to use cattail heads in dried flower arrangements, be sure to gather them early in the summer or one day you might come home to find your tidy, artistic arrangement has "exploded" and filled your house with bushels of fluff from the downy seed hairs. This fluff can be used mixed in with other material in a tinder bundle for starting fires.

These hairs are light and buoyant. This serves to carry the seeds long distances, even to isolated and newly formed wet areas. Because of this cattails can be found in many parts of the world, from the tropics to the far North.

I have a down vest that looks like one of the expensive goose down vests that have been popular with outdoor

Repairing an antique chair with twisted cattail leaves.

David Wescott

A "kitchen witch" made from cattail.

people for years — except mine's homemade and it's stuffed not with goose feathers but with down from about forty ripe cattail heads. It's very warm and though it's not as light as goose down, it has one special feature that feathers don't have: It floats! My cattail down vest doubles as a life preserver. This is quite a comfort on winter boating adventures and when I'm skating on thin ice.

I don't know if I have established that you wouldn't starve next to a cattail patch, but with all the processes I've described, you would not suffer from boredom while you were wasting away.

While we humans might barely subsist on cattails, these ubiquitous marsh plants provide a bounty of food and shelter for wildlife. Cattails are the life blood of marsh dwelling critters. It is here in the shallow water among the crowded stalks and tangled roots that the food chain starts. This is the nursery ground for the insects and the tiny fish that feed the larger fish, the amphibians and reptiles, the birds and ultimately the rest of us.

Cattail roots and shoots are the principle food of muskrats. It is often said that if you want to find muskrats, just look for cattails. Muskrats live off the starchy shoots and rootstocks

Muskrat feed beds after highwater feeding.

of cattails and they construct their lodges partially from the leaves and stalks. They dig tunnels and canals through the thick mats of roots, creating pools of open water in the dense growth that protect small fish, frogs, turtles and other creatures. Marsh wrens, rails, bitterns, red-wing blackbirds and ducks build nests in the depths of the cattail marshes while herons, raccoons, possums, otters, mink and other animals prowl among the cattails in search of prey.

Native Americans have long used the cattail not only for food but also to thatch wickiups, wigwams and other shelters and to weave mats and baskets as well.

According to an old Indian story, Coyote, that foolish trickster-creator, was out walking one evening. He was following a trail along a ridge beside a low-lying area. Suddenly he heard sounds coming from that low spot. It sounded like music. It was almost dark and he couldn't see very well but he could hear the music. Yes, there was no mistaking; that was the sound of dance rattles. There was a dance going on. There was nothing Coyote liked better than a dance. He knew he was the best dancer and he loved to get right in the middle of the dance circle and show off. So he hustled right down that hill and pushed his way into the middle of the crowd. He could hear the rhythmic rustling of the dance rattles. Swish, swish, swish, swish. There were so many of them and they were making beautiful music. Swish, swish, swish, swish. Everybody was swaying back and forth. Swish, swish, swish, swish. Coyote started doing his fanciest steps and saying things like, "You all think you know how to dance. I'll show you how I dance!" And he started really strutting his stuff. But nobody seemed to notice. They just crowded around him and kept swaying back and forth. And the dance rattles kept their steady rhythm. Swish, swish, swish, swish. Coyote started kicking his feet out in all directions and singing loudly. But the crowd paid him no attention. They just kept swaying back and forth, and the rattles kept the rhythm. Swish, swish, swish, swish. Coyote danced, and danced, and the crowd danced along, never stopping to rest. And the rattles played on. Swish, swish, swish, swish. They danced into the night and the music never stopped, nor did the dancers. Coyote was getting tired, but he didn't want to be the first to quit. He started bragging, "So you all think you can dance. Well I'll show you I can dance a LONG time!" And the crowd danced on into the night, never stopping, even for a moment. Swish, swish, swish, swish. Coyote was getting more and more tired, but the crowd kept on dancing. Swish, swish, swish, swish. Finally he said, "You know sometimes when we dance, we rest!" But nobody stopped to rest; they just kept swaying back and forth and the rattles kept on rattling. Swish, swish, swish, swish. The dancers kept on all night until Coyote was so exhausted, he could barely stand up. And when the dawn came he looked around and realized that he hadn't been dancing with human dancers, he had been dancing with Swamp Dancers. That's the Native American name for cattails. And as he looked around, bleary-eyed and exhausted, the swamp dancers were still swaying back and forth and they are still out there and they are still dancing. Swish, swish, swish, swish.

I hope you can get out there and join them.

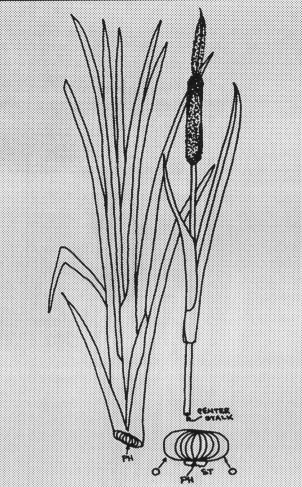

Outside leaves (O):
These are the shortest, broadest and generally the thinnest on any given stalk. Because of their rarity, the finest quality broad leaves should be saved. To flatten a leaf, cut the skin on its concave side. Edges of these broad leaves which are thin and tough are especially useful as a stitching material, for use with a needle.

Standard leaves (ST):
These leaves comprise the greatest number (about six) in any given stalk. They are concave on one side and convex on the other.

Prime Heart leaf (PH):
There is only one leaf in the heart of the vegetative stalk that is convex on both sides. Split in half on the long axis. This is the strongest and most supple leaf in the stalk.

Leaf variations:
It is suggested that you become familiar with the cattails growing over a wide range. In certain areas you may find plants that have particularly broad leaves at their bases. In other areas the plants may have a leaf which is narrower than usual.

from Bush Arts By Mors Kochanski

Mrs. Kompost's Extraordinary Cattail Leaf Visor

By Steve Watts, Photos by David Wescott

Begin with 20 leaves folded in half.

1. Start corner like this.

These initial weavers form the base for the brim of the visor. Note how the weavers start out being split and woven as "singles" at the outset, and alternate starting on the upper or lower leg (Figs. 1 & 2). This alternating split or single weaver method is required to maintain the checkerboard pattern along the brim. Once all ten weavers are put into place as singles, each weaver (with its two halves) may now be used as a single unit or double weaver for the remainder of the checkeborad pattern (Fig. 3)

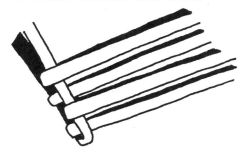

2. Initial setup - every other weaver is a single both ways

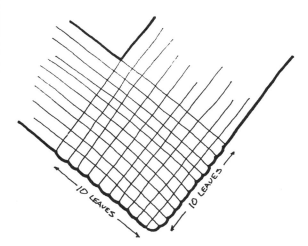

10 LEAVES

10 LEAVES

3. Checker weave 10 weavers in each direction (using both "halves)

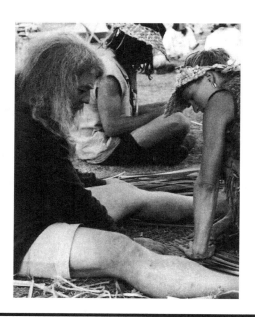

4. Fold inside double weaver back, weaving over and under to front and back. Pick up a new weaver each trip back.

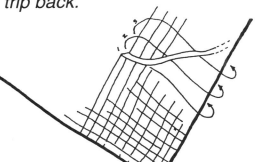

5. Continue this reduction to the ends.

Turning the inside weaver back creates a 45 degree fold in the weaver. Weave over and under with the double weaver until you reach the brim (Fig. 4). Bend the weaver around the brim and weave back. Pick up a new double weaver and begin weaving back toward the brim with both weavers until the original one runs out. Continue until they're all used up (Fig. 5).

Tie the ends together, tatoo your belly and play the flute

THE CATTAIL DOLL

Text and Illustrations By Mors Kochanski, © *1989*

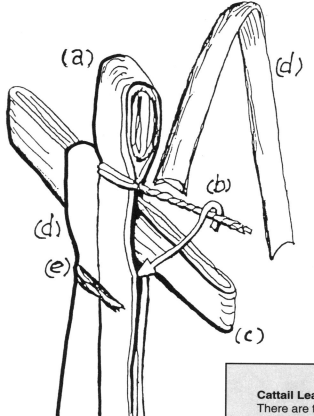

The Simple Doll

The simple doll is one that a pre-schooler can make. It is made in much the same way as the sedge doll described earlier.

(a) To make the head, neck and body core, a leaf is rolled into an oval form and covered with another leaf or two.

(b) For the tie at the neck split a small leaf down the middle, wrap its middle portion once or twice around the neck and twist the ends together until the tie is snug. Tuck the twisted end into the body core to prevent its unraveling.

(c) For the arms, a leaf is folded as shown so that it equals the height of the doll, and its ends are hidden in the body core.

(d) For a coat, a few leaves are placed over each shoulder.

(e) The waist is bound like the neck but the twisted end is tucked under the waist binding. Trim the doll to complete it.

Cattail Leaves

There are two types of cattail plant, the seed-bearing and the vegetative. The seed-bearing plant sports the familiar mace or head and the vegetative one consists entirely of leaves. The leaves from the seed-bearing stalk are seldom used as they are inferior in shape or length compared to those of the vegetative stalk and can be classified as seen in the diagram on page 13.

Harvesting Cattail

For the applications described in this book, a good time to gather cattail is in the fall as soon as the plant has turned brown. By mid-winter the leaves may be so deteriorated from weathering by wind and sun that they become sodden rather than soft when soaked. They also become more fragile. Gather the leaves when they can be folded into bundles of a size that can be easily stuffed into a large plastic bag. Ideally, this should be done after a rain when the leaves are supple enough to fold without cracking. The leaves should be dried for storage or they will mold. Properly stored, they will remain suitable for crafting for years. They should be well soaked and perhaps wrapped with an old towel or cotton shirt and kept in a plastic bag for a day or two before use, for maximum pliability.

The cattail doll in its many forms is one of the most universally popular natural crafts. This type differs from the corn husk doll in that cattail leaves are longer and coarser. The dolls in this article are patterned after an Ojibway doll found near Lake Winnepeg, Canada.

The Standard Doll

The standard doll is the simple unembellished form that is the starting point for more complex dolls.

(a) This is what this doll looks like. It requires about six vegetative cattail stalks (PH).

(b) The head of the doll is two standard size leaves that are wound into a ball, as if winding string. As the head should be more an egg shape than spherical, squeeze the ball now and again to make it more oval. The completed ball is one-seventh to one-eighth the height of the doll.

(c) The ball is now covered with about six smaller or narrower-than-average leaves as these tend to produce a better effect. All are made to cross at the very top of the head and are overlapped so that the ball is covered neatly and completely. Once this is done the neck is twisted slightly to tighten the covering a little more. The neck is then tied with a prime heart leaf.

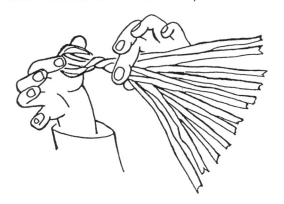

(d) Gather a small bundle of leaves about four times as long as the doll is tall. Lay some leaves in the opposite direction to make the bundle of a more even thickness. At a point one-third from an end, double the bundle and begin twisting the first arm. About seven twists will produce a length of arm that is half the height of the doll. At a point one-third from the remaining end, double the bundle and twist until the base of the first arm is reached.

(e) The completed arms should form a T.

(f) Part the body core in the middle and insert the arms. Fold leaves over each shoulder until a desired bulk is achieved and tie at the waist. Trim the bottom of the dress. The standard doll shown at (a) is now complete.

ADVENTURES WITH THE VERSATILE TULE

*Text, Illustrations and Photos
By Jim Riggs, © 1994*

Dennis Torresdal

"What's a tule?"

When my friend Rusty returned from Boy Scout camp, I asked him about his adventures. He said that because of this minor infraction of the rules, he had spent a lot of time on "tule detail" -- pulling tules (too-lees) from the lake margin to clear the camp swimming hole. I didn't know what a tule was, nor could I imagine that far into the future I would voluntarily spend a lot of my own time pulling tules.

Tules, genus *Scirpus* of the sedge family, are distributed in a variety of species worldwide. Also known as bulrushes, the dark green tules are distinguished easily from cattails (*Typha*) and other marsh vegetation by their tall, un-branched round stems, which reach 10 or more feet in Oregon. Tules often grow in pure stands of several acres. Had I grown up aboriginally almost anywhere in the Great Basin or Columbia Plateau regions of the Intermountain West, tules would have been integral to my life from birth. Since I have been teaching aboriginal life-skills courses, I've researched and experimented considerably with the multifarious uses of the tule that I missed in my own childhood.

Even a cursory inspection of Western native cultures reveals certain plants of utmost importance: red cedar bark and wood, for fiber and construction materials along the Northwest coast, and sagebrush, fulfilling those same functions in the Great Basin, are but two examples. Tules were prolific along streams, lakes and fresh or saltwater marshes over the entire area and had the distinction of being used by nearly all tribes.

Each spring the new tule shoots spurt upward from perennial rhizomes (underground stems) and reach full height in a few short weeks. In early June in the Malheur National Wildlife Refuge, I've watched the tules grow several inches in one day. With the frosts of fall, the green stems die, fade through yellow to brownish and are bent and broken by the winter winds. These dense tangles provide the protective cover necessary for early nesting waterfowl the next spring before new vegetation emerges.

Muskrats cut the abundant tules, eat the succulent bases and pile the stems in large conical heaps for their well-insulated winter lodges. At Utah Lake in the late 1820s, mountain man Jedediah Smith wrote in his journal

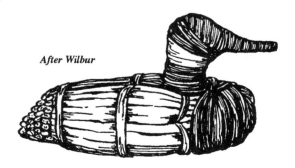

After Wilbur

that we "passed through a large swamp of bulrushes, when suddenly the lake presented itself to our view. On its bank were a number of buildings constructed of bulrushes, and resembling muskrat houses. These we soon discovered to be wigwams, in which the Indians remained during the stay of the ice." It is entirely possible these dwellings were patterned after muskrat lodges, for we humans have learned much from the animals.

Tule houses seen by Smith were probably the common Great Basin type. A dozen stout but pliable freshly cut willows were planted upright in the ground in a circle 10 to 12 feet across. At 7 to 8 feet high, the tops were pulled nearly together to form a semi-dome (a smokehole was left open at top center). Thinner willows were tied horizontally around the uprights to hold the dome's shape. This frame was covered with several "prefabricated" panels of tules and/or cattail leaves held together with willows.

Each panel, about 5 feet long and 5 feet wide, was constructed quite simply. Two or three willows were laid parallel on the ground about 18 inches apart. Quantities of tules were piled to a depth of 6 inches across these willows. A second set of willows was positioned on top, directly above those on the bottom. The corresponding willows were then tied together every few inches through the tules to tightly clamp the tules in place. These finished tule-and-willow "sandwiches" were then picked up and leaned around the willow dome.

On larger houses, two tiers of panels were used, those placed on top overlapping the ones leaned around the base. These panel walls were warmer than tule mats and less time-consuming to make, but they required considerably more tules. Living in such snug but fire-prone dwellings, it is no wonder the Great Basin peoples seldom owned no more articles than they could quickly grab at a moment's notice and carry out in one trip.

The second major type of tule dwelling was a tepee-like structure of leaned poles covered with several layers of tule mats. In the northern Great Basin, these conical houses were about the same size as the tule-paneled domes; but over much of the Columbia Plateau, tule mat lodges often reached massive proportions. One lodge along the Clearwater River in Idaho, described by Alvin M. Josephy Jr. in **The Nez Perce Indians and the Opening of the Northwest**, housed an entire village: "It was about 150 feet in length and contained 24 fires down its center and about twice that many families."

The typical Plateau lodge frame was like an elongated tepee; the semicircular ends were connected by a long horizontal ridgepole and subsidiary poles. Mats intended for lodge coverings were commonly 10 or 12 feet long and as wide as the tules were tall, usually 6 to 8 feet. The tules were laid on the ground, the thicker butts alternating with the thinner tops, and strung together with several rows of fine cordage hand-twisted from dogbane fibers. The tules were flattened along each seam to retard splitting, and a row of fiber twining reinforced the edges of each mat. These long mats, laid and tied in shingle fashion over the pole frames, would shed rain admirably. Additional poles were frequently leaned against the outside of the mats to further secure them during windy weather.

Winter lodges were used only part of the year and were usually dismantled each spring as the inhabitants prepared to begin their seasonal food harvesting rounds. Mat construction was a tedious job, but well-made mats would last two or three winters if they were carefully rolled up and cached during the off seasons in dry pits or caves. Worn or frayed mats were recycled into interior floor coverings,

TULE MAT LODGE   WILLOW FRAME →   TULE or CATTAIL & WILLOW HOUSE ←→

Two Common Northern Paiute Winter Dwellings

bedding and wrappings for cached foods.

Soon after many of the Plateau cultures (such as Nez Perce, Spokane and Umatilla) obtained horses, they began annual trips eastward in late summer to the buffalo ranges of western Montana and Wyoming. During this period of increased contact with the Plains groups, the familiar tepee came into vogue, and lodge coverings of skin and, later, canvas nearly replaced those of tule mats. Have you ever seen a tule-mat lodge at the Pendleton Round-Up?

Of all the native groups who made some use of the tule, the Klamath, who specifically adapted their culture to the south-central Oregon marshes and lakes, were the champions of tule knowledge. From the locally prolific styles -- infant cradles, sandals, boots, leggings, aprons, skirts, capes, hats and hoods, mittens, spoons, plates, trays, dolls and other toys, games, arrow quivers, cordage, storage and carrying bags and myriad basketry forms for all conceivable uses. Most of these articles were manufactured by a finger-weaving technique called twining, in which the long elements, the warps, were bound together by twisting additional tule stems, the wefts, around them.

The nature of the tule stem makes it well suited to primitive manufactures. Properly prepared, the smooth green stems are pliable and easy to manipulate. The stem core is much like Styrofoam, a lightweight froth filled with tiny air pockets that provide bulk, excellent insulation and floatation. For immediate, temporary use, fresh stems were quickly twisted into open-weave carrying bags and rough baskets that were casually and just as quickly discarded.

In preparation for making more permanent articles, however, the fresh stems were harvested and spread on the ground to partially dry. During this "controlled wilting," the tules dehydrated, shrank somewhat and became stronger.

The bulk of twined tule work was of whole or split stems in various combinations, but the finest baskets were made by striping away only the tougher green outer covering, hand twisting the long lengths of fiber into uniform two-ply cords and twining these together. Some coiled baskets of tule also were made. The small, dark brown tule roots were incorporated into either weave to create bicolored designs.

Besides its versatility in manufacture, the tule contributed significantly to the aboriginal diet. In late summer quantities of ripe seeds were harvested, parched, winnowed and ground into flour for breads and mush. The long, snake-like rhizomes were pulled from the silt and muck of the marsh bottoms, washed and baked in pit ovens to make their starchy interiors more digestible. New shoots and succulent cores of the mature stem bases were eaten fresh or baked. Both rhizomes and stem bases were dried and ground into flour, either raw or after baking. All the edible parts of the tule have an agreeable, though bland, flavor. Like the more familiar cattail, the underwater parts of the tule can be collected for food at any time of the year, and they were especially important in late winter when previously stored foods ran low. Breaking the ice, wading in the numbing water and groveling in the muck for tule rhizomes in near-zero weather was doubtless not a preferred activity (I've tried it), but it beats starving!

Earlier in this century, the small matted wads of tule fiber commonly excavated from Great Basin caves perplexed interpretive archaeologists. Were these the result of some unknown fiber-cleaning process? They seemed awfully tangled to be of much use. As archaeology became more holistic, and the aboriginal diet was examined, these mystery wads were determined to be "quids," the discarded by-products of aborigines masticating tule rhizomes to extract the nutritious starch.

Tule rhizomes or stem bases may have had another important function. In his book **Stone Age in the Great Basin**, Emory Strong reports, "Edward Palmer, before 1870, saw desert Indians chew the roots as a preventative of thirst before starting a long journey" and "Dr. Walter P. Cottam of the University of Utah reported that he experienced neither hunger nor thirst during one day of strenuous field work while he chewed the sweet starchy roots."

I have also tried this with some success during desert travel and intend to experiment further.

Tule sandal made by "close-twining" method.

In late summer, little green aphids (mealy plum aphids) often cover the stalks of tules, the common reed (*Phragmites*) and other emergent vegetation. These aphids suck the plant juices, process them through their bodies and excrete them back into the stems as clear, sweet droplets called "honey-dew." When an aphid-infested stand was located, the aborigines would collect these droplets in quantity, roll the sticky crystals into little balls and eat them as a sugary candy, one of the few natural sweeteners available.

Years ago, when I first encountered a colony of these aphids, I hazily remembered reading of honey-dew, but I couldn't remember all the particulars. I gathered my fortitude (this is real experimental archaeology) and ingested a large lick of the aphids. They tasted green and mushy, but not sweet. Then I sampled the dried crystals and knew I'd found the real honey-dew. Honey Lake, ringed with extensive tule stands, in far northeastern California was probably named after this valued substance.

Of all the articles aboriginal peoples created from tules, I think the most wondrous is the tule boat. Like most material culture items made in the Great Basin, the underlying motivation in constructing the tule boat was to aid in the food-collecting process. I first read of the boat in Margaret Wheat's exceptional book **Survival Arts of the Primitive Paiutes** and immediately incorporated its construction into my aboriginal life-skills courses.

With nothing more than knives, a tolerance for mosquitoes and a convenient stand of tall tules, half a dozen eager people can create a tule boat in about three hours. The tules are cut and laid, all facing the same direction, in two piles, each a little more than 2 feet in diameter at the butt ends. Long braided or twisted ropes of cattails, tules or other sedges are quickly made, and each pile is wrapped and bound at several points to form a solid bundle. The two bundles are then bound side-by-side to form the hull of the boat. The narrow ends of the bundles are drawn up together and with more rope to form the pointed, raised bow. A gunwale of smaller tule bundles is laced onto the "deck," and the boat is completed.

It is during the boat-building process, perhaps from the tedium of cuttings, carrying and piling hundreds of tules, that the "tule jokes" begin:

"After the boat, let's build a tule hang glider!"

A student struggling to maintain balance on a boat listing into the wind hears a helpful suggestion yelled from a classmate on shore: "Don't lean windward, lean tule."

I'll spare you more; perhaps this is tule many already.

Each boat will fully support one person kneeling at the stern, where the bundles are thickest. In the shallow marshes, the boat was normally pushed along with a pole, rather than paddled. In the Great Basin, tule boats were used by the Paiutes to scour the marshes for waterfowl eggs and to herd young birds and adults, especially the ubiquitous coot or mudhen during its midsummer flightless eclipse plumage phase, into nets strung across narrow channels of open water. The gunwales on the boat kept the pile of eggs and dead birds from falling off, and the successful hunter often found himself wading in the water pushing his food-laden raft ahead of him.

The boats generally were used for a few consecutive days until the desired quantity of birds or eggs was harvested, then were casually abandoned. Larger, more carefully constructed boats of tules and similar plants were used by aboriginal peoples around the world. Thor Heyerdahl, in **The Ra Expeditions**, demonstrated that a primitively made

Close-up of a portion of a twined tule mat.

reed boat could be seaworthy enough to cross the Atlantic Ocean [See also **BPT #6**].

The arid Great Basin is a land of seeming contradictions and extremes - parched high deserts and alkali flats juxtaposed with snowcapped mountains and freshwater marshes and lakes, with summer temperatures of more than 100 degrees and sub-zero winters. Life there was not easy, but aboriginal man learned to manipulate the available natural resources to his advantage and cope with the factors he couldn't change. Life surely would have been harder without the versatile tule.

Introduction To Tule Ethnobotany

By Norm Kidder

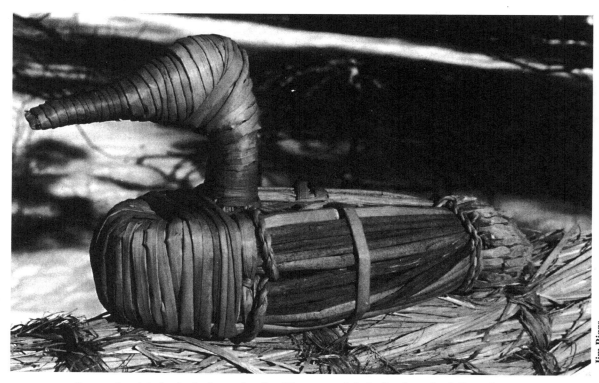

Canvasback tule duck decoy by Jim Riggs, modeled after Lovelock Cave types.

In many parts of the world tules, reeds, bulrushes and their relatives have been used by local groups as building material. The Egyptians used papyrus for paper and boats (more technically called balsas, or floats). A statue of King Tut shows him spearing hippos from a reed 'surfboard', while multi-ton slabs of stone are known to have been transported on large ocean going reed vessels. (See Thor Heyerdahl, the Ra Expeditions). Natives in other parts of Africa, the Marsh Arabs of Iraq, and Indians of South America, Mexico, and California also used the versatile reeds for watercraft. In this article I will stick to the uses of tule reeds by the Indian peoples of Central California and neighboring Nevada.

Tule, seems to be both a general term for freshwater marshes and also for the sedges of the genus Scirpus. The term Tule Fog refers to moisture rising from the ground. The Spanish called the seasonally flooded center of the San Joaquin Valley the "tulares". In the San Francisco Bay area, the Common Tule is Scirpus acutus. This tule grows up to over 16 feet tall, has a round dark green stem, and only vestigial leaves. Its seed head is an open tassel normally 2 inches or less across. A similar looking relative, Scirpus californicus, or California Tri-square differs in having a lighter green and triangular stem, and a larger

seed head. The tri-square also has a larger internal cell structure which makes it inferior for most construction purposes. A number of other species are found around the country, and may or may not prove suitable for making useable items.

In Central California, Tules were made into:

baskets - *from loose berry baskets to water carriers (Yokuts);*
clothing - *Pomo 'grass' skirts and leggings to Yurok sun visors;*
mats - *to thatch a house or sit on, or rolled up for storage;*
dolls and toys - *slings, quivers, swaddling clothes, arrow skippers;*
balsa boats and rafts - *from one man floats to small islands;*
duck decoys - *plain, painted, and feather covered.*

WORKING WITH TULES

Cut tules anytime after they have reached full height. They will tend to get firmer from late summer into fall. They can be cut in the fall until wind and rain have broken and dried them. The feel of the stem is the real determining factor. Be careful when cutting to keep the tules neatly stacked in the same direction so they don't bend or break. I tie them into bundles about 8 inches thick at the base with cords near each end and one in the middle. Always carry the bundles with the butt ends forward to avoid breakage.

Once cut, the stems must be dried before use. Depending on when they are cut, they may shrink up to 50% in diameter as they dry. When they are uniformly light green they are just dry enough, although yellow or tan is better. While drying, be sure to allow for good ventilation, and don't stack the tules too thickly, or mold and mildew will result. I prefer to dry tules in the shade. It takes longer, but they acquire a leathery texture. Drying in the sun is quicker (a few days instead of a few weeks), but the stems end up more crisp and brittle.

TWINING

Twinging is easily confused with weaving, but differs in a fundamental way. Weaving involves a single strand passing in and out between the standing stock or ribs. Twining involves two (or three) strands which pass around the ribs in sequence, while intertwining around each other (Fig. A). This results in a 'locked' stitch compared to weaving's looser wrapping. Twining done without ribs (twisting) results in a two (or three) ply rope.

TULE MATS AND SUCH

To twine tules into mats or other items, begin as you would for rope, twisting together three or four inches of single ply cord. Instead of twisting the plys together, place the twisted section around a small bunch of tules with each twist. You should have the tules laid out roughly. Pass the strand which lies on top of the first bunch over the strand which comes up from beneath, and then this strand passes beneath the second bunch of tules and then comes back out to the working face. Repeat this - over, behind and out - until you have completed a row. Add in additional pieces of tule as needed to maintain the thickness of the strand. As the row progresses, each 'stitch' should slant at the same angle across the face of the project (Note the photo below of two painted decoys resting on a twined mat.). At the end of a row, twine the tule strands into rope until it is long enough to reach the next spot you want a row to begin, then turn and twine the row. Continue this process until you have finished. End the last row with a knot, then tuck the ends back into the work.

Fig. B The "Kink"

Fig. A *Weaving*   *Twining*

Fig. C The start for 2-ply cordage.

TWISTING

Twisting is used to turn fibers into string, or in this case using whole or split tules to make tule rope. To begin, grasp a bundle of at least two tules at each end and twist them between your fingers until the tules begin to 'kink' back on themselves (Fig. B). Move your hands closer together as the tule strands are twisted, and the kink begins to twist into a 2-ply strand (Fig C). Attach the end to something (your teeth?), and now, as you twist clockwise, pass the strand over each other counterclockwise, switching hands. Repeat this endlessly, adding in new tules (fat end first) into each side as needed (See BPT #2 for a complete description of the string making process).

Two painted and decorated decoys, by Jim Riggs, resting on a twined tule mat.

TULE DUCK DECOYS

From observations by early explorers, decoys of tules and feathers were used over a wide area in the West. A cache of decoys was found, wrapped in a tule mat, in a dry cave in Nevada in 1924. Most were painted and partly feathered, others plain. A bag of feathers was found with it. Paiute Indians have continued to make tule duck decoys to this day. Jimmy George, a Paiute shaman, is shown making a decoy in Margaret Wheat's book Survival Arts of the Primitive Paiutes (Univ. of Nevada Press, 1967) in the 1940's. I have a decoy I believe was made by his son some years later, and we have recently purchases two decoys from Daren George, the grandson.

There appear to be two styles of decoys. One was finished by pinning a fresh duck skin to a body of tule (shown in Wheat), and adding the stuffed head. The other type (from Lovelock Cave) has the whole figure made from tule, with paint and feathers applied over it to define the species of duck (or goose). The following instructions are for making the second type, leaving decoration up to the user.

Decoys were commonly set out in a marshland where they would attract a flight of ducks to land. A concealed hunter then pulled up a net, weighted with stones (so as to sink out of sight), and attached on the opposite bank, ensnaring the flock. Other methods included shooting with arrows equipped with 'skip bomb' heads which would skip along the surface of the water and into the swimming group of birds; and nets thrown into the landing or leaving flock.

Tule decoys made in recent times have been primarily for decoration, but there is no reason a motivated primitive hunter couldn't give the old ways a try.

All photos and artifacts for this article provide by Jim Riggs

A PAIUTE TULE DUCK DECOY
(Based on a model made by Davin George)

1. Tie off a 2' bunch of tules, 2" in diameter in the middle with dampened cattail leaf, twisted into a cord.

2. Twine into 3 bundles with cattail cord, about 3" from middle. The 1st bundle should use half of the tules, the second bundle use 2/3 of what remains, and the 3rd bundle uses what's left.

3. Bend the bundle in the middle and continue on across to the other side, twining into 3 parts, going from smallest to largest.

4. Twine a 2nd row of 6 bundles across the whole ducks body, about 3" from the 1st row. Then tie the whole body together another 3" from this 2nd row with a cattail cord. Sculpt the body to shape, making sure the base is open and wide. Cut off the excess tail at an angle.

Cut

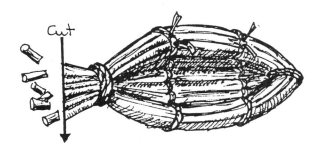

Fold

TIE OFF INSIDE

5. Use tule to make the basic head shape, with each coil of tule passing through the top of the body. Make sure the neck sticks up only about 2". Then wrap with dampened cattail leaf or split tule until the desired shape is achieved. Finish by running the end of the wrapper into the body and tying it off. Add paint and feathers as desired.

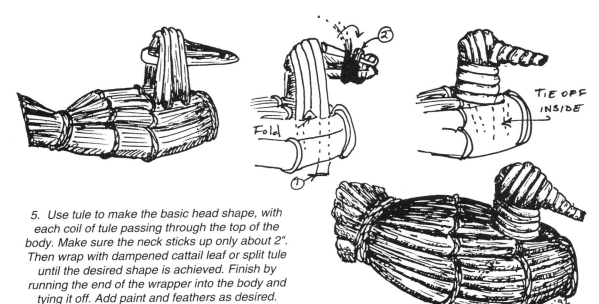

KIDDER '92

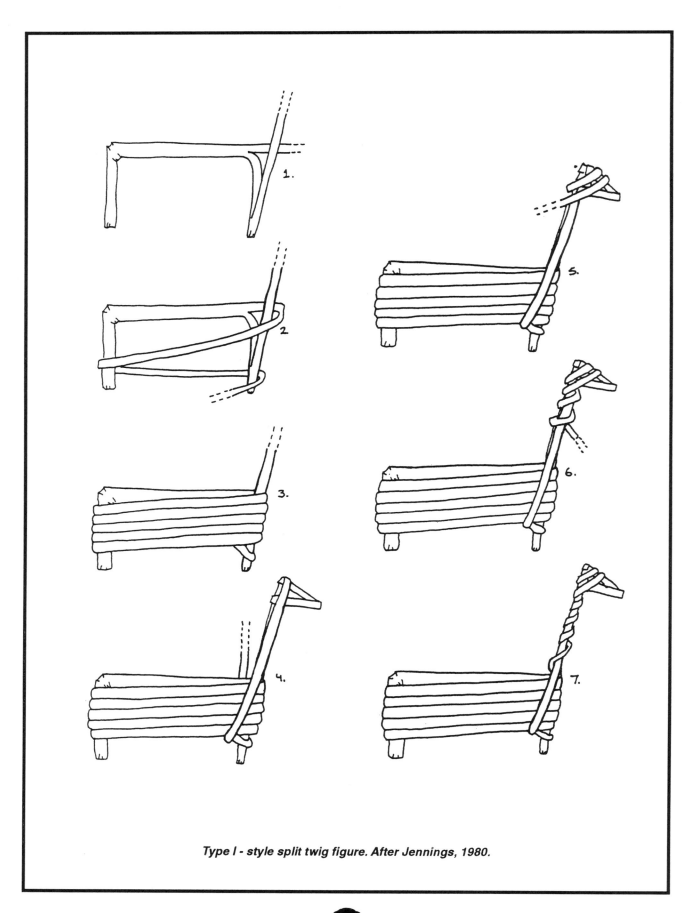

Type I - style split twig figure. After Jennings, 1980.

THE ANCIENT ART OF SPLIT WILLOW SCULPTURE

By Tom Elpel, Photos By Upcountry

People have always loved constructing useful and decorative objects from soft and pliable willow twigs and branches.

"Archaeologists have found split-willow figures of deer made by Southwest cultures thousands of years ago", Jim Riggs, of Wallowa, Oregon, an instructor at a recent primitive living skills gathering, told students.

"Archaeologists believe the figures may have first been used in hunting rituals; in later times they were likely used as kids' toys", said Riggs. He displayed two different styles of willow figures and then led the class through the procedure of making them. The instructions that follow are the steps for making these simple figures.

Step One

Select a slender, green willow twig at least 30 inches in length. It should not have any branches growing off of it. Run your fingers down the willow to strip the leaves off. Then cut an inch or so off the small end of the willow. Stick your fingernails into the end of the twig where you cut it, and split it apart. Split it down the length of the willow as shown in **Fig. 1**. If the split becomes uneven with one half

Step Two

Kink the willow twig 90 degrees about 1 and 1/2 inches from the end, right where the split ends in the willow (**Fig. 2**). This first section forms the back legs of the deer; the next section becomes the backbone. Leave about 2 inches for the backbone, with both halves of the willow together. Then kink only the piece that is on top down at 90 degrees to begin shaping the front leg. Make the front leg the same length as the back leg, then kink the willow back on itself, so that the bark is showing. The end of the willow will stick straight up.

Step Three

The "bottom half" of the backbone which is sticking straight out (or straight up from the back leg, as in **Fig. 2**) is used to fill in the body. Wrap it around the front and back legs again and again until you run out of twig. Then tuck the end of the twig back inside the body to hold it in place (**Fig. 3**). The other half twig is kinked at about 1 and 1/2 inches up from the body to form the neck. Kink it back on itself so that the bark is showing. Bring the end back down and wrap it around the body to lock it in place (**Fig 4**). Bring the willow back up to the top of the neck and bend it over the stub that forms the neck, shaping the head to look like the number "4". The tricky part is to hold everything together as you work As Riggs said, "It would help to have a little hand at the end of

Fig. 1 Splitting the willow

Fig. 2 Bending the split willow to form the back and legs.

of the twig bigger than the other, then bend the fatter side more sharply as you work; this will re-position the split back to the center of the twig. Split the length of the willow, but stop about 1 and 1/2 inches from the big end.

each finger." Your work should now look like the example in **Fig. 5**.

Fig. 3 Wrap the entire body and tuck the end into the wrap.

Fig. 4 The neck is approx.1" to 2 "long.

Step Four

The remaining willow is wrapped around the neck and back to the nose. Start at the nose and wrap around the head again and again until the whole head is wrapped. Next, wrap the neck with the remaining length of willow and tuck the end under part of the wrap to lock it in place (Fig. 6). The action of wrapping from the head around to the neck will cause the head to turn to one side or another, depending on which direction you are wrapping. Riggs said, "Archaeologists found that roughly 75% of the split willow figures they found had the heads turned one way and the other 25% had the heads turned the other way. Archaeologists once thought there was some ritual significance to which direction the head was turned". But Riggs pointed out that the head turns automatically as you work, and suggested that each person just naturally works around the head from one side or the other. In our own test, my wife and I found that all of hers consistently turned one way and all of mine consistently turned the other.

Step Five

At this point your split willow figure is finished. You may, however have too much or not enough length of twig to finish the job. If there is extra then just cut it off. If it is short then it may look just fine with only part of the neck or head wrapped. The measurements suggested here for different parts of the body are only approximations. As you make more split willow figures you will learn to adjust the proportions of the body for the length of the willow you work with.

Split willow figures are quick to make. After you stumble through the first one or two then the rest are easy. At the end of our hour-long class we had quite a herd of deer around us. And as I write this article, a new herd is forming on my desk.

Split willow figures are fun to make for adults or kids, and make great Christmas ornaments.

Fig. 5 The head is shaped as a simple "four".

Fig. 6 Wrap the neck, and the figure is complete.

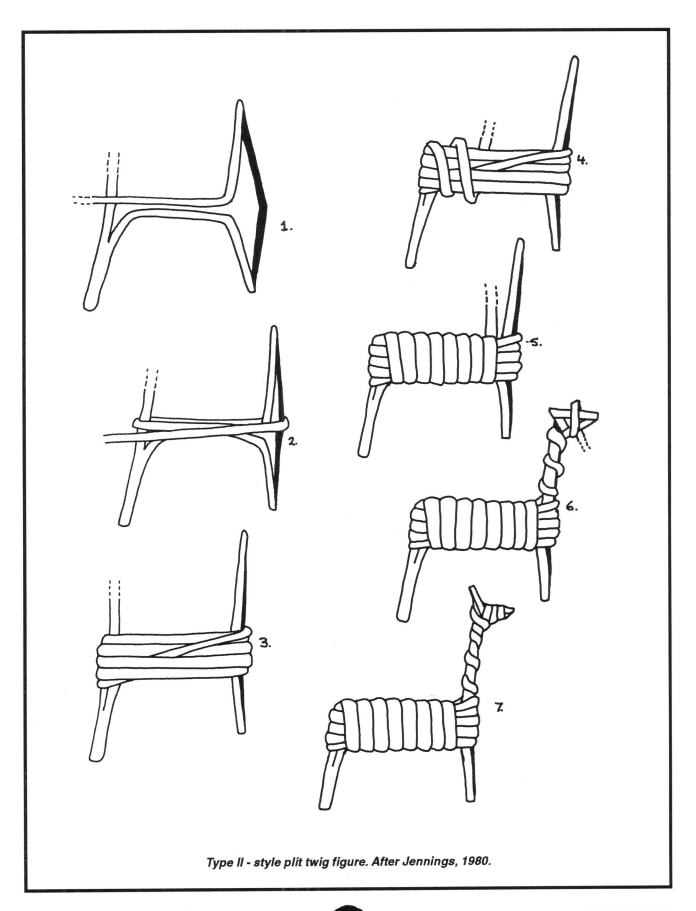

Type II - style plit twig figure. After Jennings, 1980.

Mogollan Plaited Yucca Sandals

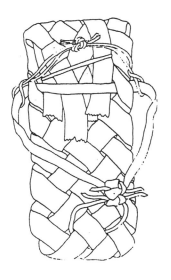

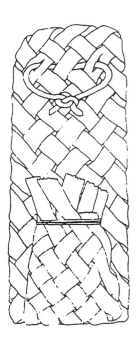
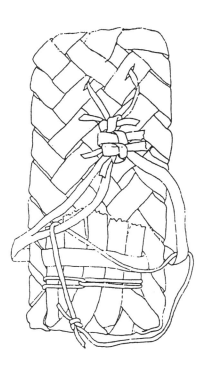
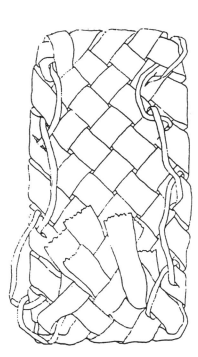

Figure 1. Plaited Sandals from Tularosa and Cordova Caves: variations on a theme. Lower right example is likely a winter type; side loops may have held grass or bark insulation by means of cross ties. (Drawings by Gustaf Dalstrom in Martin 1952)

PLAITED WHOLE LEAF YUCCA SANDALS

By Paul Douglas Campbell

A pair of Mogollon sandals can be completed in a couple of hours. But it was their simple beauty which first caught my attention. The clean diagonal weave of a thousand year old sandal with frayed remnants of toe and heel tie hung in a dimly lit glass case of the basement of the Southwest Museum. My vague browsing stopped short, awed by the mind which saw in the leaf of the yucca this beautifully plaited sandal. The crafting in turn reflected the character of the plant whose long tough leaves grace many a mountainside of the southwest. In the spring thick stalks replete with cream-white blossoms grow from the yucca center and both stalk and flowers provided food for Indian groups from the Cahuilla to the Pueblo.

I studied the incased sandal for an hour or more until I captured its secret. Luckily, the yucca plant does not have to die so we might be shod. We need only four leaves per sole plus another for the ties. Yuccas are widespread throughout the American Southwest. The Mogollon used the banana yucca (*Yucca baccata*) common in southwestern New Mexico where many of these sandals have been uncovered in ancient caves. In Los Angeles I used the yucca common to the Los Angeles region called simply yucca or Our Lord's Candle (*Yucca whipplei*). The banana yucca leaf is thicker and softer but the Los Angeles yucca suffices.

Comfortable and durable sandals can be plaited from the unprocessed and green leaves of the yucca. However, as the leaves dry over the weeks, they shrink, and open spaces appear in the weave (especially with the thinner *whipplei* leaves). This can be overcome by lightly pounding the leaves with a smooth stone against a log or also using two leaves paired for each plait, doubling the number of leaves. Archaeologists digging the Mogollon caves of west-central New Mexico felt most of the sandals they found were made from essentially whole unprocessed leaves but some seemed to have been made from leaves which had been pounded or crushed. They also found sandals where the leaves had been doubled.

Cutting green fibrous leaves from a live yucca (especially the *Yucca whipplei*) with a sharp stone or knife is trying work, and the razor edged neighboring leaves can lacerate your hand in the process. Dead dried leaves on the other hand pull out easily. The ends of the yucca leaves, one too curved and too wide and the other too sharp, can be trimmed off by holding the edge on a stationary stone.

Dried leaves should be soaked for about twenty-four hours before you begin bending them to shape; otherwise, they crack.

The sandal described is the standard sandal found by archaeologists in Mogollon sites. Of twenty-seven sandals recovered from four Mogollon caves of west-central New Mexico during excavations by the Chicago Natural History Museum's 1952 expedition under Paul D. Martin, twenty-four were of plaited whole yucca leaves. Twice that number of whole leaf plaited sandals had been found earlier by the museum in Tularosa and Cordova caves from the same west-central New Mexico region—all on tributaries of the Gila River. Generally archaeologists found no difference in the manufacture of left or right sandals, but some from Tularosa Cave were more rounded in front on one side or the other so that lefts could be distinguished from rights. A simpler version of these woven sandals with only three plaits or leaves was also found. Smaller, split-leaf varieties had apparently been worn by children.

Anasazi sandals, such as from Pueblo III sites of northeastern Arizona, are also plaited but of very narrow elements. However, the whole leaf Mogollon style has been found in the southern Anasazi Pueblo IV sites of Camp Verde and Canyon Creek. Plaited sandals first appear amongst the Anasazi in Basketmaker III sites and are of the wider or whole leaf elements.

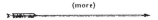

(more)

A Mogollon-style plaited fiber sandal apparently of bark is in the possession of the Santa Barbara Museum of Natural History. Amazingly, the sandal is said to have been found in a dry cave on Anacapa Island. If true, this the most common sandal of the ancient Mogollon of New Mexico was probably worn by a Chumash Indian of Southern California.

The Secret Revealed

I have found seven simple steps to a completed sandal:

1) Bend a leaf approximately in the middle, perpendicularly, right over left, making a right angle open to the left. Now bend the left side—the base of the angle—under and parallel to the first bent half, leaving an approximately one to two inch perpendicular section between them as shown below.

2) Bend a second leaf once in the middle, right side over left, bringing the two halves side by side in a near parallel arrangement and overlapping the perpendicular section of the first leaf between the two parallel elements. Repeat steps one and two for a second set of leaves. (If you are doubling each leaf and the sandal is for a long adult foot, it may be advantageous to overrun the leaves of each doubled pair making a longer bundle, thinner at each end.)

3) Face the two sets diagonally and begin to loosely plait them, using the left set as weft into the right warp. The pattern is first leaf (the right leaf of the left set) over, under, over, under. Next leaf (the second from the right) under two, over two. The next or third leaf is over two, under one; and finally the last leaf goes under one, over two which will be the pattern for all subsequent weaves.

4) Tighten the plaiting completed as much as you can—this is most important. Then continue with your weave, pulling and tightening after each weaver has been passed through the warp, bent under one, over two, from the left and over one, under two, from the right, bending each leaf at a ninety degree angle and pulling tight, until the leaves are used up. To keep the weave from unraveling you might tie a thin strip of yucca around the completed end.

5) Measure your foot to the piece and bend over excess at the loose end to form the heel; mash it down forcefully and put something heavy to hold it that way while you cut a one quarter inch to one half inch wide strap to pass through two side weaves about two inches from the back of the heel (see sketches of Mogollon sandals). This strap holds down the extra material which overlaps the heel and also forms an instep brace. Secure it in front of the foot with a square knot. Trim excess from the loose ends of the heel overlap.

6) Cut an approximately one eighth inch wide piece for the toe strap and place it under the first long warp element in the center front, bringing it around the second and third toes and securing it to the instep brace with a square knot, adjusting to your foot all the while. Keep the ends of the straps wet to facilitate tying. The straps themselves dry fairly stiff.

7) Cut the final ankle tie string one sixteenth to one eighth inch wide and soften it by wetting and holding the ends and running it a couple of times back and forth around a soft surface—a sapling for example. Put the sandal on, adjust it; place the tie over the front of the foot and loop the tie ends over, around and under each side of the instep brace and back over the tie string itself and fasten in a square knot at the back of your ankle; or just bring it from the back, loop around the instep brace and tie it in back. For a custom fit, wear the sandal as much as you can as it dries out over the next few days.

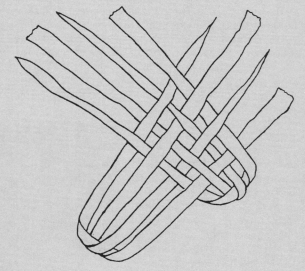

Figure 2. The simple secret of the plaited Mogollon sandal revealed. While there are variations or "mistakes," this seems to be the classic Mogollon weave. The pattern continues with loose weavers on the left bending under one, over two, and those from the right, over one, under two until completed.

MAKE YOUR OWN HIDE GLUE
By Jim Riggs, © 1991

In the beginning ...

Finding a natural glue evaded me for years. On my first to yew bows, short, fat-limbed Northern California style, I used regular Elmer's white glue with

Well-made hide glue, your very own hide glue, will forever bond you to its wondrous merits.

not-very-refined sinew. It worked fine, though no glue would have held down those chunky sinew ends forever! But native peoples did not use Elmer's to back their bows or haft points and blades. I wanted something natural, something I could produce myself from raw materials. The ever-present but low-key search was on.

Back in the 60's and early 70's there seemed to be neither a lot of people into primitive skills, processes and technologies, nor much awareness of, nor contact among, those of us who were. Nor was there a lot of good, specifically written "how-to" information. The old Ben Hunt books had their limitations! In our "isolated compartments" we ferreted out what information we could and experimented along, trail and error, having to solve needs and problems mostly via our own ingenuities. In 1967 Larry Olsen's **Outdoor Survival Skills** was published and, figuratively at least, initiated the more recent and widespread revival of interest in aboriginal skills. Numerous newer books, Abo gatherings and networking have made a plethora of knowledge and information readily available. Nowadays one can learn in a single article or workshop methods and skills that have taken many of

us 20 years or more to figure out on our own.

I was living in a little log cabin two miles up a trail in the Southern Oregon Cascades immersed in a variety of primitive projects. Periodically, after running into enough dead-ends or accumulating enough questions, I'd make a trip out to do some library research. References to glue and binding agents were generally brief and ambiguous: pitch, pitch and charcoal, other plant juices, asphaltum, fish skin, sturgeon noses, bladders and something from along the backbone, bone joints, cartilage, sinew, antler, hooves and hide. At the time, I tended to amalgamate all of these into a somewhat ephemeral, surrealistic vision similar to the Macbeth witches' "Double double toil and trouble, fire burn, cauldron bubble." Gee, maybe eye of newt and toe of frog would make glue too!

My early mentor, Buckskin Slim, used Elmer's for backing most of his bows, but had also used boiled down salmon skin glue. I'd eaten hundreds of boiled trout on survival trips and knew how sticky the skins became, but at the time it made more dietary sense to eat the skins rather than experiment with glue making (Perhaps Tim Baker will relate his experiments with fish skin glue).

The category "hide glue" sounded simplest and stuck somewhat dormantly in my mind. I was not then aware that commercial "rabbit skin" glue existed. Finally, about 15 years ago, the need for glue and the impetus for addressing that particular experiment coincided; I had finished a nice Serviceberry bow, wanted to sinew-back it and was determined not to use Elmer's!

The Original Experiment . . .

Since I'd been brain-tanning buckskin for several years, I always kept a stash of hides, and found some scrap pieces of deer and elk rawhide laying around. As whole hides, these had been fleshed while fresh, laced into frames to dry and the hair scraped off. The vast expanses had been used for quivers, other containers, knife sheaths, etc. With tin-snips I cut up a handful of dry scraps into 1-2" square pieces and plopped them into a #10 can of water boiling on the stove. An hour or so   later,

(more)

besides the interesting aroma that pervaded the house, I noticed the skin scraps were swelling and becoming somewhat gelatinous to the touch. As the water boiled away, I added enough more so as to not burn the skin. A couple times I'd quickly dip a finger into the soup, but noticed no discernible stickiness. A couple hours later it had again boiled down, seemed a little thicker than plain water and was becoming a translucent brownish color. I again dipped in a forefinger, smeared it on thumb to an evenly thin layer, blew on it a couple times to evaporate a bit more moisture, then tightly squeezed thumb and index finger together for about 30 seconds. The result surprised me, amazed me . . . and freaked me out -- I honestly could not pull finger and thumb apart. Eureka, I've finally discovered glue! However, I still had this problem. Fortunately, I more rationally remembered the glue is water soluble, and a rinse in warm water returned my use of thumb and finger as separate appendages.

Since that enlightening day I've made and used gallons of hide glue and can better describe my own "how-to" process in a sequential series of steps, tips, do's and don'ts, though I'm sure there is more to learn.

The Hides . . .

I suppose almost any skin will produce some glue, but larger, thicker hides as deer or elk seem more energy-efficient. If a hide has been salted for storage, I think it advisable to thoroughly soak and repeatedly rinse it in water to dissolve away as much salt as possible. You can use any pieces of skin, green or dried, but they should be fleshed clean of any meat or fat, and I prefer to have scraped off the hair prior to boiling them up. Initially, the hair is not detrimental, it just adds extraneous bulk, but you don't want hair in your final glue. Once I've boiled the mass to the point where the skin is well-cooked (swollen and gelatinous) and the glue has gone into the water, I pour all the liquid through a piece of window screen to strain out all skin pieces and hair. Cheesecloth or similar fabric is a bit slower but even more thorough in straining out hair.

For the last several years I've refined my glue process even more by using hide shavings, a natural by-product of making buckskin. In the dry-scrape buckskin tanning process I begin with a clean fleshed deerhide. It can be freshly peeled from the carcass, or most often is one I've previously dried or salted for storage, then soaked in plain water 24 hours or so until it's thoroughly wet and pliable. Either way, I cut inch-long slits parallel to the edge of the hide, 1/2" in from edge, every 3/4" around the hide perimeter. Then I lace or tie it into a rectangular pole or two-by-four frame fairly tightly and evenly stretched. As it dries over a day or two it shrinks and becomes even tighter, so some practice is required in not stretching so tightly at first that, as it dries, it rips out some of the ties. When dry, I begin scraping off the hair and epidermal layer of skin which lies beneath it. The scraper is a steel blade roughly 4" long, 1 1/2"

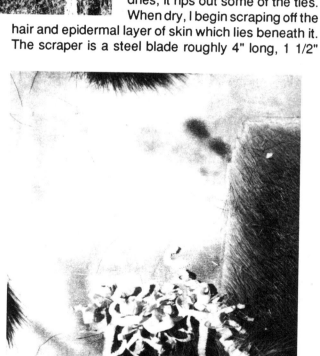

Note the curls of skin - seperate from hair for glue making.

wide, 1/8" thick, with a rounded cutting edge sharpened on a single bevel. This blade is lashed or screwed onto an elbow-shaped handle of wood, antler or flat angle-iron (see illustration).

If my goal is just getting the hide adequately scraped for the next step in making buckskin, I quickly shear off both hair and grain (epidermis) together with only one or two brisk strokes at any specific area as I work down and across the whole hide. When I want shavings for glue, however, I scrape more lightly to remove only the hair. When done, I clear it away from the base of the frame. Then I go back over the whole hide again shearing off the now mostly hairless epidermis.

> **Eureka, I've finally discovered glue! However, I still had this problem. Fortunately, I more rationally remembered the glue is water soluble, and a rinse in warm water returned my use of thumb and finger as separate appendages.**

With long smooth strokes of the scraper blade, this comes off in thin curled shavings much like a plane removes shavings of wood. I then collect all these shavings which, since dry, will not spoil and store them until I need a batch of glue. Some hair remains in the root follicles of the shavings and other fluffs of hair unavoidable get mixed in, but are immaterial at this stage.

Making Glue . . .

My standard, all-purpose, old reliable camping pots, stew pots, tea pots and glue pots are #10 cans (roughly 2-3 lb. coffee can size). I punch opposite holes just below the rims and attach wire bails for easy manipulation. For glue, I jam a couple big compressed handfuls of hide shavings into the pot, say, a well-packed 2/3 full, and fill with hot or cold water to 3/4 full. Since the shavings are so thin, they immediately soak-up a lot of water. I bring this to a rolling boil, pot uncovered to reduce boil-over potential. And maintain the boil for an hour or so, adding more water as needed. At this stage don't worry about too much water--more is better than less to prevent burning the skin. I stir this glop frequently. After an hour the shavings should be swollen and gelatinous. I pour off all

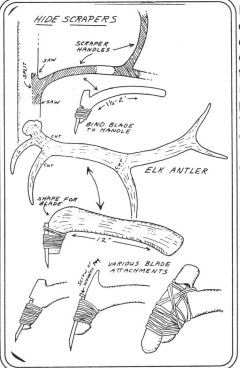

the liquid through a screen or strainer into a second pot, refill and reboil the first for another half hour, then strain that into the second pot. This time I also hand-squeeze the skin glop to get most liquid out and discard the skin as compost. By this time most of the glue from the skin should be in the water.

Besides the fact the skin shavings soak and boil up quickly, I believe this mostly epidermal layer contains proportionately more glue than the rest of the hide, though this theory remains objectively untested. In my experience with shavings, one pot's worth makes enough glue to easily back one bow, with considerable glue left over. Again, for an expected ration of raw skin to finished glue, more experimentation could be done; I'm simply not into the real statistical end of it!

Whether you've boiled up fresh skin, dry skin, hairy skin, skin shavings, etc. and strained the liquid, you now have quite a pot of milky to tan-colored soup, free of most hair and actual pieces of skin, but still way too thin as is for glue. As you further boil this down and as water evaporates to a quarter pot or less, the "incipient glue" should become more viscous and somewhat darker. I use different viscosities of glue for different jobs, but generally seek a consistency slightly thinner than the commercial LaPage's mucilage in the pear-shaped bottle with the pink rubber spreader on top (the stuff you probably used in grade school, if you're old enough, anyway!). To check your glue for adequate adhesive qualities, just try the previously described finger/thumb test. If not sticky enough, boil it down further. Make sure you cool it down enough before use though, or it'll cook and rubberize your sinew! And for immediate use, that should do it, but, there is definitely more to know about your newly-made glue.

The Nature and Care of Hide Glue . . .

I must confess that I consider hide glue, like sinew, to be a nearly magical medium, sort of like a living organism with a mind of its own! By most of our contemporary concepts of logic and application, it should not be able to accomplish what we know it can (by the laws of physics, a bumblebee should not be able to fly either), but we must produce, manipulate and treat it within its own necessary parameters for it to serve us well. Ignore or forget it too long in the wrong condition (that can mean you, or the glue!) and it'll turn fickle quite rapidly on you, molding or rotting with the stench of death.

Let's say you've made a batch of glue but aren't going to use it right away or have glue left over after a project and want to store it. Since I feel I've already done almost everything wrong with hide glue at least once, I feel qualified to offer some do's and don'ts. The only way I know to store hide glue indefinitely is to completely dry it down, and this is an active process using a direct heat source. Without heat, a pot of glue, even perhaps only 1-2" deep, if left to just sit will soon glaze over and begin to harden on top, but remain liquid beneath that and soon spoil. The glue does not have to be boiling to be drying, though with low heat the surface glaze should be broken through periodically to allow quicker evaporation from beneath. Refrigeration or freezing may delay spoilage or mold for a few days, but I've had small cans of glue go bad within a week, whether frozen or just cold. The other two "safe" but temporary conditions are actively reconstituting dry pieces or crystals with water and heat to the consistency for use, or actively drying it back out after use.

My wood heater is perfect for either process as the heat source is continuous and the temperature adjustable by the amount and kind of wood and by moving a glue pot to different areas of the stove surface. I also keep a grate set on a couple bricks a few inches above the stove top and have drying screens above and behind the stove. Thus, when I add water the glue is reconstituting and after use it is automatically drying back out. With a large pot of glue intended for storage, I usually just dry it down to a solid layer and leave it in the can. When thoroughly dry, this hard, flat translucent disc of brownish glue has shrunk away from the sides and bottom of the pot and can be removed for travel or storage elsewhere if desired. Dry chunks can be pounded or ground into finer pieces or crystals like the commercial hide glue. The crystals of course reconstitute faster than chunks. In actively drying down a pot of glue, it naturally becomes thicker

Nowadays one can learn in a single article or workshop methods and skills that have taken many of us 20 years or more to figure out on our own

and thicker until it congeals into the "Jello" phase, thence through the rubber and leather phases on its way to the inert rock phase. Once it is no longer liquid, care must be taken not to burn it. When congealed and dry enough to be rubbery and not sticky to the touch, the entire glob can usually be eased from the can with a butter knife and dried on a screen as is or sliced like cheese into thinner slabs for quicker drying. If you don't have time to carefully boil a whole batch all the way down, you can rapidly boil it until quite viscous but still liquid, then pour a thin layer into a flat pyrex or enamel casserole dish, onto a non-greasy cookie sheet or even foil and sun dry or place in an oven set on warm. A thin layer will usually dry quickly with little chance of spoilage. Unless preparing to back a bow, I normally need only small amounts of glue, but quite regularly, for hafting, fletching, etc., so I always keep a tuna can with some dried down glue near the wood heater. This requires only a dash of water and a couple minutes of heat to be usable, and quickly dries back out.

The Open-ended Finis . . .

There is a definite satisfaction in doing more with less and being directly familiar with and responsible for all phases and materials in any aboriginal project one undertakes. The ability to make your own glue is one such endeavor, one useful product of a process. As with any process repeated enough, you'll eventually learn what you must do to be successful, what you must not do and, yes, what you can get away with! Well-made hide glue, your very own hide glue will forever bond you to its wondrous merits.

Mummy Varnish, Spruce Gum
and Other Sticky Stuff

By Scott K. Silsby

As interpreted from archeological findings, the history and prehistory of adhesives stretches back to the earliest signs of hafting. Some of the earliest are the late Mousterian tool kits associated with Neanderthal culture. They certainly had a wide range of adhesives from which to choose, as nature's warehouse offered an inexhaustible range of plant resins, rosin, pitch, tar, sap, gum, oil, sugar, starch, latex, bitumen and such not including the various animal glues and products like shellac, bees wax and propolis. From a replication standpoint, knowing the time, place and culture of an artifact would help narrow down what choices were available for adhesives.

Some formulas for hide and fish glues read like an alchemist's worst nightmare. In **Turkish Archery and the Composite Bow** (Klopsteg, 1934), he summarizes Turkish bow glues and describes the several day process of simmering sinew in rainwater, fat

> *As interpreted from archaeological findings, the history and prehistory of adhesives stretches back to the earliest signs of hafting. Some of the earliest are the late Mousterian tool kits associated with Neanderthal culture.*

skimming and rendering it into a form "like leeches". Fish glue was obtained from the skin of the roof of the mouth of the Danube Sturgeon (in these days: *Gadus morrhica*). It was fried and shipped to market, resoaked, pounded with a wooden cudgel on a marble slab. The cudgel was frequently moistened with the tongue since water was said to spoil the glue at that stage. Some of these "hot" hide glues are rated at 20,000 pounds per square inch. In some cases the two glues were combined. A good bit of this early primitive technology was highly sophisticated and efficient. Keep in mind primitive means first, not worst. The early archery records of these ancient folk still stand as testimony to this.

One basic adhesive that was used extensively throughout most of the world for a wide range of purposes and is well documented are the various conifer resin products referred to as Naval Stores in the commercial track. This industry antedates the Christian era in the Mediterranean region. In his article **Naval Stores: The Industry** (Ward, 1949), Jay Ward tells of early accounts of the process used where natives gathered resins or gums of trees and cooked them in open pots until a thick pitch was left in the bottom. They stretched fleecy sheep skins over the tops of the pots to catch the oily vapors that arose from the boiling gum then wringing out the wet fleece to recover the oils. He goes on to tell that one of the uses was varnish for mummies. He further describes a vast commercial operation in the production of tar, pitch, rosin and turpentine that supplied products to all the wooden sailing vessels of all the European nations. The industry through time shifted from Scandinavia and the Baltic countries to New England then through New Jersey into Virginia, winding up in the Carolinas where, at its peak, 1,998,400 drums of gum rosin at 520 pounds each were produced. That's a lot of sticky stuff.

> *Keep in mind that "primitive" means first.... not worst.*

The French, Spanish and Native Americans were busy making war on the conifers, as well, for their own needs. The unsurpassed birch bark canoes of the past incorporated carefully prepared resins for waterproofing and strengthening joints.

For many of us, our interest in all this is more towards the practical aspect of finding a workable natural material suitable for hafting stone to wood, bone and such. While many things work, spruce gum has become my resin of choice. My experience with the stuff occurred when I tried to arm my giant ragweed

(more)

stem arrows with slate "error-heads" (concrete slab ground, notches punched with a nail). Although that was nearly forty years ago, my failure with hot hide glues for that aspect of gluing and success with raw pine pitch and kite string (cotton) is well remembered today: Good glue—wrong use! As hide glue dries, it continues to shrink until an equilibrium is reached with the humidity. In dry regions it becomes quite brittle. In humid regions, it stays flaccid. In hafting stone to wood, it keeps shrinking. As it pulls the wood haft area tight, it breaks loose from the stone and becomes nothing more that a filler in the haft area. When damp, it's like tight rubber bands.

> *From a replication standpoint, knowing the time, place, and culture of an artifact would help narrow down what choices were available.*

• •

A system I worked out through trial and error over the years since that first discovery has given me good service so I pass it along as one way to get it done, although not the only way.

Don't be too picky about whether it's spruce, pine, fir or such. Spruce seems best but a mixture of conifer resins is fine or all pine does well also. If damaged resin-bleeding trees can be had, use them. Second choice is collecting rosin balls and drippings that are dry to semi-dry. Scrape them into a sealable jar, add turpentine (half and half) and periodically shake the mix over a day or two until it appears dissolved. Strain out bark, bugs and needles then either set in the sun with the lid off to evaporate excess turpentine or rig up a double boiler outside to speed it up. Turpentine vapors are quite flammable and give off thick black soot and heavy turpentine odors if they catch fire. Never cook it in a sealed container and smother flash pot fires with an old loose fitting lid to prevent explosions.

I dislike the process of slashing trees to bleed them so will skip over that technique. Any National Forest with camping areas will be rich in vandalized trees as well as the edges of construction sites.

Now we are at the stage of having a pot full of either fresh conifer sap or reconstituted conifer pitch, thick and sticky. Some folks use it in this state and pat charcoal powder on the surface to protect from getting the sap on their body as in the old bark canoes where high flexibility was needed.

For hafting, I prefer "Scotty's Deluxe Formula". Using a double boiler of earthenware, soapstone or tin cans (If you didn't catch Maria Sidoroff's excellent article on ceramics in the bulletin of Primitive Technology Vol. 1 No. 1). Slowly heat the batch to evaporate the turpentine and other remaining fluids. For a one cup batch, take it off the heat after ten minutes for the first test. Dip an arrow shaft sized stick into the hot glop then dip the stick and glop in cool water until you feel it's around 72 degrees all the way through. It will chill on the surface while remaining hot in the center. Allow this core heat to resurface and test by lightly pressing the blob. Don't squeeze hard; it may erupt! Once at or near 72 degrees, press your fingernail into it. It should dent 1/32" at 6 pounds pressure. Catch the indentation with your nail or a dull knife and pry up slowly. It should move a smidgen (1/4 tad) before popping out or off, a small conchoidal-like spall. If you can squeeze the blob flat between your fingers, it's still a little soft for hafting use. If it's weak and brittle and shatters then you have over cooked it. Back in the turpentine dissolution jar for over brittle batches. For harder, less flexible batches, mix crushed rock dust and short plant fibers into the batch while cooking. I prefer red hematite and limonite dust for color and wolfs bane (dogbane to the civilized world) fibers with the outer bark included for the burnt sienna color. One-fourth inch fibers add some flexible strength to the batch.

> *If you squeeze the blob flat between your fingers, it's still a little soft for hafting use.*

To use this stuff in hafting stone to wood such as in an arrowhead into a pre-formed socket, preheat the arrowhead and the wood socket to drive off moisture and warm the haft area. Dip the hot arrowhead's base into the hot resin mix and join the two while both are still hot. Center and balance the point by spinning the arrow with the tip down on a smooth hard wood surface and no, don't use Aunt Ethel's cherry side board. Adjust the point while the whole thing is warm and reheat over a low fire if required. Use small wood shavings as shims, if needed, until the whole arrow and point spin true. Needless to say, start with a straight arrow. Use small blade flakes of heat-tolerant flint or a dull knife (native copper, of course), both hot, to remove excess rosin to sculpt the haft area. Allow the haft area to completely cool then bind with hide glue soaked sinew. **[Stay away from commercial liquid hide**

glues and use the granular type as handled by a few dealers in the Resource Directory and Bulletin Board of the S.P.T.].

      After twelve to twenty-four hours of drying time, depending on heat and humidity, excess rosin will ooze out of the notch from the shrinking sinew. Pop off these "oozettes" with your finger nail. Remoisten and rub vigorously with your fingers to spread the hide glue and to remelt and smooth the rosin. You can now shoot your arrow into green hardwood. The point may break or perhaps the shaft but if you did correctly the haft area will survive seven times out of ten shots.

REFERENCES

Klopsteg, Paul E.
1934 *Turkish Archery and the Composite Bow.*

Ward, Jay
1949 *Naval Stores: The Industry in Trees.* **The Yearbook of Agriculture, U.S.D.A.** *G.P.O. Wash., D.C.*

Sidoroff, Maria
1991 *Introduction to Ceramic Replication.* Bulletin of Primitive Technology *Vol. 1, No.1.*

For many of us, our interest in all of this is more towards the practical aspect of finding a workable natural material suitable for hafting stone to wood, bone and such.

MEMBERS RESPOND - Adhesives

Making Pitch Sticks
By Evard H. Gibby

As a follow-up to the section on adhesives in the Fall 1991 BPT, storing pitch on sticks is a handy and makes the use of it simple in the field.

Collect a batch of pitch from conifer trees and heat it near a fire in a small can or pot. As it is melting add up to 1/2 its volume of finely ground wood ash and stir until the mixture is melted and well mixed.

Take several small twigs (3 - 4 inches long) and begin dipping them in the hot mixture, and setting them aside to cool. Re-dip them several times like dipping candles, until a small hot dog shaped blob of pitch is on each stick. As each stick is dipped it can be dipped into cold water to help cool it faster if desired. When sufficient pitch coats each stick and it has partially cooled it can be rolled back and forth in the palms to help shape the pitch stick.

Store a few of these sticks in your possibles bag or pack for ready use in the field. To use the pitch stick, in hefting for example, heat the end of the pitch stick over a small flame and either let the melted pitch drip into the notch of the handle or daub it in with the pitch stick. When the desired amount of pitch lines the notch (reheat the pitch in notch over the flame if needed) insert the blade and wrap with cordage or sinew.

Another method described by Charles Robbins of the Anasazi Post is to melt the pitch, mix in the ground charcoal, and let the mixture begin to cool. When it begins to firm up, pour it onto a flat surface and roll it into a long coil about the diameter of a pencil. After it has completely cooled, break it into pieces several inches long for convenient storage and use. Jim Woods of the Herrett Museum, Twin Falls, Idaho describes the Australian aboriginal method of making pitch sticks as follows:

Collect pitch (in our case use conifer pitch) and heat in a container until it melts. While it is heating take some charcoal out of the fire and grind into a fine powder and place this in a small cone shaped depression in the ground. When the pitch is melted pour it into the depression with the charcoal. When it begins to cool, start mixing the pitch and charcoal together by hand. Pull out small blobs and mix it similar to pulling taffy. Then roll between hands to make small cigar shaped pitch sticks. set aside and make another until all the pitch is used. The ratio is roughly 1/2 charcoal to 1/2 pitch. The pitch sticks are used as described above.

Mr. Woods suggests the primitive Americans may have added ground up dried grass fibers to their pitch to give it strength. He also suggests that there are several unanswered questions regarding the preparation of pitch adhesives.

How long should the material be heated for best results? Should it be boiled or just heated up? Can it be overcooked and become too brittle? Can the pitch be reheated several times and still be effective? What were the additives, and how much were used by the primitives?

Trying to find the answers to these and other questions about pitch adhesive would be a beneficial research project says Woods. Any takers?

One way to keep pine pitch glue from becoming brittle is by adding a small amount of beeswax to the pitch when melted. This causes the pitch to become tacky and reduces the chances of shattering.

Beeswax, however, is not readily available in the wilderness in a primitive or survival situation, but milkweed plants are often found. When melting a batch of pine pitch, cut a few stalks of milkweed and allow the juice to drip into the container with the melting pitch. This will also give the pitch glue a tacky property. Some experimentation should be done to determine how much juice to add to get the desired result. Different types of milkweed may have different amounts of latex in their juice. The plant that I have used in southern Idaho is Asclepias speciosa.

A Word On Pitch
By Errett Callahan

In his article, *Making Pitch Sticks*, in **BPT #6**, Evard Gibby asks for comments on evaluating pitch mixtures. Having used various pine pitch mixtures for over 20 years and consulted with Swedish pitch users, I'd like to offer Gibby, Jim Woods, and our readers a word or two on the subject.

Various members of the Swedish Society of Prehistoric Technology have graciously shared their years of experience with me, experience founded upon traditional use patterns ages old in Scandinavia. Pitch is typically mixed about 50-50 with finely powdered charcoal, extremely finely powdered (i.e. lampblack). I was at first under the impression that the less the pitch was heated the better, but not so. You don't just heat it till it melts, you boil the tar out of it (or into it). (Just as with pine tar.) The longer you boil it down the better, but watch out it doesn't catch fire. I can't see that cooking reduces the volume any, but it does seem to make it tougher and more resilient. Still, at its best, pine pitch mixtures are but fillers, not glues. Nor can it compare with the Australian spinifax gum, which allows hafting of stone tools without the use of binding.

Additives include, in various parts of the world, charcoal powder, hardwood ashes, unfired ceramic clay powder, and dried dung flakes (of grass eaters). I haven't tried them all so can't evaluate their relative merits. A mixture with beeswax (40% to 60%

pitch) improves its flexibility. But remember, the North American Indian didn't have the honey bee. Other natural waxes, however, have yet to be investigated. So I'll close by asking, as Gibby did, if there are any takers on the use of waxes other than beeswax, either for pitch mixes, sealers, varnishes, or mummy gum. (Shades of Silsby, BPT #2.)

About Animal Glues
By Errett Callahan

The bad news: I have just been informed that some art supply houses are now withdrawing their animal hide glues (rabbit skin glue) from the market. This seems to be because of protests by misinformed "animal rights" activists who think rabbits are being slaughtered solely for the glue. (Haven't they seen the meat for sale in the frozen food section of their grocery stores?) So those who are paranoid about making bows without sinew backing will now have to learn real bowmaking skills or make their own glue.

The good news: Tim Baker sent me a sample bottle of fish glue which seems to be of superior quality in a liquid state (unlike liquid animal hide glues which are very weak). It's made by Garrett Wade Co., Inc. , 161 Avenue of the Americas, NYC 10013 (phone: 800-221-2942). Yes, they take phone orders. I don't know the cost, but I'm very impressed with the strength. Yes, you can use it for sinew bows.

Pitch sticks ready for just about any job. Evard Gibby.

Section 5

Projectiles
Power From The Human Hand

Thong-Thrown Arrows and Spears

By Tim Baker

Payne-Gallwey, in "**Crossbows**", his 1903 study of balistic machines, describes an ancient pastime among men of Yorkshire: arrow-throwing. A string is wrapped around the arrow and the index finger, the string acting somewhat like a flexible atlatl. Gallwey reports distance of up to 372 yards!

To put this in perspective, a 70lb bow is about the comfortable draw-weight limit for a typical archer. Such a bow can be expected to cast a normal weight hunting arrow about 250 yards. An average atlatl thrower will reach about 125 yards.

But 370 yards ! And by hand ! ? !

Gallwey had to be wrong. And there was a simple way to prove it.

Following Gallwey's instructions, one end of a knotted string was wrapped around a standard target arrow, the other end around my index finger. The arrow was thrown toward a pile of hay at the end of my driveway. Then two unexpected things happened: 1. a surpisingly heavy tug as the arrow was released -- real work was being done; 2. the arrow disappeared.

Then there was silence in the neighborhood. A long,

uncomfortable silence, followed in time by the distant but unmistakable sound of a 125-grain steel field point imbedding in wood siding. Gallwey was onto something.

Upon reflection, 300-plus distances are not surprising. Near-equal amounts of energy are expended by the arm and body when throwing either a 1,000-grain atlatl dart, or a 300-grain arrow (One once = 437 grains). In addition, compared to the atlatl, a string's lighter mass makes more of that energy available to the arrow. Obviously a lighter arrow should travel farther than a heavier dart. Recent experiments by Oregon flintknapper and atlatl researcher, Craig Ratzat support this thinking. Craig reaches far greater distances when using lighter darts.

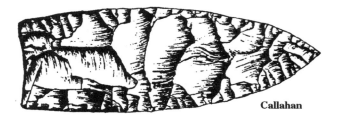

Callahan

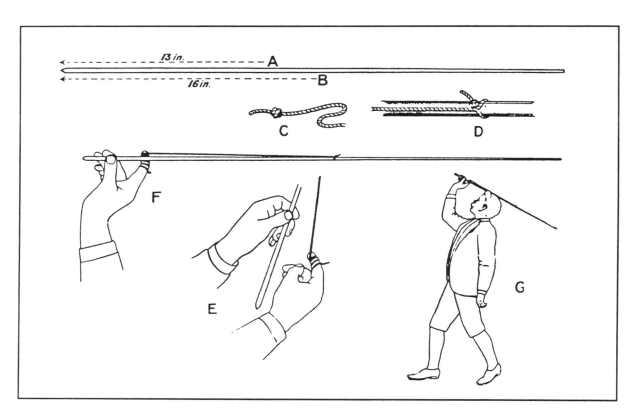

Gallwey's Yorkshire arrow throwers used hazel shafts about the thickness of a man's little finger. Hazel was selected because of its light pithy center and strong, thin wood shell. Arrows were 31" in length, and well dried. Shafts were made without weighted heads, fletching, or nocks. To fly straight and true each shaft was slightly tapered, blunt end forward. Shaft diameters were 3/16 at the small end, 1/4 at the center, and 5/16 at the head. Each weighed about one-half ounce. A proper shaft's balance point was about 13" from it's head.

Here are Gallwey's throwing instructions verbatim:

1. Make a pencil mark around the arrow at 16 inches from the head. Fig. B.
2. Take a piece of hard, strong string, 1/16" in diameter and 28" long. Tie a double knot at 1/2" from one end of the string. Fig. C.
3. Hold the head of the arrow towards you in your left hand, and hitch the knot firmly around the pencil mark, as shown in Fig. D.
4. Next, and still holding the head of the arrow towards you in the left hand, twist the loose end of the string around the first joint of the first finger of the right hand, until the inside edge of this finger is 3" from the point of the arrow along its' shaft. Keep the string tightly stretched from the finger to the knot. The knot will not slip if the string is kept taut. Fig. E.
5. Now grip the arrow close to its' head between the thumb and second and third fingers of the right hand (the first finger keeping the string tight); and turn it from you in the direction of its' intended flight. Fig. F.
6. Hold the arrow at arms length in front of you, then draw it back and with a powerful jerk of the arm, cast it forward and high as if throwing a stone, its' line of flight being at an angle of about 45 degrees to the ground.

Pointers to remember-

1. Remember that the knot is merely hitched to the arrow and not tied to it.
2. During the process of winding the string on the forefinger of the right hand, the left hand should grasp the arrow and the string together a few inches below the knot, so a s to prevent the latter from slipping. The part of the string (about half its' length) which is wrapped around the finger may be unravelled so as not to cut the skin. The unravelled portion may be stopped by a knot from unwinding too far.

Arrow throwing is not extinct. Utah paleontologist, Don Burge has been throwing arrows for twenty years. He uses tamarisk, dogwood, or even Port Orford cedar shafts. Each is feathered, and weighted as per normal hunting arrows. Throwing 500-grain arrows, Don reaches distances of 200 yards, equaling the performance of a 65lb bow. He reports his students typically reach these distances after 20 minutes practice.

As when stringing a child's spinning top, the string is held in place by pressure against the knot. At release, as the string exceeds a 90-degree angle relative to the arrow, the knot is freed and the string falls free.

Don uses a well-worn leather shoestring, sometimes dampened for traction. He places the knot near the fletching and wraps the thong one-quarter turn around the shaft. The knot faces forward, permitting the string to slip free on release. Don has thrown 185-grain arrows over 300 yards.

Don ready to release. The arrow is thrown very much like a rock or baseball. The Fingers will release their grip instinctively.

Trapper, flintknapper, George Stewart uses a different launching technique learned from his father, Elmer, who in turn learned it around the turn of the century from Cherokee Indian boys in Stillwell, Oklahoma. Arrows are launched with a 30" throwing stick. A four-inch leather thong attaches to the stick's end; a one inch-long sliver of bone is tied to the thong's end. A small barb is tied at the balance point of a normal-weight arrow. The bone sliver catches in the barb. The rear of the arrow is held in the left hand, throwing stick in the right. Aim is taken, and the arrow is snapped forward, atlatl-style.

George believes this system to be more accurate than a simple thong release. Although it seems to have been used only for sport, it is evident, as George points out, that an emergency weapon could be constructed in very short order, which in practiced hands would be fairly affective.

Cherokee bowmaker, Al Herrin corroborates the use of this arrow-throwing method, and its' use principally as a toy. But he is not convinced of its' Indian origin. He reports that by tradition, throwing-arrows were made from shingles. Al feels it quite possible that arrow-throwing originated with early European settlers.

Thong-thrown shafts were not always used for sport. Greeks used thonged spears in war. Their method of thong attachment, and release is depicted on vases of the period. Atlatls would likely have been more effective, but may not have been known in the Mediterranean world of the time. Far more ancient use of thong-thrown shafts is suggested by SPT member Paul Comstock elsewhere in this issue.

Atlatls have greater range, and are more accurate and penetrating than thong-thrown spears or arrows. Bow-shot arrows have greater range, are far more accurate, and sufficiently penetrating for large game. This, no doubt, accounts for the present obscurity of thong-thrown shafts. In the age of mega-fauna, heavy thong-thrown shafts would have been practical. In a pinch, thong-thrown arrows and light spears could be used for today. But as in the post bow-and-arrow- past, the chief value of thong-thrown projectiles is sport.

To prevent the knot disengaging, tension must be kept on the string.

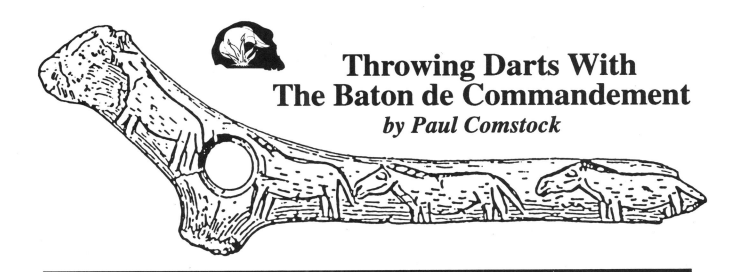

Throwing Darts With
The Baton de Commandement
by Paul Comstock

From 23,000 to 12,000 years ago, across of wide expanse of Europe, a tool was made that is today called the *baton de commandement*. Surviving artifacts are made of antler. They usually have a tine intersection at one end. This usually forms a T or Y shape. At the minimum, there is always a swelling of the antler at one end. There is always a hole drilled through the antler below the T, Y, or swelling. The batons are usually under a foot in length.

When these artifacts were first discovered more than 100 years ago, they were considered to be emblems of status or authority, hence the name *baton de commandement*. Many of the batons were highly decorated, contributing to the conclusion of earlier archaeologists.

It is usually assumed the batons were some type of tool. Many uses for the batons have been suggested. Perhaps the most widely suggested is the batons were shaft straighteners. One of the more esoteric explanations is the batons represent sexual symbols, specifically the combination of female orifice and phallic antler.

While the batons can be the subject of much speculation, they have one trait that can be clearly demonstrated. They are very effective spear throwers. A cord is needed to throw a spear or dart with a baton. The cord is fastened to the baton and the loose end is knotted. The knotted end is wrapped around the dart, in the manner described by Tim Baker in a separate article on arrow throwing. Using only my hands, I can throw a 66-inch, 1,500-grain (97.4 gram) feathered dart about 30 yards. If I secure a cord to the dart (ie., the arrow-throwing method) I can throw the dart about 43 yards. If I use a baton and cord, I can throw the dart up to 68 yards.

The batons first appeared 9,000 years before the atlatl was invented. If the batons were used to throw spears, ancient hunters would have found the baton allowed them to double the force they could obtain

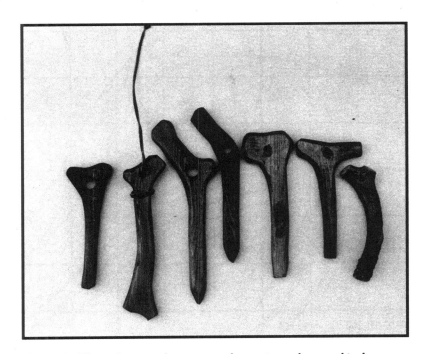

Figure 1. These batons de commandement *can be used to increase the force of a hand-thrown spear or dart. The baton at the right is made of a whitetail deer's right antler, and is for a right-handed thrower. The wooden batons are copies of Paleolithic artifacts. Each baton is shown as a right-handed thrower would see it when looking at his hand, palm-up.*

with a hand-thrown spear. This would have made a baton a very valuable item. With an 11,000-year life span covering an area from France to Moscow, it seems the batons were indeed valued by Paleolithic hunters.

Cro Magnon Man (By Tom Prideaux, Time-Life Books, 1975) says the oldest atlatl artifacts come from the cave of La Placard, France, and are about 14,000 years old. These artifacts consist of the hook, or spur end, of the thrower. Made of antler, many of these artifacts are more highly decorated than most batons. When the atlatl appeared, the baton began to slowly disappear. Using a 28-inch atlatl, I can send the 1,500-grain dart mentioned earlier 78 yards. The well designed atlatl is more efficient than the baton.

I have made proportionately accurate copies of 11 different baton artifacts. All are equally effective in dart-throwing. They range from 6 to 8 inches in length. The biggest baton artifact I have seen described in a book was 13 inches long. Copying a baton artifact is fairly easy since many are depicted in books. If the above baton illustration is enlarged with a copying machine, it becomes a pattern to make a wooden replica.

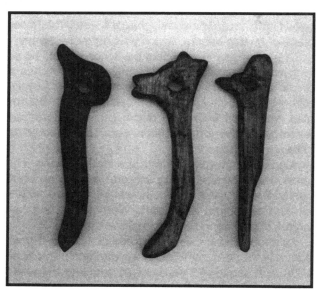

Figure 2. Here are copies of baton de commandement artifacts which appear to have been worked to accentuate the curve of the handle, or to create a recess to accomodate the base of the thumb. Such batons allow effective dart-loading while enabling the thrower to keep his eyes on his target.

The Paleolithic batons were made of red deer or reindeer antler. It also is possible to make a baton out of whitetail deer antler. The main beam of whitetail

deer antler curves much more sharply than red deer or reindeer antler. For this reason, the right-handed thrower may find he needs to make his baton from the whitetail's right antler. And vice-versa for the left-handed thrower. The straighter red deer and reindeer antlers are more likely to produce ambidextrous batons. Many batons have a definite front and back side. These batons cannot be expected to work if held in the incorrect position.

The hole serves a critical element in baton function. Each of my 11 baton replicas works well when one end of the cord is tied around the baton shaft. The loose end is passed through the hole and appears on the front side of the baton. From there, the cord passes

Figure 3. This is the typical appearance of a dart loaded into a baton. The cord was twisted one full revolution around the dart, in a counter-clockwise motion toward the dart tip.

over the top of the baton and is twisted around the dart. Some of these batons also work best when the cord is twisted around the dart in a counter-clockwise direction when viewed from the dart's point. (See photo) Others require a clockwise twist. Correct twisting of the cord passed through the hole will keep the dart from falling off the baton until the throw begins. This is the most critical function of the baton's hole. Conceivably, some batons could work with no hole. But the loading process would be far more cumbersome. A T or Y shape at the end of the baton increases tolerance of variations in cord-twisting.

Some batons have curved handles. These batons should be held so the handle curves away from the wrist. Some straight-handle batons can be held with either side facing up and still produce good results. With some batons, the cord can come out the hole on the back side of the baton. Another option may be to tie the cord directly through the baton hole, instead of around the baton handle and passed through the hole. Variables in the throwing process include cord length, number of revolutions the cord is wrapped around the dart, baton length, dart length, and dart center of gravity.

For accurate and stable dart flight, it seems the cord should extend from the baton 8 inches. For a quicker throw, a 10 to 12-inch cord may yield better results. The number of revolutions the cord circles the dart affects dart flight and accuracy. The 66-inch 1,500-grain feathered dart requires one complete revolution of the cord for best results. A 45-inch 500-

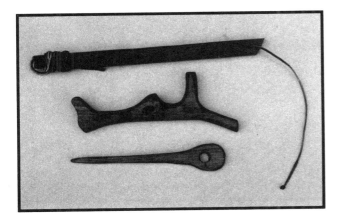

Figure 4. When throwing darts with a baton, technique is more important than baton design. The baton at top is a hypothetical model 13 inches long and an inch wide. Used correctly, it is as effective as a routine baton. The bottom two are copies of artifacts, and are also reliable throwers.

grain feathered dart only needed 3/4 of a turn. Too many turns will greatly reduce dart velocity.

Roots of Civilization (By Alexander Marshack, Moyer Bell Ltd., 1991) includes two depictions of cave paintings showing darts that are unmistakably fletched. In one scene, 19 fletched darts are flying at a horse. In the other, a rhinoceros has been hit with four such darts.

To subject the baton-thrower concept to a severe test, a hypothetical baton was made, 13 inches long and only an inch wide. It was first used with a shallow V in the end, and later used with a flat, angled end. With both configurations, the 1,500-grain dart flew as well as it did from a normal baton. The hypothetical baton required a cord twist of 1 1/2 revolutions. The baton user must experiment with such variables for the best results. The good performance of the hypothetical baton shows proper technique is far more important than baton design.

The 1,500-grain dart works well with the wrap beginning at the dart's mid-point. The 500-grain dart worked well with the wrap starting at the dart's center of gravity. The easiest darts to use will be quite nose-heavy. The 1,500 and 500-grain darts were made of river cane, with the thick end as the tip. They yielded good flight more consistently than a 45-inch feathered piece of broom handle, which was not nose-heavy.

There is reason to suspect the baton should be as long as possible, while still allowing about 12 inches of the dart to extend beyond the throwing hand. Longer batons work better with longer darts. Short batons also work well with long darts, but the increased leverage of the longer baton can be expected to improve dart speed.

A good cord for some darts is a leather thong. The knotted and twisted thong will grip a wooden shaft tightly. It may tend to slip, however, if used with a modern aluminum atlatl dart. Wetting the last few inches of the thong usually improves the grip.

As another example of the force of a baton-thrown dart, one throw of my 1,500-grain dart accidentally hit a 7/8-inch sapling 15 yards away, splitting the wood from one side to the other and leaving the dart pinned in the tree.

Other darts used include a regular wooden archery arrow. Best results can be expected when the baton is not much longer than about six inches. An arrow seems to fly best with 1 1/2 twists of the cord, but it is difficult to throw an arrow without some wobble. The 45-inch piece of cane made a better dart.

At the other end of the extreme, I have tried a six-foot spear that weighed a whopping 1.375 pounds (626.7 grams or 9,604 grains). This monster put tremendous strain on the baton cord. An otherwise tough leather thong would break with a hard throw, or if the cord was given too much tension before the throw. A Dacron cord held up without breaking. Throwing such a heavy dart in an aboriginal setting would require a sturdy cord of rawhide or sinew.

The effectiveness of the baton-thrower — combined with the fact batons ultimately disappeared following the invention of the atlatl — is perhaps the greatest reason to suspect the batons were used this

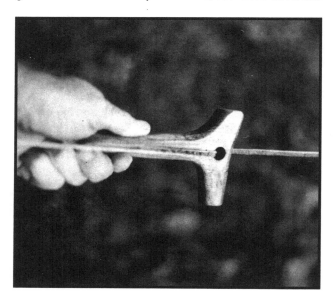

Figure 5. This is M.C. Burkitt's concept of thong-softening, to explain apparent "wear" traces on some batons de commandement. This "wear" could have been intentionally worked into batons to improve reliability when throwing heavy darts.

way at 20,000 B.C. There are other subtle hints.

The Old Stone Age: A Study of Palaeolithic Times (by M.C. Burkitt, New York University Press, 1955) suggests the batons were used to work stiff thongs to make them soft. He shows an illustration of such a thong threaded through a baton hole (see photograph). He says some baton artifacts show this kind of wear — at the bottom of one side of the hole and at the top of the other side. This is exactly the kind of wear that could result with a baton thrower when the cord is tied around the handle, and passes out the front hole of the baton, going over the top of the baton. What may be more likely, however, is the baton-makers worked the holes this way intentionally to

remove sharp edges that could cut or fray the cord under the great strain of throwing a heavy dart. The same thing could be accomplished by cutting the hole at an angle or making the hole wider at the surface than in the interior. Both methods are displayed with some Paleolithic batons. The angled hole is described in ***Ancient Hunters and Their Modern Representatives*** (by W.J. Sollas, The MacMillan Co., 1924). A baton with a wide-throated hole is shown in ***The Old Stone Age.***

Many batons could certainly have been used as shaft straighteners. But not all shafts could be straightened with batons, and not all batons could straighten a shaft.

Cro Magnon Man shows a photo of an open Russian grave containing two boys buried 23,000 years ago. Visible in the picture is a baton. Also visible are spears or lances made of mammoth ivory, lying next to the boys. Not only are these ivory spears too large to fit in the hole of the baton, but at their widest points they are as thick as the baton's handle.

Man and Culture in the Late Pleistocene: A Case Study (by Richard G. Klein, Chandler Publishing Company, 1969) shows artifacts unearthed in Russia that appear to be hide scrapers or polishers. They have flattened, spoon-like ends, often serrated around the edges. One of these artifacts, labeled an "art object," has a hole drilled through the middle of the spoon. The artifact is depicted from two sides, and the

Figure 6. This copy of a spoon-shaped Russian baton requires pinching the handle with the fingertips for reliable dart-throwing.

spoon-like section is quite thin, too thin to straighten a shaft without badly denting the shaft or creating strain that would threaten to break the spoon. Yet this artifact was drilled for some apparent purpose. A wooden copy of this artifact is a reliable thrower of the 1,500-grain dart. Modifying the customary grip when using this baton (see photo) keeps the dart in place before the throw. Another baton shown in *Ancient Hunters* has four holes and is a good dart-thrower. Perhaps it and the Russian spoon baton were designed as dual-purpose implements.

As mentioned earlier, a curved-handle baton has definite advantages when loading the dart. Some batons were carved to increase the natural curve of the antler. *The Old Stone Age* shows an attractive baton carved to the form of an animal's head around the hole. The handle was worked to form a gradual and graceful S-curve. Another such baton is depicted in *Ancient Hunters*. The curve at the end of the handle was accentuated by carving, giving the end of the handle the shape of an elongated knob. A variation on this theme is another baton depicted in *Ancient Hunters*. The handle was shaped to make a concavity that fits against the base of the thumb when the baton is used as a thrower.

Figue 7. This carving on a fragment of a baton de commandement from La Madeleine, France, shows a man holding a stick just as he would if about to throw it with a baton. (Redrawn from "Ancient Hunters and Their Modern Representatives.")

Also depicted in *Ancient Hunters* is a carving on a fragment of a baton from La Madeleine, France. It shows a man slightly crouched and leaning forward, as if he is about the throw the stick in his hand, held with one end over his shoulder. Instead of holding the stick in the middle, he is gripping it nearer its tip, just as he would if throwing it with a baton. *Roots of Civilization* shows a photograph of this fragment. Toward the end of the figure's stick are two lines that may be intended to depict barbs on the stick.

The case for the Paleolithic baton spear-thrower is compelling. The baton spear-throwers that work well today could have worked well long ago, when there were no atlatls and no archery. Could Ice Age hunters have made batons for 11,000 years without discovering they could double the force of a hand-thrown spear?

Here is a suggested loading-throwing sequence for a right-handed thrower:

• The thrower holds the dart and the loose end of the baton cord. The dart point is to his left, the butt to his right. The baton dangles free at this point.

• The end of the cord circles the dart shaft and the cord is wrapped behind the knot on the end.

• The thrower removes his right hand from the dart and grabs the baton. If watching the target, he slides his hand down the cord until it reaches the baton.

• If he is using a curved-handle baton, the thrower can tell the baton is right-side-up by the feel of the baton in his hand. And if the cord is passed through the hole correctly, the baton and cord are automatically in the correct position in relation to the dart. If using a straight-handle baton, the thrower can confirm correct position of the baton by feeling for the cord coming out of the front side of the hole with his thumb.

• The cord is then twisted around the dart, toward the dart tip. If using a one-revolution twist, the thrower can keep his eyes on the target. He can use his left hand to make sure the knot is on the same side as the dart as the baton, assuring a complete revolution.

• The thrower next pulls the baton toward the dart tip, so the cord is under at least slight tension. He next grips the dart with his right thumb and forefinger (just like gripping an atlatl dart) and removes his left hand from the dart.

• The thrower throws the dart at the target similar to throwing a hand-held spear. The throw must be a perfect overhand movement. As with the atlatl, any sideways movement can spoil the throw. At the point of release, he opens his right thumb and forefinger.

ATLATLS: Throwing For Distance
By Craig Ratzat

Most of the papers and books on the atlatl produced thus far are trying to prove if the atlatl weight improves or hinders performance. Performance being measured by the distance that a dart can be thrown. I'm no engineer, but with all the engineers that have worked on self bows if a weight worked in the middle of a bow limb you could go to the store and buy a bow with weights attached. The atlatl weight does work as a counter balance to the dart so that it can be held in the ready position in a hunting situation for an extended period of time without the wrist and arm tiring out, thus measuring performance at the dinner table, rather than distance (fig. 1).

Figure 1: The author with a target or hunting style atlatl ready to throw. Atlatl is 24", and the dart is 67".

Look at the atlatl as a held bow that when matched with the right spined dart, both the atlatl and dart will flex with stored energy that will cast the dart like an arrow from a bow. Although using the flex-spine theory for better performance, the weighted atlatl and dart set for hunting is different in length and weight than those used for long distance throwing. For maximum distances there are a number of factors to keep in mind:

1-length of the atlatl	4-dart spine
2-weight of atlatl	5-dart balance
3-dart weight	6-throwing style

A longer atlatl has increased tip speed causing faster dart travel. The increase is due to the amount of additional time that force is applied to the dart due to the expanded radius of the arc created by the longer atlatl. Dart speed at time of release gives the dart its distance.

Weight of the atlatl is increased by longer length so to keep the speed high you must keep the weight down. To illustrate, hold a three foot long 2x4 in one hand and move it in an arc over your head as fast as you can. Then use a willow shoot the same length. Weight not length make the speed difference. Shaping the atlatl like half a bow, with the hand grip being the heaviest and then tapering to the spur, will give the best weight balance to keep your tip speed high. This design will also give the atlatl flex. If there is deflex there is reflex and this can add more tip speed just before the dart is released.

Figure 2: The author with atlatl and dart ready to throw long distances. Atlatl is 42.5", and the dart is 52"

The dart weight will determine how much you want the atlatl to flex. If the atlatl does not flex enough then it is not storing any of the energy that you are producing during the throw. Instead of the dart shooting off the spur with a boost of deflexed stored energy you only get what you generate through brute strength. If the dart spine/flex is to great for the atlatl reflex, it may cause the dart to rupture prior to release. If the atlatl flex is too great for the weight of the dart then the stored energy is not released until after the dart has left the spur. A heavy dart may also overstress the atlatl to the breaking point. If you can keep the dart weight as light as possible then you keep the tip speed of that atlatl and dart as high as possible. Carefully consider different material, length, and diameter when making lighter darts.

The dart spine is how much the dart will flex or bend. This bending is storing up energy to be released at the time the dart leaves the atlatl spur. If the spine is too stiff then little or no energy is released. If the spine is too soft, then the energy is released from the dart after it leaves the spur. Watch out for darts that in the first part of their flight bend one way and then the other several times before straightening out for level flight. All aluminum darts that I have seen do this badly. Any dart that has the same diameter its full length will do this because of a middle balance point. Since the force is applied to one end, the notch end will try to pass the tip end. This is corrected in two ways: fletching the butt end and/or weighting the tip. With fletching you can stabilize the shaft but you will have that early bending boing, boing, boing effect.

With proper dart balance you can leave off the fletching.

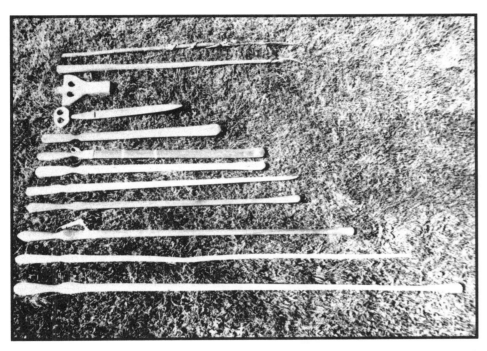

Figure 3: Just a few of my atlatls. The short one is 8" long, and the longest is 48" long. The two on the top use a cord to either nock a dart like an arrow, or nock a dart in the middle of the shaft. The second from the bottom is the atlatl described in the article and shown in figure 2.

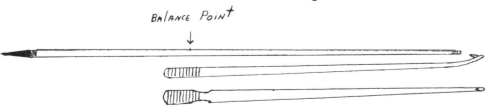

Fletching stabilizes the dart by dragging the air especially in the boing part of the flight, reducing speed. The dart should be a tip heavy tapered shaft and balance on a knife edge about two-fifths of the overall dart length. If this dart boings on release the spine is too soft. You can sometimes cut a little off the smaller diameter nock end to stiffen the spine.

Different materials the same diameter and length can vary a lot in both balance and spine, so one has to experiment for best combinations.

Figure 2 shows the atlatl and dart in the position ready to throw long distances. On July 8, 1990 I made my first throws over 500 feet using this throwing style and atlatl/dart set. The atlatl is made from yew wood with an antler nocking spur tied on with sinew. It is 42.5 inches long and weighs 103 grams and even with the following dart it will flex over 6 inches during the throw. The dart is made from my favorite material, cattail. It has a hardwood point and nock glued in and sinew wrapped around the shaft to keep it from splitting. It's 52 inches long, weighs 20 grams, is 3/8 inch in diameter at the point and 1/4 inch at the nock (fig. 3). It will balance on a knife edge 21.75 inches from the point.

In my efforts to throw as far as I can, I have made over 40 different atlatls ranging from 6 to 54 inches long, with various nocks and types of wood (fig. 4). Since I'm making a half bow with weight as a factor I use the lightest bow woods available: juniper, red cedar, and yew wood. The 150 plus darts have been made from every kind of bush, berry, reed, cane, and shoots from around the USA that I can find or trade. Broad leaf cattail from Oregon is my first choice, but rag weed from the East is showing good promise. The dart length only needs to be long enough to hold on to as it is thrown. Who says that a dart has to be longer that the atlatl? A well made 18 inch dart will fly just as well as a 90 inch dart when thrown from an atlatl that was made to fit the dart.

The best set combination for me may not be the best for you. The length of your arms and your strength will make enough difference that you will have to play around with lengths and weights or both atlatls and darts in order to improve your distance. But PLAYING AROUND is what it's all about.

PRIMITIVE
HUNTING EQUIPMENT:
JABBING AND THROWING SPEARS
By Scooter Cheatham

* Notes taken from Errett Callahan's chart on projectiles

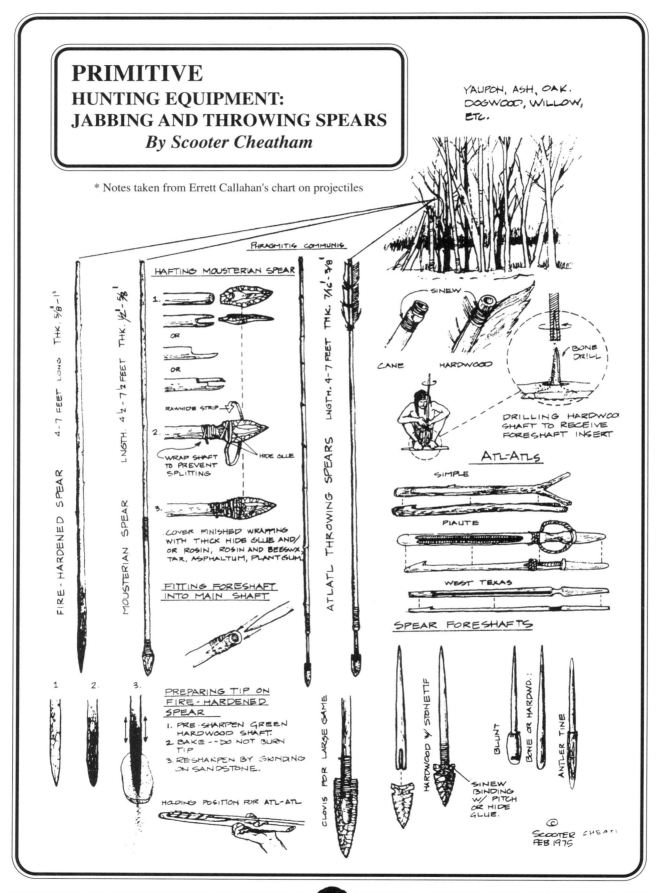

YAUPON, ASH, OAK, DOGWOOD, WILLOW, ETC.

PHRAGMITIS COMMUNIS

FIRE-HARDENED SPEAR   4-7 FEET LONG   THK. 5/8"-1"

MOUSTERIAN SPEAR   LNGTH. 4½-7½ FEET   THK. ½'-5/8'

HAFTING MOUSTERIAN SPEAR

1.

OR

OR

RAWHIDE STRIP

2.

WRAP SHAFT TO PREVENT SPLITTING

HIDE GLUE

3.

COVER FINISHED WRAPPING WITH THICK HIDE GLUE AND/OR ROSIN, ROSIN AND BEESWX, TAR, ASPHALTUM, PLANT GUM.

FITTING FORESHAFT INTO MAIN SHAFT

ATLATL THROWING SPEARS   LNGTH. 4-7 FEET   THK. 7/16'-3/8'

SINEW

CANE   HARDWOOD

BONE DRILL

DRILLING HARDWOOD SHAFT TO RECEIVE FORESHAFT INSERT

ATL-ATLS

SIMPLE

PIAUTE

WEST TEXAS

SPEAR FORESHAFTS

1.   2.   3.

PREPARING TIP ON FIRE-HARDENED SPEAR

1. PRE-SHARPEN GREEN HARDWOOD SHAFT.
2. BAKE -- DO NOT BURN TIP
3. RESHARPEN BY GRINDING ON SANDSTONE.

HOLDING POSITION FOR ATL-ATL

CLOVIS FOR LARGE GAME

HARDWOOD W/ STONE TIP

SINEW BINDING W/ PITCH OR HIDE GLUE.

BLUNT

BONE OR HARDWD.

ANTLER TINE

© SCOOTER CHEATH
FEB 1975

Reconstructing A Generic Basketmaker Atlatl

By David Wescott

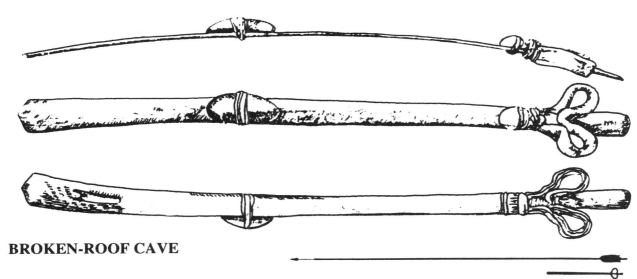

BROKEN-ROOF CAVE

Ever since my early exposure to **Outdoor Survival Skills** by Larry Olsen, I have been fascinated by the design and function of the atlatl. I have made many and always had a few in my collection of tools. But it wasn't until the 1988 Rabbit Stick Rendezvous where I saw Jim Riggs' quiver of Great Basin reproductions that I realized there was more to this stick than I had imagined. His collection contained a wide variety of local types and displayed his pride in knowing the indigenous culture of his home. I decided right then to make a study of the Basketmaker culture of my home and collect as much data as possible.

Laying the Foundation

The first and most obvious task was to locate pictures and measurements of existing artifacts. In doing this, it was interesting to note the wide variety of style and materials used in the Great Basin as compared to the almost identical shape, scale and materials common to the southwest. I also obtained a printout from an Australian museum that listed the specs of 289 woomera specimens in their collection. Once again the variety was limited only to the taste and skill of the maker.

Once the specimens were identified, I wanted to see some of them up-close. It's hard to get a feel for the shape, scale and beauty of an object from a copy of a photo or anthropological description. A friend was visiting some museums in the southwest to study collected rabbitsticks and bullroarers, so I went along to find as many atlatls as I could. I pressed my nose up against many cases and fogged up the plexiglass covers to try get an overall view of the few I was able to locate. In most cases photos were difficult and measurements impossible.

I found out what I could and ended up going back to the literature to confirm what first-hand information I did obtain. It was also helpful to see the real thing in order to get a better framework for comparing the data in the literature. We saw fragments, weathered specimens, some oddities, and 4 complete artifacts. Knowing the basics and comparing data to what we did see, we came to the conclusion that some of the information in print was inaccurate, inconsistent in its collection and reporting, and incomplete.

Most current research and experimentation is limited to the controversy over weight use, location and implications. Ethnographic and archaeological reports were most helpful in getting measurements and photos. From the reports, I chose specimens with the most consistent styles. They dominated the literature and are clearly representative of what could be called "Basketmaker Style" atlatls. Rare designs that are "out of the ordinary", as is common in Great Basin specimens, are essentially nonexistent.

The Process

The best representative specimen was located at the Museum of Northern Arizona in Flagstaff - the Sand Dune Cave specimen. It was on display and could not be measured, but it was completely intact and had been thoroughly studied in a number of anthropological reports. Its only oddity was the style of fastening the finger loops in place. This was compared to a very recent find now housed at the

(more)

BASKETMAKER ATLATLS: A Comparative Analysis (approx. 100BC - 500AD)

SITE	LENGTH	THICKNESS	WIDTH	SPUR	MATERIAL	LOOPS	FETISHES	SURFACES	WEIGHTS	SOURCE
Sand Dune Cave	59cm (23")	6.5-10mm (1/4-3/8")	15-26mm (3/8-1")	Integral Female	Oak?	leather over sinew core	bast fiber cord blue feathers	polished and top flat back convex	None	AP 98
Broken Roof Cave	53.4cm (20 3/4")	0.6cm (1/4")	2.5cm (1")	Integral Female	Oak	3-ply split leather sinew wraps	small black nut in loop moonstone	shorter & thinner than ave.	dark red stone 56 grams	HB#9 (1921)
Grand Gulch #1 & 2	(64cm) 25"	(0.9cm) 3/8"	(2.5cm) 1"	Integral Female	Split Hardwood	leather & sinew	Extensive * "Heart of the fetish bird"	slight groove on top, runs from spur	blk. limonite yucca fiber 2 quartzite	Mus. Jr. 1928 (1895)
White Dog Cave #1	62.0cm (24 1/4")	0.6cm (1/4")	3.4cm (1 3/8")	Integral Female	Oak	Single loop split hide folded	see weights	top pitch covered plano-conv.	3 loaf-shape green stones fossilized tooth	BAE #65 (1916)
Whte Dog Cave #2	(60.3 cm) 23 1/2"	NA	NA	Integral Female	Oak	leather & sinew	none	ligature marks from loop & wghts.	wh. limestone disk 1" bone pin green satin spar chipped stone	BAE #65 (1916)
Kin Boko Cave #1	66.0cm (25 3/4")	NA	2.2-3.3cm (7/8-1 1/4")	NA	Oak	NA	NA	No photo	limestone 28.0 grams shaped & drilled	World Arch 1966 (1919)
Lukachukai	(61cm) 23 3/4"	(.10cm) 1/4-3/8"	(2.6cm) 1"	Integral Mixed	Red Oak maybe Hickory	leather over sinew leather	Rattlesnake skin, braided	Superior work flat surfaces ornam. groove	none evidence of previous	Mus. Jr. 1928 (1902)
Baylor Rock Shelter	43.8cm (17")	0.7cm (1/4")	2.5cm (1")	NA	Mesquite	NA	NA	No photo	gypsum wght.	World Arch. 1966 (1902)
NC Cave	53.9cm (21")	0.9-1.2cm (3/8-1/2")	1.5-2.1cm (5/8-7/8")	NA	Hardwood	NA	NA	NO photo	sandstone 30.3 grams	World Arch. 1966 (1982)

Proximal=handle
Distal=spur tip

Measurements in parenthesis is approximate conversion from information contained in descriptions found in the literature.
* 4 turquoise beads, wildcat tooth, dyed cotton yarn, brown fur, lightening stone, chipped calcedony cleaver.

1mm =.04"
1cm =.39"

Anasazi State Historical site in Boulder, Utah. It was very weathered, but not to the point of losing measurements or specific features. With this much to guide me, I decided to make a reproduction of the MNA-Sand Dune model, also a Generic model using average measurements, adornments, and finger loops compiled from the accompanying graph, as well as up-to-date information on the affects of weights and tuning principles.

The Sequence

The wood of choice was clearly scrub oak (Querqus gambelli). It is very strong and can maintain a stiff spine with very little material (see chart for measurements). Green wood was cut for the MNA model, and a fire-killed stand was used for the Generic model. The green wood was split with a machete and baton, and the two halves tied together with string. Spacers were placed between the halves to allow for moisture loss. The staves were loosely wrapped in a plastic bag for 1 week to slow the drying process, thus reducing checking and warping. The fire-killed stave was split with a celt and wooden wedges and worked immediately.

A cardboard template was made from the measurements of each design. The Generic model was designed from averages taken from the selected specimens on the graph. Length-60.2cm; Width distal-2.7cm; Width at narrowest-1.5cm; Width proximal-2.2cm; Thickness distal-1.2cm; Thickness proximal-.63cm. This was traced onto the stave as a guideline. The stave is then roughed-in with a machete, adze, and knife. Final shaping was done with a rasp, spokeshave, and bow scraper. Care must be taken to check the spine and make sure that the wood you are using is dense enough to let you match the measurements of the original yet still maintain strength. Not all pieces of wood are the same. Check the growth rings for density. The MNA model only had three rings, and wood was taken only from the belly.

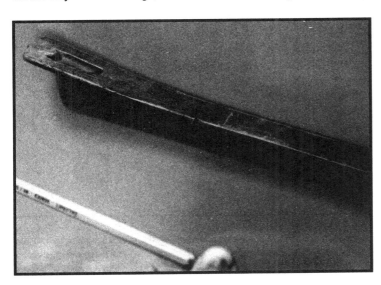

The spur and trough are cut into the stave using a small chisel. Chert flakes were also used with very good results on the dryer wood, and a beaver tooth gouge worked well on the green wood. Final tuning was done with an obsidian scraper and spoke shave. An atlatl must be tested for spine (modified tiller) to check its deflex. Deflex should be

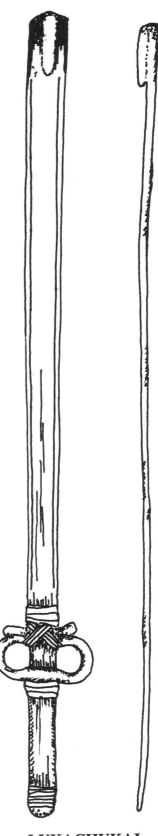

LUKACHUKAI

tested by bending the atlatl towards its back (not towards the belly as in bow making), occur at about the mid-point, and not bend more than about 1". The point of flex is where the weight is placed if you choose to use one.

All finely crafted wood specimens I have seen are burnished with an antler tine and finished by hand polishing. This closes the grain and makes the wood less vulnerable to weathering.

At this point the atlatl was tested with a light dart made of Canary Reed Grass (Phragmites communus) that is fletched and has a willow foreshaft and small obsidian point attached. Dart fragments found in southwestern caves are commonly of reed grass or some other very light material. Because of the thinness of this model, a heavy cane or willow dart could overpower and snap the atlatl.

Lastly, the finger loops are attached along with any other adornments, fetishes/medicines, and technologies such as weights. Materials such as ochre, feathers, claws, teeth, gems, fiber cordage, etc. all reflect the taste of the maker.

The following description of the finger loops and how they were applied is taken from University of Utah Anthropological papers related to the basketmaker cave excavations in Arizona and Utah.

This particular loop system had some unique additions, but is basically a common model. The diagram is a detail of the construction of the loops: details on the left are the back, and those on the right show the front of the atlatl.

"The grips were formed of a strip of leather about 14.5 cm long rolled up around a piece of sinew. This was then perforated in the center and slid up the shaft to a point 9.5 cm from the end. The ends of the leather were brought forward to form the grips, tied to the shaft and then back on themselves with sinew. The center of the strip was also secured with sinew. Shallow notches had been cut on either side of the shaft to allow more room for the fingers. An additional piece of leather, with two long "tails" had been attached to the back with sinew; then the tails were wrapped around the loops and shaft and secured with sinew, thus concealing some of the loop attachment. Sinew and leather wraps continue up the shaft, just forward of the finger loops. Fiber cordage and blue bird feathers are applied over these wraps."

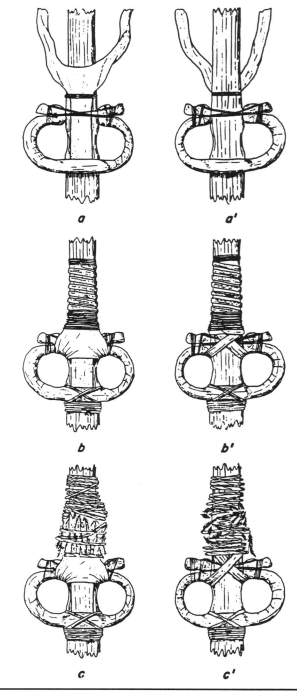

a   a'

b   b'

c   c'

Where are they now? Through my research, I was able to uncover mention of 28 separate specimens or fragments. Locating specimens from reports, however, is difficult as they do not tell where to look for them. The majority of specimens were listed in the following sources: **Great Basin Atlatl Studies, Stone Age In The Great Basin, Handbook of the North American Indian #11, U of U Anthropological Paper #93, and U of U Anthropological Paper #104.** Some of the atlatls mentioned have been discussed elsewhere in this issue of the BPT. Unfortunately, the majority are still in collections, a few are on display, but no listing of their present locations has been compiled. Do you know where these atlatls are housed? If so please contact the SPT and let us know. We are interested in compiling an inventory of eastern specimens and/or any other western ones we have missed to this point.

Great Basin Specimens - Lovelock Cave, Plush Cave, Roaring Springs Cave 1 & 2, McClure, Nicolarsen, Cowbone Cave/Winnemucca Lake, Hogup Cave, Council Hall Cave, Last Supper Cave, Kramer Cave, Juke Box Cave, Cowboy Cave, Potter Creek Cave.

Basketmaker Specimens - Broken Roof Cave, Grand Gulch 1 & 2, White Dog Cave 1-2-3, Kinboko, Lukachukai, Baylor Rock Shelter, N.C. Cave, Leonard Rock Shelter, Etna Cave, Gypsum Cave, Humboldt Cave.

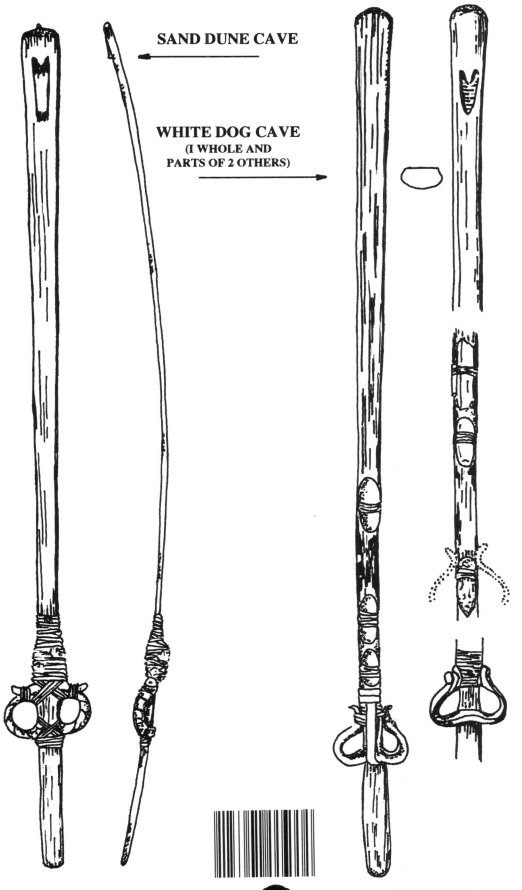

SAND DUNE CAVE

WHITE DOG CAVE
(I WHOLE AND
PARTS OF 2 OTHERS)

PRIMITIVE
HUNTING EQUIPMENT:
JABBING AND THROWING SPEARS
By Scooter Cheatham

* Notes taken from Errett Callahan's chart on projectiles

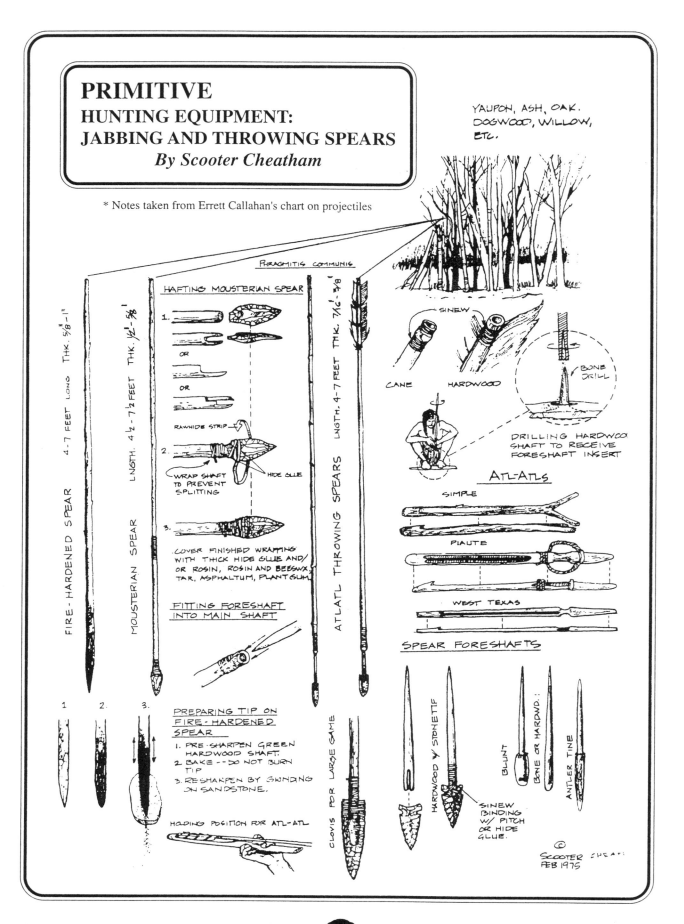

YAUPON, ASH, OAK. DOGWOOD, WILLOW, ETC.

PHRAGMITIS COMMUNIS

FIRE-HARDENED SPEAR   4-7 FEET LONG THK. 5/8-1"

MOUSTERIAN SPEAR   LNGTH. 4½-7½ FEET THK. ½-5/8'

ATLATL THROWING SPEARS   LNGTH. 4-7 FEET THK. 7/16-5/8'

HAFTING MOUSTERIAN SPEAR

1.

OR

OR

RAWHIDE STRIP

2. WRAP SHAFT TO PREVENT SPLITTING   HIDE GLUE

3.

COVER FINISHED WRAPPING WITH THICK HIDE GLUE AND/OR ROSIN, ROSIN AND BEESWX, TAR, ASPHALTUM, PLANT GUM.

FITTING FORESHAFT INTO MAIN SHAFT

1.   2.   3.

PREPARING TIP ON FIRE-HARDENED SPEAR
1. PRE-SHARPEN GREEN HARDWOOD SHAFT.
2. BAKE -- DO NOT BURN TIP
3. RESHARPEN BY GRINDING ON SANDSTONE.

HOLDING POSITION FOR ATL-ATL

SINEW

CANE   HARDWOOD

BONE DRILL

DRILLING HARDWOOD SHAFT TO RECEIVE FORESHAFT INSERT

ATL-ATLS

SIMPLE

PIAUTE

WEST TEXAS

SPEAR FORESHAFTS

CLOVIS FOR LARGE GAME

HARDWOOD W/ STONE TIP

SINEW BINDING W/ PITCH OR HIDE GLUE.

BLUNT

BONE OR HARDWD.

ANTLER TINE

ⓒ SCOOTER CHEATH. FEB 1975

Throwing Atlatl Darts

Photos By David Wescott & David Holladay

Holding Dart with Baseball Grip

Baseball Grip

Holding Dart with Split-Finger Grip

Split-Finger Grip

ABOVE: Throwing for distance . Note high angle of release. BELOW: Throwing for accuracy. Note flat trajectory.

Sample Rabbit Stick Patterns

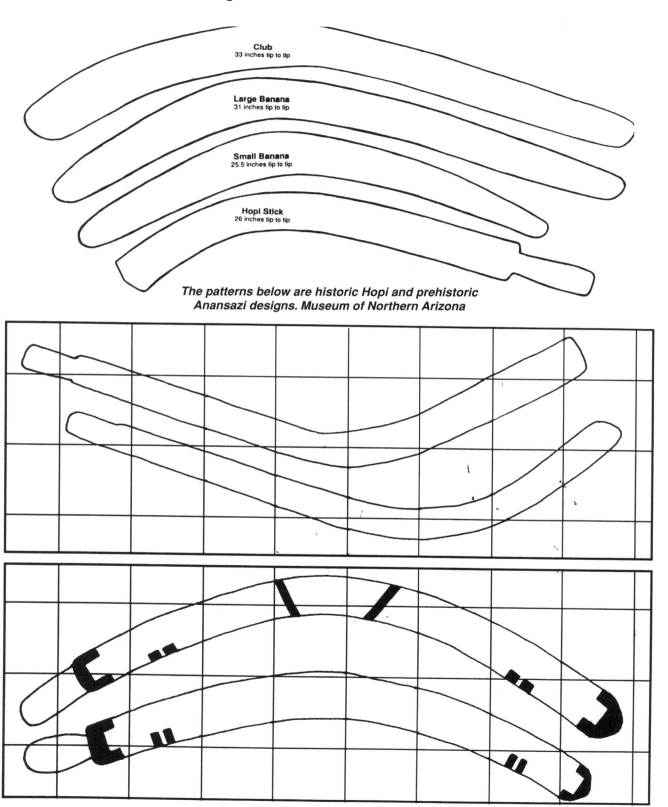

Club
33 inches tip to tip

Large Banana
31 inches tip to tip

Small Banana
25.5 inches tip to tip

Hopi Stick
26 inches tip to tip

The patterns below are historic Hopi and prehistoric Anansazi designs. Museum of Northern Arizona

HAND-THROWN PROJECTILES
Things That Fly - Part 1

"In the early days of the Dreamtime, people had to crawl on their hands and knees because the sky was nearly touching the ground. An old chief came to a magic pool and he stooped down to drink. As he did so, he saw a beautiful straight stick in the water and he reached in and picked it up. Then he suddenly thought, 'I can push up the sky with this stick and we'll be able to stand up.' So he pushed and pushed until he pushed the sky to where it is today and the trees began to grow and the possums ran about in the branches and the kangaroos started hopping for joy. Then he looked at his stick and saw it was terribly bent. Thinking it was no longer good, he threw it away but it came back to him. He tried again and it came back again. So he kept the stick and called it the boomerang."

--Australian Aboriginal legend as told by Les and Arthur Janetski

No one can be sure of the boomerang's origins. The twisting path of a falling leaf or seed may have inspired the first experiment, or it may have evolved from simple throwing [clubs].

The oldest wooden boomerangs so far discovered date from 8 - 10,000 years ago. Boomerangs also appear in Arnhem Land rock paintings, thought to be more than 15,000 years old.

Despite this antiquity, the world's oldest boomerang is possibly not Australian. A boomerang made from a mammoth's tusk was found in southern Poland during 1987 and has been dated to 23,000 years ago. Other prehistoric boomerangs have been found in Jutland [Denmark] (7,000 years) and are depicted in North African cave paintings [Ethiopia] (9,000 years).

Australian Aborinals were joined as boomerang throwers by the Hopi Indians, Eskimos, peoples of India, Ancient Egypt, Indonesia, the New Hebrides, Spain, Holland, and Germany. In most of these places the boomerang was made obsolete by the bow and arrow.

Aborigines have used boomerangs for thousands of years. It is not surprising to find a great diversity in their form and function. Specific uses have led to specialized forms.

Despite their specialized forms, some types of boomerang had several uses. In arid Australia for example, a boomerang was used as a hunting and fighting weapon: a ceremonial percussion instrument: a utensil for digging, clearing the ground, making or tending

THE VERSATILE BOOMERANG

The boomerang that the aboriginal uses for hunting (B) is fairly straight and streamlined in cross section (F). It is thrown directly at game and does not return. A picklike tip may be added (A) to make a more lethal fighting weapon. Returning boomerangs (C, D) are lighter, have an airfoil shape (E) and are used as toys and in sporting contests.

fire and for cutting meat. Boomerangs could be used as toys by children or adults, or could become sanctified as religious objects.

Q. What do you call a boomerang that doesn't come back?
A. A stick.

The fact is that most boomerangs did not come back. Of the popular fallacies associated with the boomerang perhaps the most widespread and deep-rooted is the belief that all boomerangs are of the returning type. As a matter of fact, returning boomerangs constitute only a very small percentage of Australian boomerangs, a percentage difficult to estimate accurately but which under normal aboriginal conditions may have been exceedingly small. There are parts of Australia, particularly in the North, where the return boomerang is unknown.

Surprisingly, the non-return boomerang is aerodynamically more complex than the returning boomerang.

Both types of boomerang share the same essential characteristic, which is that the lift generated by their rotating wings gives them a greatly extended flight. For a return boomerang, the flight path is approximately circular, whereas for a straight-on boomerang the flight

This section is a compilation of articles and discussions with some of the top experts in the field of boomerangs and throwing sticks. Thanks goes to Ray Rieser, Benjamin Ruhe, and Bob Foresi for contributions to our better understanding of Throwing Sticks.

path is nearly linear. But both are capable of travelling 200 m or more through the air--much further than one can throw a simple throwstick, which makes no use of aerodynamic lift and has a range of about 60 m.

Another reason for calling both the return and non-return weapons 'boomerangs' is that by judiciously heating and twisting the wings it is in many cases possible to convert a return boomerang to a non-returner, and vice versa.

Some authors confuse the 'non-return boomerang' with the simple ballistic throwstick/club.

"Any weapon that is thrown by hand, such as a rock, spear or club, has a limited range. To maximize this range one must aim high or throw very hard. For a hunter using such a weapon, this means that he must either get very close to his prey or sacrifice accuracy by aiming high and throwing with a lot of force. On semi-arid plains with little cover the problem of getting close to an animal target is acute. The boomerang, although it appears simple in form, is actually a sophisticated aerodynamic device designed to cope with this problem facing hunters.

The non-returning boomerang is generally larger and heavier than the returning variety and is only moderately curved. It is used for hunting and war, and designed to fly in a fairly straight line parallel with the ground. It is a formidable weapon ideally suited to use on the open plains. It leaves the hunter's hand at a speed of 60 miles per hour and rotating ten time per second, and will kill or injure anything in a path approximately one meter wide and 200 meters long." **Rieser**

What then, apart from the flight, is the difference between a return boomerang and a straight-flying boomerang?

Return boomerangs develop an overturning moment as well as lift, and it is this moment which makes the boomerang turn and so return. If one wants a boomerang to fly straight, one must obtain lift but eliminate the overturning moment. This is usually achieved by twisting each wing so that the inner part provides the usual positive lift, but the outer part provides negative lift.

The plane of rotation at launch is normally about 20 degrees above the horizontal (70 degrees to the right of the vertical) so that there is some lateral movement to the left of the thrower as the boomerang flies away.

With its near linear flight, the straight-flying boomerang can be aimed more accurately than the return boomerang and so is preferred for general hunting purposes.

Although boomerangs are one of Man's oldest weapons, a quantitative analysis of their flight presents many difficulties; and the only way one can at present determine the precise trajectory of a boomerang is by **throwing it.**

Most of the bibliography was sent in by Ben Ruhe and Ray Rieser, two notables in the field of stick throwing. For more information on boomerangs, both returning and non-returning, contact; Ray Rieser,2900 Edgecliff Rd., Lower Burrell, PA 15068. 412-335-5216; Ben "Guru" Ruhe, 1882 Columbia Rd. N.W., Washington, D.C. 20009. 202-234-9208.; or Bob Foresi, Springfield, MA 413-733-7403.   **Bibliography**
Anderson, Christopher and Philip Jones. Boomerang - booklet produced for the exhibitionof the same name at the South Australian Museum. Feb 27-July 19, 1992.
Borkensha, Peter. The Pitjantjatjara and Their Crafts- book
Foresi, Robert. In Support of Non-Returners. Unpublished paper.
Foresi, Robert. Some Modern Ideas On The Construction of Non-Returning ThrowSticks. Unpublished paper.
Hess, Felix 1975. Boomerangs, Aerodynamics and Motion. Doctoral Thesis, Germany. July 7, 1975.
Musgrove, Peter. Many Happy Returns - magazine article.
Rieser, Ray 1985. Using Natural Wood Elbows. Many Happy Returns, Spring -p15-18.
Rieser, Ray 1987. Boomerangs. Carnegie Magazine. May/June, p34-39.

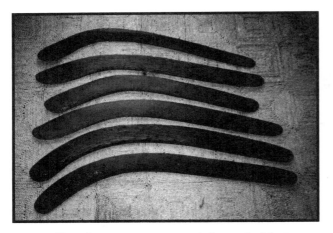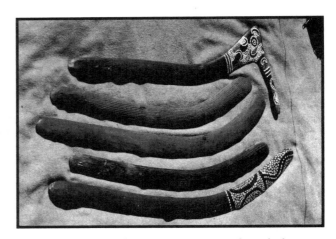

Most boomerangs are not decorated, but some are painted and others have patterns carved on their surfaces. Some Aborigines put small gouges on the top surface of the weapon; this is done, some say, for more than decoration. Like the dimples on a golfball, these fluted areas may extend its flight range.Central Australian Non-Returning sticks from the Ben Ruhe Collection.

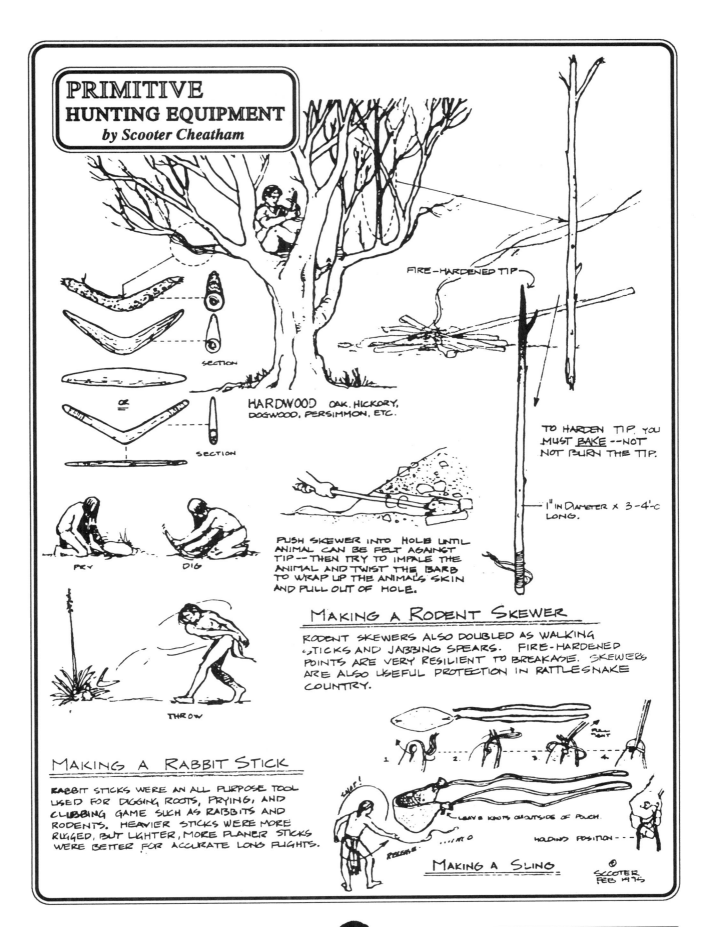

PRIMITIVE HUNTING EQUIPMENT
by Scooter Cheatham

SECTION

SECTION

HARDWOOD OAK. HICKORY, DOGWOOD, PERSIMMON, ETC.

PRY

DIG

THROW

FIRE-HARDENED TIP

TO HARDEN TIP, YOU MUST BAKE -- NOT NOT BURN THE TIP.

1" IN DIAMETER X 3-4'-C LONG.

PUSH SKEWER INTO HOLE UNTIL ANIMAL CAN BE FELT AGAINST TIP -- THEN TRY TO IMPALE THE ANIMAL AND TWIST THE BARB TO WRAP UP THE ANIMAL'S SKIN AND PULL OUT OF HOLE.

MAKING A RODENT SKEWER

RODENT SKEWERS ALSO DOUBLED AS WALKING STICKS AND JABBING SPEARS. FIRE-HARDENED POINTS ARE VERY RESILIENT TO BREAKAGE. SKEWERS ARE ALSO USEFUL PROTECTION IN RATTLESNAKE COUNTRY.

MAKING A RABBIT STICK

RABBIT STICKS WERE AN ALL PURPOSE TOOL USED FOR DIGGING ROOTS, PRYING, AND CLUBBING GAME SUCH AS RABBITS AND RODENTS. HEAVIER STICKS WERE MORE RUGGED, BUT LIGHTER, MORE PLANER STICKS WERE BETTER FOR ACCURATE LONG FLIGHTS.

LEAVE KNOTS ON OUTSIDE OF POUCH.

RELEASE

HOLDING POSITION

MAKING A SLING

SCOOTER FEB 1975

How To Make A Throwing Stick
The Non-Returning Boomerang
By Errett Callahan, PhD.

*Excerpts from **The Non-Returning Boomerang: Evolution and Experiment.** Virginia Commonwealth University, March 15, 1975.*

BACKGROUND

The non-returning boomerang, or rabbitstick, is one of the most efficient hunting implements ever devised by primitive man for sparsely vegetated to semi-desert conditions. It is capable of being hand-propelled in a near straight line-trajectory for over 200 yards with little deviation to left or right and with little change in elevation until the very end of its journey.

"Ballistically", if we may use that term, it's flight resembles that of modern firearms more than does any other primitive missile, arrow included. Few aboriginal bows could be made to propel a hunting arrow beyond 200 yards. Of those that were capable of this in Pope's tests (war bows) the pull was so strong as to be quite unreasonable for most types of hunting.

Despite the rapid forward velocity, the real damage of the non-returning boomerang is caused by the spinning limbs which revolve so rapidly as to greatly increase the punch upon impact with the objective. A solid 12 oz non-returning boomerang is easily capable of snapping the foreleg of a deer or comparable-sized animal at great distances.

The non-returning boomerang has been called a variety of names - besides those given it on the spot by its intended (or unintended) victims. In New South Wales, Australia, the Botony Bay Aborigines refer to the returning boomerang as "bumarin", from which we get the word "boomerang". Elsewhere, it is referred to as "wongium", "wunkun", and "wangal". The non-returning boomerang is called the "tootgundy wunkun" or "straight-on" boomerang, the "killer stick", the "war" boomerang, the "hunting" boomerang, the "kylie" and of course, the "non-returning" boomerang. The Hopi refer to their version as the "rabbitstick".

In the New World, the Hopi rabbitstick of the Southwest is the American counterpart of the non-returning boomerang. Rabbitsticks have been documented in a wider area of the Southwest than that which the Hopi occupied. The Indians of Baja California have been observed using a version of the rabbitstick. I have speculated that the rabbitstick or non-returning boomerang may have been previously used by a substantial portion of the Southwest Desert Archaic Culture. This culture system seems to have been in operation by 10,000 years BP and existed well into contact times virtually unchanged., The Baja California Indians and the Paiutes of Nevada today seem to be directly related culturally and technologically to this desert/semi-desert way of life.

The non-returning boomerang requires open or semi-desert terrain for it's successful operation. An open country without an abundance of thick trees, tall bushes, or even high grass is essential; for undergrowth, naturally, impedes the flight. For such open country the non-returning boomerang is indeed well-adapted.

The non-returning boomerang was an adaptation of a simple throwing stick. Possibly man's earliest missile, at least in wooded areas and brush country, was a simple stick. In time the sticks chosen for missiles would have become more specialized. Certain lengths, weights, diameters, materials, balances, and hardnesses would have been found more effective than others. In some culture areas the sticks would have eventually been modified over their found condition. These modified sticks would have still been basically straight and round. Such specialized "throwing sticks" have been reported from all over the world and are particularly abundant in Australia.

PREPARATION

Wood

In order to make a non-returning boomerang (NRB), one needs certain materials and tools. I will [discuss] three optional methods so that one may make his either with modern power tools, modern hand tools, or primitive stone tools.

Plywood may be used for making the NRB. But do not, if possible, use standard soft plywood. Marine plywood or aircraft plywood 5/16 to 1/2" thick is ideal as it is dense and hard. The more weight one can pack into a given diameter up to 12 oz, the farther one can throw the implement. This does not necessarily hold true for the returning boomerang, however, as lighter woods are usually sought.

Curved limbs, roots, or crotches are needed for making non-returning boomerangs the old way. It takes a lot of looking around to find a suitable curve and even more to find one of a hard, dense wood. You can get into the habit of looking for suitable boomerang limbs and saplings wherever you go so beware; it can become an obsession. One soon notices that certain tree species tend to curve more than others. Sourwood, hackberry, and buckeye are especially noted for this.

Avoid using limbs with a branch or knot at the curve or angle as this will cause a weakness. I have yet to have a

PLANS FOR "IDEAL/OPTIMUM" STICKS

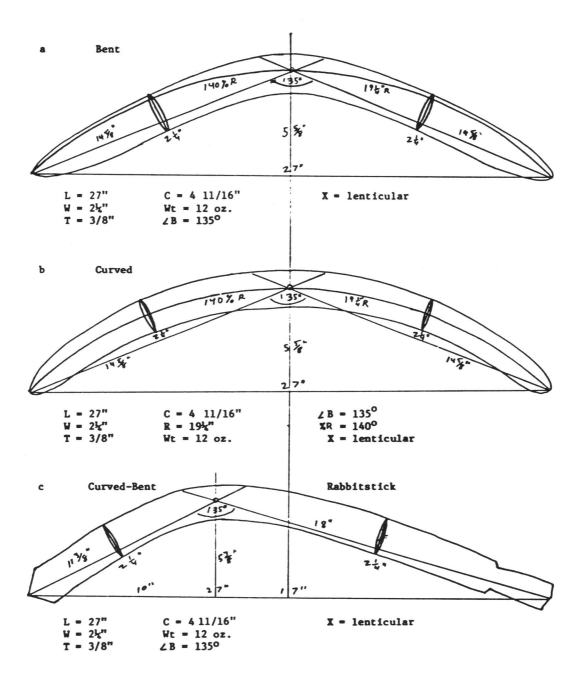

a   Bent

L = 27"   C = 4 11/16"   X = lenticular
W = 2¼"   Wt = 12 oz.
T = 3/8"   ∠B = 135°

b   Curved

L = 27"   C = 4 11/16"   ∠B = 135°
W = 2¼"   R = 19½"   XR = 140°
T = 3/8"   Wt = 12 oz.   X = lenticular

c   Curved-Bent   Rabbitstick

L = 27"   C = 4 11/16"   X = lenticular
W = 2¼"   Wt = 12 oz.
T = 3/8"   ∠B = 135°

boomerang made of such a limb last any time at all. Maximum strength is needed at the mid-point. Try to select a section which will give you limbs at least 2" wide, while 2 1/2 - 3" is preferable.

Some of the more suitable tree species in the US include apple, barberry, beech, birch, buckeye, cherry, crabapple, dogwood, elm, hackberry, hickory, holly, hop hornbeam, ironwood, locust, manzanita, maple, mesquite, oak, osage, persimmon, plum, redbud, serviceberry, sourwood, and sycamore. In Australia, mulgawood (an acacia), lancewood or sudburu (also an acacia), and blue gum (a euclyptus) are all used for making the "tootgundy wunkun". In India, non-returners are sometimes made of ivory.

In Arizona, the Hopi made their rabbitsticks of scrub oak. The bright yellow wood of Arizona barberry (Berbieris fremontii) is also suitable for making rabbitsticks. Non-returners that are too light cease rotating and "come untied", flipping face-over-face instead of cutting a horizontal slice thru space.

Suitability of material is based to a large extent on density of the wood, the denser, heavier, and harder, the better. Hardness may be increased, at least on the surface, by fire hardening. This is accomplished by gently toasting the completed or nearly completed piece on a bed of coals, avoiding flames, till the surface turns a golden brown. Keep it rotating back and forth during heating and watch out for scorching. Fire hardening may be accomplished in conjunction with skewing of limbs in order to modify flight patterns as below.

Weight may be temporarily increased slightly be soaking in water.

It is best to cut the wood during the winter when the sap is down. This reduces incidence of cracking during drying. Rough out the blank while the wood is green if using stone tools. Otherwise wait till the wood is seasoned, if feasible. Be careful to season it very slowly (in a dry place outdoors) so as to avoid splitting and warpage. (Warpage after seasoning can be corrected somewhat by heating the limbs over coals and bending in the desired direction).

Submerging the piece under water is a way of quick-seasoning green woods. The sap is removed without dehydrating the pores.

PROCESS

Power Tools - Use the sabre saw or band saw for cutting out plywood blanks. The disk or drum sander is used for grinding down the contours and getting the correct cross-section. Modern tools and materials allow you to start out with a known formula to attain predictable results.

Hand Tools - Aborigines in Australia today use a small axe, metal adze, and a piece of glass for making non-returning boomerangs. With but little experience, one can cut down a limb with a saw and split it with a maul and wedges. One can also rough out a 2 1/2" thick limb or sapling using a sharp machete in 10-15 minutes. The Surform rasp can be used to shape up the same blank into a 1/2" thin lenticular

cross-section within another 20 minutes. After test flying, further adjustments may be made, but one needn't spend more than an hour total using such tools.

Stone Tools - Natural tools and materials call for judgement. No recipes. Use the hafted axe, celt, or either kind of large adze for cutting down suitable limbs, trunks, or roots and for roughing out the general shape. The hafted flake adze is used to good advantage in leveling the surface and in trimming the blank to near its final proportions. The flake adze is hafted so that the unifacially retouched flake is aligned with the handle. Such an adze is used by placing one foot on the objective piece, grabbing the handle as one would grasp a dagger, and chopping down and into the blank, working toward the foot. The handle is held at quite a low or flat angle to the wood. One of the most efficient stone tools I have used is a snapped biface (knife-like implement). Such a tool is easy to grasp, has two very strong 90 degree edges at the point of fracture and makes for as effective a wood plane as I've ever used, metal or stone. Hold the flat part of the tool at a low angle to the wood and push this 90 degree edge along the surface of the objective piece.

After test flying, stone-tool-made boomerangs may be finished off either by continued scraping with sharp-edged flakes or scraper/flakes, by rubbing with fine dry sand held in a leather pad, or by rubbing with a piece of dry sandstone.

Give the finished implement several good rubdowns with oil, tallow, or wax (or varnish) to seal out moisture. Refinish as needed after bumps and knocks dent the surface, in order to maintain the same aerodynamic behavior.

FLYING AND TUNING

After roughing out the non-returning boomerang to a flattened shape with a lenticular cross-section, take your implement outside for some test flying.

Hold the NRB by either end if symmetrical, with the hook pointing forward as one would hold a sickle. Throw it with a side-arm throw with the plane of the axis parallel to the ground. Give it plenty of wrist snap as you let it go. Wrist snap more than forward motion is the key to throwing any kind of boomerang successfully (Ruhe 1972, a:4). Throw it gently at first then increase velocity until you have a fairly good picture of the flight pattern. You may find that it curves to left (rarely) or right (more often) consistently. If it curves to the right, try tilting the hand up so that the distal limb is no longer parallel to the ground. Usually, on symmetrically constructed implements, a favorite end will evolve.

An aerodynamically optimum non-returning boomerang will fly in a straight line when thrown horizontally to near-horizontally.

It's a good idea to take your rasp or biface plane along with you when test flying your NRB so you can make adjustments as needed on the spot.

Remove material from the top or bottom sides - or both - of each limb till you get the flight pattern you wish. Rasping at the bottom corner of the leading edge will increase lift. Approximating a convex-plano section will reduce lift. If too thick, plane down each face evenly. I prefer to test my NRB when it is about 1/2" thick and thin it down to 3/8" or so during the test session.

A method the Aborigines often used, is to shape the limbs into a plano- convex cross-section with flat side down. This is the way returning boomerangs are usually made. One may have different cross-sections in different areas of each limb.

Aborigine returning boomerangs are often made by planning down the limbs to a flat cross-section with too little thickness to afford effective lift. The limb tips are gently heated and simultaneously twisted upward in two direction. The tip itself (the last 6" or so) is given positive dihedral by being pulled upwards, much as is the tip of a bird's wing on the downward stroke and the leading edge, the lineal edge which cuts into the wind during revolution, is skewed or twisted upward several degrees. Sometimes this was done only to one limb. This now would apply to tuning non-returning boomerangs, lift may be reduced by reversing the process: bending the tip down (producing negative dihedral) and/or skewing the leading edge downward. Careful rasping of unheated limbs may accomplish a similar feature.

If one wishes to alter the flight pattern without replanning the wood and reducing the weight, heating is the technique to use. Heat the limb over the coals, not the flames, to avoid scorching. Holding the limb 3 to 4" above the coals, one to two minutes should suffice to warm the limb enough for bending. It should be a little too warm to touch with an ungloved or unpadded hand. Twist the limb in the desired direction and hold till cool.

One thus has 3 options for modifying flight patterns:
1. Replanning surfaces to make them
   a. more lenticular
   b. more plano-convex
   c. thinner
2. Bending the limb tips up or down by using heat, increasing or decreasing dihedral
3. Twisting the leading edge of the limbs up or down by using heat

I would suggest starting out with a lenticular cross-section with no positive or negative dihedral, skew, or twist and work from there. This should give you a serviceable non-returning boomerang with satisfactory flight patterns. You can then tinker around with "fine tuning" all you want depending on your preferences, aspiratons, and patience. Suggested optimum non-returning boomerangs, one with bend, and one with continuous curvature, are given.

Note: If any readers achieve flights of over 200 yds (on windless days) I would be interested in hearing so that I may keep my record list updated.
From the results of the study done in this paper, Errett produced a western-style non-returning throwing stick that flew a sustained 300+ yards at approximately 3 feet above the ground.

Using Natural Wood Elbows
by Ray Rieser

While on a recent trip to Washington, DC, Ben Ruhe was kind enough to show me a film of an aborigine constructing a boomerang. The aborigine sought out a tree with a root coming out of trunk at the "proper" angle. He made several cuts in the tree trunk and severed the root about 18 inches from the tree. He then pulled this boomerang shaped piece of wood from the living tree, sliced it longitudinally into two parts and shaped them into boomerangs (Figure #1).

In searching out natural wood formations from which to construct boomerangs, several criteria must be met. It is essential that the arms of the boomerang be in the same plane and that the angle between the arms be proper .

I soon discovered that even with the abundance of gnarled trees and exposed roots along the river bank, that finding a bent limb or a trunk and root combination that would meet the above criteria was rare. Rather than return home nearly empty handed, I decided that I would collect other

parts of trees that even remotely resembled the boomerang shape, and slice thru them to study the orientation of the grain.

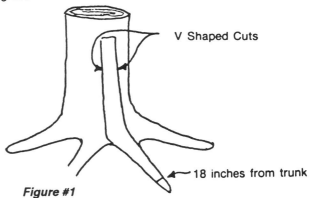

Figure #1

For maximum strength it is essential that the wood grain follow the shape of the boomerang. Otherwise, the 'rang may break upon impact (Figure 2).

After slicing thru the various formations, I discovered that it is possible to find wood suitable for boomerang construction from a trunk-limb configuration and from a Y formation. Figure 3 illustrates the regions where the grain follows the

SPECIFICATIONS FOR THE OPTIMUM NRB

Material - Variable

Length - Variation: 16 - 36" (40 - 90 cm)
- Suggested optimum: 27" (68.5 cm)

Width - Variation: 1 1/2 - 4" (3.8 -10.2 cm) (l/w ratio = 24.00 - 8.00)
- Suggested optimum: 2 1/4" (5.7 cm) (l/w ratio = 12.00; w = 1/12 length)

Thickness - Variation: 1/4 - 3/4" (.6 - 1.9 cm) (l/w ratio = 16.00-4.00)
- Suggested optimum: 3/8" (1.0 cm) (w/t ratio = 6.00; t = 1/6 width)

Circumference - Variation: 3 1/8 - 8 1/2" (8.0 - 21.5 cm)
- Suggested optimum: 4 11/16" (11.0 cm)
(equivalent of rounded stick 1 1/2" in diameter)

Cross-section - Variation: plano-convex to lenticular to convex-plano and flat
- Suggested optimum: lenticular

Weight - Variation: 5 oz - 1 lb. 8 oz (140 - 680 g)
- Suggested optimum: 12 oz (340 g) (2.25 inches/ounce or .44 ounce/inch)

Angle of Bend - Variation: 123 degrees - 145 degrees
- Suggested optimum: 135 degrees

Curvature - Variation: 115 - 175 percent
- Suggested optimum: 140 percent

Radius - Variable

Expected Forward Speed - 30 m/sec. (plus or minus)

Expected Rotational Speed - 10 r/sec. (plus or minus)

Expected Distance - 100 - 200 yards

Expected Flight Patterns - Variation: curve left to right, straight, "S" curve to reverse "S".
- Suggested optimum: straight

Note: The above range of variations and suggested optimum specifications are based on experimental research and checked as possible against ethnographic and archeological data.

outside contour of the tree.

Armed with this knowledge it is possible to increase your chances many fold of finding a natural piece of wood with proper grain orientation for boomerang construction. I found that a bow saw, sometimes referred to as a Swede saw and available at all hardware stores, was the best tool to take with you to the woods. Be sure to cut your logs longer than needed, because the ends may develop shrinkage cracks. It has been my experience that hardwoods produce the nicest blanks for making boomerangs. So far I have gathered samples from cherry, locust, oak and dogwood.

Ideal Grain Orientation

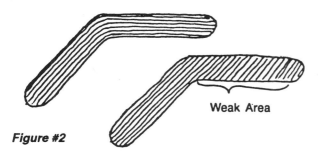

Weak Area

Figure #2

Once you have brought your logs home you must take proper care of them. Wood taken from a living fallen tree contains moisture in the form of sap or rainwater, and is referred to by woodworkers as green wood. Once cut and stored out of the weather, wood begins losing moisture until it reaches equilibrium with the moisture in the surrounding air.

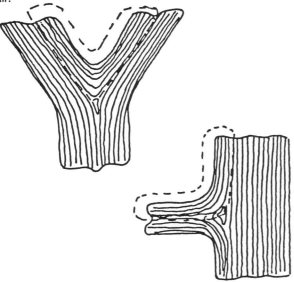

Dotted Lines Enclose Regions Suitable
For Boomerang Construction

Figure #3

As wood loses moisture it begins to shrink. In a log the wood on the ends loses moisture more rapidly than the wood in the interior of the log. With the ends trying to shrink while the interior remains swollen, enormous stress develops within the log, resulting in radial cracking known as checking. To prevent rapid end drying of a log, the ends should be coated as soon as possible. Any impervious material may be used such as wax, aluminum paint, etc.

Be sure to leave the bark on the log until you are ready to slice thru it. This helps to cut down rapid moisture loss. Some woodworkers even store freshly cut logs in sealed plastic bags to slow moisture loss. I have had a birch elbow crack completely through in less than 24 hours because it was not end-coated.

The easiest way to tell if a log has reached equilibrium with the moisture in the air is to periodically weigh it. When the weight becomes constant over a period of weeks, the moisture loss has stopped. This, however, can be very time consuming; for instance, to air dry a 1 inch thick piece of cherry may take from 2 to 7 months.

I, for one, am too impatient to wait this long. The alternative is to start slicing thru the log and see if the grain pattern is suitable. If the wood moisture content is not at equilibrium with the atmosphere the slices are going to warp (Figure 4). The easiest method is to cut them to permit good air circulation, and let them dry. Once the wood has dried and warped, simply flatten one side with a plane, joiner or sander and then plane the other side to the desired thickness.

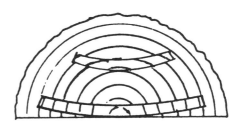

How Green Wood Slices Warp As They Dry

Figure #4

Do not cut the piece of wood to the boomerang shape until this time, because if edge cracks do develop and the slice is oversized, they can be cut away.

The process I have just described is by far the simplest method of obtaining usable blanks for boomerang construction. But with this ease comes a cost. You will find that since you must slice extra thick to allow for warpage you cannot get as many blanks from a log as you would like.

Originaly printed in **Many Happy Returns** -Quarterly Newslatter of the USBA, Spring 1985. Reprinted by permission of the author and Editor.

CROSS-SECTIONS

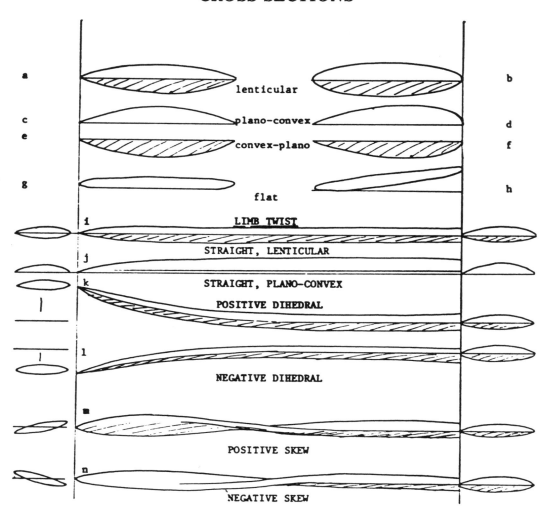

a   lenticular   b

c   plano-convex   d

e   convex-plano   f

g   flat   h

i   LIMB TWIST

    STRAIGHT, LENTICULAR

j   STRAIGHT, PLANO-CONVEX

k   POSITIVE DIHEDRAL

l   NEGATIVE DIHEDRAL

m   POSITIVE SKEW

n   NEGATIVE SKEW

FLIGHT - PATTERNS

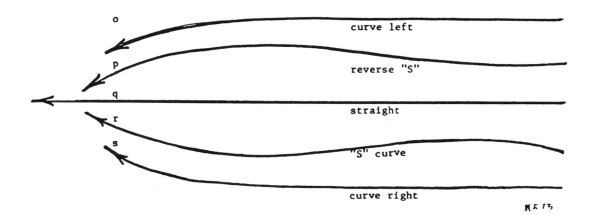

o   curve left

p   reverse "S"

q   straight

r   "S" curve

s   curve right

Tuning A Throwing Stick
By Robert Foresi

ACTUAL SIZE

camber line higher (slightly exaggerated)

leading edge

Excerpts from Some Modern Ideas On The Construction of Non-Returning Throwing Sticks. An Unpublished paper submitted by Ben Ruhe.

Tuning and Throwing

As I have advanced the theory of tuning non-returners only incrementally beyond its primitive beginnings, I have not found a "cookbook" formula for tuning them as yet. The suggestions presented here are the most successful approaches I have taken to date. Perhaps I can at least save the aspiring stick-thrower from some of the least prolific throwing sessions I have experienced.

The first rule of tuning non-returners is to forget everything you know about returning boomerangs. Forget about the bottom side of the stick being flatter than the topside. Forget about adding extra undercut to the leading edge. And forget about leading edges being blunter than trailing edges. All these factors will tend to produce a stick with too much lift. All that is desired is a slight amount of lift, enough to negate the force of gravity.

The following is the airfoil I have used with the most success. Note that the faces are flat for the central 2/3 or so of the airfoil section, and note that there is a slight built-in negative skew to the airfoil section. The skew may not be essential to obtaining the desired flight.

ACTUAL SIZE

camber line

leading edge

Make the throw stick with this airfoil section throughout its length, except no skew near the elbow of the stick. Test throw it, easy at first of course. If it rises too much, taper the topside of the leading edge a bit, or try bringing the whole camber line up a bit, as shown, or try more negative skew.

If the stick is dipping in flight too much, try tapering the trailing edge on top just slightly, or the leading edge bottom, or try bringing the whole camber line down a hair.

leading edge

It should be mentioned that the throw itself has a lot to do with the flight. Launching with more layover off vertical will of course tend to make the stick rise more, and vice versa. The desired layover angle is usually 45°-90° off vertical.

Sometimes it is helpful to flip the stick over and throw it upside down. This is admittedly sneaky, but produces results more often than one might guess.

A final rule for the enjoyment of throwing non-returners and for their advancement is safety. Any criticism of non-returners typically is centered around their potential danger and their past use as hunting implements. However, if a throw stick does not strike anything or threaten to do so, there is no danger, and throw sticks can then be regarded in the same manner as returners. Therefore, the most important safety rules are to select an expansive throwing area, and to know the flight potential of the stick you're throwing. Throw the stick easy at first, and recognize the possibility of errant throws. Especially important is to use caution when a throw stick has just been re-tuned. Vastly different ranges and curvatures of flight are often obtained from only slight adjustments to airfoiles. For long-range sticks an open field of a size 350 yds. by 250 yds. is required.

REFERENCE ARTICLES
1) "The Non-returning Boomerang - Evolution and Experiment." Errett Callahan, Virginia Commonwealth University, 1975.
2) "Australian Throwing Sticks, Throwing Clubs, and Boomerangs." D.S. Davidson, American Anthropologist, N.S., 38, 1936.

MAKING THROW STICKS BEHAVE

By Norm Kern

If the throw stick had never been developed, it seems quite unlikely that the boomerang would ever have been developed and we wouldn't be having all this fun. I believe the first boomerangs were probably defective throw sticks. Even though throw sticks are probably the parents of the boomerang, very little is written about them. I have purchased or made 13 throw sticks. Like boomerangs, each has its own personality, but throw sticks have their own set of aerodynamic behaviors, and challenges. I set out to make a few throw sticks for demonstrations. Following is an account of this learning experience.

Since the throw stick was intended for hunting, the most desirable flight patterns would be straight, long, and would be nearly parallel to the ground for sustained periods of the flight. To increase the opportunity of striking the target, the plane of rotation near the target would need to be nearly parallel to the ground. It would also be necessary for the stick to retain significant radial velocity at the time of impact. Most animals would be alarmed by the scent of the hunter if approached from upwind, so the stick must be able to fly upwind or at least cross wind. It all seemed so simple until I tried to make a throw stick behave.

My first attempts were plagued by "fatal flutter". To have the above listed properties the throw stick must spin in a plane with the flat surfaces basically parallel to the plane of rotation. When a throw stick flutters, it twists somehow along its long axis, and the flat surfaces are no longer parallel to the plane of rotation. Once the flat surfaces are exposed to the oncoming air, the throw stick quickly loses its spin, and drops to the ground.

The other type of throw stick misbehavior is soaring, and/or veering. At the end of the flight, such throw sticks curve off the straight path. For right handed throwers, the throw stick veers to the right. The throw stick may also gain altitude at the end of the flight. A variation on the soaring theme, is the throw stick which likes to gain altitude from the moment of release, and does not come close to the ground until it has lost almost all forward momentum, and so hovers down.

Figure A shows outlines of four throw sticks. I call them the Club, the Large Banana, the Small Banana, and the Hopi stick. I made all four from half inch 9 ply plywood. You should be able to obtain such wood from lumber yards or cabinet makers. I throw the Club, and the Large Banana with two hands, basically parallel to the ground, much like swinging a baseball bat. I throw the Small Banana and the Hopi stick one handed and launch with about 45 degrees of layover.

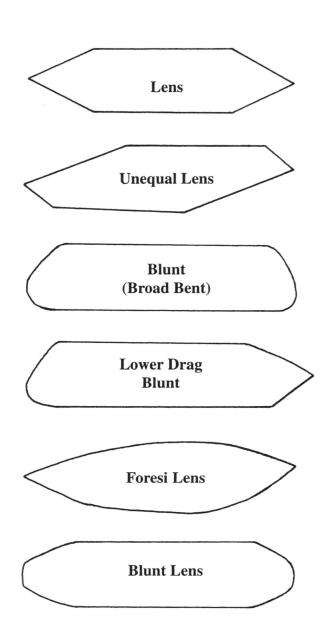

Lens

Unequal Lens

Blunt
(Broad Bent)

Lower Drag
Blunt

Foresi Lens

Blunt Lens

Throwing Stick Profiles

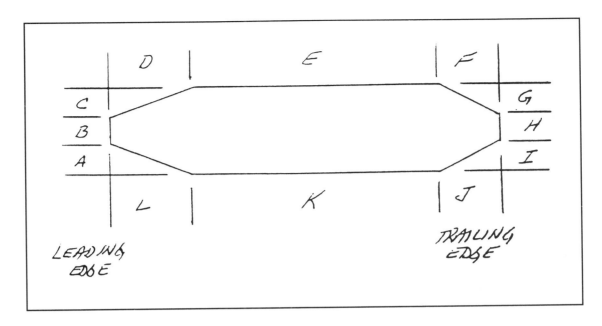

LEADING EDGE

TRAILING EDGE

Air Foils

When I began to make throw sticks, I read what I could and the common wisdom said the cross section should be that of a lens. The first throw stick I purchased had the lens cross section (Please see the cross section diagram above). The lens cross section has B and H equal to zero, C roughly equal to A, and D roughly equal to L, and likewise G equal to I, and F equal to J. This is how I made my first three throw sticks. All of them had "fatal flutter". Every throw was plagued by flutter, and there were no stable flights. My first success came on the Small Banana when I made C larger than A, and D larger than L. I also made I larger than G and J larger than F. (B, and H were zero.) This unequal lens made the Small Banana very stable, and enabled it to fly about 60 meters, but it tended to soar at the moment of release. Using the unequal lens on the other two throw sticks did not cure the flutter.

Upon discussing the flutter syndrome with Gary Broadbent, he showed me a very blunt airfoil with A much smaller than C, and I much smaller than G. and D, L, F, and J all very small. (B and H were basically zero.) I tried this approach on the Club (See the Blunt airfoil diagram). Both the leading and trailing edges were alike, and were quite similar to the leading edges of a normal returning boomerang. This provided a very stable flight but my intuition said that the blunt trailing edges must be creating drag which must be shortening the flight. I then increased F to decrease the drag. The effect was to cause the Club to soar and veer to the right at the end of flight. I lengthened the flight time, but it was certainly now a poor hunting device. I increased I and J to the current shape to reduce lift. This cured the soaring and veering, and Club had a nice level flight again.

I have four other throw sticks which have gone through similar changes with similar results. From these experiences I concluded:

1. On airfoils where B, and H equal zero, as you increase A and L (commonly called undercut), you will induce instability, and cause "flutter". The more C exceeds A, the more stable the throw stick will fly.

2. As you increase F, you will increase soaring and veering.

3. As you increase I and J, you will decrease soaring and keep the throw stick close to the ground in flight.

4. As you increase D, you decrease drag, maintain spin, and lengthen flight times and distance.

My first throw stick was made by Bob Foresi. I asked Bob to review these conclusions. He said on his current air foils he tries to "keep A and C equal, I equal to or slightly larger than G, and D greater than L and greater than F. I also keep E & K small, not so much at the center of the stick." Bob keeps B and H equal to zero. He said he agrees with the above airfoil principles with the possible exception of number 1.

Gregg Snouffer is another active throw stick maker. Gregg favors a blunt lens. It has B and H equal to about 50% of the face of the airfoil. A, C, G, and I equal about 25% of the face. The transitions are rounded. Likewise L, D, F, and J are each equal to about 20% of the cord. I tried the blunt lens on the Hopi stick and the Large Banana with excellent results. Neither stick flutters.

For all of the throw sticks I have made or purchased, the air foil shape is the same on both arms, of course taking into account which edge of an arm is the leading edge. I have not intentionally experimented with different shaped airfoils on the same throw stick.

Shape & Weight

After all of the above events, I had most of my throw sticks working without fatal flutter at least when thrown downwind. Some were not stable when thrown up wind. I had operational sticks with 4 different airfoils. I concluded there must be something about the basic shape and weight distribution of the various shapes which also affected flutter, etc. Following are the dimensions I found to be important.

Z = Length - The distance between the extremes of the tips.
Y = "Height" I placed the tips of the throw stick on the bench and used a carpenter's square to measure the highest point on the elbow region.
U = "Height" of the center of mass. I taped one end of a string to one of the tips. I let the throw stick hang from my fingers at the point the string was attached. The other end of the string was weighted so it hung straight down. I taped the other end of the string to the other end of the throw stick at the point it naturally crosses the stick. I repeated the process with another string with the other end of the throw stick on top. The center of mass and rotation is at the point the strings cross. I put the throw stick on the bench again as before and used the square to measure the "height" of the center of mass.
Weight = weight in ounces.

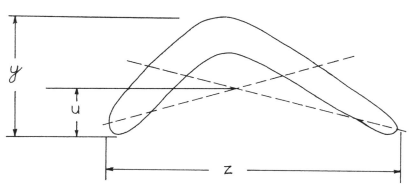

The sticks were made of a variety of materials, and were of significantly different sizes, so I could not just study the raw dimensions. I calculated ratios of these critical dimensions. Bob Foresi had indicated that the angle of the arms would be important. He believed that the lower (or more acute) the angle was, the more stable the throw stick would be. Since many throw sticks have one or both arms quite curved, I could not determine a satisfactory means to measure actual angle. The ratio of "Height" to Length relates to the angle. The higher this ratio is, the lower (or more acute) the angle will be. Based on my stick collection, the other critical ratio seemed to be weight to length. The throw sticks which weighed more per inch of length were more stable. This seemed reasonable. The wood used by the aboriginal peoples of Australia are heavier than the plywood I was using.

There was only one problem with these conclusions. One of the most stable sticks (Bob Foresi's) was the lightest and had the largest angle (as indicated by the ratio of Height to Length). It seemed there must be something else. This stick also had the "highest" center of mass as indicated by the ratio of Height of center of mass to Height. This observation took me back out to the field to experiment To "pull the center of mass up", I added lead tape to the elbow region near the balance point of the throw sticks

which tended to flutter. They became more stable. To "push the center of mass down", I added weight to the tips of stable fliers. They tended to flutter more when thrown upwind, but had less soaring and veering when thrown downwind. I believe that a good compromise can be reached for any given throw stick.

If you are trying to refine a design, you can vary the actual shape.

To decrease soaring and veering, lower the center of mass - weight the tips, narrow the cord of the elbow region, widen the tips, or make a more shallow (geometrically larger) angle. You could use any or all of these approaches in combination.

To cure flutter, raise the center of mass- weight the elbow region, narrow the tips, widen the cord in the elbow region, or make the angle more acute (geometrically smaller). Use any or all in combination.

Of course, weight, shape, air foils all interact to determine the flight of a throw stick. A shape which works in heavy wood may not work in light wood. Air foils which work on one shape may not work on all shapes.

Section 6

Art & Music
Discipline and Meaning

THE MUSIC OF PREHISTORY

By Laurence Libin

Virtually no direct evidence survives for how archaic "music" was performed, how it sounded, or even when music as we understand the concept, originated. The performance practices and instruments of modern aboriginal peoples might furnish tangible clues, but inferences drawn from comparative studies of cultures tens of thousands of years apart are of doubtful validity. Even a universally acceptable definition of music eludes musicologists, but pitch, tonal, dynamic, and rhythmic inflections of the voice and other body-produced sounds, used for expression and communication among many animals, surely lie at its root. In its most basic sense music prefigures language. Indeed, neurological experiments indicate that human musicality is dispersed among deep-seated regions of both brain hemispheres, whereas language abilities are more centralized in the left forebrain and therefore theoretically of more recent origin. Taking into account discoveries of unexpectedly complex vocalization among relatively intelligent mammals such as elephants and whales, "music" rich in esthetic content may not be a uniquely human accomplishment.

The simplest musical implements—uncrafted, found objects such as sticks and stones, intentionally manipulated to make noise—may represent an early development in human prehistory. Even if any such objects survive more or less intact, their aural function could easily be overlooked by archaeologists not used to thinking in terms of sound sources; after all, we normally ignore the acoustical aspects of caves—startling echo effects and so on—in speculating on the behavior of Paleolithic cave-dwellers. The first sound-producing artifacts doubtless served multiple purposes, of which sound production initially might have been incidental, if inevitable. Examples include eoliths used percussively, or log troughs pounded during food preparation (e.g., **BPT** 1994:1 p. 83), or stretched and plucked sinews (loc. cit., p. 38). Once the sonic potential of particularly resonant substances or shapes was recognized, such objects might have been exploited in, say, signaling, hunting, and courtship, to convey messages, decoy prey, or attract mates either ritualistically or directly.

> The first sound-producing artifacts doubtless served multiple purposes, of which sound production initially might have been incidental, if inevitable.

Improvements aimed at better replicating natural noises or projecting desirable sounds over longer distances could have led to development of utensils specifically designed to optimize tone—the first real instruments. These might well have been zoomorphic or anthropomorphic, as are many non-Western instruments today; it is no mere coincidence that violins, too, have a head, neck, belly, back, ribs, and waist, among other parts more usually associated with living creatures.

Their elementary form and nearly universal distribution suggest that idiophones (naturally sonorous solids normally struck or rubbed; notably, resonant stalactites and stalagmites) and aerophones (wind instruments, as simple as a hollow section of bone or cane without finger holes) preceded chordophoes (taut strings) and membranophones (taut skins); the latter types, which were evidently not so widely dispersed in prehistoric times, involve at least minimal technology to maintain the necessary tension of string or skin. It is significant that, with one possible exception, the chordophone family did not exist among pre-Conquest aboriginal American populations so far as is known. The only chordophone believed native (but not exclusively) to the Western Hemisphere is the mouth bow, a plucked type so primitive that it likely predated the hunting bow. (Sounding a string by rubbing it with a separate bow is a very late technique, not known in Europe until about one thousand years ago.)

Although we can never know much about archaic music, vocal or instrumental, its importance throughout human culture is undeniable. Informed speculation about prehistoric music and its tools, guided by ethnomusicology, might enrich our conception of primitive behavior, perhaps leading to fresh interpretations of some objects.

PAINT WITH PRIDE
By Doug Land

October 1971, Kaibab National Forest, Arizona. Climbing the rock cliff next to the dry stream bed was one of many small adventures enjoyed that day. The weather was clear and cool, the air dry, the sky a deep blue, a slight breeze blowing, the smell of forested pine, straw grass along the plateau, the quiet calm of nature, and a serene atmosphere that does the soul good. Even being alone in this sparse wilderness for a few days did not cause him loneliness, for nature, in its own simple way, gave comfort and brought forth continual interest. Being ever alert for snakes and other critters for which we have great respect, the climber finally reached a bench midway to the top of the plateau. There, on the wall to his front, he encountered age old evidence of other humans who had once visited this same place, found it to their liking, and left their mark. Indecipherable dots, zigzagged lines, circles, and dashes adorned the wall face and the upper portion of an overhang. Most striking of all however, was the outline of a human hand, done in a dull red pigment, the obvious work of someone who knew that any future visitor could not resist placing his hand within the outline - just as he or she had done while tracing out the fingers and palm. Needless to say, the climber couldn't resist either. When he touched the stone; magic! His soul was forever captured by these spirits and he would run in the company of the "primitive" from that day forth. He had made that special contact which fed the flames of search, the flicker of scholarly interest, and the deep devotion to inquisition in all things primitive or prehistoric.

(more)

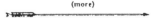

"Aboriginal Art Supplies"
By Steve Watts

Mineral Pigments:
Red - - - - - Hematite
Yellow - - - Limonite
White - - - - Kayolin Clay, Gypsum,
Chalk, Bird Droppings
Black - - - - Charcoal, Graphite,
Manganese Ores

Vehicles and Binders:
Water
Animal Fat
Plant Juices and Oils
Hide Glue
Egg Whites
Blood
Urine

Paint Containers:
Turtle Carapice
Shells
Stone Bowls
Clay Pots/Fragments
Bark Trays
Large Leaves
Skulls/Fragments
Bone and Stone Pallets
Gourd Bowls

Applicators:
Hair and Fiber Brushes
Fingers, Hands
Chewed Twig Brushes
Split Bones
Soft Sticks
Fur, Moss and Leather Bundles
Feathers
Charcoal "Pencils"
Ochre "Crayons"

Paint Preparation and Storage:
Mortar and Pestles
Grinding Stones
Water Containers
Cane and Bone Vials

"Rock Graphics"
By Steve Watts

Pictograph:

A pictograph may be created by any number of application techniques, using a wide variety of pigments, but is essentially an image painted on a rock surface. It may be a single image on a pebble, slab or free standing boulder. . . or it may take the form of a multi-imaged panel on a cliff face or canyon wall.

Petroglyph:

Petroglyphs are images formed by cutting into the surface of a rock using one or a combination of techniques. The resulting image might be shallow or deep. . .made by scratching, grooving, drilling or (as most often) pecking. Once again, the number of images may vary from one to many and the size from pebble to cliff face panel.

Petroform:

Petroforms are images formed on the surface of the earth by the placement of stones in a pattern. These images may be simple outlines or massive placements resulting in effigy mound formations.

"Neither in body nor in mind do we inhabit the world of those hunting races of the Paleolithic millennia, to whose lives and ways we nevertheless owe the very forms of our bodies and the structures of our minds. Memories of the animal envoys still must sleep, somehow, within us; for they wake a little and stir when we venture into wilderness. They wake in terror to thunder. And again they wake with a sense of recognition, when we enter any one of those great painted caves. Whatever the inward darkness may have been to which the shamans of the caves descended in their trances, the same must lie within ourselves nightly visited in sleep."

The Way of the Animal Powers
Joseph Campbell

"Phosphenes"
By Steve Watts

Certain images (circles, spirals, crosses, grids, etc.) seem to crop up again and again in aboriginal art. Is this merely coincidence or is there something else at work. Some have suggested that these images reflect the "hard wiring" of the brain . . . actual visual representations of the inner life by peoples intimately familiar with that interior landscape . . . "phosphenes"

"Phosphene comes from the Greek work for "light shows", and they are produced by excitation of the retina. Everyone who has received a severe knock on the head has seen flashes of light that seem to originate within the head. Such light patterns can also be seen when falling asleep or meditating with eyes closed. Airplane pilots report seeing similar apparitions when flying across expanses of empty sky. Astronauts have reported viewing phosphenes so tangibly in outer space that they were first believed to be caused by heavy light particles. Phosphenes appear when the opened eyes have had nothing to see for an extended period of time. Delirium tremors, fasting, high fever, hyperventilation, migraine headaches, and simple eye pressure can produce variations on the basic set of fifteen patterns., From a scientific point of view, what are these inner light shows? Phosphenes are believed to originate primarily in the retinal-optical track and the brain. Scientists think they are images reflecting neural firing patterns in the visual pathways, which makes them very important cognitive images."
Voices of the First Day
Robert Lawler, 1991

One version of the fifteen phosphene forms. From: "Phosphenes", Gerald Oster, <u>Scientific American,</u> Feb. 1970.

Taking further interest in the other diagrams and markings, he copied them down on paper, later attempting to figure out their hidden meaning And wondering when and why they were done. He noticed other colors of yellow and tan, in addition to the red. Upon returning home to New Mexico, he sent drawings and photographs, with the general location, to the Northern Arizona Museum in Flagstaff. Such was an encounter of the best kind.

November 1976, Travis County, Texas. Stumbling along the new road cut looking for flint, he couldn't help notice the patches of bright red and yellow clumps of earth, or ocher, as he would later learn. Ocher, or sometimes spelled ochre, is an earthen form of iron ore. Picking up several clumps, his mind flashed back to the pictographs in Arizona. So this is what they must have used! Further research bore this out, and much more.

Today, as in yesteryears, ocher is used as a pigment to paint such items as wooden handles and to put esoteric designs on hides and flat stones, thus recording events usually known only to the maker, or for sheer enjoyment of decoration. Personal experimentation with mixtures of ocher and animal fat, the latter becoming the medium which permitted practical application of the paint, was the next logical step. Where was the Society of Primitive Technology when you needed them? As has been stated many times before, the school of hard knocks is often long in duration and lonely, and the reinvention of the wheel or the rediscovery of knowledge is often inexacting, even for simple tasks and skills like art and self expression. There is much to be said for the members of SPT who made a conscience decision to share their hard-found knowledge with others. We applaud their noble efforts.

And yes, his first attempt at painting with this new found product was a nice, red outline of his left hand - a most satisfying, although simple, accomplishment. As in all things, one finding leads to another. What kind of application, or brush should be used? The chewed end of a wooden match stick or yucca plant worked just fine. The rendering of animal fat, short of using bacon grease, lard or the fat runoff from a juicy steak, became more involved. First, there was the problem of an appropriate container (simulated in time from before pottery or baskets) in which to contain water and meat-fat for heating. A large gourd, animal bladder, or leather pouch, placed within a hole in the ground, worked just fine. Water was more than adequately heated by placing hot stones into the gallon or so of water, which eventually came to a boil. Animal fat, boiled over a period of time, formed a thick surface which, when cooled, was used in a one-to-one ratio with the rich ocher. The paint was then stored in an oil-soaked leather pouch. It was often placed in the hollowed out portion of a soft stone that was used to crunch up the ocher before mixing with the oil. This made a handy dispenser. Colors could also be mixed and blended into various shades of red, yellow, orange and tan. Ashes mixed in with the paint would result in a dark brown paint. Ocher paint could also be used on pottery, both before and after firing. Pre-fired paints tend to wash out and leave only a slight trace and more often than not, turned a different color upon completion of firing. Fish oil can also be rendered in the same manner as above, although the smell is much worse. When mixed with ashes and rubbed on exposed body flesh, it helps keep the mosquitoes and gnats away, and others too. Texans swear by alligator grease for this latter application. Bear grease or possum grease would probably work wonders too, although you may not have many friends in close quarters.

Anyhow, reduced animal fat mixed with various colors of ocher will greatly enhance your primitive artwork. Try it with a simple hand print traced onto your finely tanned animal skins, or a series of rings and stars around your wooden ax handle. You'll believe in magic too.

ABORIGINAL AIRBRUSH

By Wylie Woods

My father came to visit me a few months ago. When he arrived I happened to be spitting diatomaceous earth against a wall, making a stencil of my hand. I tried to greet him, but my mouth was coated with microscopic silica exoskeletons and I could not speak (due to the fact that my severe grimace would not allow my lips to move correctly). I managed to choke out a "Hello." My father then told that he thought there was a better way to do what he thought I was trying to accomplish. He said that he had once observed a fellow blowing pigments through several tubes, thus creating a sort of "aboriginal airbrush".

While at the Rabbitstick Rendezvous in Rexburg, Idaho, I started asking people about this sort of device. I got a few ideas and decided to experiment. I began using different lengths and widths of bamboo. No luck, the diameters were too large and due to the chain-smoking of that day, my lungs were inadequate to expel the liquids in the device. I then tried some smaller pieces of *Phragmites* for the tubes and achieved success.

Here's How It Works

The diameter of the tubes is very important. Select materials which have a hole around 1/4 inch in diameter or smaller. Larger ones require more air pressure. In caves in Europe, such as the Lascaux site, colors were blown through bone tubes, possibly using this technique. Any hollow or pithy plants could be used such as rivercane (*Arundinaria sp.*) or elder (*Sambucus sp.*) [Bird bone is also an excellent tube material].

•The vacuum tube (see diagram) needs to be rather short. If it is too short, the paint will splatter and gurgle up. If too long it won't work at all. A working length is around 4 inches.

•The blow tube length does not seem to be that critical. A good working length would be one that allows you to see what you're doing, while holding and directing spray easily. The one I use is around 9 inches.

•The pigment container can be just about anything. I tried stone mortars, bamboo, and a cooking pot. Anything that holds liquid works. Something that can be held in one hand with a few fingers free to hold the blow tubes is most desirable [small gourds work very well].

•The angle that the blow tube is held in relation to the vacuum tube is slightly over 90 degrees. For ease of operation, I cut the tubes so that the blow tube can rest on the edge of the pigment container and touch the slightly taller vacuum tube at this angle for ease of operation (see diagram).

These are just guidelines and it is possible that other combinations of lengths and diameters of tubes will work also; so experiment. If you want colors from hematite (red) limonite (yellow) kaolin clay, gypsum, chalk, bird droppings (whites), and charcoal or manganese (blacks); mixed with hide glue, animal fat, blood, urine, or water, and you don't want to gargle with it, then try out this device. You will quickly find out the best techniques which work for you.

At Rabbitstick '95 Adam McIsacc carved a northwest-style mask, and he painted it with blue ochre, red ochre, and charcoal. We then sprayed it with a mixture of pine pitch and alcohol in order to fix the paints. The idea was to mix the paints with water so that they would be easy to use. If they dried while the painting process was still in session, then it would be convenient to simply add more water. When it was done, we would then spray this lacquer on it to set the paint and waterproof it. With a little practice, and a few beads of sweat (the paint job could have easily been ruined), we tried it. Our attempt was successful. It is feasible that a more primitive finish could be used, but this one was readily available to us.

On a related matter, Steve Watts told me of a primitive-felt-tip-marker which he once made. He took a rather pithy eider branch and peeled back the wood, leaving a large section of pith exposed. He than mixed up a watery solution of pigment and soaked the pith in it. The result, a magic maker.

I was unable to find any information on the primitive airbrush other than the existence of hollow bone tubes with pigment residue in them, and therefore do not know if it is truly a stone-age technology. If you have any information on this device, please write the Bulletin and let us know. Although using this takes the fun out of having a mouthful of charcoal, try it anyway, it is ultra cool.

REFERENCES
Ann and Gale Slevsking.
1962   The Caves of France and Northern Spain: a Guide. London, Visa Books.

"Blow" Tube
(Phragmites)

OPERATION

90°

BLOW TUBE

"Vacuum" Tube
(Phragmites)

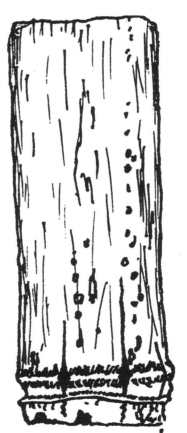

Pigment Container
(Bamboo)

IN

A Simple Glossary of Musical Instruments

In the field of ancient music the words prehistoric archaeology are all too literal; there are no records of the music of prehistoric man by definition, and archaeology is left with the instruments that have survived. These instruments are numerous and represent almost all of the major forms of music-making equipment that are used today, pipes and reeds, strings, horns, and rattles and drums.....The tragedy is however, that although we can produce sounds from these instruments we cannot know if they were those actually heard by ancient man, or in the order or intensity in which they were heard, or the occasion on which they were heard. The evidence just does not stretch this far.....The experimental work that has been done on ancient musical instruments is perhaps the most difficult to conduct without inadvertent distortion of evidence. Instruments are not mere objects to be manipulated without feeling, insensitive to the occasion upon which they were produced and played. They require as much honesty in testing as any other object whose precise function is unknown, and they cannot be given the benefits of advanced knowledge in virtuoso playing or in modern additions to the instrument. The flute, described as the voice of humanity, does not lend itself easily to dispassionate scientific analysis.

John Coles, Archaeology By Experiment

DISCLAIMER (NOT!)

Warning ! You are entering an area within the field of Experimental Archaeology that may prove hazardous to your health. Music is the only area in the field that has been responsible for the death of one of your colleagues. That's right, music.

It seems that John Coles reported in his book, **Archaeology By Experiment** that, "One of the earliest experiments concerning difficult instruments (Irish Bronze Age horns) resulted in the first and only fatality known to experimental archaeology. In the act of attempting to produce a distinct sound on a large trumpet...[the experimenter] burst a blood-vessel, and died a few days after.

So, break rocks, fire clay, explore dark continents for unknown civilizations, even voyage into the voids on boats of grass, but beware the deadly tones of the primitive music maker. Search the pages of this section with caution.

Idiophone - *instruments that are struck, rubbed or shaken.*
Most common instrument.

Composite - multiple parts or strung objects - bunch rattles of shell, hooves, bones, teeth, cocoons, etc. Suspended on a frame and played or fastened to a dancer (tinklers). Compound containers/vessels may be of clay, rawhide, plant fibers, etc.
Simple - one part or container - gourds with seeds or turtle shells with bones inside.
Sample Instruments -
lithophone - stone bells or chimes
rattle - shaken - (simple or compound) the most wide spread of all idiophones. Gourd with seeds inside, shakere, toe rattles, etc.
basket - dampened basket beaten with bundles of small sticks
wooden gong/drum - hollowed tree or plank over a hole, struck with feet
rasp - friction idiophones, very common
concussion drum - hollow gourd - open end strikes the ground
bullroarer, buzzer - parts strike the air to create a sound
ung-klung - bamboo cut to varying sizes with a clapper inside
kalimba (thumb piano), xylophone, marimba - composite idiophone
bell - clay, copper
clapper and click sticks - one item with a split, or two sticks tapped together

Aerophone - *wind/horn-like instruments, or wind created noises.*

Transverse - blown like true flute, blown perpendicular to the instrument.
Vertical - wind enters via one end of the instrument.
Oblique - blown across the top like a pop bottle.
Sample Instruments -
trumpet - shell, didjeridu, gourd
whistle - single or limited tones
pan pipe - limited evidence
flutes / flageolet - wind split by reed or beveled edge
ocarina - clay or gourd five hole instrument

Membranophones - *instruments with taut skins.*
Most widely played instrument.

Single head / Double head
Sample Instruments -
pottery drum - pot may contain water under the head
frame drum - thin with 1 or 2 heads
cylinder drum - barrel, cone, hourglass
talking drum - variable pitch drum
friction drum -

Cordophones - *instruments with taut strings.*

Pluck/strum - extensive use in other continents, but not much recorded here.
Hit - musical bows played over baskets or other resonator.
Saw - bow with tight strings dragged over tight strings on instrument. Very recent.
Sample Instruments -
mouth bow - small or large - string plucked or taped with a stick
resonator bow - berimbau
earth bow - bow placed over 2 baskets
harp, lute, zither - plucked or strummed strings
violin - Seri, Tarahumara, Apache - single or multiple strings

The Human Voice - *"One man's music is another man's noise."*

The earliest known musical instruments in the world are a group of bone whistles and flutes from late glacial sites in Europe and dating from about 30,000 years ago...All of the flutes tested, and there are many, indicate conclusively the absence of any early fixed tonal system.   John Coles

Drums and stringed instruments have a long history of use in society and ceremony, but limited evidence of prehistoric use in this country.

PRIMITIVE FLUTES OUT OF BONE:
A SOUTH AMERICAN INDIAN EXAMPLE
By Manuel Lizarralde

On the summer of 1988, Akirida (a wise Bari Indian, my friend and collaborator) and I were walking in the rain forest of northwest Venezuela, when he pointed to a plant he called *motubi*. I was surprised because I knew the term motubi means flute but I did not know that it also meant a kind of bamboo. I asked Akirida if this bamboo could be used as a flute. Akirida said "akaing" (correct) and cut a section of bamboo with his machete. In a few seconds, he made two little holes and started to play it. Then, I realized that flutes can be made of any material, but bamboo is one of the most natural plant sources for the flute. However, bone is a very good raw material that is stronger and its beauty is favorable, probably because it resembles ivory, the color preferred by many cultures. I would like to share how and what I have learned about making bone flutes.

Although I do not have much skill playing flutes, I have made many flutes that make similar sounds. I have made them out of bamboo (6), deer bones (5), lamb bones (3), and jaguar bones (1). My wife, Nerissa Russell, a zooarchaeologist working on Neolithic sites (5,400 year old) in eastern Europe, told me that bone tools tend to be made from wild animals as their bones are stronger and denser than those of domestic animals.

In the spring of 1992, at the Glass Buttes Knap-in in the Oregon desert, I managed to do something I have wanted to accomplish for some time: construct a bone flute using only stone tools. A large deer was being butchered at the site with stone tools, and I saw this as my chance to do a stone-tool bone instrument, in this case with obsidian blades.

The best bone for making flutes are tibias which are located between the ankle and knee in the front part of the rear leg . The tibia shaft has the natural shape of a pipe and the ends tend to be fairly soft and easy to work with stone tools. The tibia is more traingular than round, with three sides , wide, and its walls are thin near the ends.. The shaft is quite long (7-10 inches or 17.5-24 cm), and narrower in the center where the walls become thicker (this can be a problem when you drill the holes). Another nice characteristic is that the tibias' proportions are right for the human hands and mouth.

The first tibia bone flute I ever saw was one made by the Warao Indians. My father gave it to me in 1988. He acquired it in 1969 in the small village of Ipania along the Guiniquina Creek in the Orinoco river delta, Venezuela. According to him, the Warao Indians used to make the flutes out of human tibias, specifically from enemies killed in warfare (Karibes and Arawaks). Nowadays they make them from the tibia of white tail deer. I have since

Photo 1. The top cut is critical. The resulting hole must be close enough to at least one thin edge so that the wind is split by the bone when the flute is played (see Photo 3, and Norm Kidder's flute dawing).

Tamara Wilder

Photo 2. Joe Dabill and Manuel use a stone-tipped pump-drill to create the holes in the flute at Glass Buttes, 1993.

forest of the Sierra de Perija (near the Colombian border), the Bari indigenous people killed a jaguar and I tried to make a flute from one of the bones. Its shaft wall was too thick and the sound was not very good. Human and deer bones have thinner walls and a bigger hollow section for the marrow.

Thus, in the spring of 1993, I got the great opportunity of not only having a fresh bone at hand but also an abundance of pristine rock (obsidian) to accomplish the task with primitive pre-metal technology. I was curious about not only how long it would take to accomplish the given task, but also how hard it would be.

It is better to make bone tools or flutes when the bone is fresh because it is softer than when it is dry. To have lots of raw material is another ideal condition that I had at Glass Buttes. I was very lucky because I did this flute over a pile of obsidian flakes and near friends (most materials came from Steven Edholm) who lent me different kinds of drills and blades.

The mule deer tibia is the biggest tibia I have used for a flute. I started to cut the upper part of the bone (the end near the knee joint) about 3/4 inch from the end with some thick obsidian blades (Photo 1). You need to make the grooves progressively deeper on the three sides of the bone, until you get to the marrow. Then, it is easy to snap off.

On the far end of the bone, you make a 1/4 inch hole for the air to flow through when you blow on the flute (Photo 3). Make three or four 1/8 inch holes with a drill for creating different tones (Photo 2). I cleaned the marrow out of the bone with a stick, water and sand. With a piece of sandstone, I rubbed the bone walls to remove any soft tissues, and then used river sand and water to clean and polish the entire flute. In less than two hours, I had a working bone flute ready to be played by a primitive musician.

stores in Venezuela, four more bone flutes from the Pemon indigenous people. They had basically the same characteristics, but the deer bone was 3/4 the size of the Warao bone flute. This makes me suspect that this is the basic design and style for Venezuelan Indian flutes. It seems that jaguar bone and deer bone flutes are common in the Guyana region of South America and the North Western part of the Amazon. The Tukano indigenous people of the Vaupes region of Colombia also use jaguar tibias for their flutes.

Using the Warao Indian bone flute as the model, I made three more flutes at an experimental archaeology camp in Hungary in the summer of 1988 out of fallow deer tibias. I started with stone tools but finished the work with steel tools because the stone tools I had were not sharp enough. All three flutes produced nice sounds.

During the summer of 1990 in the Venezuelan rain

Unhafted stone drill point

(more)

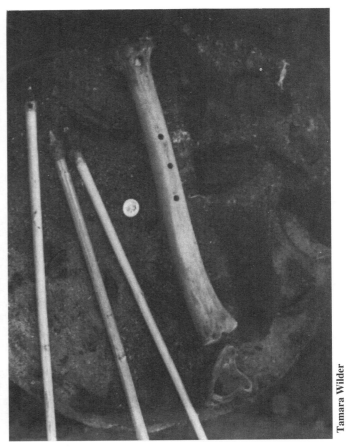

Photo 3. The correct position for playing. The marrow hole is blocked by the lower lip and chin, and the air is blown across the thin edge of the bone.

Photo 4. The finished flute and the tools used to create it. Lower left are the hafted stone drills and wooden shafts. The large flakes on the right were used for grooving and scraping the bone.

Jim Riggs Photo © 1993

Tamara Wilder

African Bottle-top Rattle
By Rob Withrow

Early visitors and traders to Africa found natives of the Belgian Congo with a sweet tooth for soda pop, especially Fanta Orange. After enjoying the drink, being a "no-discard" society, the people soon found other uses for the empty bottles and caps. One of the most honorable jobs ever given to a bottle-cap was that of achieving music. It became the tinkling, snapping, tambourinic transmitter for the little known "Ziarian Pop Shaker" rhythm instrument.

For those who undertake this project always remember, "some things need a good shaking in order to achieve that which it aren't" HA! Enjoy.

My thanks to Bill Kelso for showing me my first and allowing me to replicate and submit this information on a most unique bit of historic musical instrumentation.

Flatten the caps and then burn in fire to remove plastic coating. Quench in water to remove temper.

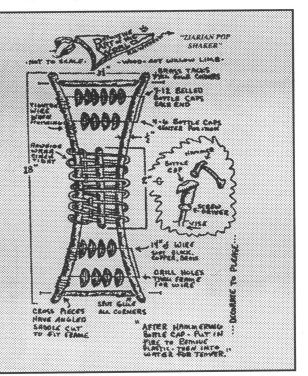

MUSICAL INSTRUMENTS OF CENTRAL CALIFORNIA

Text and Illustrations By Norm Kidder

Throughout Central California and beyond, music and dance were the media of communication with the world of 'spirits'. Songs were received from this realm during dreams or trances, and had associated powers enjoyed by the owner of the song. Songs were employed in hunting to 'charm' the spirit of the animal, during food preparation to guarantee proper results, in gambling to draw on the help of supernatural powers, in courtship to bring divine assistance to the cause of love, in ceremonies to communicate with the creative forces to restore or maintain harmony in the world, or simply to build your relationship with power (which is often called medicine). Songs were sung to greet the sun each morning, thanking it for returning to maintain its regular habits. In a world totally controlled by unseen forces, song and its visible representation, dance, were the means of maintaining the perfection of creation. The dances of the Northwest coast of California are called World Renewal dances, in Australia, men followed maps, called songlines, to periodically re-sing the world into existence, or else it might fade. In much of 'pre-contact' society, music and dance were anything but mere amusement.

The instrument most often associated with Indian dances in America today is the drum. The steady rhythm of the drum is likened to the heartbeat of the earth. In some parts of north central California, a section of hollow log was placed over a trench, and pounded

one side, it produced a looser half which could be made to clap against its partner by snapping the arm with a stiff wrist in the air, creating a sound that has been compared to castanets. The same effect was achieved by carving away wood at the base end of one side (then the top) to make it limber enough to snap in the air. These rattles were used by the members of the chorus which accompanied ceremonial dances, and sometimes during gambling and doctoring. Today, these instruments, often made of bamboo and called batons, or just bats, are used by singers to establish the rhythms of the dances. One singer in particular, known as the rock, is responsible for controlling the movements of the dance while the others concentrate on the song.

Leaf Scars

18" to 24" long

(more)

TOP VIEW

Weakening hole allows one side (top) to flap against the bottom (optional).

HANDLE

Leaf Scar

Leaf Scars

with feet or poles to produce a drum-like sound, but the skin covered drum was unknown until the arrival of Europeans. In it's place, various types of rattles took over the role of rhythm instrument.

The most common, and widely used rattle form was the split stick rattle, or clap-stick. The simplest was a piece of elderberry, bay or other straight grained wood (now also bamboo) about 2 feet long (Photo 1) which was split length-wise, leaving an unsplit handle. Any pithy center was removed (Photo 2), and the stick was struck against the opposite hand to produce a clacking sound. If the split was controlled to approach

David Wescott

Photo 1. Coastal and Inland-style (CA) clapper sticks.

Jim Riggs carving out the pithy center of an elder-berry clapper with a crooked knife. Winter Count '95.

David Wescott

Rattles may show up during other kinds of singing as well. Doctors of many specialties use rattles made of deer toes (see page 25), large moth cocoons, or the split sticks to accompany their power songs as they call upon spirits to help cure an illness, bad weather, or other disharmony which needs 'fixing'.

Whistles also served as rhythm instruments, and were used mainly by the dancers (it would be hard for the singers to blow them). They were made either of elderberry, cane, or hollow bones, had a single hole cut near the middle with a plug of pitch or asphaltum to aim the air flow against the edge of the central hole (Photo 3). The combination of clap sticks, voices, whistles and movement create a rich tapestry that is certainly enthralling to the audience of people, and I assume to the spirits as well.

Two other instruments are known from our area which were used in more personal contexts. The musical bow was sometimes made for the purpose, although a hunting bow might also be used. One end of the bow wood is held against the teeth, and the string plucked or hit with an arrow or stick. Varying tension on the string can produce a range of tones. The sound is only clearly heard inside the head of the musician, making this a private experience. The last musical instrument known from the 'old days' was the flute.

Except for the Mohave peoples of southern California who used a typical plains type flageolet (the love flute still popular today) the remainder of groups used a simple open ended flute. This was made from a hollowed elderberry tube, with the ends beveled, and four holes burned or drilled in line along the center of the tube. It is played by blowing across the open end at an angle that will produce the flute-like note. The four holes change the note, but are not standardized into a specific scale. Each flute produces it's own music. Some flutes were played from either end, producing two different scales. At times the players added complexity to the sound by humming as they blew, creating a type of harmony. These flutes were used in courtship of both future wives and possible spirit helpers. The flute is simple to make but takes consider-able practice to master. Receiving a powerful song with the aid of the flute however, would provide lasting benefit to the musician. (Songs were owned, and only worked for the original receiver, although others might sing them) (See Paul Campell's article for a more complete presen-tation of the California-style flute).

To make any of these instruments you must first find an appropriate piece of elderberry (*Sambucus sp.*). If pos-sible, harvest in the winter from a tree growing in a canyon where it gets enough sun light to grow strong, but not so much that it doesn't have to grow straight. If possible, let the piece dry completely (stripping the bark speeds this process), as it will be easier to work and won't warp later. ***Also, elderberry juice is poisonous, so don't put green elderberry in your mouth. (Some people react to elderberry juice and get a skin rash.)***

For a flute, cut a piece about an inch or inch and a quarter in diameter, and 9 - 12 inches long, cutting through a node at each end if possible. Check to see how much of the cross section is wood, and how much is soft and pithy. The ideal for a flute is a minimum of 1/8 inch thick ring of wood, to a maximum of 3/16 of an inch. After the piece has dried, gouge out the pithy center using a hard stick with the end cut to a chisel edge. Smooth and polish the inside. Cut or grind the edges of the tube to a bevel from the outside (see illustration). Draw a line down the length of the tube and mark four points along it for the holes. Placement of the holes is determined by ease of fingering. Often holes were paired, with two fingers of each hand covering a set of holes. If the holes are not centered down the length of the tube, a different scale is produced by blowing each end. I use a piece of coat hanger wire heated red hot on a stove to burn in the holes.

To play the flute, cover the holes and get comfortable, it could take a while. Hold the end of the flute to your lower lip, which should cover almost all of the opening. Tip the tube down at about a 45 degree angle, and blow across the upper edge of the flute, changing the angles until a flute-like sound is made. I find I'm almost whistling at the point where it works. Then uncover the holes to get notes.

(more)

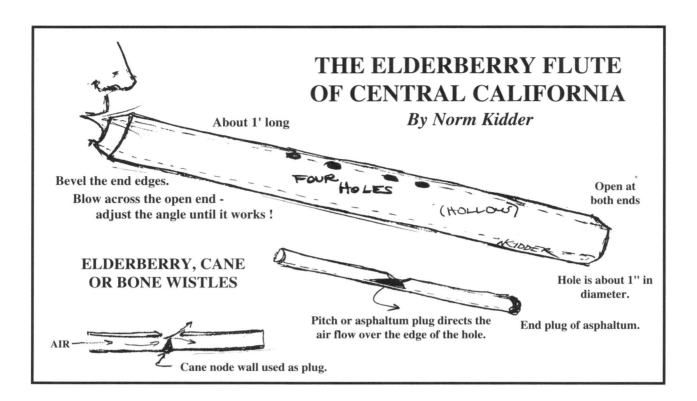

THE ELDERBERRY FLUTE OF CENTRAL CALIFORNIA
By Norm Kidder

About 1' long

FOUR HOLES

(HOLLOW)

Open at both ends

Bevel the end edges.

Blow across the open end - adjust the angle until it works !

Hole is about 1" in diameter.

ELDERBERRY, CANE OR BONE WISTLES

Pitch or asphaltum plug directs the air flow over the edge of the hole.

End plug of asphaltum.

AIR

Cane node wall used as plug.

It took me a long time to get a sound, and holding the angle requires real concentration.

To make a clap stick, find an elderberry branch between 1 and 1 1/2 inches thick, and 1 1/2 and 2 feet long. If possible, cut it so that there is a natural handle formed at one end by a leaf node. The wood thickness should be greater than for a flute, with 1/4 inch thick sides ideal. Strip off the bark and dry. Split the end away from the handle by first picking a line that will split between any leaf scars present on the 'working' end, and ending at the leaf scars forming the handle. Set a wedge or knife blade on your line and carefully split the stick down to just short of the handle. Its better to split too short than too long. If the split was successful, carefully pull the two sides just far enough apart to slip a knife between them and cut away some of the pity core. Once you have created an open channel down the center of the stick use a long hard reamer to push out and break up the remaining pith down to the handle. At this point, hitting the clapper against your hand or leg should produce the clapping sound. If not, slip a thin piece of bark, buckskin, or such down to the bottom of the split to spread it slightly. To make the more responsive instrument, pick the half of the clapper that seems the looser, and make it progressively more so by cutting away wood just above the handle (see illustration) until it flaps easily, but doesn't break.

Playing the clapper is done by slapping against anything, or by snapping in the air while keeping the wrist stiff. If you round the ends as in the drawing, the clapper can be played by rolling down the fingers on the way to the leg, creating even more rhythmic possibilities.

David Wescott

Norm Kidder carefully starts the split of an elderberry clapper-stick. Note the two-bone whistle suspended around his neck.

Removing The Hooves Of Deer
By Tamara Wilder, ©1995

Each year during hunting season we acquire the lower legs of many deer from the hunters in our area. At first we dealt with them right away and the entire process...pulling out the leg sinew, skinning off the hock skin, and pulling the hooves off with pliers...went very smoothly. However, over the next few years we started letting them dry out a few days because we were too busy dealing with the skins which were arriving at the same time. By waiting to process the legs, each step became more difficult and smelly with these somewhat dried out legs.

Some years ago we started freezing the legs until we could get to them. It was easy to remove the sinew and hock skins from the frozen legs but the hooves did not seem to slip off as easily as when they were fresh.

That same year at a braintanning seminar, we had everything spelled out for us. We were attempting to remove the hooves from a variety of legs which had been brought by different people. Some were very fresh, some frozen, and some completely dried out. After boiling in water for about three minutes, the hooves on the dried out legs were not ready to budge at all. Those on the frozen legs would slip off, but only with the right twisting motion of the pliers. Many of the hooves ripped during the process. On fresh legs, however, the hooves pulled right off with a familiar "pop' sound. With further boiling, the dried out legs were still not ready to slip off and most of them ended up separating at the joint, leaving the bone inside the hoof which then had to be cut out with a knife.

From this and similar experiences I began to give more time to the legs when they were fresh. I had never considered being able to remove the hooves without the aid of pliers, probably because we had dealt so often with frozen legs. Last year I decided that I was going to remove every hoof without pliers. The legs were very fresh and also very small which probably made the task easier. I boiled up a pot of water without the legs in it, carried the still bubbling water outside and stacked about twelve legs (toes down in the hot water) so that the water covered all of the hooves and dew claws.

After two minutes I pulled out the leg which I had put in first. The hooves were gray and slightly swollen with water at the edges where they meet the skin. I know now that this is an indication that they are probably ready. I had read of pounding the hooves off, so I tried pounding the hooves with a wooden stick which accomplished nothing more than denting the hooves. By now the leg had cooled off, so I put it back in the water.

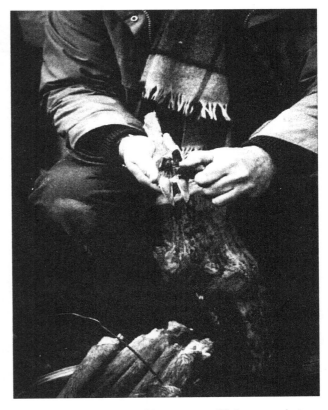

Sitting by a bucket of hot water with legs ready to work. The simple twist and pop of fresh toes and dew claws makes this project go much faster.

I pulled out another leg which was hot to the touch and grabbed hold of a dew claw between my thumb and forefinger and squeezed. Amazingly, the claw slipped right into my hand. The other did the same and I moved quickly to the hooves. They only moved slightly at first, but then by

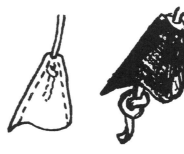

DEER-HOOF RATTLES *By Norm Kidder*

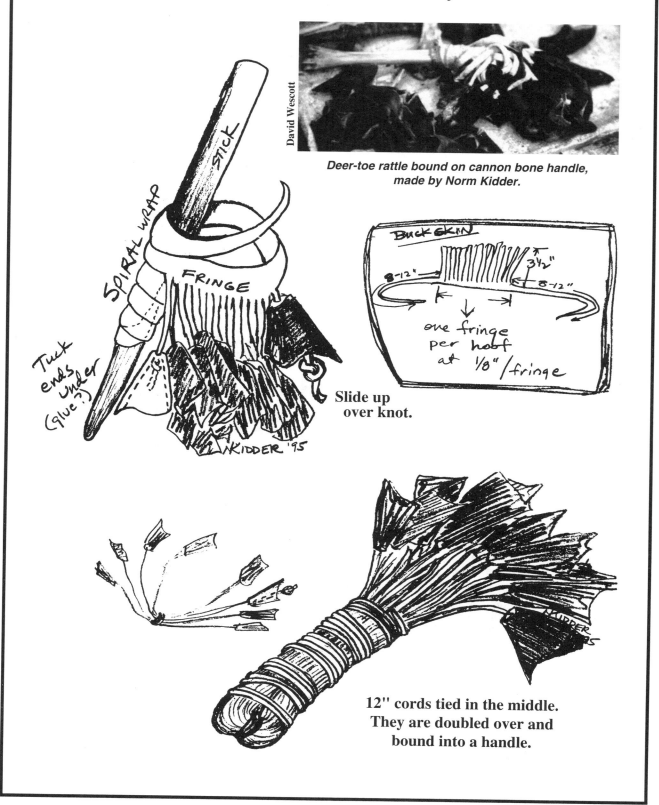

David Wescott

Deer-toe rattle bound on cannon bone handle, made by Norm Kidder.

SPIRAL WRAP

STICK

FRINGE

Tuck ends under (glue?)

KIDDER '95

BUCKSKIN

3½"

8-12" 8-12"

one fringe per hoof at ⅛"/fringe

Slide up over knot.

12" cords tied in the middle. They are doubled over and bound into a handle.

adding a little twist, they came off with that familiar "pop" sound. The next hoof had cooled so I dipped it back into the hot water for a few seconds and it came off easily.

The rest of the hooves were all easily removed without the use of pliers. While it is very important to keep everything hot, I believe that overboiling or even oversoaking can have a detrimental effect. When I was processing these legs the unfinished ones were soking in hot, not boiling,

Using a flint flake to trim the toes for stringing on a rattle.

water and I noticed that the last few were wanting to separate somewhat at the joint rather than simply slipping off the bone. Boiling or oversoaking also weakens the hooves and may cause them to rip.

Of utmost importance in processing deer legs, or any animal part for that matter, is getting into the habit of dealing with things right away instead of letting them sit and either dry out or start to rot. Fresh things are much less likely to cause infections, which can lead to blood poisoning. In addition to hoof removal, it's just plain easier to process legs when they are fresh. This is especially true of bone which is much easier to work green (fresh). It is important to cover the fresh bone with fat and let it season slowly in a cool place. This simple step minimizes cracking.

After the hooves and dew claws have been removed they are still soft and flexible and are easier to trim, clean and punch holes in than they will be once they are dry. Trim off the thin, whitish tissue when wet, as it becomes very sharp when it dries. Now is also a good time to remove the "frog"- the underside of the hoof which is made of a softer, less-shiny material. The edges can also be easily cut into designs while the hooves are still soft. It is best to punch holes at this time as well, because the hooves are less likely to split. Leave something in the hole as it dries, in case the hole tries to close up. If I am drilling the holes with a drill I prefer to do it after they have dried.

If the hooves have already been dried out they can be soaked in hot water for twenty minutes or so to be made flexible again.

As a final step, I clean the hooves with a brush, dry them in the sun and then oil them with a thin layer of deer tallow.

Davud Wescott Photos

Pile of deer toes ready to be strung and attached to a cannon bone handle.

Gadgets and Geegaws

David Wescott

1-wooden tablet painted with red ochre
2-deer-toe bone pendant
3-acid etched clam shell
4-bone disk pendant
5-bone bead
6-stone disk pedant
7-stone pendant
8-bone inlaid with turquoise & abalone
9-clame shell bead
10-turquois bead
11-deer dew claw bead
12-feather & seed bead dodad
13-elk tooth pedant
14-arrowhead pedant

15-etched clam shell
16-bone whistle bead
17-deer antler bead
18-etched clam shell bead
19-stone disk pendant
20-bone needle case

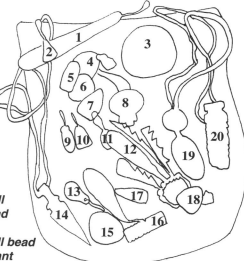

Section 7

Appendix

THE HAZARDS OF ROADKILLS

By Alice Tulloch

In your travels, you may be tempted to salvage an animal killed by traffic. Before you do, you should consider the potential legal and health consequenes.

Wildlife Law

Every State has its own set of laws and regulations that control the "taking" of wild animals. In addition, the following federal laws and international treaties may have a bearing on your actions:

* Golden and Bald Eagle Protection Act
(16 USC 663-668)
* Endangered Species Act of 1973
(16 USC 1539)
* Migratory Bird Treaty Act (16 USC 703-711)
* Fish and Wildlife Act of1956 (16 USC 742)
* Marine Mammal Protection Act of 1972
(16 USC 1371-1383)
* Lacey Act (18 USC 42 &44)
* Tariff Classification Act of 1962
(19 USC 1202)
* Title 50, Part 13, Code of Federal Regulations

These federal regulations protect hundreds of migratory and resident birds. The list includes game, non-game and rare birds of all kinds. The regulations limit or prohibit the taking or possession of these animals. But the regulations also establish a permit system for the taking or possession of these birds under carefully controlled conditions. Only certain reasons are considered justification for taking or possession of each species of bird, for instance, scientific collecting, falconry, raptor propagation, agricultural depredation, or native american religious purposes. These permits are issued by the US Fish & Wildlife Service in your state, from whom you can obtained detailed information about applying for a permit.

For birds, you may also need a State permit. States have the primary responsibility for regulating the taking of all other wildlife as well. Most people are familiar with hunting licenses for taking of game animals. Read carefully your State's published hunting regulation, that detail which animals, and the allowable seasons, times and methods of taking. Generally, picking up roadkills is not listed as an approved method of taking.

California is considered one of the most restrictive states with respect to the taking or possession of wild animal parts. Because of the state's highly diverse ethnicity, the California Dept. of Fish & Game's goal is to actively discourage the trafficking in animal parts, as the best way to keep the pressure on California native animals low. Except for deer skins and certain horns, the retail sale of any animal pelts, quills, bones, hooves, or parts is prohibited, whether game or non-game, native or introduced, killed in California or out of state. There are many exceptions and special conditions in the rules, so check with your local wildlife office for the specific pelt or part you have a question on. An example of a prohibited item is those plastic paperweights with a rattlesnake head inside. Under a trapper's license, one can take specified animals with specified methods, but only for wholesale sale out of the state. An individual may possess articles he bought out of state, made from animals (except protected and "listed" animals), but may not sell, trade or barter them. California Fish & Game has a very active sting operation that visits rendezvous, gun shows, flea markets, etc. My source adds that anything related to mountain lions is absolutely prohibited.

Regarding roadkills, CDFG says picking them up is prohibited. You are supposed to report dead animals to the local warden or highway patrol. They then put any animals in their evidence freezer. Periodically, they'll clean it out and give the animals to the raptor rescue or predator propagation programs. Animals are no longer given for human consumption due to health concerns. I've heard of the animals being given to outdoor skills schools associated with state parks. But contact your local regional office for more information.

What are the consequences for violation of the law? California imposes up to a $500 fine and 1 year in jail for all misdemeanors. Felonies can result in $20,000 fine and 5 years in jail.

Other states will have regulations, laws and penalities that differ significantly from the California example. For example, sale of bear skins and claws are okay in some places, but are a felony in California. A 20 minute conversaton with your local wildlife enforcement or protection office is a must. They may also be able to tell you about special pemits for some of your activities, beyond just a hunting license for game animals.

How are these regulations enforced? Enforcement will vary widely from area to ara. In isolated parts of Eastern Oregon, long ago, people have gotten away with bringing home one or two deer a year that collided with their pickup. But "spotlighting" deer at night was actively prosecuted. In Newfoundland, Canada, it was part of the local subsistence economy to bring home a roadkill moose, but the pickup was usually a total loss. Picking up a roadkill deer along a SF Bay Area freeway, the odds are that you'd be reported by many city drivers and vigourously prosecuted by the local war-

(more)

dens. The fellows shooting European red squirrels in Golden Gate Park in San Francisco went to jail.

Community sentiments change over time, especially if some event of abuse has been highly publicized. A California Fish & Game warden told me that their main focus is on deterring the blatant or commercial exploitation of wildlife. A lot of publicity has been put out to deter the poaching of bear gall bladders for the Asian market. But the low-key individual with a flicker feather on their rear-view mirror is not so problematic for the authorities. The best advice is to err on the side of discretion and compliance with the law. Keep your license or permit with you at all times.

Protecting Your Health

Wildlife is considered a vast reservoir of some of the most gruesome and ancient diseases effecting man. A couple of the most devastating new diseases, HIV and New Mexico hemorrhagic pneumonia, are also associated with wildlife. Below is a synopsis of some of the diseases carried by wildlife in North America and how they are transmitted. Below are some important safety practices you should observe any time you handle wildlife, whether roadkills or game animals.

Rabies is most commonly transmitted by a bite from an infected animal. But in handling a dead animal, exposure of an opening in your skin to the animal's body fluids could also transmit the disease. The best prevention is avoidance of infected animals or suspect carcasses. Rabies is 99.9% fatal unless treated.

Tularemia was first associated with the skinning and dressing of wild rabbits, in 1911, near Tulare Lake, CA. It can also be carried by squirrels, moles, muskrats, beavers, and many birds, amphibians, fish, and insects (including ticks, mosquitos, and deer flies). It is transmitted by direct handling of animals, by insect bites, and by inhalation of spores. The disease begins with an abrupt fever, cough, vomiting, has relapses after several days, and can effect many parts of the body.

Plague has devastated human populations in 3 big epidemics: the 6th Century plague of Justinian, the "Black Death" of the Middle Ages and just recently in China. The Chinese epidemic began in the mid 19th Century, and spread to the Western US by 1900. In the US, there are two focal reservoirs of plague among wild animals:

  1) Northern New Mexco, northeast Arizona,
       southern Colorado and southern Utah.
  2) California, southern Oregon, and western
       Nevada but it can occur throughout
       the West.

Plague is transmitted by flea bites. It is characterized by fever, vomiting, diarrhea, and abdominal pain. If it spreads to the blood stream, it is 100% fatal. It can be treated with antibiotics, if caught early.

Prevention includes avoidance of wild rodent fleas, elimination of rodent shelter like wood and junk piles, and insecticides. Picnic and camp grounds have been the site of many exposures in the US, due to the attraction of rodents to garbage.

Anthrax is very rare in the US, but can still be deadly. The respiratory form of the disease begins with the inhalation of spores from infected animals. Respiratory symptoms show up in 3-5 days, followed within hours by cyanosis, shock, and death. It is treatable by antibiotics, but avoidance of exposure is wiser.

Cellulitis is the name for an acute spreading inflammation of the soft tissues by streptococcus, staphylococcus and other bacteria. This infection is pretty common among folks that do brain-tanning. Infection is transmitted through a cut or crack in the skin. Strep and staph are always present on human skin, and certainly multiple in an animal hide soaking in water for several days. The infection can progress rapidly, and may lead to gangrene. The best prevention is good hygiene, avoid exposure to open wounds, and protective clothing.

One added note here. Some people have developed a rash or blisters, a contact reaction to the iodine in some antibacterial soaps. Test a soap before using it intensively during a day of brain-tanning, to see if you react to any iodine.

Tetanus shots are the best protection against tetanus, or "lockjaw." The bacteria transmitted through a wound excrete a neurotoxin. Within 7-21 days, spasms begin, followed by localized or general weakness, difficulty swallowing or chewing, increasing muscle rigidity, whole body spasm or rigidity, intense pain with spasms, bone fractures, respiratory failure and cardiac arrest.

Hantavirus is the formal name for New Mexico hemorrhagic pneumonia, the disease identified as the cause of 13 sudden deaths in the Four Corners region in 1993. It is a serious and usually fatal disease that begins flu-like, and progresses rapidly to respiratory distress caused by accumulation of fluid in the lungs. The virus is carried by rodents and excreted in their saliva, urine and feces. Inhalation of the dust of deer mice nests, while cleaning out a shed was identified as the vector in some cases. Prevention includes avoidance of mice feces and nests, wetting down of mice nests before cleaning, and breathing protection devices. Effective treatment has not yet been determined.

Trichinosis is a parasite transmitted by eating incompletely cooked foods. Food must be thoroughly cooked to170 degrees F. Freezing, drying or microwaving the meat is not effective. In addition to swine, the parasite is known to be carried by bear and walrus. Flu-like symtoms are followed by muscle pain, skin rash, deafness, seizures, congestive heart failure and sudden death after a 3-4 week illness. Drug treatment is available.

Salmonella is one of the many bacteria responsible for food poisoning. Transmission is by ingestion of contaminated food or water. The symtoms include abdominal cramps, diarrhea, vomiting, fever. If the bacteria invade the blood stream, it becomes typhoid fever. Prevention includes proper washing of food in potable water and proper cooking.

Rocky Mountain Spotted Fever can occur in all the States, southwest Canada and Mexico. The highest rate of occurrence is in Oklahoma, North Carolina, Kansas, Texas, South Carolina and Maryland. 623 cases were reported in 1989, with a 3-4% fatality rate. The bacteria is transmitted by tick bites. Fever, headache, chills, muscle tenderness, stiff neck, vomiting, diarrhea, photophobia, cardiovascular abnormalities, characteristic skin spots especially on palms and soles, and renal dysfunction can be followed by death from renal failure. Antibiotics are effective. Protect against tick bites.

"Contrary to popular belief, application of petroleum jelly, isopropyl alcohol, finger nail polish or a hot match are not effective ways to remove ticks from persons or animals. A tick can be removed safely and effectively be grasping it with a pair of forceps or tweezers and pulling gently. After removal, the site of the tick bite should be disinfected. Ticks should not be squeezed, crushed or disrupted, as their fluids may be infectious. Ticks should be disposed of by soaking in alcohol or flushing them down the toilet, after which one should wash hands with soap and water." (Gorbach, 1992)

Lyme Disease is transmitted by the deer tick, smaller than the common tick. Outbreaks have focused around the Great Lakes, the West Coast, Texas and the East Coast. Symptoms include fever, stiff neck, fatique, distinctive rash at the bite site, neurologic or cardiac involvement, and arthritis. Treatment has not yet been worked out. The best protection is prevention of exposure to ticks.

SAFETY TIPS

1. Look bothways before crossing the road.
2. Keep your tetanus immunization up to date.
3. If you transport a carcass in your car, tightly bag or containerize it to keep fleas and ticks from getting loose.
4. Process any carcass well away from any habitation or food or drink.
5. Process any carcass as soon as possible. If fresh enough for meat, refrigerate or freeze right away.
6. If you freeze or refrigerate any unprocessed, whole carcass, do not put it in a freezer or refrigerator with other foods.
7. While processing any carcass, wear protective clothing, including gloves and even a face mask. Work in a well ventilated place. Be cautious of air-borne spores or dust. Avoid touching your face or scratching your skin.
8. Do not process any animal if you have an open wound, scratch, cracked skin, hangnail, etc.
9. Wash your hands thoroughly after each contact, with an antibacterial soap.
10. Remove and separately wash all protective clothing before returning to habitation or food.
11. Thoroughly wash and disinfect all surfaces and utensils used in processing an animal.
12. Carefully dispose of any remains.
13. Isolate the hide until any fleas or ticks are dead or gone.
14. Wear light-colored clothing and check yourself often for ticks during and after handling a carcass.

It's too common among long time practitioners of primitive skills to hear all kinds of horror stories. This discussion may be a little intimidating, but with compliance with the law and attention to safety precautions, you should have few problems. I am no doctor, so naturally if a problem arises, please contact your doctor for advice. And please be careful when standing in the middle of the road.

REFERENCES

Auerback, P.S., MD, et ux
1989   *Management ofWilderness and Environ mental Emergencies*, 2 ed., C.V. Mosby Co.
Duchin, J.S., MD, et al
1994   Hantavirus Pulmonary Syndrome: A Clinical Description of 17 Patients with a Newly Recognized Disease", in **New England Journal of Medicine**, April 7.
Gorbach, S.L., MD, et al
1992   *Infectious Diseases*, W.B. Saunders Co.
Gubler, D.J., MD, et al
1994   "A Field Guide to Animal-Borne Infections," In **Patient Care**, October 15, 1994.
Pearson, S, US Fish and Wildlife Service, Sacramento
1995   Personal Communication
Reimer, Larry, MD, Dept. of Infectious Disease,
1995   University of Utah Medical Center Personal Communication
Stada, Tony,
1995   California Dept. of Fish & Game, Region 4 Personal Communication

15. Don't eat spoiled meat.
16. Thoroughly cook all meats, to above 170 degrees F.
17. Consider whether the nature of the animal's demise is evidence of the bizarre behavior of rabies, or the sudden death of anthrax or plague. Avoid all contact with any suspect animals, and report them to the authorities.
18. If your skin develops a rash, if a wound develops an infection or red streaks up your arm or leg, or if you develop fever within 2 weeks of contact, immediately see a doctor.
19.If you get a tick bite, remove the tick as soon as possible, in a safe manner, and inform your doctor of the bite if any of the above symptoms occur. Even if you're not aware of a bite, if you develop symptoms, tell your doctor if you've been in a tick area.
20. Keep children and immune-compromised people away from carcasses, processing areas, remains or animal parts until the vectors of infection have been removed or disinfected.
21. If you find mice nests in your hides, do not shake or brush them out. First, wet down the hide before cleaning off the nest, and avoid breathing any dust.
22. Avoid eating meat from an animal where the intestine or urinary tract has been ruptured.
23. Wash meat for consumption only with disinfected water.

Ethics For Modern "Primitives"
By Alice Tulloch

Many of us begin learning about aboriginal life skills for simple reasons such as learning some basic survival skills, or the pleasure of mastering a complex technology. But inevitably our character and our integrity are transformed by our growing involvement.

From the new found skills comes self-esteem and a profound respect for the people before us who relied on these skills for their livelihood. From our teachers comes a greater sense of how sharing these skills, one to one, enhances our reliance on each other.

But we are creatures of today's culture as well. Sometimes the influences of that consumptive and rushed lifestyle overshadow the lessons of the old ones. We need to take time to step back and regain our perspective on life's meaning, on how our conduct in primitive activities reflects our understanding of the deeper lessons of the ages.

In each skill we learn, there seems to be an element of right behavior. Flintknappers learn to avoid disturbing archaeologically significant quarries, or "pothunting" and picking up artifacts. They sign their work and properly dispose of their debitage to avoid confusing the archaeological record. These kinds of measures apply to all skills that leave durable products.

Those who collect plant materials also need to consider the consequences of their actions. Collecting rare or endangered species is unconscionable and prohibited. Loss of habitat and the pressure of range animals is continuing to deplete these plant populations.

Even the collecting of common plants may involve ethical questions. Many useful food, tool and basketry plants survive on private property where laws of trespass apply. Obtain permission to enter such lands. Many "primitives" are chagrined to have to obtain permits for collecting on public lands. But these permits are a response to abuses that have occurred. Two recent examples: It is reported that on the Klamath River drainage, a floral supply company, with a permit for a small amount of beargrass leaves, removed truck loads of whole beargrass plants for export. Due to the outcry of the local basket weavers who have struggled for years for protect this important traditional basket material, this company has now been denied access to many of the northern California national forests. In another case, someone used a backhoe to remove large amounts of obsidian from the archaeologically significant Warner Mountain quarries, and now permits are required for everyone. With increasing population pressure on even these simplest resources, everyone needs to be aware of the impact of their actions.

Another aspect of plant material collecting is respecting someone's territory, even on public lands. It is still common practice among many native people to cultivate certain plants year after year, to encourage quality materials. Newcomers may not be aware of the effort, and unknowingly or uncaringly take the prime materials cultivated by others. Each person needs to develop his own sites, or ask permission of the cultivator.

The taking of animals gives pause to all of us. Laws related to hunting are today's society's best guess on the proper management of game populations. Those rules have evolved and will continue to evolve as game management agencies learn more about the dynamics of the ecosystems in which these animals live. But each of us has an obligation to consider our motives in taking an animal. Attitudes have swung away from hunting for sport, to a more respectful and complete utilization of the gift of the animal's life. This attitude can apply to the use of any animal, plant or mineral resource as well.

Artifakes and fraud are all too common a problem in the world of hand-made products. "Primitives" and artisans today have a high degree of skill and knowledge of the old ways of manufacture. Some are able to exactly reproduce the techniques, materials, shapes and designs of objects made throughout human history. Out of respect for all their forebearers, they should not misrepresent their products when they sell or give them away. To their shame, some dealers and collectors have not been exempt from fraudulent practices either, even when the object's maker has been honest with them. The news too often reports about fraudulent objects making their way even to the large auction houses. How many slip through undetected? And how is this altering and obscuring the story of prehistory that the genuine objects have yet to tell us?

At the end of the day, our thoughts return to our teachers. We've learned respect for their skill and dedication. We honor the long line of teachers that have trusted us with these skills. It is not easy to live up to these standards. Each of us can tell of our temptations and transgressions. But hopefully, this discussion has given you time to reflect. Certainly as we practice and live with primitive skills, we become more in tune with the greater interconnectedness of the earth. Our time on the earth is short. But what's important is that we pass on the traditions as faithfully as they were given to us.

ABOUT OUR LOGO: Our logo was designed by David Callahan, using his and Jack Cresson's sketches, with suggestions from the board. The skull of our common ancestor, Neanderthal, becomes a cavern into which we peer to see a campfire swirling about, symbolizing the spirit of our movement. The ancient technologies, long forgotten, await our rediscovery, to unite us all.

Join the Society of Primitive Technology

P.O. Box 905, Rexburg, ID 83440
or call (208) 359-2400.

Subscriptions include the beautiful **Bulletin of Primitive Technology** which comes out twice a year (May 1 & November 1). The Bulletin focuses on how-to's, project reports, ethnographic discoveries, newsworthy notes, timely articles, society business, and the popular *Resource Directory.*

Membership shows that you support one of the most unique movements in the field. The **Society of Primitive Technology** networks with others working towards the preservation of our prehistoric and world culture. **This is your organization. If you are interested in what the Bulletin and Society stand for, don't just sit back, get active!**

Letters, articles, questions, announcements, news, etc. should be sent "Attention Editor." Memberships should be sent to the SPT Subscription Secretary at the Rexburg, ID address.

The SPT Bulletin is a vehicle to support networking, problem solving and education in the primitive/prehistoric arts and technologies. Do you have a specialty that you want help perfecting, a discovery you want to share, or a question you wish to explore? Get those communications flying and join us. Membership in the Society is $25 for US members, and **$35 International/Canada**.

Back issues available - $10 each for Bulletins, $3 for Newsletters.

All membership fees must be paid in U.S. funds.

A Membership Directory is published annually. If you wish your name to remain off this list, please indicate. _____

NAME: _____

ADDRESS: _____

CITY:_____ STATE:_____ ZIP: _____

COUNTRY:_____ PHONE: _____

MAIN INTEREST AREA: _____

Please print clearly

FREE NOTICE IN BULLETIN BOARD (20 words or less) 1 ISSUE PER YEAR.
PLEASE INDICATE ISSUE NOTICE TO APPEAR: SPRING ____ FALL ____

$25 per year - U.S
$35 per year - International/Canada

Credit Card Number: _____ Exp. Date: _____

Mail application and membership fee to : S.P.T., P.O. Box 905, Rexburg, ID 83440
or phone and apply via Mastercard or VISA - (208) 359-2400.